ANN ARBOR DISTRICT LIBRARY
31621210845870

D1416280

Internet links

There are lots of useful websites where you can find out more about physics. We have created links to some of the best sites on the Usborne Quicklinks Website. To visit the sites, go to **www.usborne-quicklinks.com** and type the keywords "physics dictionary". Here are some of the things you can do on the Internet:

- Try online puzzles, games, quizzes and experiments
- Take an interactive journey through modern physics
- Email your questions to online science experts

Internet safety

The websites recommended in Usborne Quicklinks are regularly reviewed. However, the content of a website may change at any time and Usborne Publishing is not responsible for the content of websites other than its own. We recommend that children are supervised while on the Internet.

The Usborne Illustrated Dictionary of Physics

Corinne Stockley,
Chris Oxlade and Jane Wertheim
Revision editor: Kirsteen Rogers
Designers: Karen Tomlins and Verinder Bhachu
Digital illustrator: Fiona Johnson

Scientific advisors:
Dr. Tom Petersen, John Hawkins, Dr. John Durell and Jerry McCoy

ABOUT PHYSICS

Physics is the study of the properties and nature of matter, the different forms of energy, and the ways in which matter and energy interact in the world around us. In this book, physics is divided into six color-coded sections. The areas covered by these sections are explained below.

Mechanics and general physics

Covers the main concepts of physics, e.g. forces, energy and the properties of matter.

Electricity and magnetism

Explains the forms, uses and behavior of these two linked phenomena.

Heat

Explains heat energy in terms of its measurement and the effects of its presence and transference. Includes the gas laws.

Atomic and nuclear physics

Examines atomic and nuclear structure and energy, radioactivity, fission and fusion.

Waves

Looks at the properties and effects of wave energy and examines sound, electromagnetic and light waves in detail.

General physics information

General material – charts and tables, also information on the treatment of experimental results.

CONTENTS

Mechanics and general physics

Heat

Waves

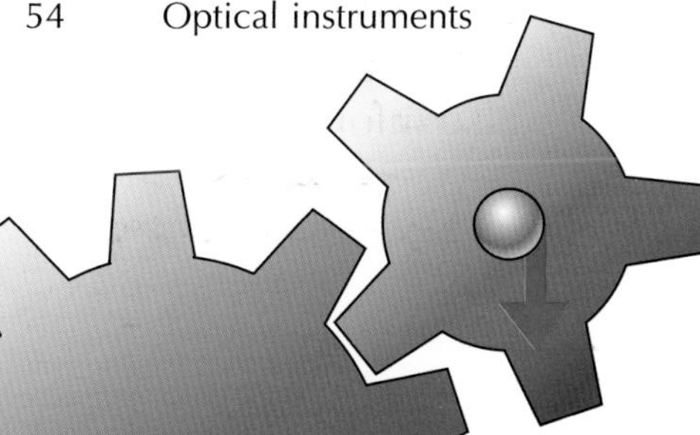

Electricity and magnetism

Atomic and nuclear physics

General physics information

ATOMS AND MOLECULES

The Ancient Greeks believed that all matter was made up of tiny particles which they called **atoms**. This idea has since been expanded and theories such as the **kinetic theory** have been developed which can be used to explain the physical nature and behavior of substances in much greater detail. Matter can exist in three different **physical states**. The state of a substance depends on the nature of the substance, its temperature and the pressure exerted on it. Changes between states are caused by changes in the pressure or temperature (see **changes of state**, page 30).

Atom
Table tennis ball
Earth

If atoms were the size of table tennis balls, by the same scale, table tennis balls would be as big as the Earth.

Atom

The smallest part of a substance which can exist and still retain the properties of the substance. The internal structure of the atom is explained on pages 82-83. Atoms are extremely small, having radii of about 10^{-10}m and masses of about 10^{-25}kg. They can form **ions*** (electrically charged particles) by the loss or gain of **electrons*** (see **ionization**, page 88).

Diagram showing relative sizes of some atoms

Oxygen (O) *Magnesium (Mg)* *Carbon (C)*

Molecule

The smallest naturally-occurring particle of a substance. Molecules can consist of any number of **atoms**, from one (e.g. neon) to many thousands (e.g. proteins), all held together by **electromagnetic forces***. All the molecules of a pure sample of a substance contain the same atoms in the same arrangement.

Molecule of oxygen (O_2)

Molecule of magnesium (Mg)

Molecule of carbon dioxide (CO_2)

Note that many substances do not have **molecules**, for example:

Compound** of **anions and **cations*** (**ionic compound**).*

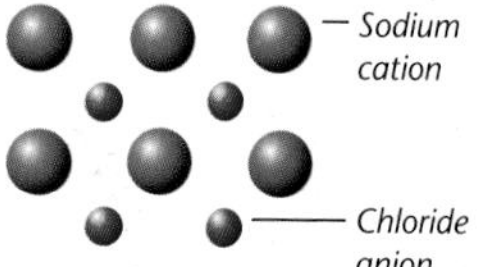
Sodium cation
Chloride anion

***Atomic lattice** of **atoms** all bonded together.*

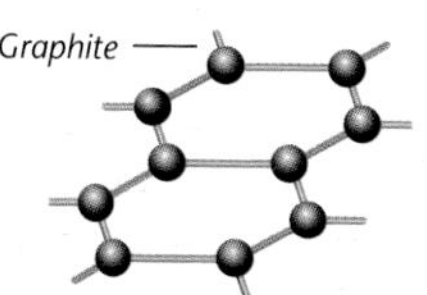
Graphite

Element

A substance which cannot be split into simpler substances by a chemical reaction. All **atoms** of the same element have the same number of **protons*** in their **nuclei*** (see **atomic number**, page 82).

Compound

A substance whose **molecules** contain the **atoms** (or **ions***) of two or more **elements**, chemically bonded together, and which can thus be split into simpler substances. A **mixture** has no chemical bonding and is therefore not a compound.

***Element** 1*

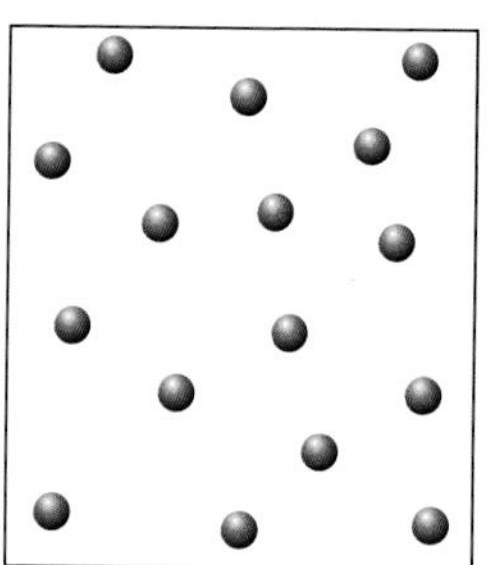

***Element** 2*

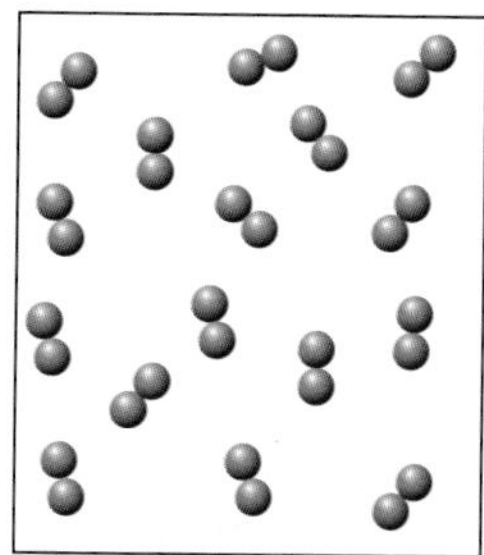

***Compound** of elements 1 and 2 – elements bonded together.*

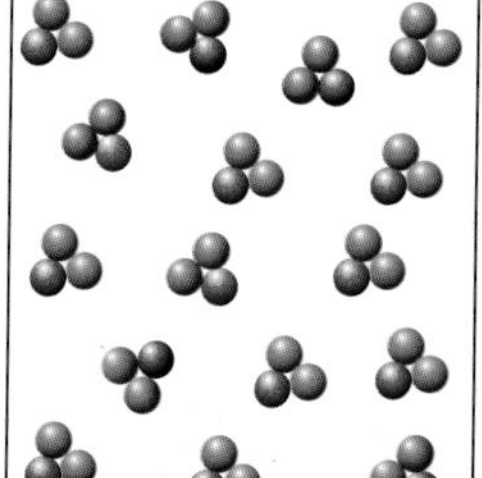

***Mixture** of elements 1 and 2 – no chemical bonding.*

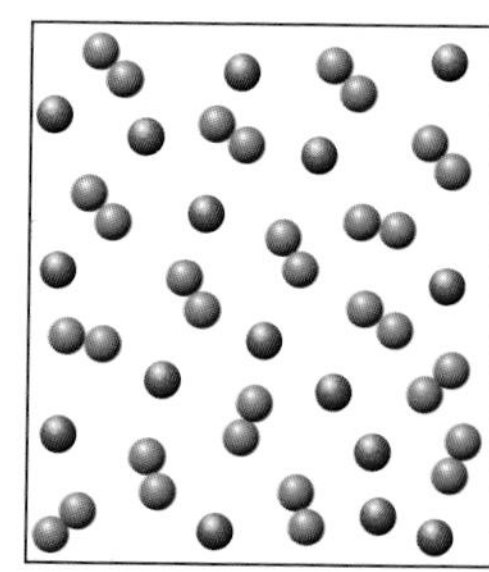

* **Anions**, **Cations**, 88 (**Ionization**); **Electromagnetic force**, 6; **Electrons**, 83; **Ions**, 88 (**Ionization**); **Nucleus**, **Protons**, 82.

Physical states

Solid state
A **state** in which a substance has a definite volume and shape and resists forces which try to change these.

Liquid state
A **state** in which a substance flows and takes up the shape of its containing vessel. It is between the **solid** and **gaseous** states.

Gaseous state
A **state** in which a substance expands to fill its containing vessel. Substances in this state have a relatively low density.

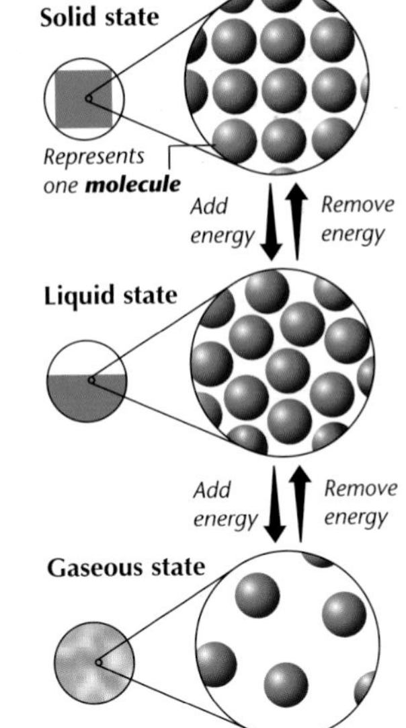
Solid state
Represents one molecule
Add energy
Remove energy
Liquid state
Add energy
Remove energy
Gaseous state

__Molecules__ vibrate about mean positions, having __molecular potential energy__ and __vibrational kinetic energy__*.*

Average energy of molecule much less than that needed by it to break free from other molecules.

Energy added breaks down regular pattern – molecules can move around and thus have both __translational__ and __rotational kinetic energy__.*

Average energy of molecule is just enough for it to break free from neighboring molecules, only to be captured by the next ones along.

Molecules have very large separation – they move virtually independently of each other – __intermolecular forces__ can be ignored.*

Average energy of molecule much greater than needed to break free from other molecules.

Gas
A substance in the **gaseous state** which is above its **critical temperature** and so cannot be turned into a liquid just by increasing the pressure – the temperature must be lowered first, to create a **vapor**.

Vapor
A substance in the **gaseous state** which is below its **critical temperature** (see **gas**) and so can be turned into a liquid by an increase in pressure alone – no lowering of temperature is required.

The kinetic theory

The **kinetic theory** explains the behavior of the different physical states in terms of the motion of **molecules**. In brief, it states that the molecules of **solids** are closest together, have least energy and so move the least, those of **liquids** are further apart with more energy, and those of **gases** are furthest apart with most energy. See above right.

Brownian motion
The observed random motion of small particles in water or air. It supports the kinetic theory, as it could be said to be due to impact with water or air **molecules**.

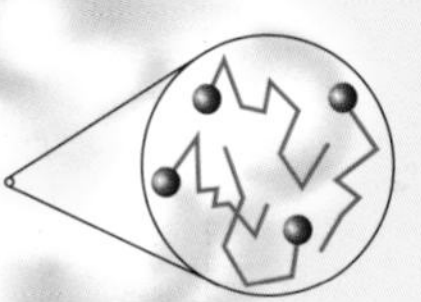

***Brownian motion** of smoke particles as they are hit by **molecules** in the air.*

Diffusion
The mixing of two **gases**, **vapors** or **liquids** over a period of time. It supports the kinetic theory, since the particles must be moving to mix, and gases can be seen to diffuse faster than liquids.

***Molecules** of two **gases** diffuse together over time.*

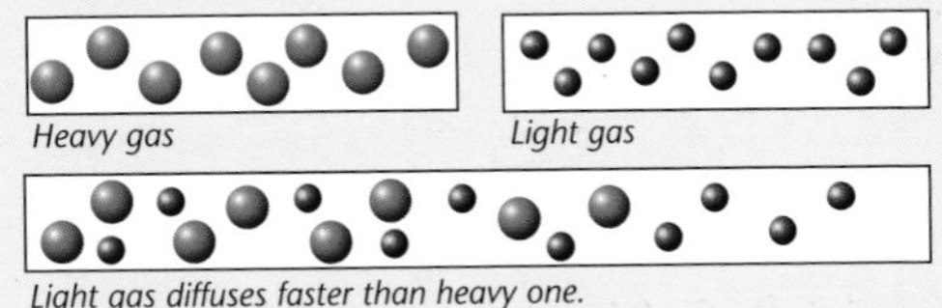
Heavy gas
Light gas

Light gas diffuses faster than heavy one.

Graham's law of diffusion
States that, at constant temperature and pressure, the rate of **diffusion** of a **gas** is inversely proportional to the square root of its density.

$$\text{Rate of diffusion} \propto \sqrt{\frac{1}{\text{density of gas}}}$$

* **Intermolecular forces**, 7; **Molecular potential energy**, 8; **Rotational**, **Translational** and **Vibrational kinetic energy**, 9 (**Kinetic energy**).

FORCES

A **force** influences the shape and motion of an object. A single force will change its velocity (i.e. **accelerate*** it) and possibly its shape. Two equal and opposite forces may change its shape or size. It is a **vector quantity***, having both magnitude and direction, and is measured in **newtons**. The main types of force are **gravitational**, **magnetic**, **electric** and **strong nuclear**. See pages 104-107 for a comparison of the first three of these.

*The Earth's **gravitational force** makes seeds fall to the ground.*

Showing forces in diagrams

***Forces** are shown by arrowed lines (the length represents magnitude and the arrow represents direction).*

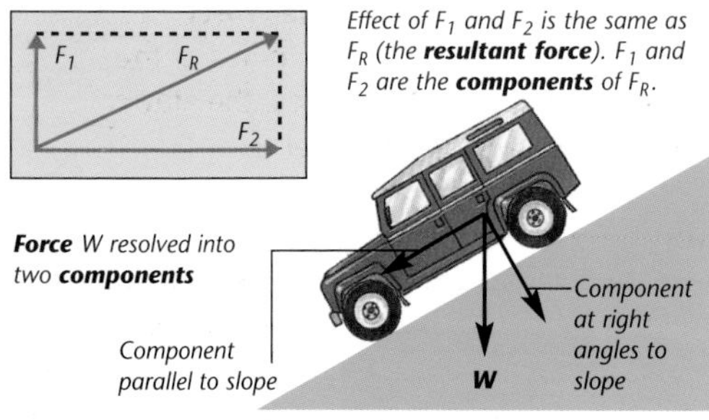

F_1
F_R
F_2
Effect of F_1 and F_2 is the same as F_R (the **resultant force**). F_1 and F_2 are the **components** of F_R.
Force W resolved into two **components**
Component parallel to slope
W
Component at right angles to slope

Newton (N)

The **SI unit*** of force. One newton is the force needed to accelerate a mass of 1kg by 1m s^{-2}.

Force field

The region in which a force has an effect. The maximum distance over which a force has an effect is the **range** of the force. Force fields are represented by lines with arrows, called **field lines**, to show their strength and direction (see also pages 58 and 72).

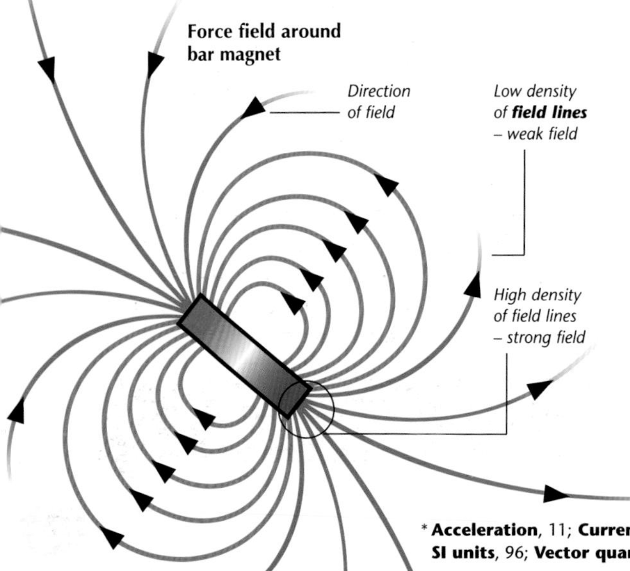

Force field around bar magnet
Direction of field
Low density of **field lines** – weak field
High density of field lines – strong field

Gravitational force or gravity

The force of attraction between any two objects which have mass (see also pages 18-19). It is very small unless one of the objects is very massive.

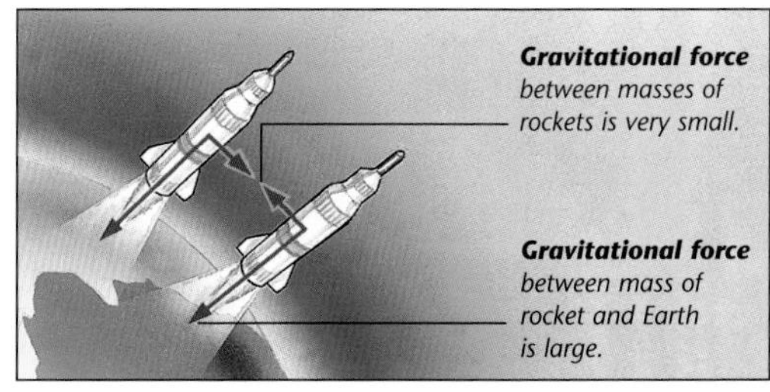

Gravitational force between masses of rockets is very small.
Gravitational force between mass of rocket and Earth is large.

Electromagnetic force

A combination of the **electric** and **magnetic forces**, which are closely related and difficult to separate.

Electric or electrostatic force

The force between two electrically-charged particles (see also page 56). It is repulsive if the charges are the same, but attractive if they are opposite.

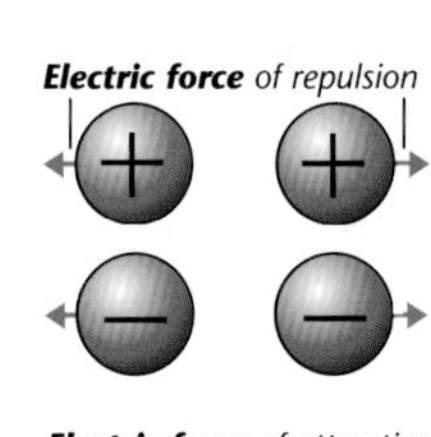

Electric force of repulsion

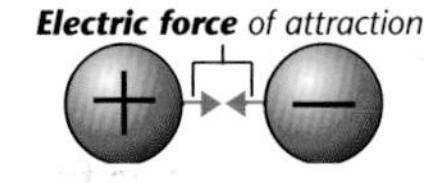

Electric force of attraction

Magnetic force

A force between two moving charges. These moving charges can be electric **currents*** (see also page 60) or **electrons*** moving around in their **electron shells***.

Magnetic forces in electric wires

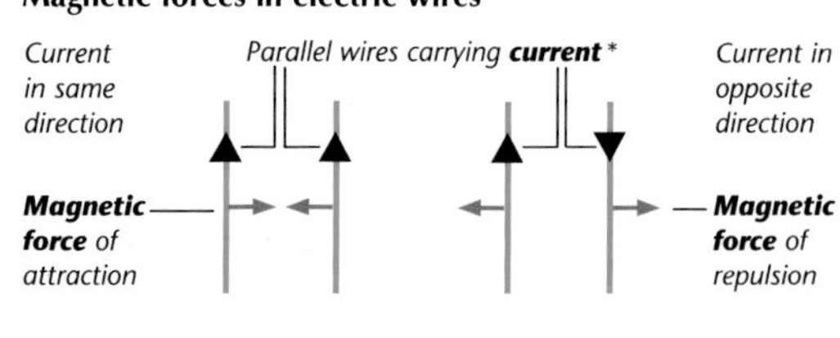

Current in same direction
Parallel wires carrying **current***
Current in opposite direction
Magnetic force of attraction
Magnetic force of repulsion

* **Acceleration**, 11; **Current**, 60; **Electrons**, **Electron shells**, 83; **SI units**, 96; **Vector quantity**, 108.

Intermolecular forces

The **electromagnetic forces** between two molecules. The strength and direction of the forces vary with the separation of the molecules (see diagram below).

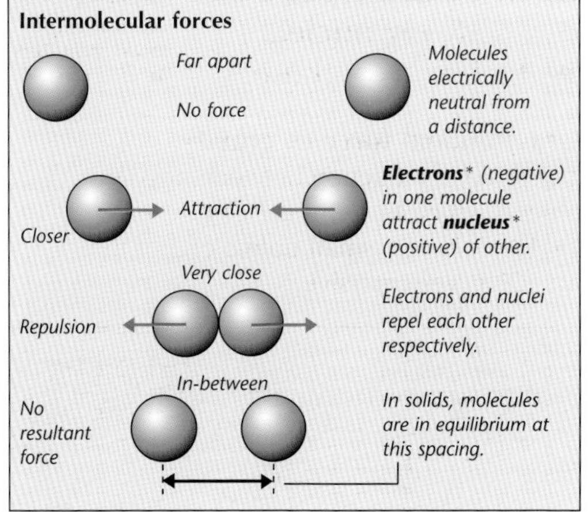

Intermolecular forces
Far apart
No force
Molecules electrically neutral from a distance.
Closer
Attraction
Electrons* (negative) in one molecule attract nucleus* (positive) of other.
Very close
Repulsion
Electrons and nuclei repel each other respectively.
In-between
No resultant force
In solids, molecules are in equilibrium at this spacing.

Tension

Equal and opposite forces which, when applied to the ends of an object, increase its length. They are resisted by the **intermolecular force** of attraction.

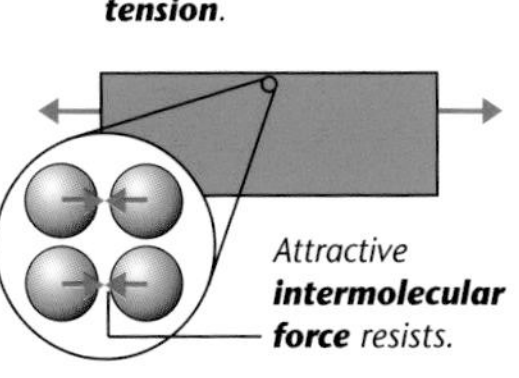

Attractive intermolecular force resists.

*Molecules pulled apart by **tension**.*

Compression

Equal and opposite forces which decrease the length of an object. They are opposed by the **intermolecular force** of repulsion.

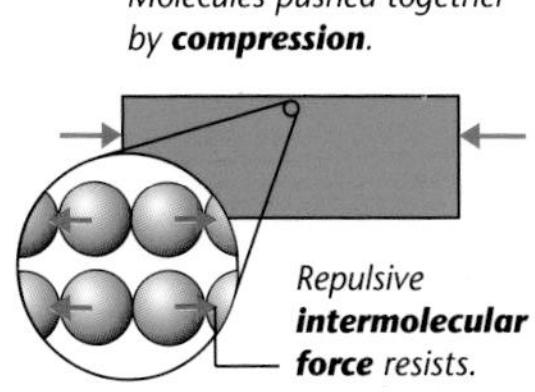

Repulsive intermolecular force resists.

*Molecules pushed together by **compression**.*

Contact force

The **intermolecular force** of repulsion between the molecules of two objects when they touch.

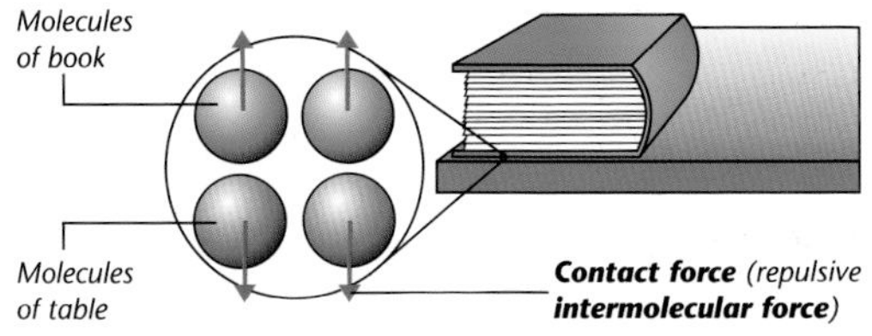

Molecules of book
Molecules of table
Contact force (repulsive intermolecular force)

Strong nuclear force

The force of attraction between all the particles of an atomic **nucleus*** (the **protons*** and **neutrons***). It prevents the **electric force** of repulsion between the protons from pushing the nucleus apart (see also page 84).

*Particles in an atomic nucleus are held together by the **nuclear force**.*

Frictional force or friction

The force which acts to oppose the motion of two touching surfaces over each other, caused by the **intermolecular force** of attraction between the molecules of the surfaces. There are two types, the **static** and the **kinetic frictional force**.

Static frictional force

The **frictional force** between two touching surfaces when a force is applied to one of them but they are not moving. The maximum value of the static frictional force occurs when they are on the point of sliding over each other. This is called the **limiting force**.

Kinetic frictional force or sliding frictional force

The **frictional force** when one surface is sliding over another at constant speed. It is slightly less than the **limiting force** (the maximum **static frictional force**).

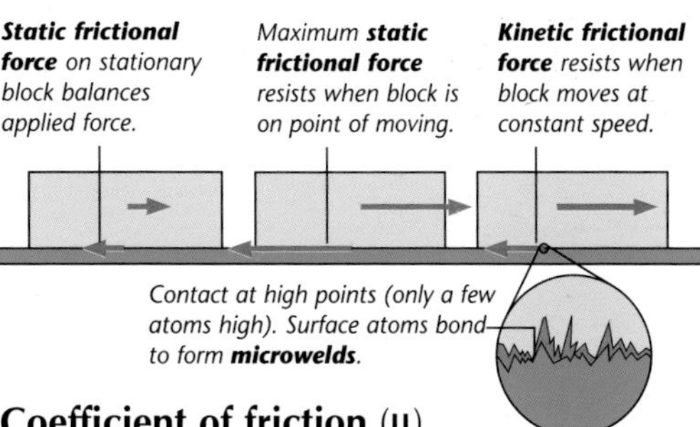

Static frictional force on stationary block balances applied force.
Maximum static frictional force resists when block is on point of moving.
Kinetic frictional force resists when block moves at constant speed.
Contact at high points (only a few atoms high). Surface atoms bond to form microwelds.

Coefficient of friction (μ)

The ratio of the **frictional force** between two surfaces to that pushing them together (the **normal contact force**). There are two values, the **coefficient of static friction** and the **coefficient of kinetic friction**.

Coefficient of friction $\mu = \frac{\text{frictional force } (F)}{\text{normal contact force } (R)}$

* **Electrons**, 83; **Neutrons**, **Nucleus**, **Protons**, 82.

ENERGY

Work is done when a force moves an object. **Energy** is the capacity to do work. When work is done on or by an object, it gains or loses energy respectively. Energy exists in many different forms and can change between them (energy **conversion** or **transformation**), but cannot be created or destroyed (**law of conservation of energy**). The **SI unit*** of energy and work is the **joule** (**J**).

The energy from the Sun is the equivalent of that supplied by one million million million power stations.

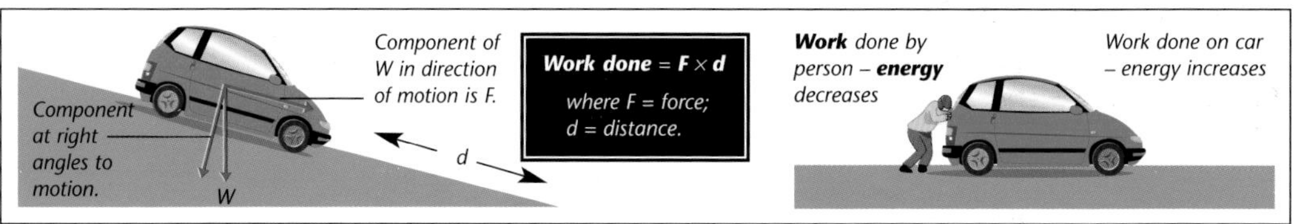

Component at right angles to motion.
W
Component of W in direction of motion is F.
d
Work done = F × d
where F = force; d = distance.
Work done by person – energy decreases
Work done on car – energy increases

Potential energy (P.E.)

The energy of an object due to its position in a **force field***, which it has because work has been done to put it in that position. The energy has been "stored up". The three forms of potential energy are **gravitational potential energy**, **electromagnetic potential energy** and **nuclear potential energy** (depending on the force involved).

Gravitational potential energy

The **potential energy** associated with the position of an object relative to a mass which exerts a **gravitational force*** on it. If the object is moved further from the mass (e.g. an object being lifted on Earth), work is done on the body and its gravitational potential energy is raised.

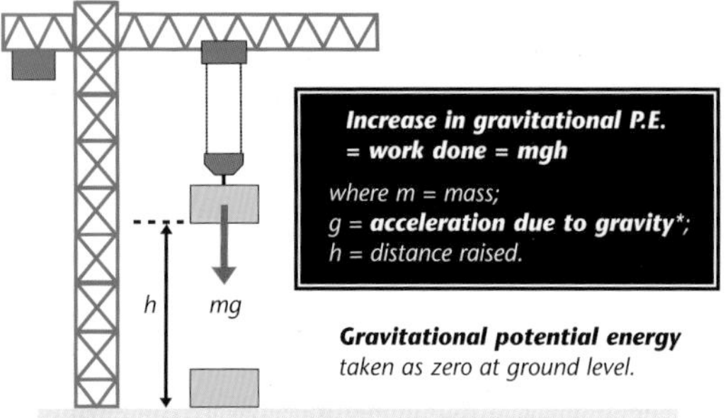

Increase in gravitational P.E. = work done = mgh
where m = mass;
g = acceleration due to gravity*;
h = distance raised.
h
mg

Gravitational potential energy *taken as zero at ground level.*

Nuclear potential energy

The **potential energy** stored in an atomic **nucleus***. Some nuclear potential energy is released during **radioactive decay***.

Electromagnetic potential energy

The **potential energy** associated with the position of a body in a **force field*** created by an **electromagnetic force***.

Molecular potential energy

The **electromagnetic potential energy** associated with the position of molecules relative to one another. It is increased when work is done against the **intermolecular force***.

Elastic potential energy or strain energy

An example of the **molecular potential energy**, stored as a result of stretching or compressing an object. It is the work done against the **intermolecular force***.

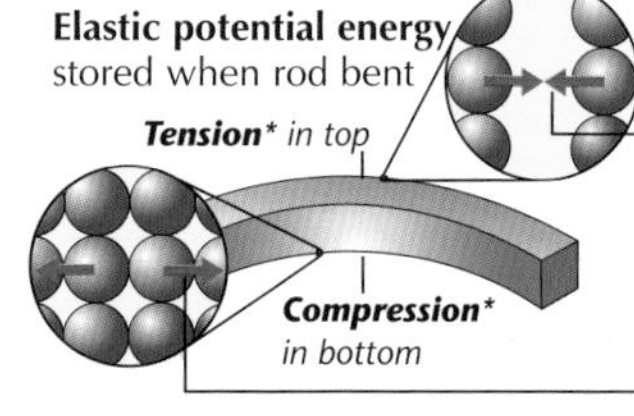

Elastic potential energy stored when rod bent
Tension* in top
Compression* in bottom

Attraction between particles (see ***intermolecular forces****, page 7).* ***Molecular potential energy*** *stored.*

Repulsion between particles (see ***intermolecular forces****, page 7).* ***Molecular potential energy*** *stored.*

Chemical energy

Energy stored in substances such as fuels, food, and chemicals in batteries. It is released during chemical reactions, e.g. as heat when a fuel burns, when the **electromagnetic potential energy** of the atoms and molecules changes.

Plants convert energy from sunlight into food – a store of ***chemical energy****.*

* **Acceleration due to gravity**, 18; **Compression**, 7; **Electromagnetic force**, **Force field**, **Gravitational force**, 6; **Intermolecular forces**, 7; **Nucleus**, 82; **Radioactive decay**, 87; **SI units**, 96; **Tension**, 7.

Kinetic energy (K.E.)

The energy associated with movement. It takes the form of **translational**, **rotational** and **vibrational energy**.

Kinetic energy of two objects linked by a spring

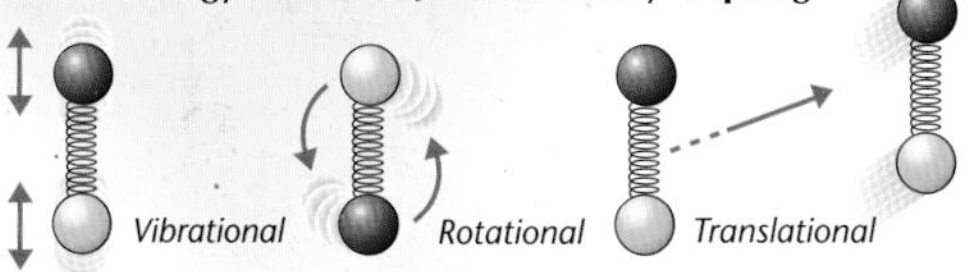
Vibrational
Rotational
Translational

K.E. = $\frac{1}{2}mv^2$ where m = mass; v = velocity.

Mechanical energy

The sum of the **kinetic energy** and **gravitational potential energy** of an object.

*The **mechanical energy** of a pendulum is constant (if resistive forces are neglected).*

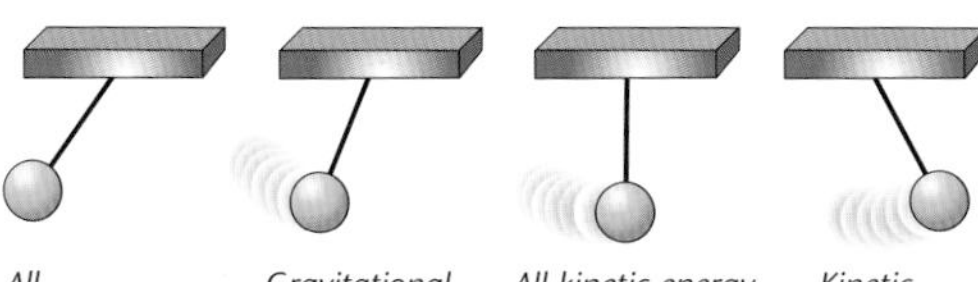

*All **gravitational potential energy***

*Gravitational potential energy to **kinetic energy***

All kinetic energy (gravitational potential energy taken as zero here)

Kinetic energy to gravitational potential energy

Internal or thermal energy

The sum of the **kinetic energy** and the **molecular potential energy** of the molecules in an object. If the temperature of an object increases, so does its internal energy.

Internal energy and temperature

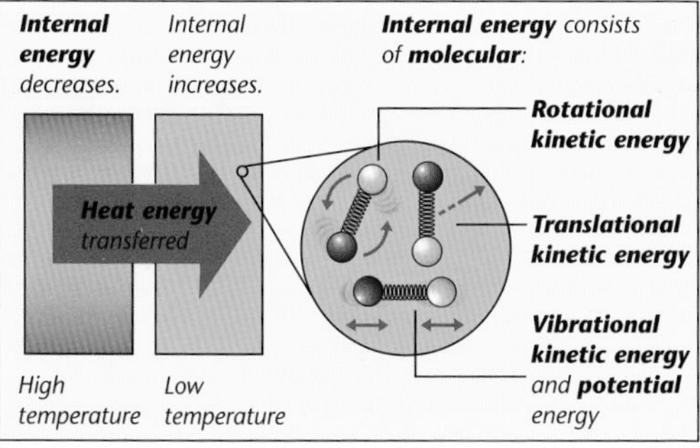
Internal energy decreases.
Internal energy increases.
Internal energy consists of molecular:
Heat energy transferred
Rotational kinetic energy
Translational kinetic energy
Vibrational kinetic energy and potential energy
High temperature
Low temperature

Heat energy or heat

The energy which flows from one place to another because of a difference in temperature (see pages 28-33). When **heat energy** is absorbed by an object, its **internal energy** increases (see diagram above).

Wave energy

The energy associated with wave action. For example, the energy of a water wave consists of the **gravitational potential energy** and **kinetic energy** of the water molecules.

Electric and magnetic energy

The types of energy associated with electric charge and moving electric charge (current). They are collectively referred to as **electromagnetic energy**.

Radiation

Any energy in the form of **electromagnetic waves*** or streams of particles. See also pages 29 and 86-87.

Power

The rate of doing work or the rate of change of energy. The **SI unit*** of power is the **watt** (**W**), which is equal to 1 joule per second.

Energy conversion in a power station

*Coal is a type of fuel called a **fossil fuel**, made up of the fossilized remains of plants that grew long ago. It is a store of **chemical energy** that came from the Sun.*

*Furnace in power station burns fuel and boils water. Here, **chemical energy** is converted to **internal energy** of steam.*

*Steam turns **turbines***. Internal energy of steam is converted to **rotational kinetic energy** of the turbine.*

Generator converts kinetic energy to **electric energy**.*

*Appliances such as heaters, lamps and audio equipment convert electric energy into **heat energy**, light (**wave energy**) and sound (wave energy).*

* **Electromagnetic waves**, 44; **Generator**, 78; **SI units**, 96; **Turbine**, 115.

MOTION

Motion is the change in position and orientation of an object. The motion of a **rigid** object (one which does not change shape) is made up of **translational motion**, or **translation**, i.e. movement of the **center of mass** from one place to another, and **rotational motion**, or **rotation**, i.e. movement around its center of mass. The study of the motion of points is called **kinematics**.

*A satellite spinning in orbit displays **rotational motion** (1) and **translational motion** (2).*

Linear motion

Linear or **rectilinear motion** is movement in a straight line and is the simplest form of **translational motion** (see introduction). The linear motion of any rigid object is described as the motion of its **center of mass**.

Center of mass

The point which acts as though the total mass of the object were at that point. The center of mass of a **rigid** object (see introduction) is in the same position as its **center of gravity** (the point through which the Earth's gravitational force acts on the object).

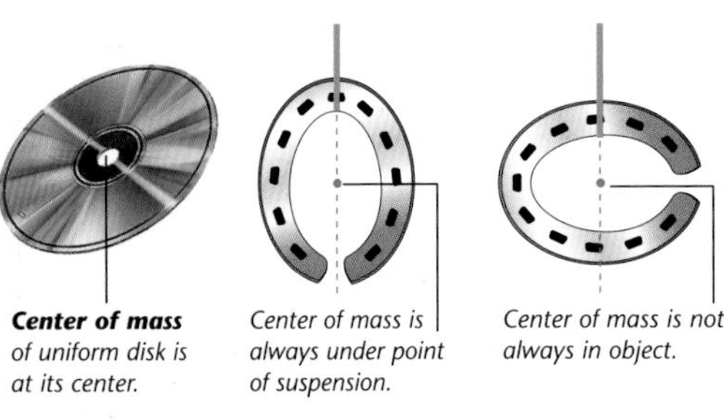

***Center of mass** of uniform disk is at its center.*

Center of mass is always under point of suspension.

Center of mass is not always in object.

Displacement

The distance and direction of an object from a fixed reference point. It is a **vector quantity***. The position of an object can be expressed by its displacement from a specified point.

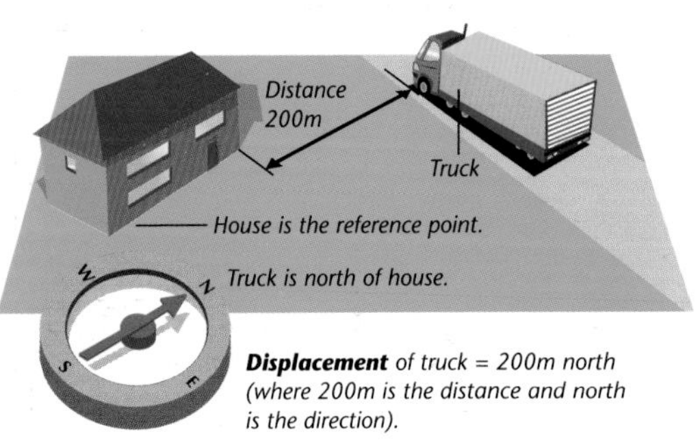
Distance
200m
Truck
House is the reference point.
Truck is north of house.
W
N
S
E
Displacement of truck = 200m north
(where 200m is the distance and north
is the direction).

Speed

The ratio of the distance traveled by an object to the time taken. If the speed of an object is constant, it is said to be moving with **uniform speed**. The **average speed** of an object over a time interval is the distance traveled by the object divided by the time interval. The **instantaneous speed** is the speed at any given moment.

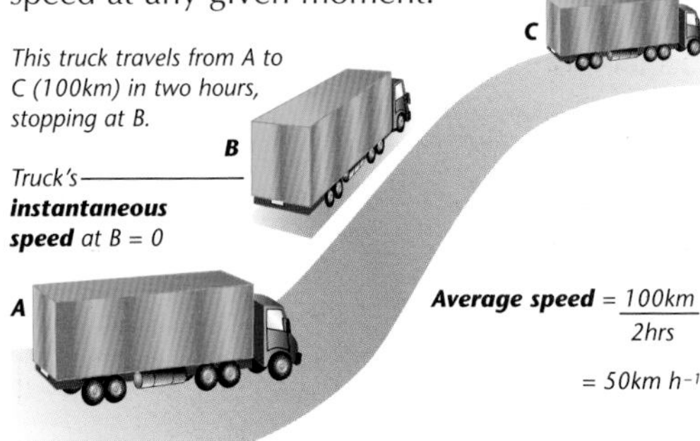
This truck travels from A to
C (100km) in two hours,
stopping at B.
C
B
A
Truck's
instantaneous
speed at B = 0
Average speed = 100km / 2hrs
= 50km h^-1

Velocity

The **speed** and direction of an object (i.e. its **displacement** in a given time). It is a **vector quantity***. **Uniform velocity**, **average velocity** and **instantaneous velocity** are all defined in a similar way to **uniform speed** etc. (see **speed**).

A displacement-time graph for an object which moves in a straight line from A to B and back to A (showing velocity calculation)

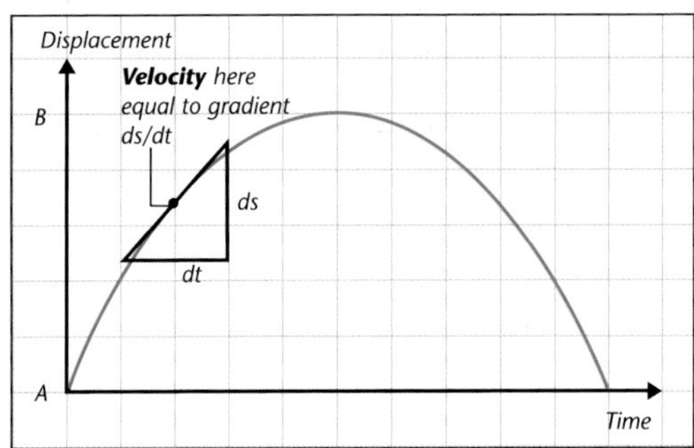
Displacement
Velocity here
equal to gradient
ds/dt
ds
dt
B
A
Time

* **Vector quantity**, 108.

Relative velocity

The **velocity** which an object appears to have when seen by an observer who may be moving. This is known as the velocity of the object relative to the observer.

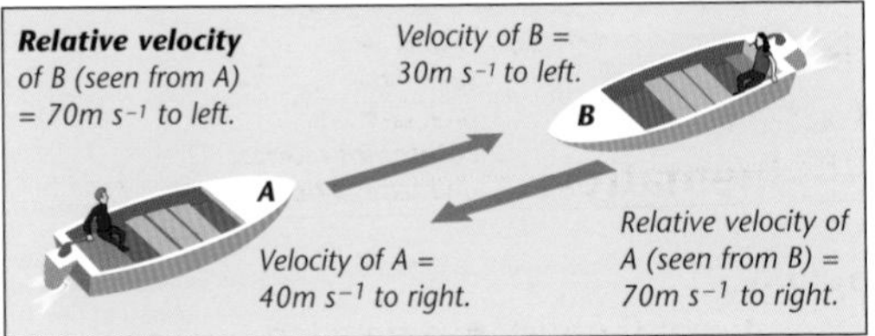

Relative velocity of B (seen from A) = 70m s⁻¹ to left.
Velocity of B = 30m s⁻¹ to left.
B
A
Velocity of A = 40m s⁻¹ to right.
Relative velocity of A (seen from B) = 70m s⁻¹ to right.

Acceleration

The ratio of the change in **velocity** of an object to the time taken. It is a **vector quantity***. An object accelerates if its **speed** changes (the usual case in **linear motion**) or its direction of travel changes (the usual case in **circular motion***). **Deceleration** in one direction is acceleration in the opposite direction (negative acceleration). An object whose velocity is changing the same amount in equal amounts of time is moving with **uniform acceleration**.

Graphs of velocity versus time showing acceleration

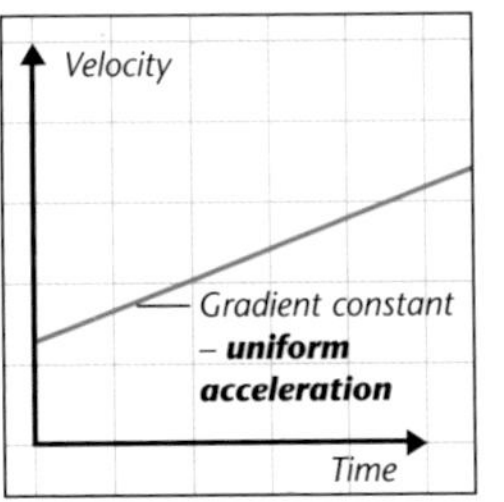

Velocity
Gradient constant – uniform acceleration
Time

Distance traveled in equal time intervals increases.

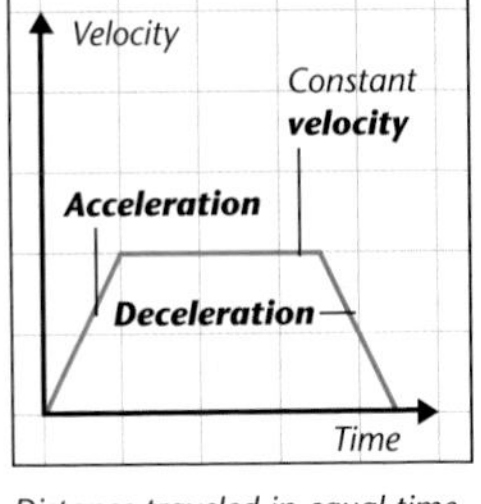

Velocity
Constant velocity
Acceleration
Deceleration
Time

Distance traveled in equal time intervals increases, remains constant, then decreases.

Rotational motion

The movement of an object about its **center of mass**. In rotational motion, each part of the object moves along a different path, so that the object cannot be considered as a whole in calculations. It must be split into small pieces and the **circular motion*** of each piece must be considered separately. From this, the overall motion of the object can be seen.

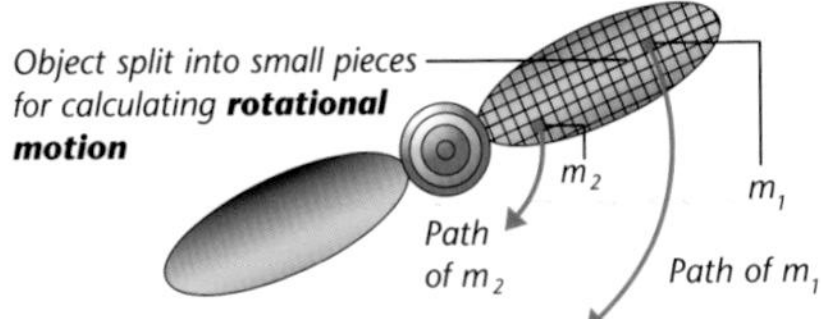

Object split into small pieces for calculating rotational motion
m2
m1
Path of m2
Path of m1

Equations of uniformly accelerated motion

Equations which are used in calculations involving **linear motion** with **uniform acceleration**. A **sign convention** must be used (see below). The equations use **displacement**, not distance, so changes of direction must be considered.

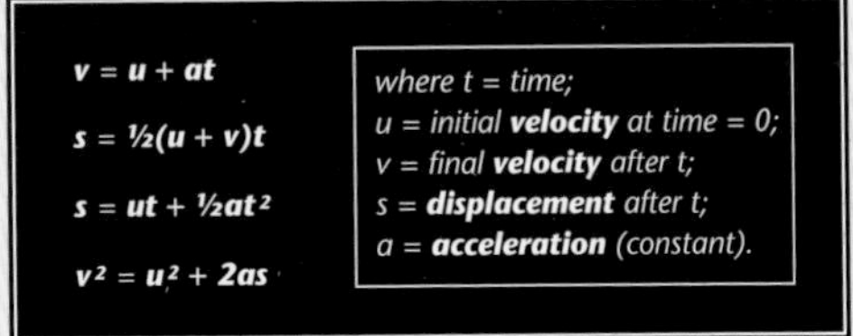

$v = u + at$

$s = \frac{1}{2}(u + v)t$

$s = ut + \frac{1}{2}at^2$

$v^2 = u^2 + 2as$

where t = time; u = initial **velocity** at time = 0; v = final **velocity** after t; s = **displacement** after t; a = **acceleration** (constant).

Sign convention

A method used to distinguish between motion in opposite directions. One direction is chosen as positive, and the other is then negative. The sign convention must be used when using the equations of motion (see above).

Sign convention

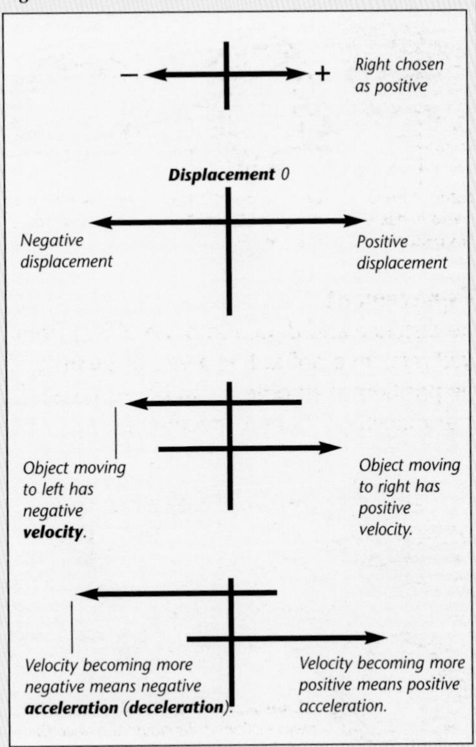

–
+
Right chosen as positive
Displacement 0
Negative displacement
Positive displacement
Object moving to left has negative velocity.
Object moving to right has positive velocity.
Velocity becoming more negative means negative acceleration (deceleration).
Velocity becoming more positive means positive acceleration.

* **Circular motion**, 17; **Vector quantity**, 108.

DYNAMICS

Dynamics is the study of the relationship between the motion of an object and the forces acting on it. A single force on an object causes it to change speed and/or direction (i.e. **accelerate***). If two or more forces act and there is no resultant force, the object does not accelerate, but may change shape.

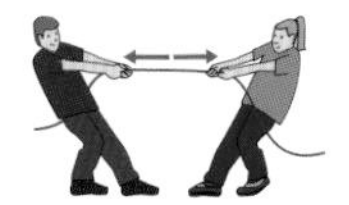

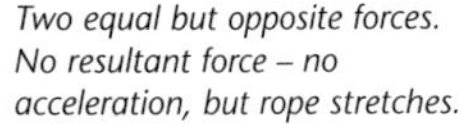

Two equal but opposite forces. No resultant force – no acceleration, but rope stretches.

Forces not equal. Rope still stretches, but also accelerates to left due to resultant force.

Mass

A measurement of the **inertia** of an object. The force needed to accelerate an object by a given amount depends on its mass – a larger mass needs a larger force.

Momentum

The **mass** of an object multiplied by its **velocity***. Since velocity is a **vector quantity***, so is momentum. See also **law of conservation of linear momentum**.

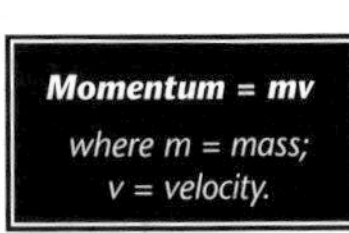

Momentum = mv
where m = mass;
v = velocity.

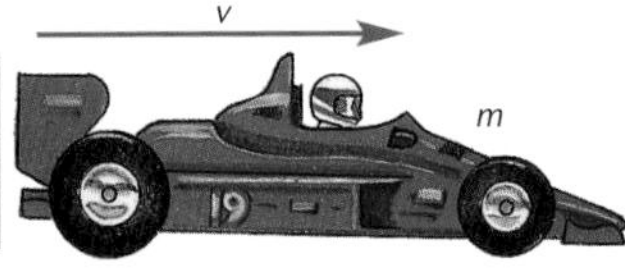
v
m

Inertia

The tendency of an object to resist a change of **velocity*** (i.e. to resist a force trying to **accelerate*** it). It is measured as **mass**.

*The large ship has much greater **inertia** (and therefore **mass**) than the little boat – a much larger force is needed to **accelerate*** it.*

Impulse

The force acting on an object multiplied by the time for which the force acts. From **Newton's second law**, impulse is equal to the change in **momentum** of an object. An equal change in momentum can be achieved by a small force for a long time or a large force for a short time.

Impulse = Ft
where F = force;
t = time.

*Since force is rate of change of **momentum** (see **Newton's second law**) then:*

Impulse = change in momentum

*"Crumple zone" in the front of a car increases **collision** time – this makes force smaller.*

Crumple zone

Newton's laws of motion

Three laws formulated by Newton in the late 1670s which relate force and motion.

Newton's first law

An object will remain at rest or in uniform motion unless acted upon by a force.

Forces on the object below are equal – no resultant force, so no acceleration.

Object at rest

Force exerted by grass

Force due to gravity (weight)

Newton's second law

If the **momentum** of an object changes, i.e. if it **accelerates***, then there must be a resultant force acting on it. Normally, the **mass** of the object is constant, and the force is thus proportional to the acceleration of the object. The direction of the acceleration is the same as the direction of the force.

$$\textbf{Force} = \frac{\textbf{change in momentum}}{\textbf{time}}$$

*If **mass** remains constant, then:*

Force = mass × acceleration

* **Acceleration**, 11; **Vector quantity**, 108; **Velocity**, 10.

Collision

An occurrence which results in two or more objects exerting relatively large forces on each other over a relatively short time. This is not the everyday idea of a collision, because the objects do not necessarily have to be in contact.

Example of collision without contact

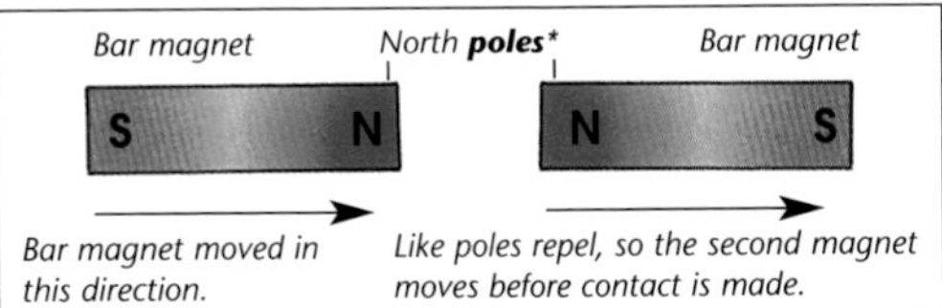
Bar magnet
North **poles***
Bar magnet
S
N
N
S
Bar magnet moved in this direction.
Like poles repel, so the second magnet moves before contact is made.

Law of conservation of linear momentum

If there is no external force on an object, then its linear **momentum** remains constant. If the system is considered just before and just after the **collision**, forces such as friction can be ignored.

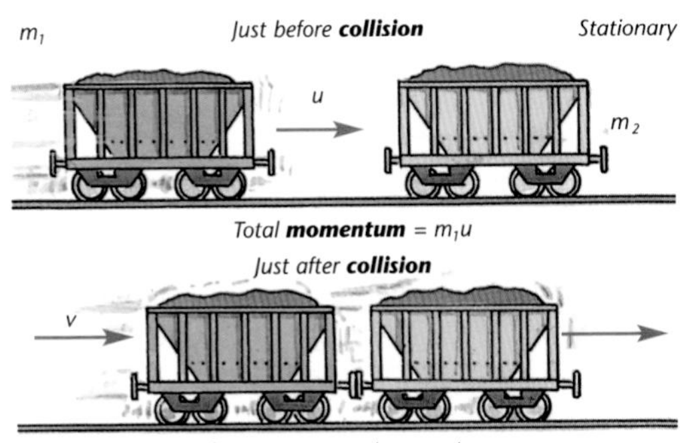
m_1
*Just before **collision***
Stationary
u
m_2
*Total **momentum** = m_1u*
*Just after **collision***
v
*Total **momentum** = $(m_1 + m_2)v = m_1u$*

Mass** increases – **velocity decreases to conserve momentum.*

Rocket engine

An engine which produces a high **velocity*** stream of gas through a nozzle by burning fuel held on board. The **mass** of gas is small, but its high velocity means it has a high **momentum**. The rocket gains an equal amount of momentum in the opposite direction (see **law of conservation of linear momentum**). Rocket engines are used in space because other engines require air.

Rocket engine

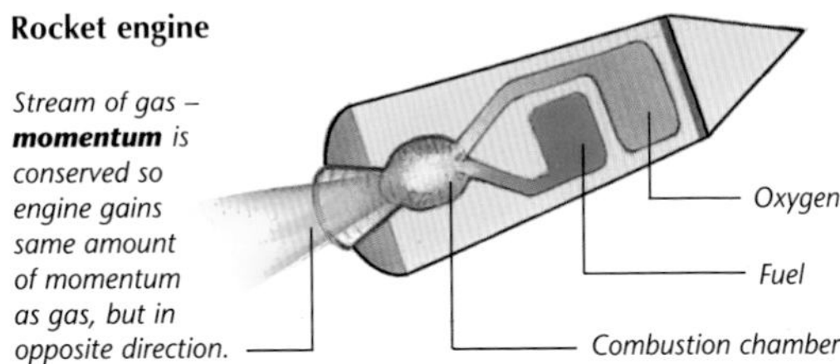
Stream of gas – **momentum** is conserved so engine gains same amount of momentum as gas, but in opposite direction.
Oxygen
Fuel
Combustion chamber

Jet engine

An engine in which air is drawn in at the front to burn fuel, producing a high **velocity*** jet of gas. The principle is the same as that for the rocket engine, except that the gas is produced differently and the engine cannot be used in space because it requires air.

Jet engine

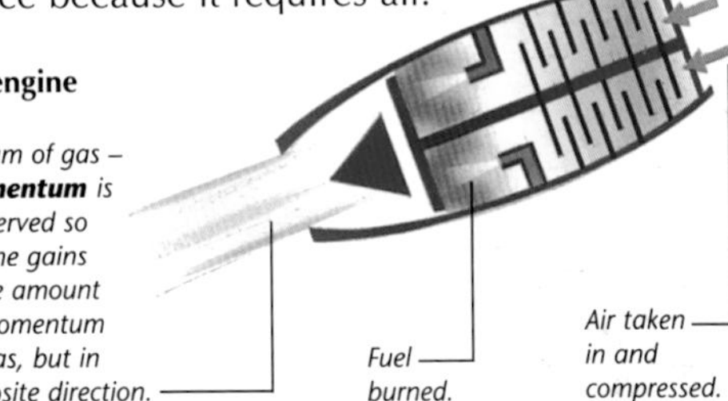
Stream of gas – **momentum** is conserved so engine gains same amount of momentum as gas, but in opposite direction.
Fuel burned.
Air taken in and compressed.

Example of Newton's second law

*A tennis ball hit by a racket undergoes a change of **momentum**.*

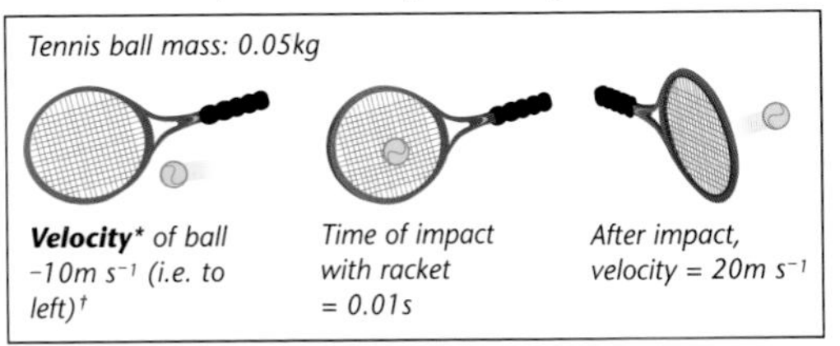
Tennis ball mass: 0.05kg
Velocity* of ball −10m s⁻¹ (i.e. to left)†
Time of impact with racket = 0.01s
After impact, velocity = 20m s⁻¹

Resultant force found as follows:

$$\text{Force at impact} = \frac{\text{change in momentum}}{\text{time}} = \frac{(0.05 \times 20) - (0.05 \times -10)}{0.01} = 150N$$

Or:

$$\text{Force} = \text{mass} \times \text{acceleration} = \frac{\text{mass} \times \text{change in velocity}}{\text{time}}$$

$$= \frac{0.05 \times 30}{0.01} = 150N$$

Newton's third law

Forces always occur in equal and opposite pairs. Thus if object A exerts a force on object B, object B exerts an equal but opposite force on A. These forces do not cancel each other out, as they act on different objects.

Example of Newton's third law

Bat exerts force on ball, accelerating it in opposite direction.

Ball exerts equal and opposite force on bat (felt as sudden slowing down of bat).

* **Pole**, 70; **Velocity**, 10.

† *Movement to right considered as positive (see **sign convention**, page 11).*

TURNING FORCES

A single force produces an **acceleration*** (see **dynamics**, page 12). In **linear motion***, it is a **linear acceleration.** In **rotational motion***, **angular acceleration*** (spinning faster or slower) is caused by a turning force or **moment** acting about the axis of rotation (the **fulcrum**).

*The rear rotor blades of a helicopter apply a **moment** to the helicopter which prevents it from spinning.*

Moment or torque

A measure of the ability of a force to rotate an object about an axis (the **fulcrum**). It is the size of the force multiplied by the perpendicular distance from the axis to the line along which the force acts (see diagram below). The **SI unit*** of moment is the **Newton meter** (**Nm**).

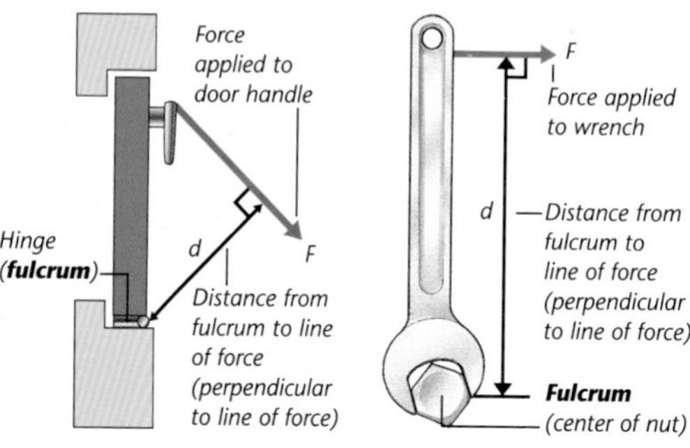
Force applied to door handle
Hinge (fulcrum)
d
F
Distance from fulcrum to line of force (perpendicular to line of force)
F
Force applied to wrench
d
Distance from fulcrum to line of force (perpendicular to line of force)
Fulcrum (center of nut)

In each case:

Moment = Fd

When considering moments, the axis about which they are taken must be stated and a **sign convention*** must be used to distinguish between clockwise and counterclockwise moments. The **resultant moment** is the single moment which has the same effect as all the individual moments acting together.

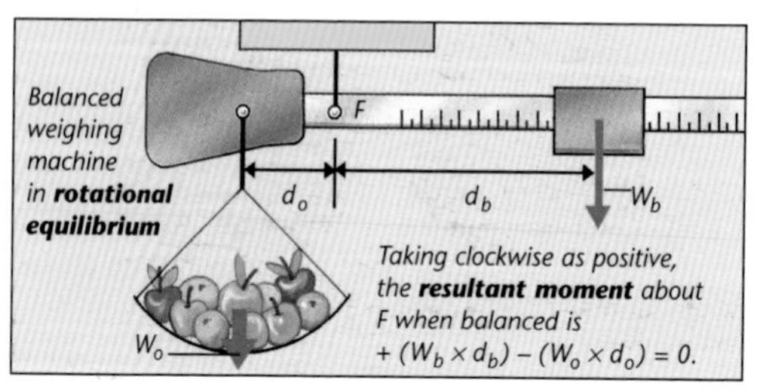
Balanced weighing machine in rotational equilibrium
F
d_o
d_b
W_b
W_o
Taking clockwise as positive, the resultant moment about F when balanced is
$+ (W_b \times d_b) - (W_o \times d_o) = 0.$

Couple

Two parallel forces which are equal and opposite but do not act along the same line. They produce a turning effect only, with no resultant acceleration of the **center of mass***. The **resultant moment** produced by a couple is the sum of the moments produced, and equals the perpendicular distance between the lines along which the forces act, multiplied by the size of one force.

*Equal and opposite forces (a **couple**) on a steering wheel cause it to turn.*

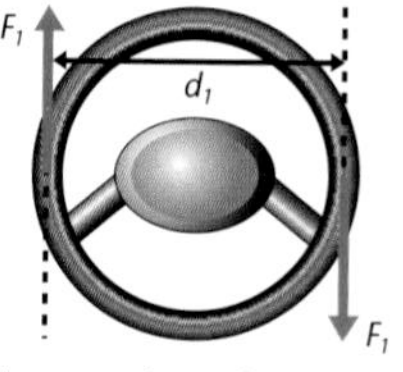
F_1
d_1
F_1

***Moment** of **couple** = $F_1 \times d_1$*

In this case, one force applied to wheel by hand – the other by steering column.

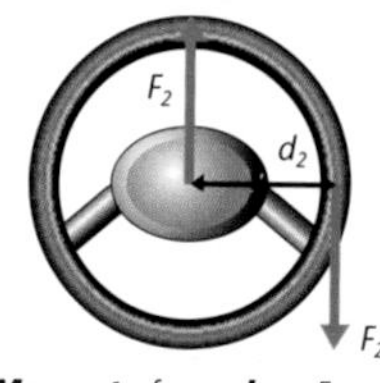
F_2
d_2
F_2

***Moment** of **couple** = $F_2 \times d_2$*

Toppling

A condition which occurs if the vertical line through the **center of mass*** of an object does not pass through the base of the object. If this occurs, a **couple** of the weight and the **normal contact force*** rotates the object further over.

*Slightly tilted – **couple** will return it to level.*

Toppling – couple now acts to turn further over.

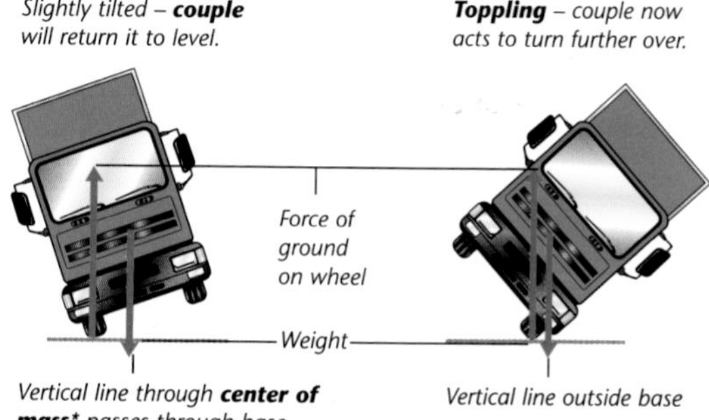
Force of ground on wheel
Weight

*Vertical line through **center of mass*** passes through base.*

Vertical line outside base

*A low **center of mass*** and wide base make a race car very stable.*

* **Acceleration**, 11; **Angular acceleration**, 17; **Center of mass**, **Linear motion**, 10; **Normal contact force**, 7 (**Coefficient of friction**); **Rotational motion**, **Sign convention**, 11; **SI units**, 96.

Equilibrium

When an object is not accelerating, it is said to be in **equilibrium**. It can be in **linear equilibrium** (i.e. the **center of mass*** is not accelerating) and/or **rotational equilibrium** (i.e. not accelerating about the center of mass). In addition, both cases of equilibrium are either **static** (not moving) or **dynamic** (moving).

Linear equilibrium

The state of an object when there is no acceleration of its **center of mass***, i.e. its speed and direction of motion do not change. The resultant force on the object when it is in linear equilibrium must be zero.

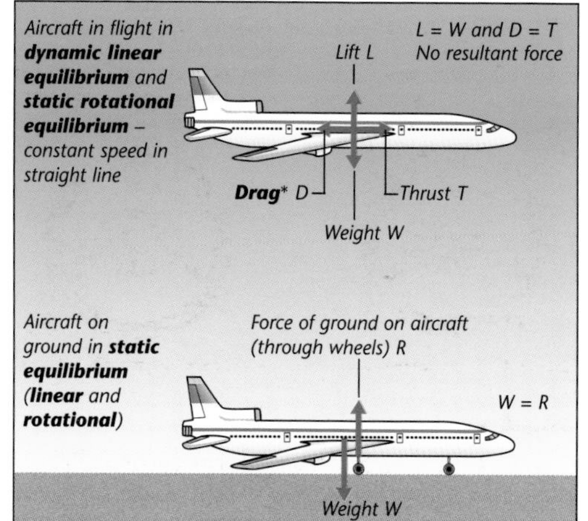

Aircraft in flight in **dynamic linear equilibrium** and **static rotational equilibrium** – constant speed in straight line
L = W and D = T
No resultant force
Lift L
Drag* D
Thrust T
Weight W
Aircraft on ground in **static equilibrium** (**linear** and **rotational**)
Force of ground on aircraft (through wheels) R
W = R
Weight W

Rotational equilibrium

The state of an object when there is no **angular acceleration***, i.e. it spins at constant **angular velocity***. If an object is in rotational equilibrium, the **resultant moment** (see **moment**) about any axis is zero.

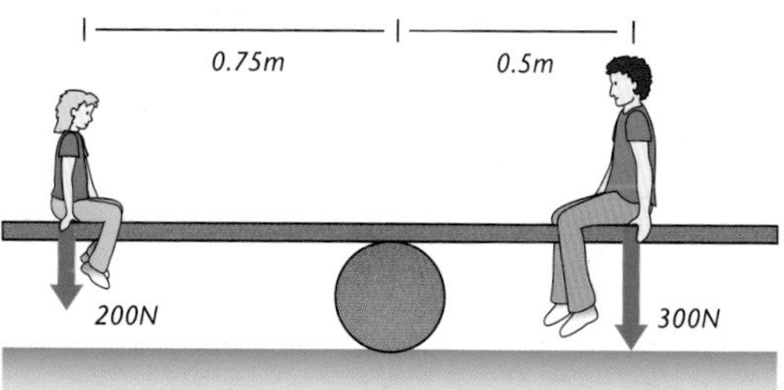

0.75m
0.5m
200N
300N

*Beam in **static rotational equilibrium**, since 200 × 0.75 = 300 × 0.5*

Stable equilibrium

A state in which an object moved a small distance from its equilibrium position returns to that position. This happens if the **center of mass*** is raised when the object is moved.

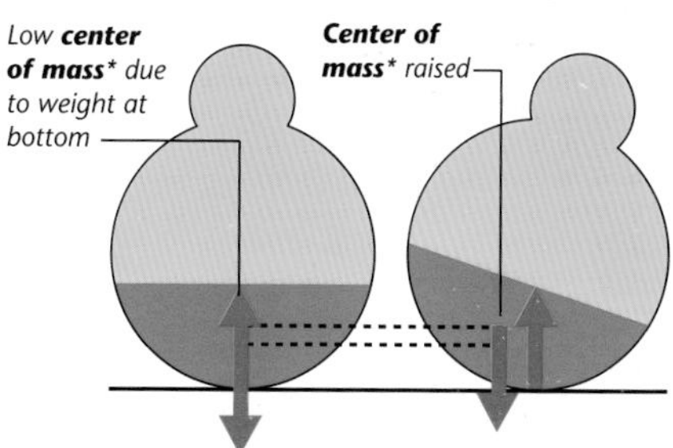

Low **center of mass*** due to weight at bottom
Center of mass* raised

*Weight and force from ground form **couple** to turn toy upright.*

Unstable equilibrium

A state in which an object moved a small distance from its equilibrium position moves further from that position. This happens if the **center of mass*** is lowered when the object is moved.

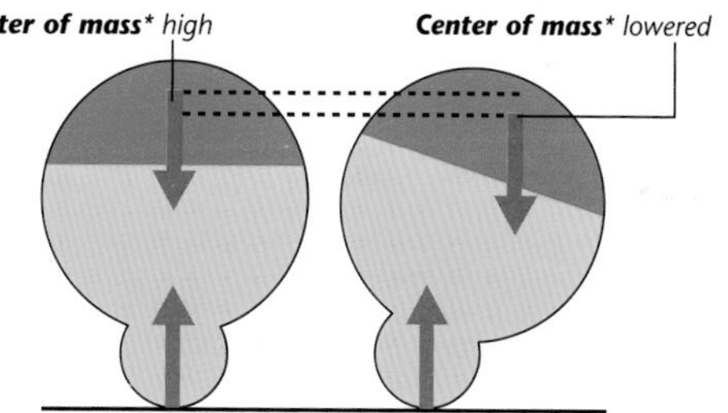

Center of mass* high
Center of mass* lowered

*Weight and force form **couple** which turns toy further over.*

Neutral equilibrium

A state in which an object moved a small distance from its equilibrium position remains in the new position. This happens if the **center of mass*** remains at the same height.

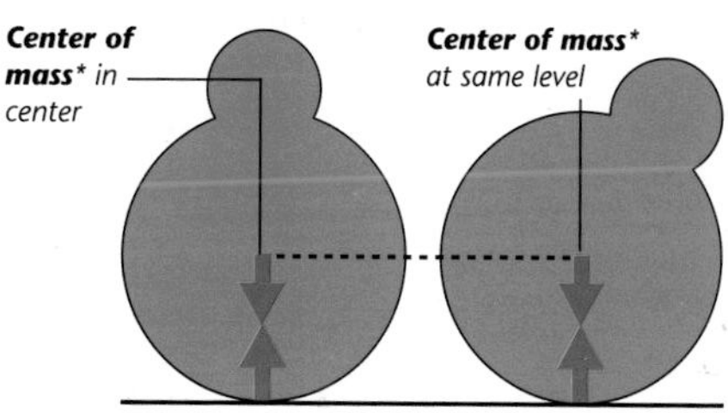

Center of mass* in center
Center of mass* at same level

*Weight and force on same line – no **couple** so toy stays in new position.*

* **Angular acceleration**, **Angular velocity**, 17;
Center of mass, 10; **Drag**, 19 (**Terminal velocity**).

PERIODIC MOTION

Periodic motion is any motion which repeats itself exactly at regular intervals. Examples of periodic motion are objects moving in a circle (**circular motion**), the swing of a pendulum and the vibration of molecules. **Wave motion*** consists of the periodic motion of particles or fields.

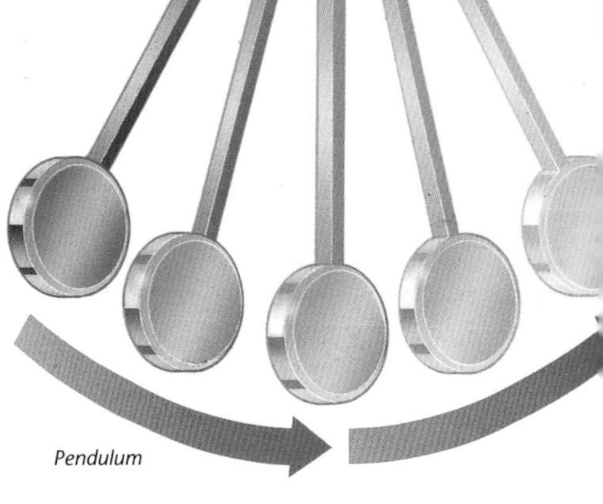
Pendulum

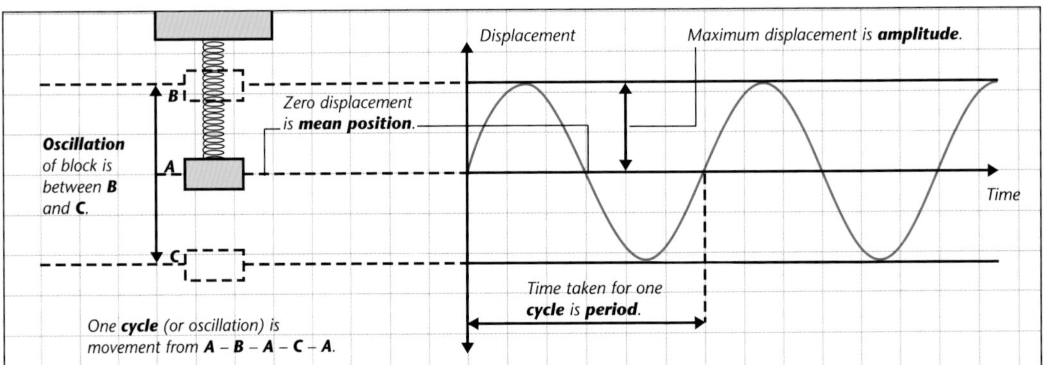
Displacement
Maximum displacement is **amplitude**.
Zero displacement is **mean position**.
Oscillation of block is between **B** and **C**.
B
A
C
Time
Time taken for one **cycle** is **period**.
One **cycle** (or oscillation) is movement from **A – B – A – C – A**.

Cycle

The movement between a point during a motion and the same point when the motion repeats. For example, one rotation of a spinning object.

Oscillation

Periodic motion between two extremes, e.g. a mass moving up and down on the end of a spring. In an oscillating system, there is a continuous change between **kinetic energy*** and **potential energy***. The total energy of a system (sum of its kinetic and potential energy) remains constant if there is no **damping**.

Period (T)

The time taken to complete one **cycle** of a motion, e.g. the period of rotation of the Earth about its axis is 24 hours.

Frequency (f)

The number of **cycles** of a particular motion in one second. The **SI unit*** of frequency is the **Hertz** (**Hz**), which is equal to one cycle per second.

$$f = \frac{1}{T}$$ where f = **frequency**; T = **period**.

Mean position

The position about which an object **oscillates**, and at which it comes to rest after oscillating, e.g. the mean position of a pendulum is when it is vertical. The position of zero displacement of an oscillating particle is usually taken as this point.

Amplitude

The maximum displacement of an **oscillating particle** from its **mean position**.

Damping

The process whereby **oscillations** die down due to a loss of energy, e.g. shock absorbers in cars cause oscillations to die down after a car has gone over a bump in the road.

Damping in an oscillating system

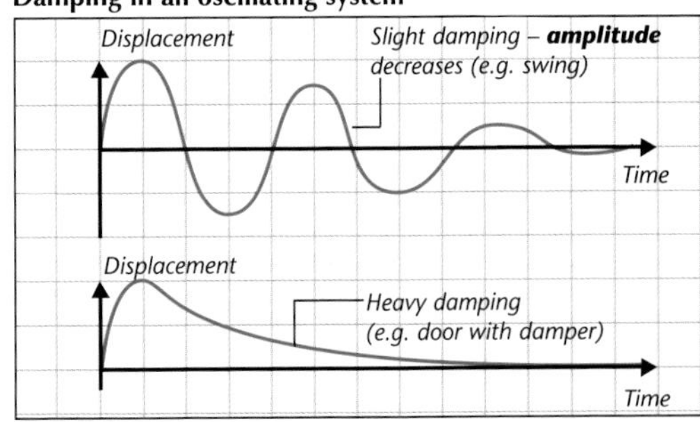
Displacement
Slight damping – **amplitude** decreases (e.g. swing)
Time
Displacement
Heavy damping (e.g. door with damper)
Time

* **Kinetic energy**, 9; **Potential energy**, 8; **SI units**, 96; **Wave motion**, 34.

Natural or free oscillation

The **oscillation** of a system when left after being started. The **period** and **frequency** of the system are called the **natural period** and **natural frequency** (these remain the same as long as the **damping** is not too great).

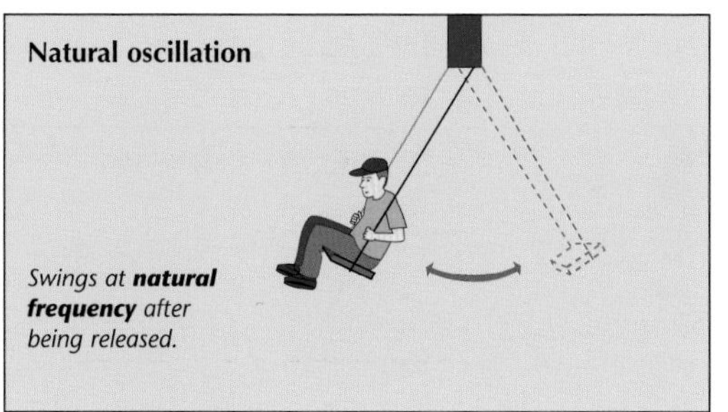
Natural oscillation
Swings at **natural frequency** after being released.

Forced oscillation

The **oscillation** of a system when given a repeated driving force (a force applied to the system) at regular intervals. The system is made to oscillate at the **frequency** of the driving force, irrespective of its **natural frequency**.

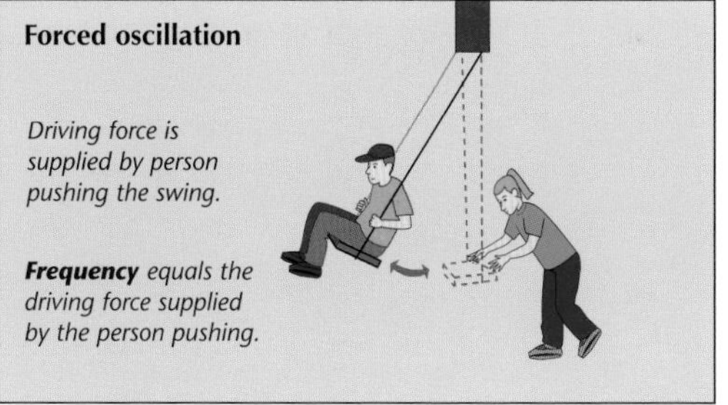
Forced oscillation
Driving force is supplied by person pushing the swing.
Frequency equals the driving force supplied by the person pushing.

Resonance

The effect exhibited by a system in which the **frequency** of the driving force (a force applied to the system) is about the same as the **natural frequency** of the system. The system then has a large **amplitude**.

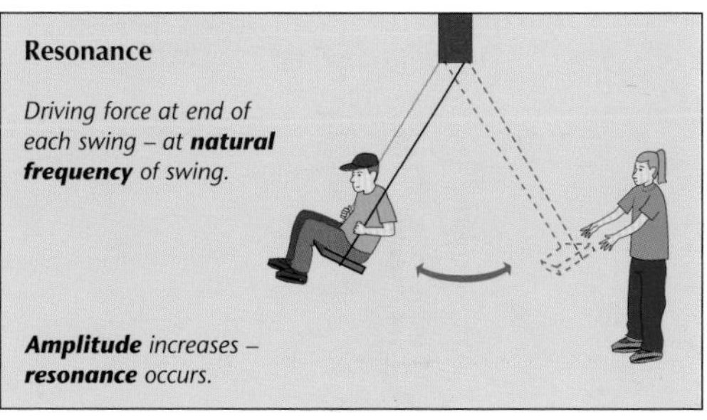
Resonance
Driving force at end of each swing – at **natural frequency** of swing.
Amplitude increases – **resonance** occurs.

Circular motion

Uniform circular motion

The motion of an object in a circle at constant speed. Since the direction (and therefore the **velocity***) changes, the object is constantly **accelerating*** toward the center (**centripetal acceleration**), and so there is a force acting toward the center. Circular motion can be considered in terms of **angular velocity**.

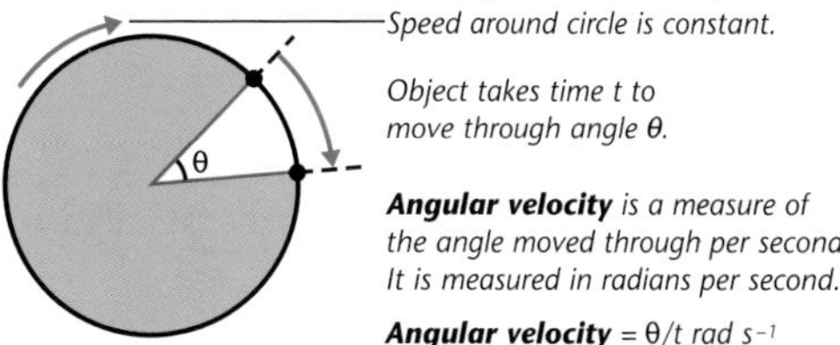
Speed around circle is constant.
θ
Object takes time t to move through angle θ.
Angular velocity is a measure of the angle moved through per second. It is measured in radians per second.
Angular velocity = θ/t rad s⁻¹

Centripetal acceleration (a)

The **acceleration*** of an object in circular motion (see above) acting toward the center of the circle.

Centripetal force

The force which acts on an object toward the center of a circle to produce **centripetal acceleration**, and so keeps the object moving in a circle.

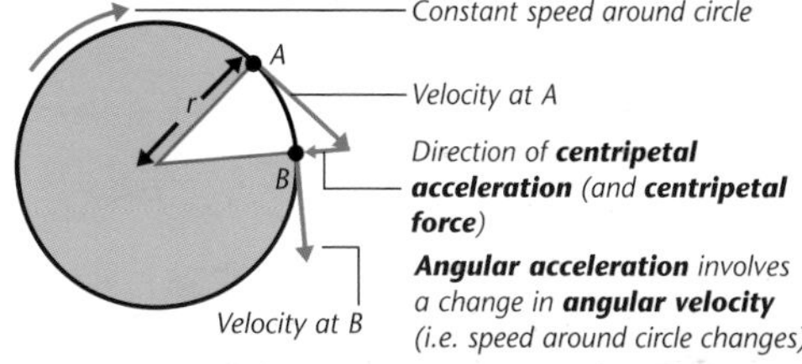
Constant speed around circle
A
r
B
Velocity at A
Direction of **centripetal acceleration** (and **centripetal force**)
Angular acceleration involves a change in **angular velocity** (i.e. speed around circle changes).
Velocity at B

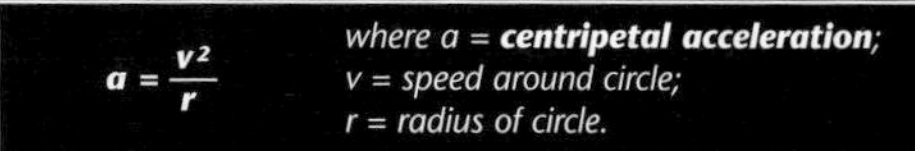

$$a = \frac{v^2}{r}$$

where a = **centripetal acceleration**; v = speed around circle; r = radius of circle.

Centripetal force has an equal and opposite reaction (see **Newton's second law**, page 12), called **centrifugal force**. It does not act on the object moving in the circle so is not considered in forces calculations.

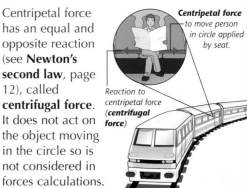

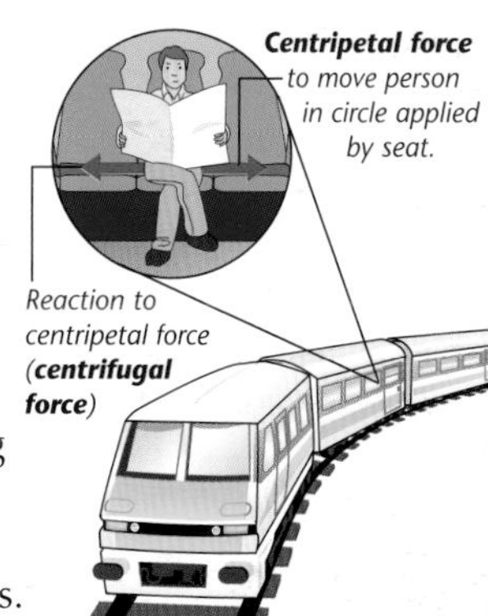
Centripetal force to move person in circle applied by seat.
Reaction to centripetal force (**centrifugal force**)

* **Acceleration**, 11; **Velocity**, 10.

GRAVITATION

Gravitation is the effect of the **gravitational force*** of attraction (see also page 104) which acts between all objects in the universe. It is noticed with massive objects like the planets, which remain in orbit because of it. The gravitational force between an object and a planet, which pulls the object downward, is called the **weight** of the object.

F

Mass M

d

Saturn with Tethys, one of the 18 moons that orbit it.

F

Mass m

The gravitational force between two objects can be calculated from their masses (M and m) and the distance between them (d).

Newton's law of gravitation

States that there is a gravitational force of attraction between any two objects with mass which depends on the masses of the objects and the distance between them. The **gravitational constant** (**G**) has a value of $6.7 \times 10^{-11} Nm^2\ kg^{-2}$, and its small value means that gravitational forces are negligible unless one of the masses is very large.

$$F = G\frac{Mm}{d^2}$$ where G = ***gravitational constant***.

Weight

The gravitational pull of a massive object (e.g. a planet) on another object. The weight of an object is not constant, but depends on the distance from, and mass of the planet. Hence, although the mass of an object is independent of its position, its weight is not.

Weight of mass of 100kg alters with position:

Weighing scales measure the force exerted on them. At the surface of the Earth, the weight of mass 100kg is 980N.

On surface of Moon (smaller than Earth), weight of mass 100kg is 160N.

At 10,000km above surface of Earth, weight of mass 100kg is 150N.

Acceleration due to gravity (g)

The **acceleration*** produced by the gravitational force of attraction. Its value is the same for any mass at a given place. It is about $9.8 m\ s^{-2}$ on the Earth's surface, and decreases above the surface according to **Newton's law of gravitation**. The value of $9.8 m\ s^{-2}$ is used as a unit of acceleration (the **g-force**).

Object
(mass m)
Planet (mass M)

*From **Newton's law of gravitation** and **Newton's second law***:*

$$\text{Force on mass } (= mg) = G\frac{Mm}{d^2}$$

*So **acceleration due to gravity (g)**:*

$$g = G\frac{M}{d^2}$$

*During tight turns, pilots experience high **g-forces** (e.g. 5g – five times the normal) which can lead to blackout.*

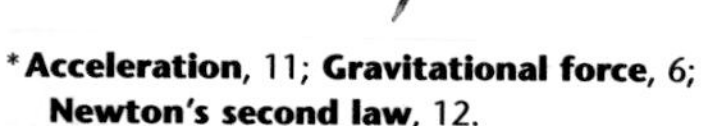

*__Acceleration__, 11; __Gravitational force__, 6; __Newton's second law__, 12.

Terminal velocity

The maximum, constant **velocity*** reached by an object falling through a gas or liquid. As the velocity increases, the resistance due to the air or liquid (**drag**) increases. Eventually, the drag becomes equal to the **weight** of the object, and its velocity does not increase any more.

*Just after the sky diver jumps, **velocity*** = 0, so **drag** = 0 and **acceleration*** = g.*

Velocity increases, drag increases, acceleration less than g.

Drag

Force down = **weight**.

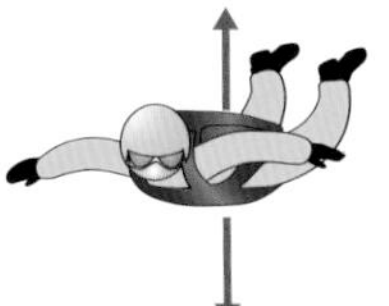

*At **terminal velocity**, drag same as weight, acceleration = 0.*

Parachute open, drag much greater, terminal velocity less.

Escape velocity

The minimum **velocity*** at which an object must travel in order to escape the gravitational pull of a planet without further propulsion. It is about 40,000km h^{-1} on Earth.

Free fall

The unrestricted motion of an object when it is acted upon only by the gravitational force (i.e. when there are no resistive or other forces acting, e.g. air resistance).

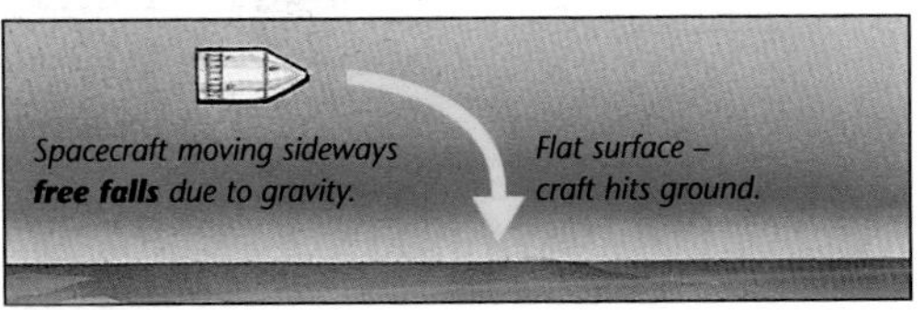
Spacecraft moving sideways **free falls** due to gravity.
Flat surface – craft hits ground.

Surface is curved.
Planet's surface falls away as quickly as spacecraft free falls.
Spacecraft gets no nearer to planet and therefore orbits.

Weightlessness

The state in which an object does not exert any force on its surroundings.

True weightlessness

Weightlessness due to an object being in a gravity-free region.

Apparent weightlessness

The state of an object when it is as if there were no gravitational forces acting. This occurs if two objects **accelerate*** independently in the same way.

*Astronaut inside an orbiting spacecraft **free falls** in same way as spacecraft and is therefore **apparently weightless** inside it.*

Geo-stationary or parking orbit

The path of a satellite which orbits the Earth in the same direction as the rotation of the Earth so that it stays above the same place on the surface all the time. The satellite has a **period*** of 24 hours.

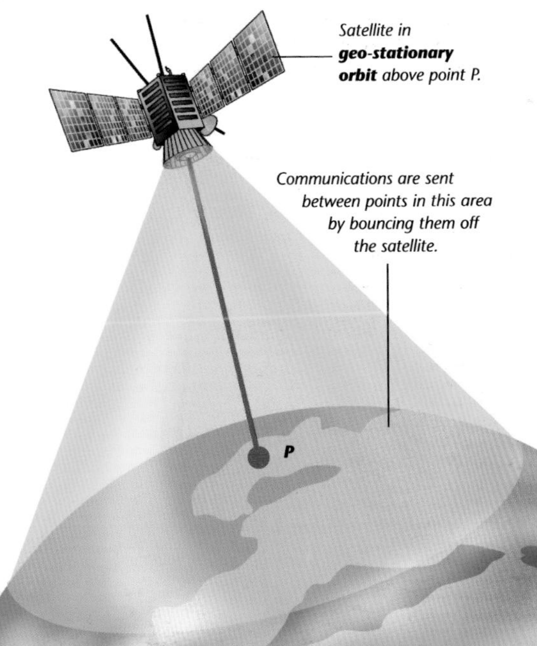
Satellite in **geo-stationary orbit** above point P.
Communications are sent between points in this area by bouncing them off the satellite.
P

* **Acceleration**, 11; **Period**, 16; **Velocity**, 10.

MACHINES

A **machine** is a device which is used to overcome a force called the **load**. This force is applied at one point and the machine works by the application of another force called the **effort** at a different point. For example, a small effort exerted on the rope of a **pulley** overcomes the weight of the object being raised by the pulley.

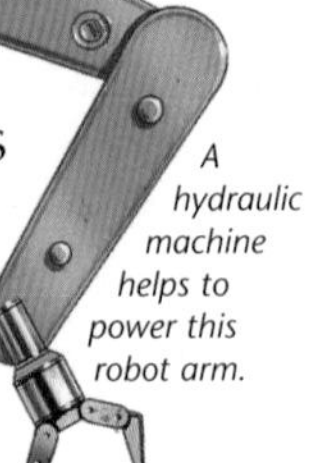
A hydraulic machine helps to power this robot arm.

Pulley system – an example of a machine

(See also page 21.)

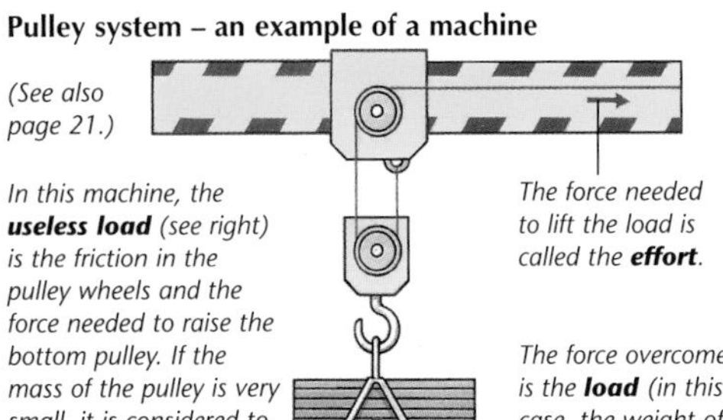

*In this machine, the **useless load** (see right) is the friction in the pulley wheels and the force needed to raise the bottom pulley. If the mass of the pulley is very small, it is considered to be a **perfect machine**.*

*The force needed to lift the load is called the **effort**.*

*The force overcome is the **load** (in this case, the weight of the object).*

Useless load

The force needed to overcome the **frictional forces*** between the moving parts of a machine and to raise any of its moving parts.

Perfect machine

A theoretical machine, with a **useless load** of zero. Machines in which the useless load is negligible compared to the load can be considered as perfect machines.

Mechanical advantage (M.A.)

The load (L) divided by the effort (E). A mechanical advantage greater than one means that the load overcome is greater than the effort. The mechanical advantage of any given **perfect machine** remains the same as the load increases. The mechanical advantage of any given real machine increases slightly with load because **useless load** becomes less significant as the load increases.

$$\text{M.A.} = \frac{L}{E}$$

Diagram of screwjack showing effort, load and work done

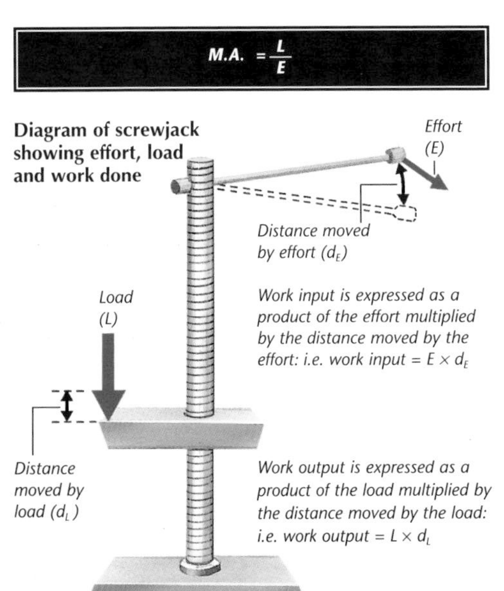
Effort (E)
Distance moved by effort (d_E)
Load (L)
Distance moved by load (d_L)

Work input is expressed as a product of the effort multiplied by the distance moved by the effort: i.e. work input = $E \times d_E$

Work output is expressed as a product of the load multiplied by the distance moved by the load: i.e. work output = $L \times d_L$

Efficiency

The **work** done (force × distance – see page 8) on the load (work output) divided by the work done by the effort (work input), expressed as a percentage. All real machines have an efficiency of less than 100% due to **useless load**. **Perfect machines** are 100% efficient.

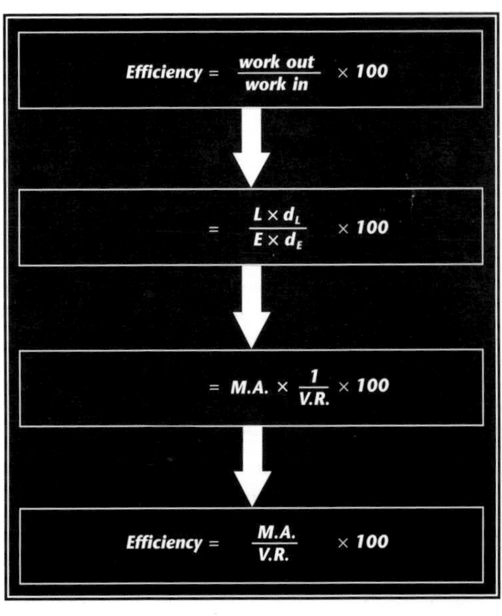

$$\text{Efficiency} = \frac{\text{work out}}{\text{work in}} \times 100$$

$$= \frac{L \times d_L}{E \times d_E} \times 100$$

$$= \text{M.A.} \times \frac{1}{\text{V.R.}} \times 100$$

$$\text{Efficiency} = \frac{\text{M.A.}}{\text{V.R.}} \times 100$$

*In a **perfect machine** (100% efficiency):* **M.A. = V.R.**

* **Frictional force**, 7.

Examples of machines

Hydraulic press

A large and small cylinder connected by a pipe and filled with fluid, used to produce large forces.

Hydraulic press

Volume of liquid moved = $a \times d_E$ = $A \times d_L$ so ***V.R.*** *$(d_E / d_L) = A / a$*

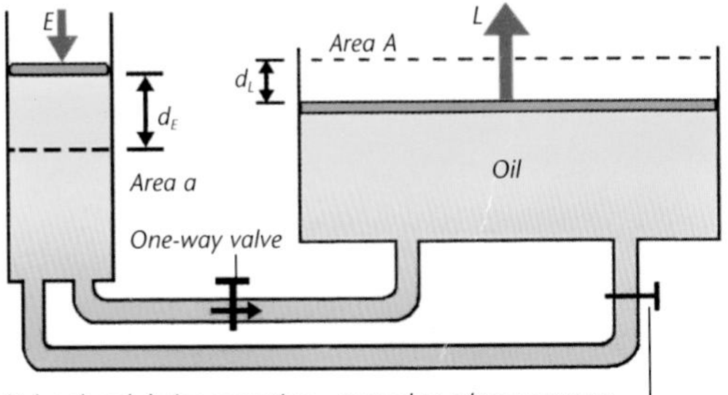

E
L
d_L
Area A
d_E
Area a
Oil
One-way valve

Valve closed during operation – opened to release pressure

Lever

Any rigid object which is pivoted about an axis called the **fulcrum** (**F**). The load and effort can be applied on either or the same side. There are three classes of lever, shown below.

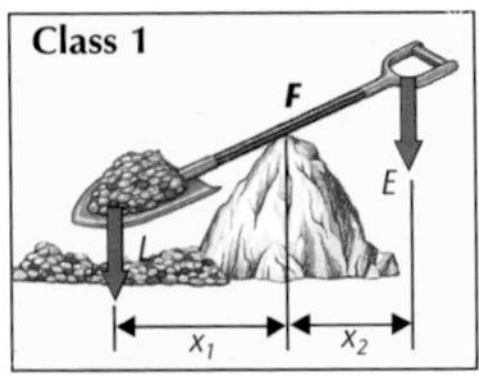

Class 1
F
E
x_1
x_2

Fulcrum between effort and load.

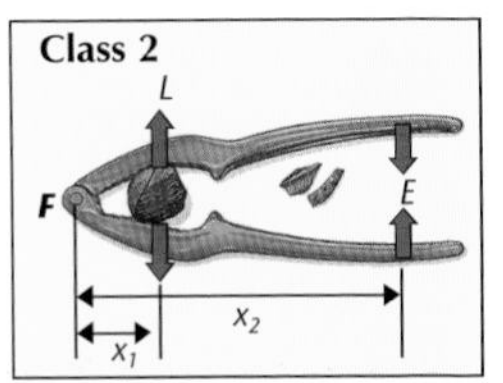

Class 2
L
F
E
x_2
x_1

Load between effort and fulcrum.

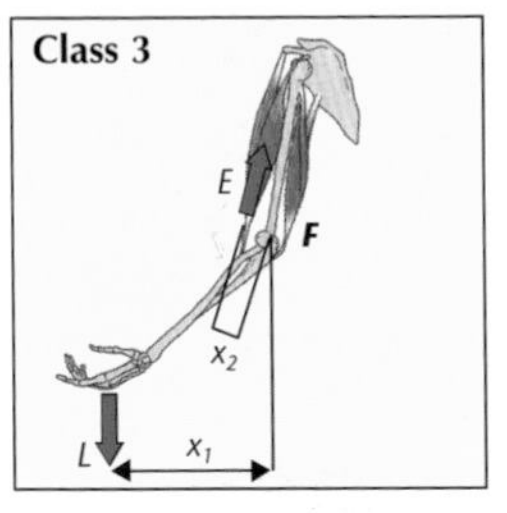

Class 3
E
F
x_2
L
x_1

Effort between fulcrum and load.

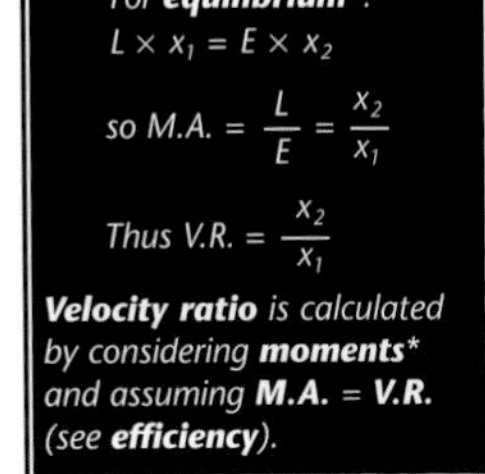

For ***equilibrium******:

$$L \times x_1 = E \times x_2$$

$$\text{so M.A.} = \frac{L}{E} = \frac{x_2}{x_1}$$

$$\text{Thus V.R.} = \frac{x_2}{x_1}$$

Velocity ratio *is calculated by considering* ***moments***** and assuming* ***M.A.* = *V.R.*** *(see* ***efficiency****).*

Gear

A combination of toothed wheels used to transmit motion between rotating shafts.

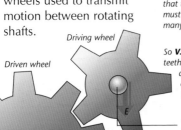

Driving wheel

Driven wheel

E

L

Twice as many teeth on the driven wheel means that the driving wheel must rotate twice as many times.

So ***V.R.*** *= number of teeth on driven wheel divided by number of teeth on driving wheel.*

Shafts of same diameter

Pulley system

A wheel (or combination of wheels) and a rope, belt or chain which transmits motion.

Pulley system on a crane

Pulley systems

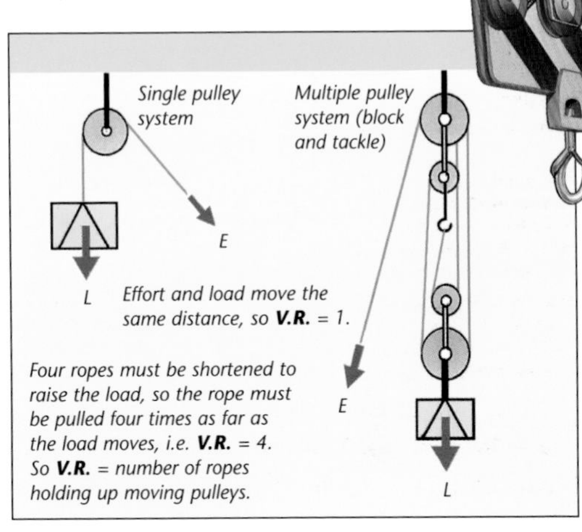

Single pulley system
Multiple pulley system (block and tackle)
E
L
Effort and load move the same distance, so V.R. = 1.
Four ropes must be shortened to raise the load, so the rope must be pulled four times as far as the load moves, i.e. V.R. = 4.
So V.R. = number of ropes holding up moving pulleys.
E
L

Inclined plane

A plane surface at an angle to the horizontal. It is easier to move an object up an inclined plane than to move it vertically upwards.

Inclined plane

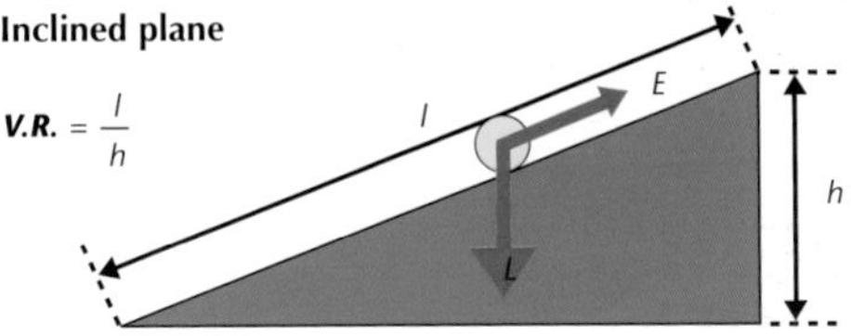

V.R. = l / h
l
E
L
h

Screw jack

A system in which a screw thread is turned to raise a load (e.g. a car jack). The **pitch** is the distance between each thread on the screw.

Screw jack

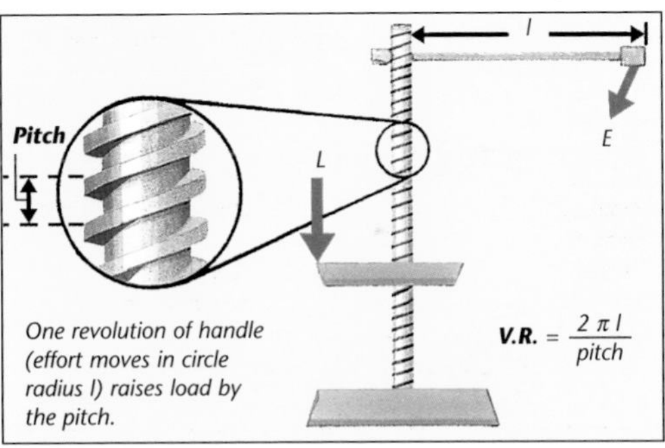

l
E
Pitch
L
One revolution of handle (effort moves in circle radius l) raises load by the pitch.
V.R. = 2 π l / pitch

* **Equilibrium**, 15; **Moment**, 14.

MOLECULAR PROPERTIES

There are a number of properties of matter which can be explained in terms of the behavior of molecules, in particular their behavior due to the action of the forces between them (**intermolecular forces***). Among these properties, and explained on this double page, are **elasticity**, **surface tension** and **viscosity**. See also pages 4-5 and 24-25.

Elasticity

The ability of a material to return to its original shape and size after distorting forces (i.e. **tension*** or **compression***) have been removed. Materials which have this ability are **elastic**; those which do not are **plastic**.

*Cool wax is **plastic** (the seal leaves a permanent impression in the wax).*

Elasticity is a result of **intermolecular forces*** – if an object is stretched or compressed, its molecules move further apart or closer together respectively. This results in a force of attraction (in the first case) or repulsion (in the second), so the molecules return to their average separation when the distorting force is removed. This always happens while the size of the force is below a certain level (different for each material), but all elastic materials finally become plastic if the force exceeds this level (see **elastic limit** and **yield point**).

*Balloons are **elastic** – they return to their original shape after stretching.*

Hooke's law

States that,
when a distorting force is applied to an object, the **strain** is proportional to the **stress**. As the size of the force increases, though, the **limit of proportionality** (or **proportional limit**) is reached, after which Hooke's law is no longer true (see graph, page 23).

Strain and stress in a stretched wire

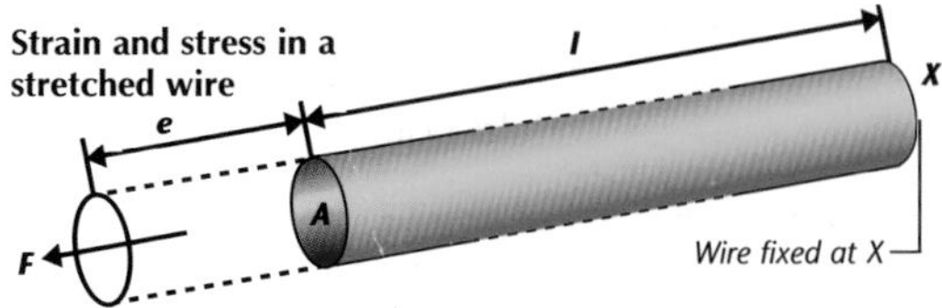

l
X
e
A
F
Wire fixed at X

***Strain** is stated as change in length per unit length.*

Strain $= \frac{e}{l}$ *where e = change in length; l = original length.*

***Stress** is stated as force applied per unit area.*

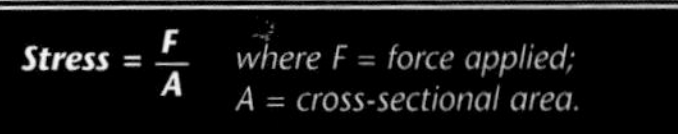

Stress = F/A
where F = force applied;
A = cross-sectional area.

***Spring balance** uses **Hooke's law** to measure force. Spring is extended in proportion to force applied.*

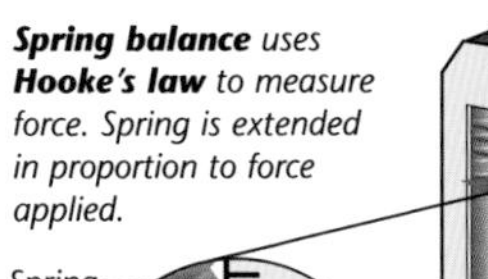

Spring
5

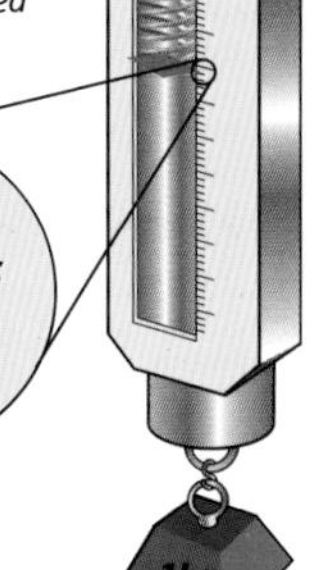

1kg

*Scale **calibrated*** so that length of spring gives size of force in **newtons***.*

*For an object in **tension*** or **compression**, **stress** divided by **strain** (see above) is always same figure for a given material (**Young's modulus** – see page 112) until **limit of proportionality** is reached.*

Elastic limit

The point, just after the **limit of proportionality** (see **Hooke's law**), beyond which an object ceases to be **elastic**, in the sense that it does not return to its original shape and size when the distorting force is removed. It does return to a similar shape and size, but has suffered a permanent strain (it will continue to return to this new form if forces are applied, i.e. it stays elastic in this sense).

* **Calibration**, 115; **Compression**, **Intermolecular forces**, 7; **Newton**, 6; **Tension**, 7.

Yield point

The point, just after the **elastic limit**, at which a distorting force causes a major change in a material. In a **ductile*** material, the internal structure changes – bonds between molecular layers break and the layers flow over each other. This change is called **plastic deformation** (the material becomes **plastic**). It continues as the force increases, and the material will eventually break. A **brittle** material, by contrast, will break at its yield point. The **yield stress** of a material is the value of the **stress** at its yield point. See graph below.

Stress/strain graph for a ductile* material

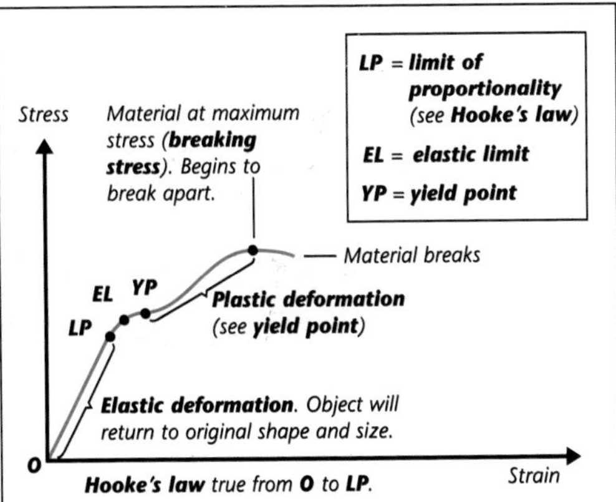

LP = limit of proportionality (see Hooke's law)
EL = elastic limit
YP = yield point
Stress
Material at maximum stress (breaking stress). Begins to break apart.
Material breaks
EL
YP
LP
Plastic deformation (see yield point)
Elastic deformation. Object will return to original shape and size.
O
Strain
Hooke's law true from O to LP.

Viscosity

The ease of flow of a fluid. It depends on the size of the **frictional force*** between different layers of molecules as they slide over each other.

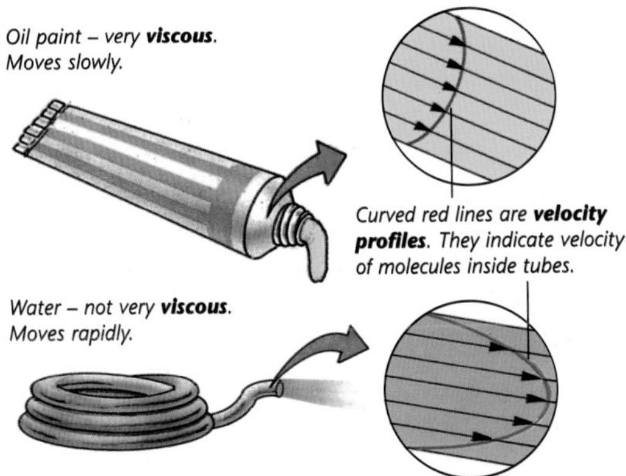

Oil paint – very viscous. Moves slowly.
Curved red lines are velocity profiles. They indicate velocity of molecules inside tubes.
Water – not very viscous. Moves rapidly.

*Outer layers of fluid slowed by **frictional force*** between them and sides of container. Working inwards, friction gradually loses effect. Effect lost much faster in water than oil paint.*

Surface tension

The skin-like property of a liquid surface resulting from **intermolecular forces*** which cause it to contract to the smallest possible area.

Two examples of surface tension

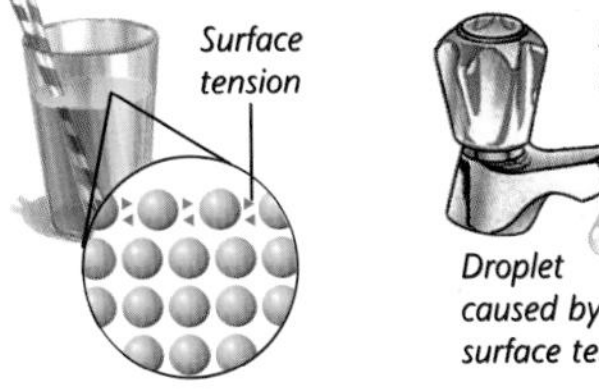

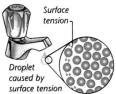

Surface tension
Surface tension
Droplet caused by surface tension

At the surface, the molecules are slightly further apart than the inner ones, and at a separation such that they attract each other (see **intermolecular forces**, page 7). The molecules cannot move closer because of equal forces on either side. The surface molecules are therefore in a constant state of tension, giving the surface elastic properties.

Water bug on water's surface

Adhesion

An **intermolecular force*** of attraction between molecules of different substances.

***Capillary action** or **capillarity** is a result of **adhesion** or **cohesion**.*

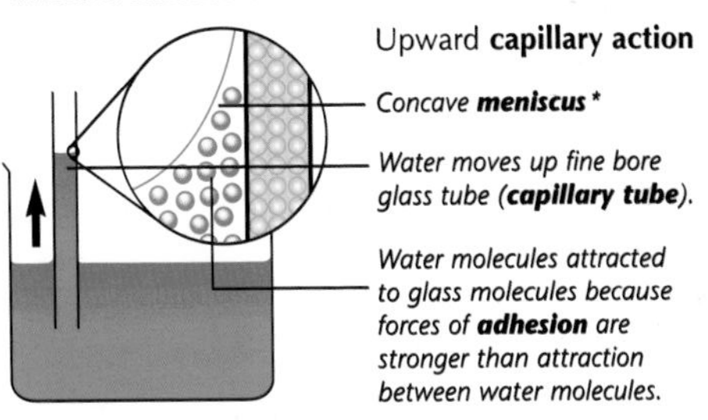

Upward capillary action
Concave meniscus *
Water moves up fine bore glass tube (capillary tube).
Water molecules attracted to glass molecules because forces of adhesion are stronger than attraction between water molecules.

Cohesion

An **intermolecular force*** of attraction between molecules of the same substance.

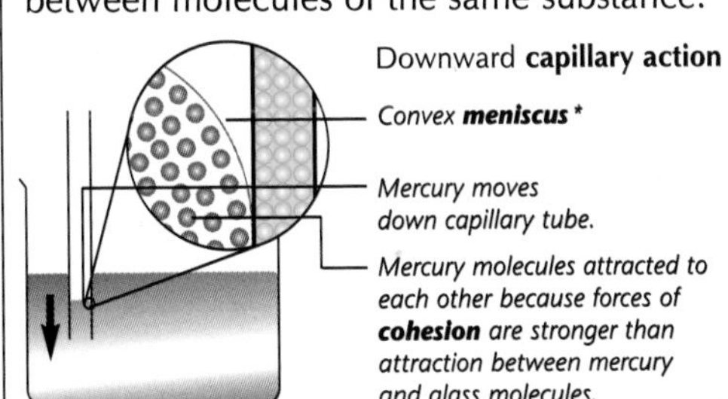

Downward capillary action
Convex meniscus *
Mercury moves down capillary tube.
Mercury molecules attracted to each other because forces of cohesion are stronger than attraction between mercury and glass molecules.

* **Ductile**, 115; **Frictional force**, **Intermolecular forces**, 7; **Meniscus**, 115.

DENSITY AND PRESSURE

The **density** (ρ) of an object depends on both the mass of its molecules and its volume (see formula, right). For example, if one substance has a higher density than another, then the same volumes of the substances have different masses (the first mass being greater than the second). Similarly, the same masses have different volumes.

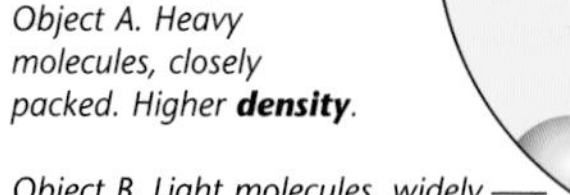

*Object A. Heavy molecules, closely packed. Higher **density**.*

Object B. Light molecules, widely spaced. Lower density.

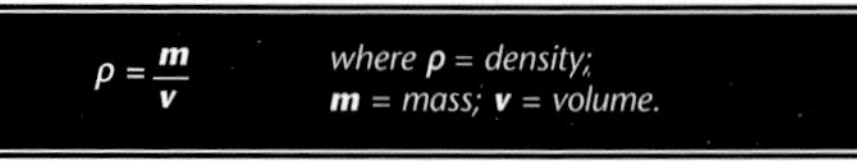
$\rho = \frac{m}{v}$
where ρ = density; m = mass; v = volume.

Hence $m = \rho \times v$

v is the same for objects A and B, so object A has greater mass.

*The **SI unit** * of density is the kg* m^{-3}.

Relative density or specific gravity

The density of a substance relative to the density of water (which is 1,000kg m^{-3}). It indicates how much more or less dense than water a substance is, so the figures need no units, e.g. 1.5 (one and a half times as dense). It is found by dividing the mass of any volume of a substance by the mass of an equal volume of water.

Eureka can

A can used to measure the volume of a solid object with an irregular shape, in order to calculate its density. The volume of water displaced is equal to the volume of the object. The density of the object is its mass divided by this volume.

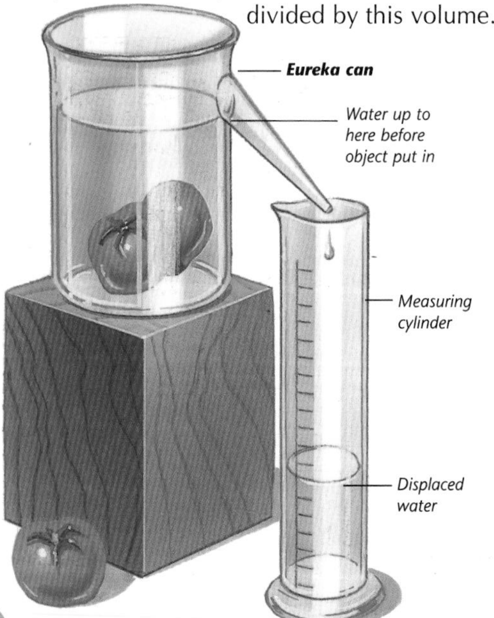
Eureka can
Water up to here before object put in
Measuring cylinder
Displaced water

Density bottle

A container which, when completely full, holds a precisely measured volume of liquid (at constant temperature). It is used to measure the density of liquids (by measuring the mass of the bottle and liquid, subtracting the mass of the bottle and dividing by the volume of liquid).

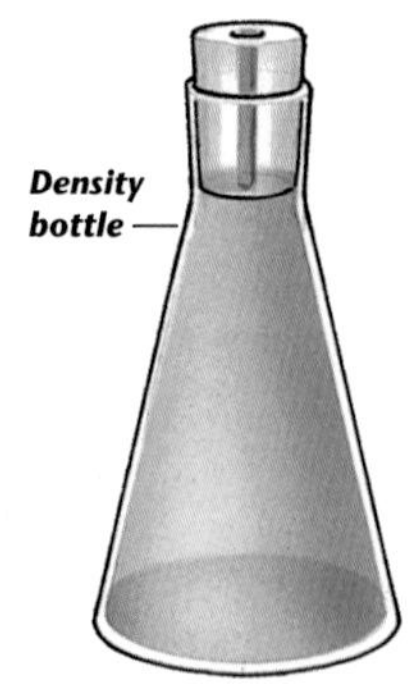
Density bottle

*Fine bore tube (**capillary tube**) in glass stopper. Bottle filled, stopper inserted, excess liquid rises through tube and runs out – ensures same volume each time.*

Hydrometer or aerometer

An instrument which measures the density of a liquid by the level at which it floats in that liquid. If the liquid is very dense, the hydrometer floats near the surface, as only a small volume of liquid needs to be displaced to equal the weight of the hydrometer.

Hydrometer

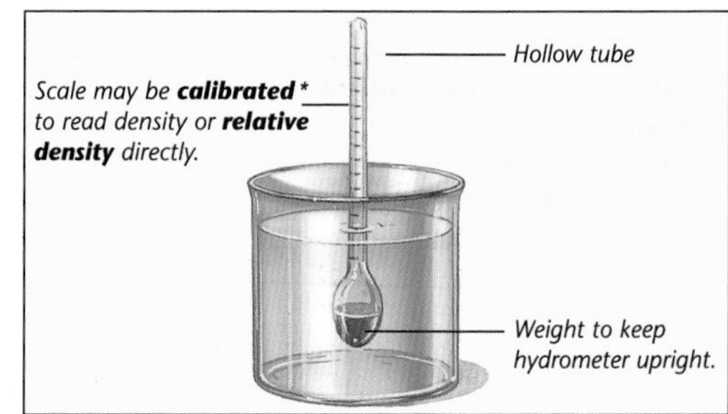
Hollow tube
Scale may be calibrated * to read density or relative density directly.
Weight to keep hydrometer upright.

* **Calibration**, 115; **SI units**, 96.

Pressure

Pressure is the force, acting at right angles, exerted by a solid, liquid or gas on a unit area of a substance (solid, liquid or gas).

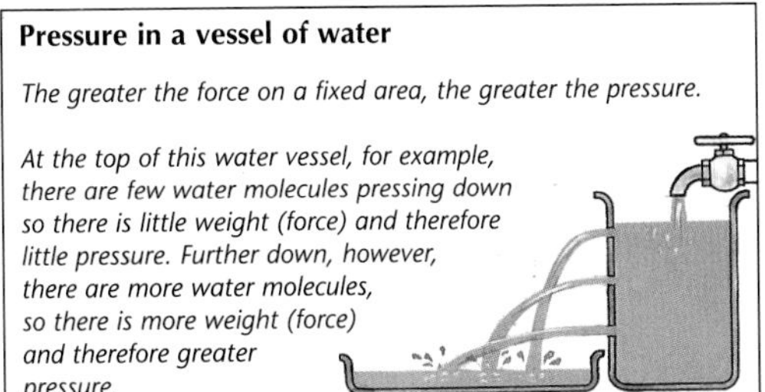

Pressure in a vessel of water

The greater the force on a fixed area, the greater the pressure.

At the top of this water vessel, for example, there are few water molecules pressing down so there is little weight (force) and therefore little pressure. Further down, however, there are more water molecules, so there is more weight (force) and therefore greater pressure.

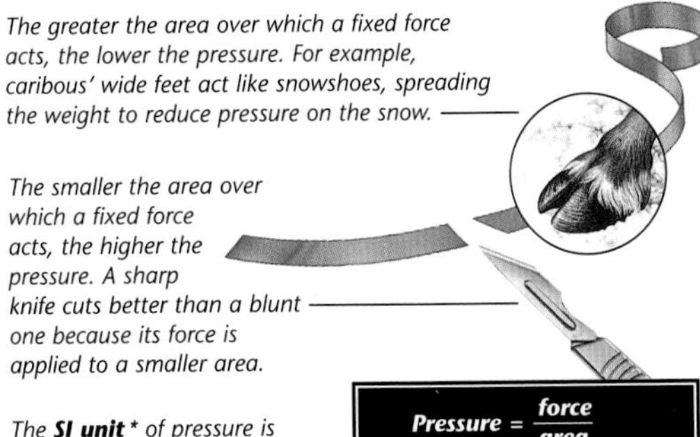

The greater the area over which a fixed force acts, the lower the pressure. For example, caribous' wide feet act like snowshoes, spreading the weight to reduce pressure on the snow.

The smaller the area over which a fixed force acts, the higher the pressure. A sharp knife cuts better than a blunt one because its force is applied to a smaller area.

*The **SI unit*** of pressure is the **pascal** (Pa).*

$$\text{Pressure} = \frac{\text{force}}{\text{area}}$$

Barometer

An instrument used to measure **atmospheric pressure** – the pressure caused by the weight of air molecules above the Earth. There are several common types.

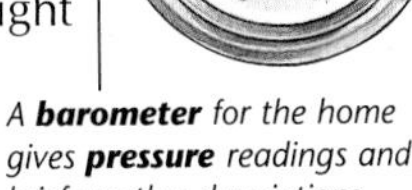

*A **barometer** for the home gives **pressure** readings and brief weather descriptions.*

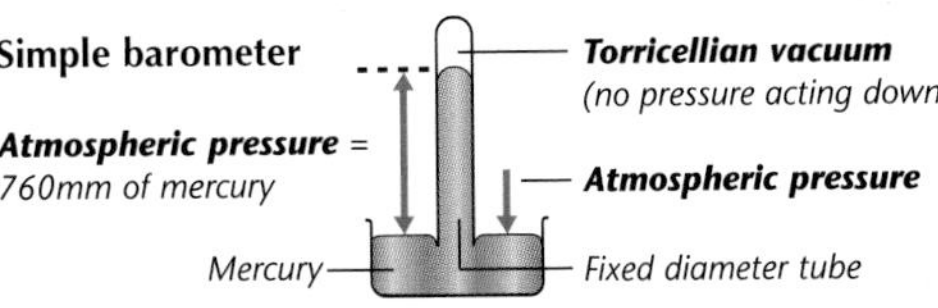
Simple barometer
Torricellian vacuum
(no pressure acting down)
***Atmospheric pressure** =*
760mm of mercury
Atmospheric pressure
Mercury
Fixed diameter tube

Manometer

A U-shaped tube containing a liquid. It is used to measure difference in fluid pressures.

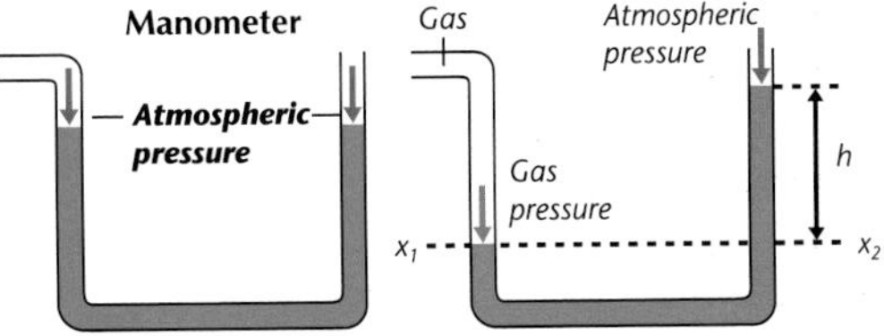
Manometer
Atmospheric pressure
Gas
Atmospheric pressure
Gas pressure
h
x_1
x_2

Pressures at x_1 and x_2 (same level) must be the same.
So pressure of gas = pressure at x_2
= atmospheric pressure + pressure of height (h) of liquid.

Objects in fluids

An object in a fluid experiences an upward force called the **buoyant force**. According to **Archimedes' principle**, this is equal to the weight of the fluid displaced by the object. The **principle of flotation** further states that, if the object is floating, the weight of displaced fluid (buoyant force) is equal to its own weight. It can be shown (see below) that whether an object sinks, rises or floats in a fluid depends entirely on density.

Archimedes' principle

Buoyant force = weight of fluid displaced

Principle of flotation

For a floating object: ***U = W*** — *where **U** = buoyant force; **W** = weight of object.*

Weight = mass (m) × acceleration due to gravity (g)
Mass = density (ρ) × volume (v)
So weight (of object or fluid displaced) = ρvg

*Submarines demonstrate **Archimedes' principle** and the **principle of flotation**. Altering air/water mix in ballast tanks alters density.*

*Submarine has two forces acting on it – its own weight and the **buoyant force**.*

***1**. If U = W, sub remains at a given depth.*

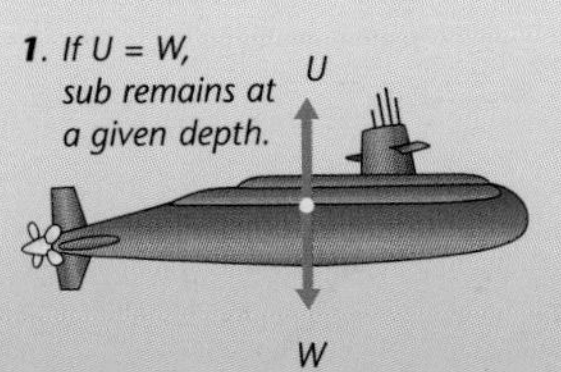
U
W

***2**. If U > W, sub starts to rise.*

Sub breaks surface and floats. U = W, though density still less than that of water (see below), because now volume of water displaced is less.

***3**. If **U** < W, sub starts to sink.*

Both W and U = ρvg (see above). v and g are the same for both, and density (ρ) of water is constant. So 1, 2 and 3 can be brought about by altering the density of the sub. In 1, the sub's density is the same as that of water, in 2 it is less and in 3 it is greater.

* **SI units**, 96.

TEMPERATURE

The **temperature** of an object is a measurement of how hot the object is. It is measured using **thermometers** which can be **calibrated*** to show a number of different temperature scales. The internationally accepted scales are the **absolute temperature scale** and the **Celsius scale**.

*On Venus, the **temperature** is approximately 480°C, or 753K. This is because thick clouds trap the Sun's radiation and prevent the heat from escaping.*

Thermometer

An instrument used to measure temperature. There are many different types and they all work by measuring a **thermometric property** – a property which changes with temperature. **Liquid-in-glass thermometers**, for example, measure the volume of a liquid (they are **calibrated*** so that increases in volume mark rises in temperature).

Liquid-in-glass thermometer

A common type of **thermometer** which measures temperature by the expansion of a liquid in a fine bore glass tube (**capillary tube**). A glass bulb holds a reservoir of the liquid, which is usually either mercury or colored alcohol. These substances are very responsive to temperature change – mercury is used for higher temperature ranges and alcohol for lower ones.

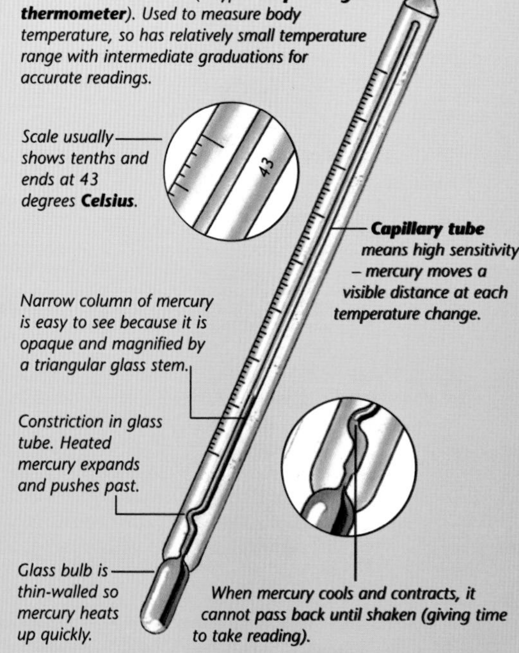

Clinical thermometer (a type of liquid-in-glass thermometer). Used to measure body temperature, so has relatively small temperature range with intermediate graduations for accurate readings.
Scale usually shows tenths and ends at 43 degrees Celsius.
43
Capillary tube means high sensitivity – mercury moves a visible distance at each temperature change.
Narrow column of mercury is easy to see because it is opaque and magnified by a triangular glass stem.
Constriction in glass tube. Heated mercury expands and pushes past.
Glass bulb is thin-walled so mercury heats up quickly.
When mercury cools and contracts, it cannot pass back until shaken (giving time to take reading).

Temperature scales

Fixed point

A temperature at which certain recognizable changes always take place (under given conditions), and which can thus be given a value against which all other temperatures can be measured. Examples are the **ice point** (the temperature at which pure ice melts) and the **steam point** (the temperature of steam above water boiling under **atmospheric pressure***). Two fixed points are used to **calibrate*** a thermometer – a **lower** and an **upper fixed point**. The distance between these points is known as the **fundamental interval**.

Using fixed points to calibrate* the Celsius scale on a thermometer

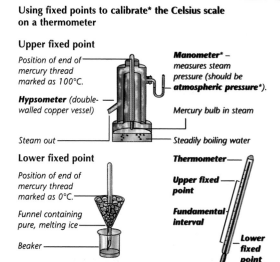

Upper fixed point

Position of end of mercury thread marked as 100°C.

***Hypsometer** (double-walled copper vessel)*

Steam out

Manometer – measures steam pressure (should be **atmospheric pressure***).*

Mercury bulb in steam

Steadily boiling water

Lower fixed point

Position of end of mercury thread marked as 0°C.

Funnel containing pure, melting ice

Beaker

Thermometer

Upper fixed point

Fundamental interval

Lower fixed point

* **Atmospheric pressure**, 25 (**Barometer**); **Calibration**, 115; **Manometer**, 25.

Maximum and **minimum thermometers**

Special **liquid-in-glass thermometers** which record the maximum or minimum temperature reached over a period of time. They contain a metal and glass **index** (see picture below) which is pushed up or pulled down (respectively) by the liquid **meniscus***. The index stays at the maximum or minimum position it reaches during the time the thermometer is left. It is reset using a magnet.

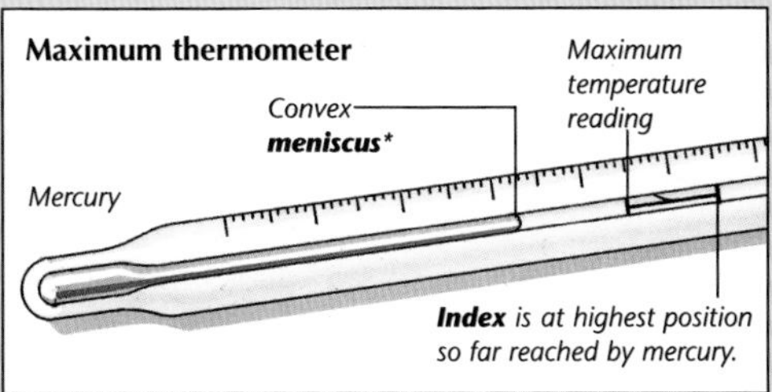
Maximum thermometer
Convex **meniscus***
Maximum temperature reading
Mercury
Index is at highest position so far reached by mercury.

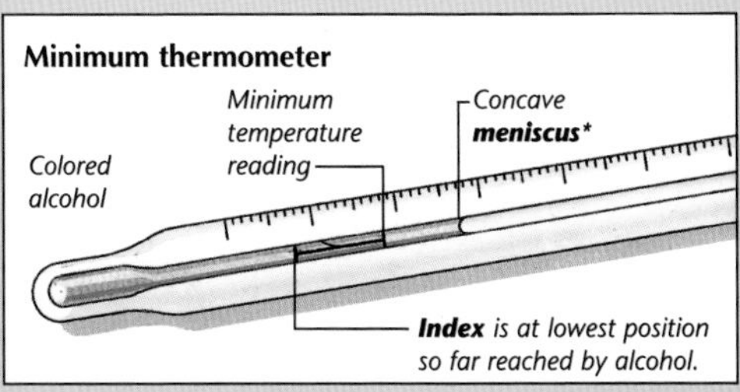
Minimum thermometer
Minimum temperature reading
Concave **meniscus***
Colored alcohol
Index is at lowest position so far reached by alcohol.

Other types of thermometer

Resistance thermometer

Measures temperature from change in **resistance*** it causes in a coil of wire. Similar devices, e.g. under aircraft wings, use resistance change in **thermistors***.

*Aircraft have **thermistors*** under their wing surfaces to measure the air temperature.*

Liquid crystal thermometer

A thermometer containing liquid crystals that change color when they are heated.

35
36
37
38
39
40

*A **liquid crystal thermometer** on the skin shows its temperature.*

Digital thermometer

A thermometer with a heat-sensitive electric component.

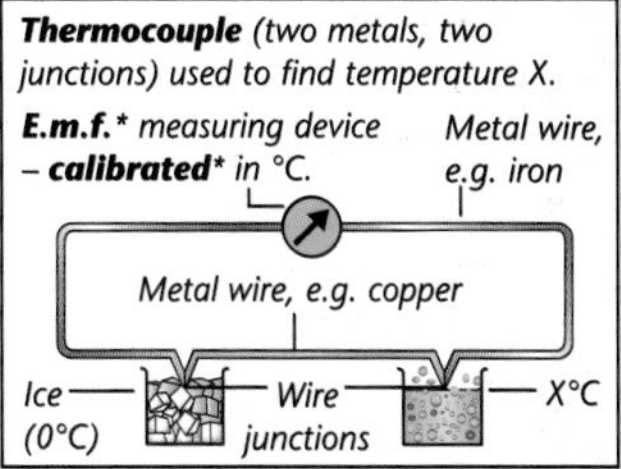

Digital display shows temperature.

Thermocouple

A device which uses the **e.m.f.*** produced across metal junctions to measure temperature difference.

Thermocouple *(two metals, two junctions) used to find temperature X.*

E.m.f. measuring device – calibrated* in °C.* *Metal wire, e.g. iron* *Metal wire, e.g. copper* *Ice (0°C)* *Wire junctions* *X°C*

Absolute or **thermodynamic temperature scale**

A standard temperature scale, using units called **kelvins** (**K**). The zero value is given to the lowest possible temperature theoretically achievable, called **absolute zero**. It is impossible to have a lower temperature, as this would require a negative volume (see graph, right) which cannot exist.

Celsius scale (°C)

A standard temperature scale identical in graduations to the **absolute temperature scale**, but with the zero and one hundred degree values given to the **ice point** and **steam point** respectively (see **fixed point**).

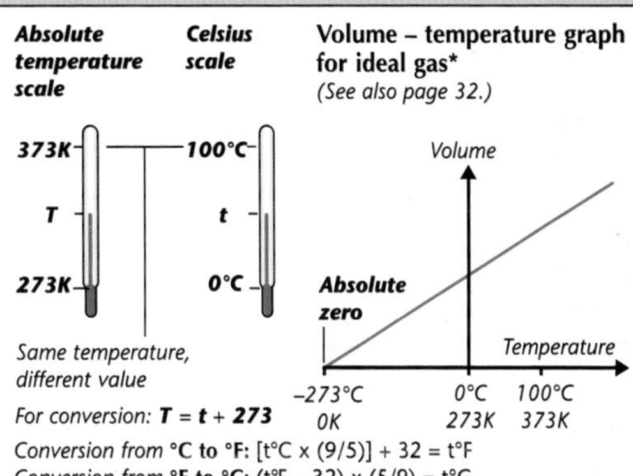
Absolute temperature scale
Celsius scale
373K
T
273K
100°C
t
0°C
Same temperature, different value
For conversion: T = t + 273
Volume – temperature graph for ideal gas*
(See also page 32.)
Volume
Absolute zero
Temperature
–273°C
0K
0°C
273K
100°C
373K

Conversion from °C to °F: [t°C x (9/5)] + 32 = t°F
Conversion from °F to °C: (t°F – 32) x (5/9) = t°C

Fahrenheit scale (°F)

An old scale with the values 32°F and 212°F given to the **ice point** and **steam point** respectively (see **fixed point**). It is rarely used in scientific work.

* **Calibration**, 115; **Electromotive force (e.m.f.)**, 60; **Ideal gas**, 33; **Meniscus**, 115; **Resistance**, 62; **Thermistor**, 65.

TRANSFER OF HEAT

Whenever there is a temperature difference, **heat energy** (see page 9) is transferred by **conduction**, **convection** or **radiation** from the hotter to the cooler place. This increases the **internal energy*** of the cooler atoms, raising their temperature, and decreases the energy of the hotter atoms, lowering theirs. It continues until the temperature is the same across the region – a state called **thermal equilibrium**.

*Gliders are lifted up by **convection currents** of warm air (see bottom of page).*

Conduction or thermal conduction

The way in which heat energy is transferred in solids (and also, to a much lesser extent, in liquids and gases). In good **conductors** the energy transfer is rapid, occurring mainly by the movement of free **electrons*** (electrons which can move about), although also by the vibration of atoms – see **insulators** (bad conductors), below.

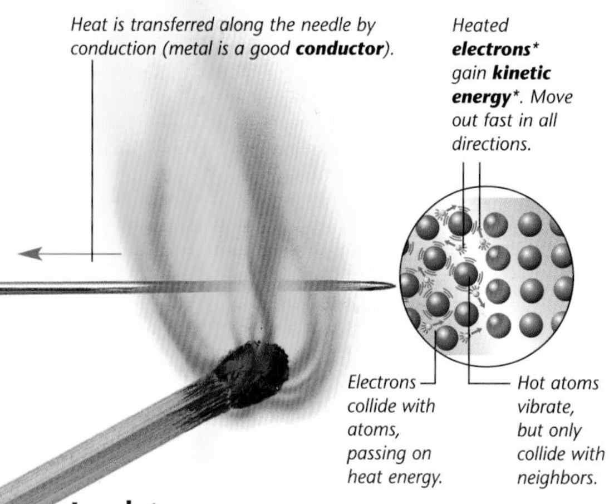
Heat is transferred along the needle by conduction (metal is a good conductor).
Heated electrons* gain kinetic energy*. Move out fast in all directions.
Electrons collide with atoms, passing on heat energy.
Hot atoms vibrate, but only collide with neighbors.

Insulators

Materials such as wood and most liquids and gases, in which the process of **conduction** is very slow (they are bad **conductors**). As they do not have free **electrons***, heat energy is only transferred by conduction by the vibration and collision of neighboring atoms.

Conductivity or thermal conductivity

A measure of how good a heat **conductor** a material is (see also page 112). The rate of heat energy transfer per unit area through an object depends on the conductivity of the material and the **temperature gradient**. This is the temperature change with distance along the material. The higher the conductivity and the steeper the gradient, the faster the energy transfer that takes place.

Metal pan – high conductivity (good conductor)
Plastic handle – low conductivity (bad conductor)
1
x
2
Flow of heat energy

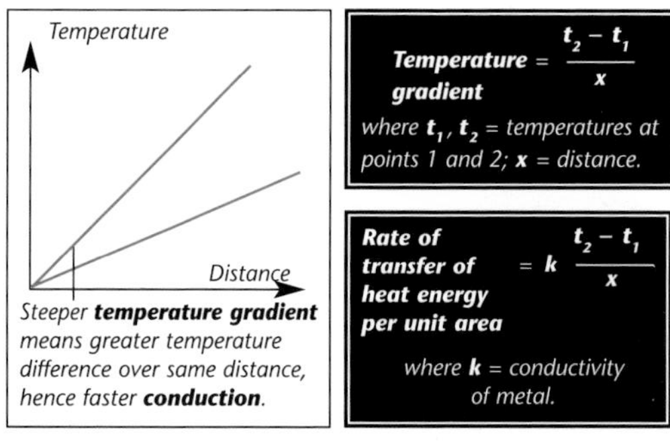
Temperature
Distance

*Steeper **temperature gradient** means greater temperature difference over same distance, hence faster **conduction**.*

$$\textbf{Temperature gradient} = \frac{t_2 - t_1}{x}$$

where t_1, t_2 = temperatures at points 1 and 2; x = distance.

$$\textbf{Rate of transfer of heat energy per unit area} = k\,\frac{t_2 - t_1}{x}$$

where k = conductivity of metal.

Convection

A way in which heat energy is transferred in liquids and gases. If a liquid or gas is heated, it expands, becomes less dense and rises. Cooler, denser liquid or gas then sinks to take its place. Thus a **convection current** is set up. The picture on the right shows how convection currents cause daytime coastal breezes, a process which is reversed at night.

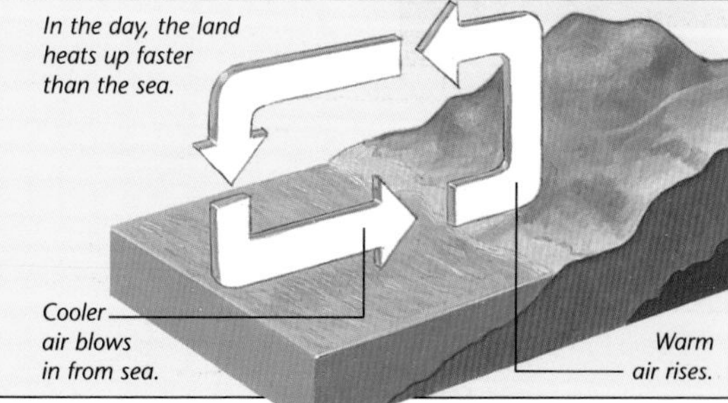
In the day, the land heats up faster than the sea.
Cooler air blows in from sea.
Warm air rises.

* **Electrons**, 83; **Internal energy**, **Kinetic energy**, 9.

Radiation

A way in which heat energy is transferred from a hotter to a cooler place without the **medium*** taking part in the process. This can occur though a vacuum, unlike **conduction** and **convection**. The term radiation is also often used to refer to the heat energy itself, otherwise known as **radiant heat energy**. This takes the form of **electromagnetic waves***, mainly **infra-red radiation***. When these waves fall on an object, some of their energy is absorbed, increasing the object's **internal energy*** and hence its temperature. See also **Leslie's cube**, right.

Use of radiation to supply hot water

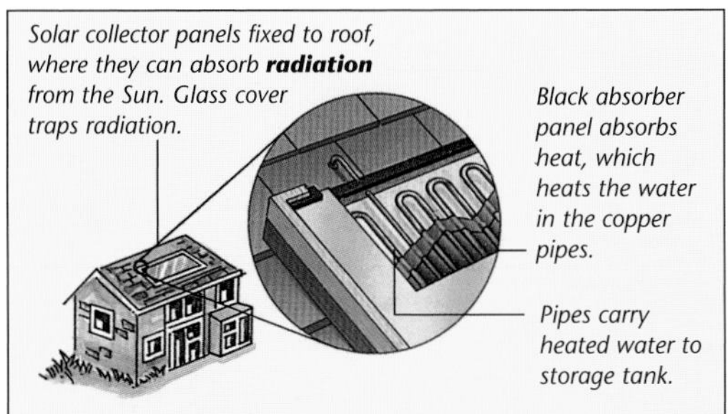
Solar collector panels fixed to roof, where they can absorb **radiation** from the Sun. Glass cover traps radiation.
Black absorber panel absorbs heat, which heats the water in the copper pipes.
Pipes carry heated water to storage tank.

Thermopile

A device for measuring **radiation** levels. It consists of two or more **thermocouples*** (normally over 50) joined end to end. Radiation falls on the metal junctions on one side and the temperature difference between these hot junctions and the cold ones on the other side produces **e.m.f.*** across the thermopile, the size of which indicates how much radiation has been absorbed.

Thermopile

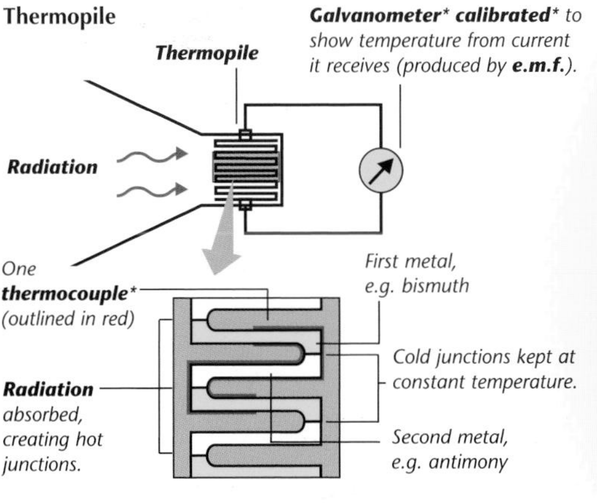
Thermopile
Galvanometer* calibrated* to show temperature from current it receives (produced by e.m.f.).
Radiation
One thermocouple* (outlined in red)
First metal, e.g. bismuth
Cold junctions kept at constant temperature.
Radiation absorbed, creating hot junctions.
Second metal, e.g. antimony

Leslie's cube

A thin-walled, hollow cube (good **conductor**) with different outside surfaces. It is used to show that surfaces vary in their ability to **radiate** and absorb heat energy. Their powers of doing so are compared with an ideal called a **black body**, which absorbs all radiation that falls on it, and is also the best radiator.

__Leslie's cube__ used to compare powers of __radiation__ – numbers show best (1) to worst (4) surface.

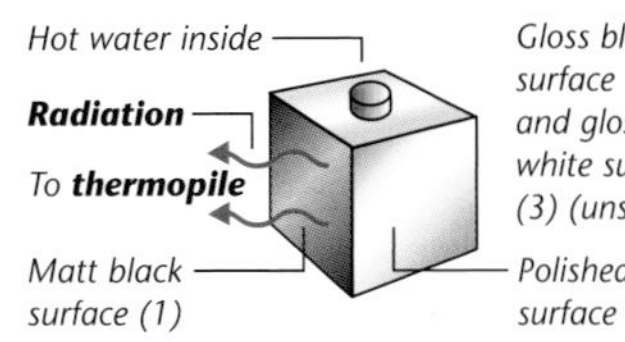
Hot water inside
Radiation
To thermopile
Matt black surface (1)
Gloss black surface (2) and gloss white surface (3) (unseen)
Polished metal surface (4)

Vacuum flask

A flask which keeps its contents at constant temperature. It consists of a double-walled glass container, with a **vacuum*** between the walls (stopping heat energy transfer by **conduction** and **convection**) and shiny surfaces (minimizing transfer by **radiation**).

Vacuum flask

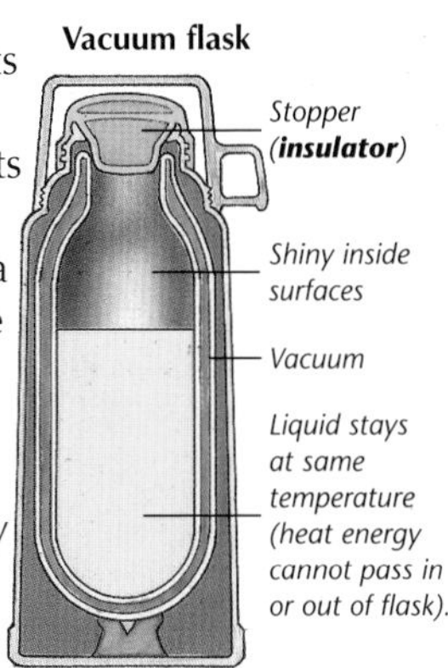
Stopper (insulator)
Shiny inside surfaces
Vacuum
Liquid stays at same temperature (heat energy cannot pass in or out of flask).

Greenhouse effect

The warming effect produced when **radiation** is trapped in a closed area, e.g. a greenhouse. The objects inside absorb the Sun's radiation and re-emit lower energy radiation which cannot pass back through the glass. Carbon dioxide in the atmosphere forms a similar barrier, and its level is increasing, hence the Earth is slowly getting warmer.

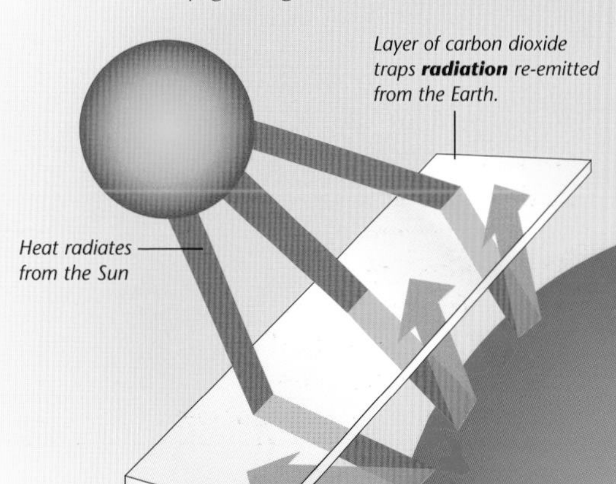
Layer of carbon dioxide traps radiation re-emitted from the Earth.
Heat radiates from the Sun

* **Calibration**, 115; **Electromagnetic waves**, 44; **Electromotive force (e.m.f.)**, 60; **Galvanometer**, 77; **Infra-red radiation**, 45; **Internal energy**, 9; **Medium**, 115; **Thermocouple**, 27; **Vacuum**, 115.

EFFECTS OF HEAT TRANSFER

When an object absorbs or loses **heat energy** (see pages 28-29), its **internal energy*** increases or decreases. This results in either a rise or fall in temperature (the amount of which depends on the **heat capacity** of the object) or a **change of state**.

During evaporation, molecules escape from the surface of a liquid.

Changes of state

A **change of state** is a change from one **physical state** (the solid, liquid or gaseous state) to another (for more about **physical states**, see page 5). While a change of state is happening, there is no change in temperature. Instead, all the energy taken in or given out is used to make or break molecular bonds. This is called **latent heat** (**L**) – see graphs, page 31. The **specific latent heat** (**l**) of a substance is a set value, i.e. the heat energy taken in or given out when 1kg of the substance changes state.

Evaporation

The conversion of a liquid to a vapor by the escape of molecules from its surface. It takes place at all temperatures, the rate increasing with any one or a combination of the following: increase in temperature, increase in surface area or decrease in pressure. It is also increased if the vapor is immediately removed from above the liquid by a flow of air. The **latent heat** (see above) needed for evaporation is taken from the liquid itself which cools and in turn cools its surroundings.

Vaporization

The change of state from liquid to gaseous at a temperature called the **boiling point** (when the liquid is said to be **boiling**). The term is also used more generally for any change resulting in a gas or vapor, i.e. including also **evaporation** and **sublimation**.

Condensation

The change of state from gas or vapor to liquid.

Melting

The change of state from solid to liquid at a temperature called the **melting point** of the solid.

Freezing

The change of state from liquid to solid at the **freezing point** (the same temperature as the **melting point** of the solid).

Sublimation

The conversion of a substance from a solid directly to a gas, or vice-versa, without passing through the liquid state. Iodine and carbon dioxide are two substances that **sublime**.

Changes of state
Temperature remains constant (see graphs, page 31).

Changes due to heating

*Heat energy taken in, which would have raised the temperature, used instead (as **latent heat**) to break bonds.*

Changes due to cooling

*Heat energy which would have been lost (lowering temperature) used instead (as **latent heat**) to make bonds between molecules.*

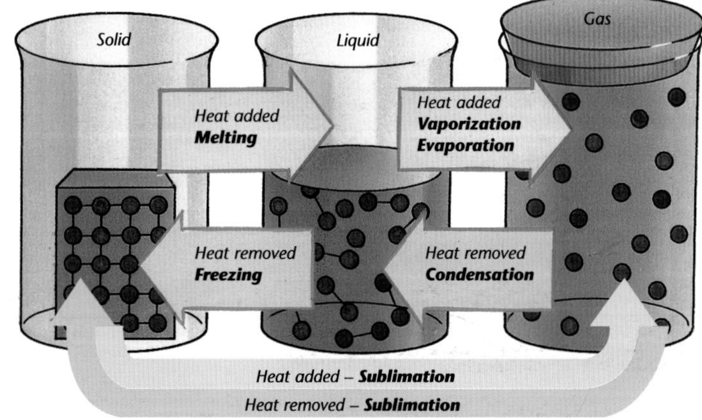
Solid
Liquid
Gas
Heat added
Melting
Heat added
Vaporization
Evaporation
Heat removed
Freezing
Heat removed
Condensation
Heat added – Sublimation
Heat removed – Sublimation

* **Internal energy**, 9.

Graph showing increase of temperature with heat added

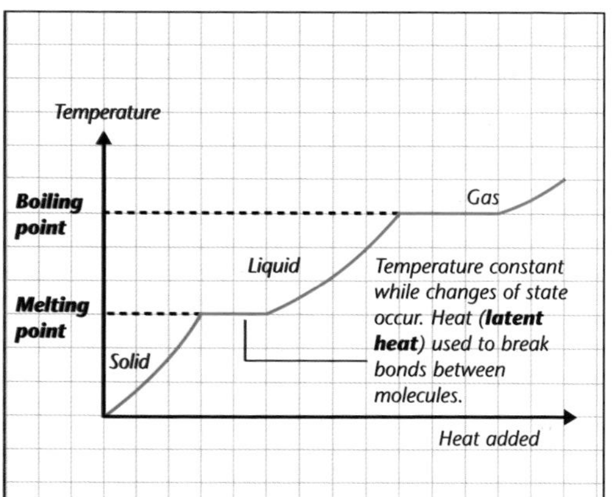
Temperature
Boiling point
Melting point
Gas
Liquid
Solid
Temperature constant while changes of state occur. Heat (**latent heat**) used to break bonds between molecules.
Heat added

Graph showing decrease of temperature as object cools

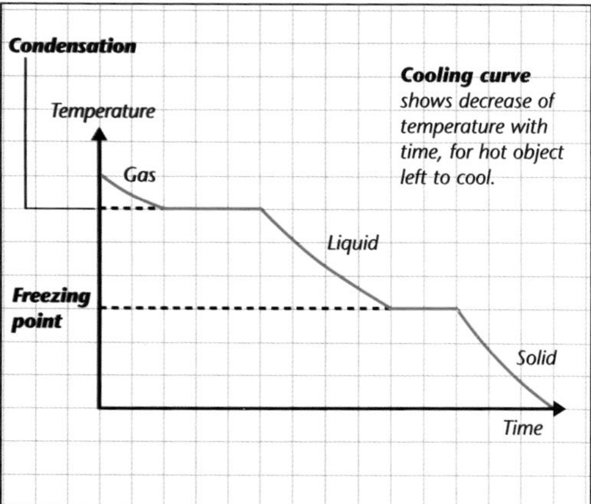
Condensation
Temperature
Gas
Liquid
Freezing point
Solid
Time
Cooling curve shows decrease of temperature with time, for hot object left to cool.

Specific latent heat of vaporization

The heat energy taken in when 1kg of a substance changes from a liquid to a gas at its **boiling point**. It is the same as the heat given out when the process is reversed.

Specific latent heat of fusion

The heat energy taken in when 1kg of a substance changes from a solid to a liquid at its **melting point**. It is the same as the heat given out when the process is reversed. See also page 112.

$Q = ml$ *where Q = heat energy lost or gained by object; m = mass; l =* ***specific latent heat****.*

The ***SI unit**** *of* ***specific latent heat*** *is the joule per kilogram (J kg^{-1}).*

Heat capacity (C)

The heat energy taken in or given out by an object per temperature change by 1K. It is a property of the object and depends on both its mass and the material(s) of which it is made (as well as the temperature and pressure), hence its value is different for every object.

$Q = C(t_2 - t_1)$ *where Q = heat energy lost or gained; C = heat capacity; t_1 and t_2 = initial and final temperatures respectively.*

The ***SI unit**** *of* ***heat capacity*** *is the joule per kelvin (J K^{-1}).*

Specific heat capacity (c)

The heat energy taken in or given out per unit mass per unit temperature change. It is a property of the substance alone, i.e. there is a set value for each substance (though this changes with temperature and pressure). See also page 112.

$Q = mc(t_2 - t_1)$ *where m = mass; c =* ***specific heat capacity****; Q, t_1, t_2 as above.*

The ***SI unit**** *of* ***specific heat capacity*** *is the joule per kilogram per kelvin (J kg^{-1} K^{-1}).*

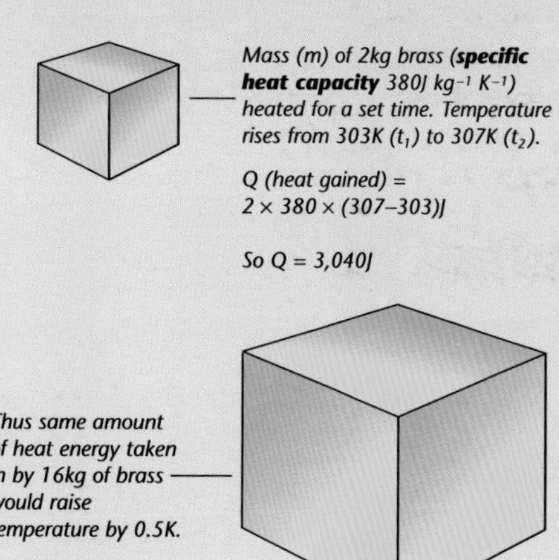
Mass (m) of 2kg brass (**specific heat capacity** 380J kg^{-1} K^{-1}) heated for a set time. Temperature rises from 303K (t_1) to 307K (t_2).
Q (heat gained) = 2 × 380 × (307–303)J
So Q = 3,040J
Thus same amount of heat energy taken in by 16kg of brass would raise temperature by 0.5K.

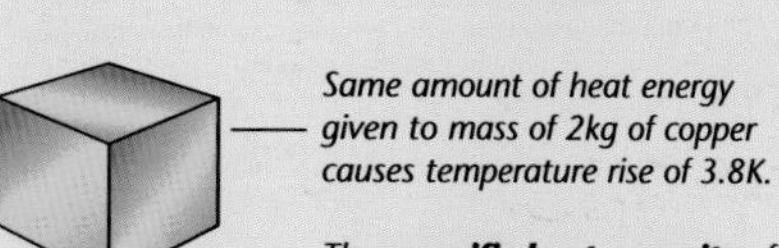
Same amount of heat energy given to mass of 2kg of copper causes temperature rise of 3.8K.
Thus **specific heat capacity** of copper is 400J kg^{-1} K^{-1}.

* **SI units**, 96.

EXPANSION DUE TO HEATING

Most substances expand when heated – their molecules move faster and further apart. The extent of this expansion (**expansivity**) depends on **intermolecular forces***. For the same amount of heat applied (at constant pressure), solids expand least, as their molecules are closest together and so have the strongest forces between them. Liquids expand more, and gases the most.

Expansion of solids on heating must be taken into account in building work.

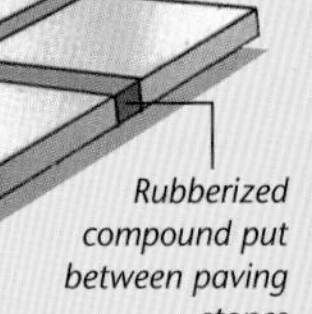

Rubberized compound put between paving stones

Bimetallic strip

A device which shows the expansion of solids due to heating. It is made up of two different strips of metal, joined along their (equal) length. When heated or cooled, both metals expand or contract (respectively), but at different rates, so the strip bends. Such strips are used in **thermostats**.

Thermostat (temperature regulator)

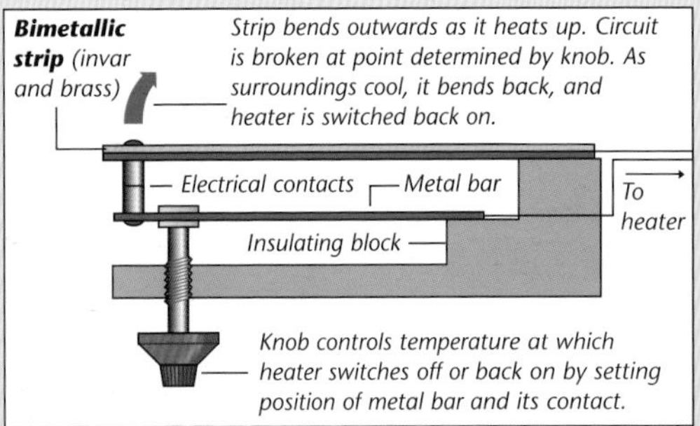

Bimetallic strip (invar and brass)
Strip bends outwards as it heats up. Circuit is broken at point determined by knob. As surroundings cool, it bends back, and heater is switched back on.
Electrical contacts
Metal bar
To heater
Insulating block
Knob controls temperature at which heater switches off or back on by setting position of metal bar and its contact.

Linear coefficient of expansion (α)

A measurement of the fraction of its original length by which a solid expands for a temperature rise of 1K.

Areal coefficient of expansion (β)

A measurement of the fraction of its original area by which a solid expands for a temperature rise of 1K.

For solids or liquids:

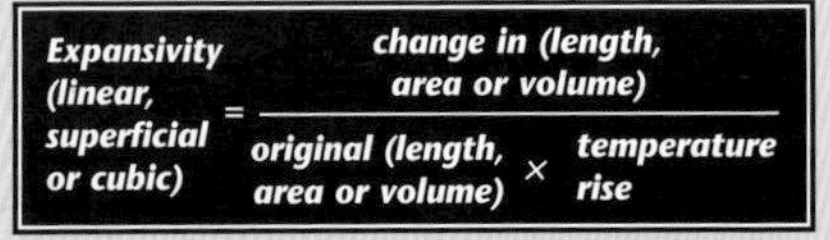

Expansivity (linear, superficial or cubic) = change in (length, area or volume) / original (length, area or volume) × temperature rise

Note the only relevant measurement for liquids is ***cubic expansivity****. It is either* ***real*** *or* ***apparent*** *(see right), therefore so also is the change in volume in formula.*

For gases:

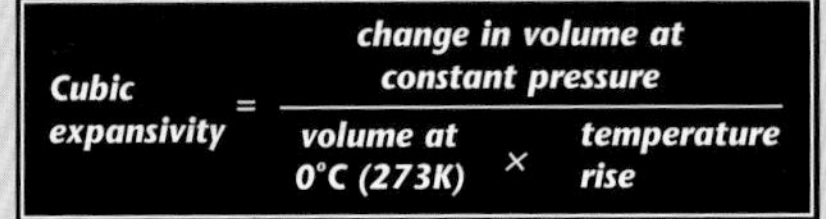

Cubic expansivity = change in volume at constant pressure / volume at 0°C (273K) × temperature rise

Volume coefficient of expansion (γ)

A measurement of the fraction of its original volume by which a substance expands for a temperature rise of 1K. It is the same for all gases (at constant pressure) when they are assumed to behave as **ideal gases**. Since gases expand by very large amounts, the original volume is always taken at 0°C so that proper comparisons can be made (this is not necessary with solids or liquids as the changes are so small).

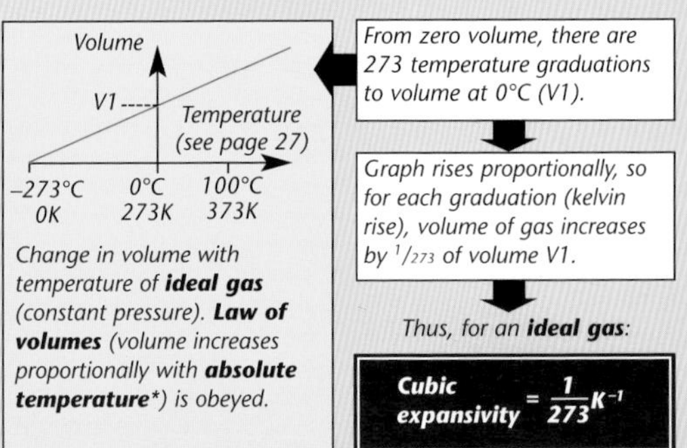

Volume
V1
Temperature (see page 27)
–273°C 0K
0°C 273K
100°C 373K
From zero volume, there are 273 temperature graduations to volume at 0°C (V1).
Graph rises proportionally, so for each graduation (kelvin rise), volume of gas increases by 1/273 of volume V1.
Thus, for an ideal gas:
Cubic expansivity = 1/273 K⁻¹

Change in volume with temperature of ***ideal gas*** *(constant pressure).* ***Law of volumes*** *(volume increases proportionally with* ***absolute temperature****) is obeyed.*

Real or absolute cubic expansivity

An accurate measurement of the fraction of its volume by which a liquid expands for a temperature rise of 1K.

Apparent cubic expansivity

A measurement of the fraction of its volume by which a liquid apparently expands for a temperature rise of 1K. In fact, the heat applied also causes very slight expansion of the container, so its calibrated measurements are no longer valid.

Anomalous expansion

The phenomenon whereby some liquids contract instead of expanding when the temperature rises within a certain range (e.g. water between 0°C and 4°C).

* **Absolute temperature scale**, 27; **Intermolecular forces**, 7.

Behavior of gases

All gases behave in a similar way, and there are several **gas laws** which describe their behavior (see below and right). An **ideal gas** is a theoretical gas which, by definition, exactly obeys **Boyle's law** at all temperatures and pressures, but in fact also obeys the two other laws as well. When real gases are at normal temperatures and pressures, they show approximately ideal behavior (the higher the temperature and the lower the pressure, the better the approximation), hence the laws may be generally applied.

Boyle's law

The volume of a fixed mass of gas at constant temperature is inversely proportional to the pressure. For example, if the pressure on the gas increases, the volume decreases proportionally – the molecules move closer together. Note that the pressure exerted by the gas increases (the molecules hit the container walls more often).

Boyle's law

$$V \propto \frac{1}{P} \quad \text{or} \quad PV = constant$$

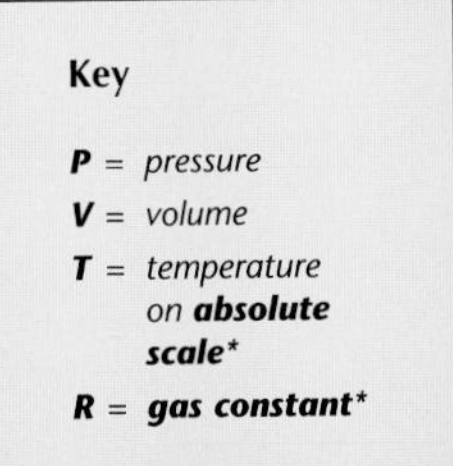
Key
P = pressure
V = volume
T = temperature on absolute scale*
R = gas constant*

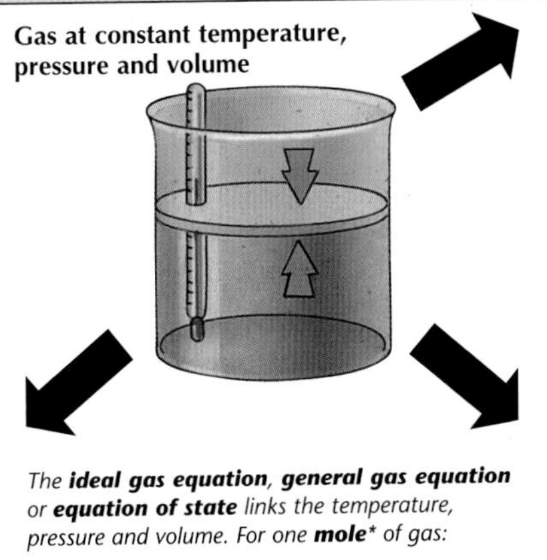
Gas at constant temperature, pressure and volume

*The **ideal gas equation**, **general gas equation** or **equation of state** links the temperature, pressure and volume. For one **mole*** of gas:*

$$\frac{PV}{T} = R \quad \text{or} \quad PV = RT$$

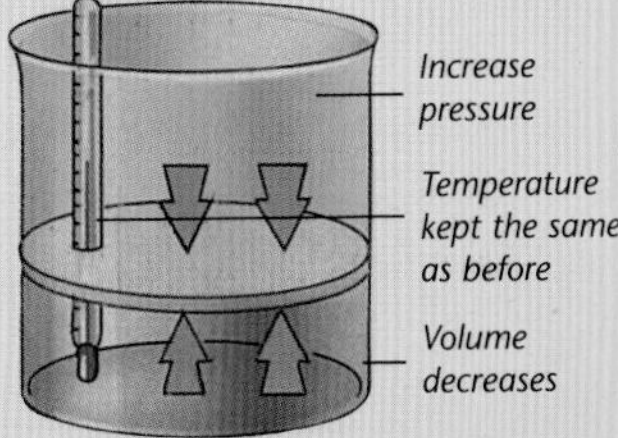
Increase pressure
Temperature kept the same as before
Volume decreases

Pressure law

The pressure of a fixed mass of gas at constant volume is proportional to the temperature on the **absolute scale***. For example, if the temperature increases but the volume is kept the same, the pressure inside the gas increases proportionally – the molecules move faster, and hit the container walls more often. Note that the pressure exerted on the gas to keep the volume constant must increase.

Pressure law

$$P \propto T \quad \text{or} \quad \frac{P}{T} = constant$$

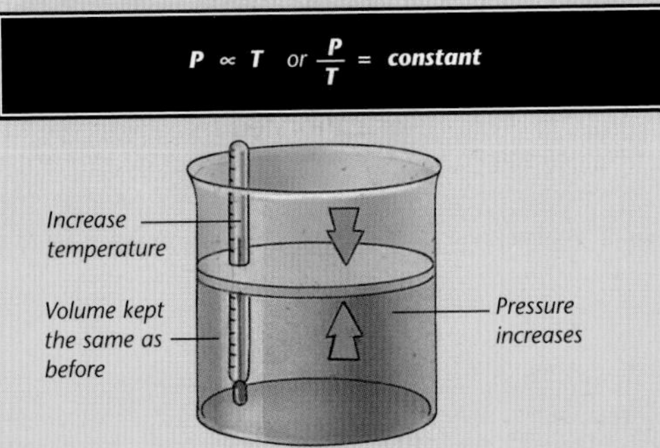
Increase temperature
Volume kept the same as before
Pressure increases

Law of volumes

The volume of a fixed mass of gas at constant pressure is proportional to the temperature on the **absolute scale***. For example, if the temperature increases and the pressure is kept the same, the volume increases proportionally (given an expandable container) – the molecules move faster and further apart. Note that the pressure exerted by the gas remains constant (the molecules hit the walls at the same frequency – they have more space, but greater energy).

Law of volumes

$$V \propto T \quad \text{or} \quad \frac{V}{T} = constant$$

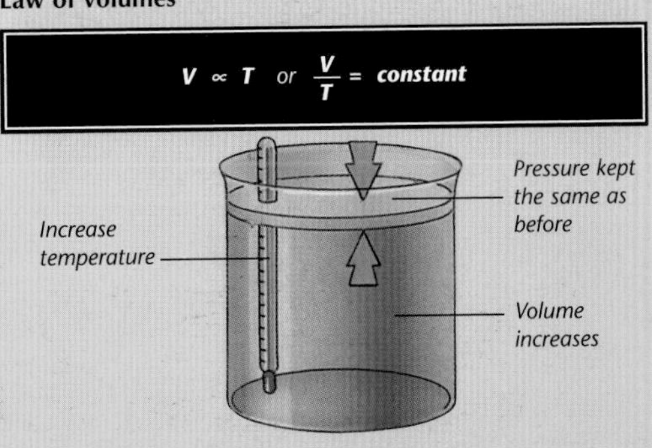
Pressure kept the same as before
Increase temperature
Volume increases

* **Absolute temperature scale**, 27; **Gas constant**, 113; **Mole**, 96.

WAVES

All **waves** transport energy without permanently displacing the **medium*** through which they travel. They are also called **traveling waves**, as the energy travels from a source to surrounding points (but see also **stationary wave**, page 43). There are two main types – **mechanical waves**, such as sound waves, and **electromagnetic waves** (see page 44). In all cases, the **wave motion** is regular and repetitive (i.e. **periodic motion** – see page 16) in the form of **oscillations** – regular changes between two extremes. In mechanical waves it is particles (molecules) that oscillate, and in electromagnetic waves it is electric and magnetic fields.

Mechanical wave (**transverse wave**) *passes along string.*

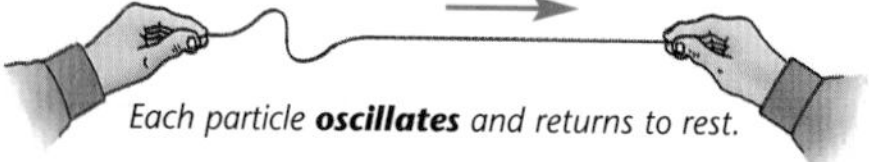
Each particle oscillates and returns to rest.

Displacement/time graph for oscillation of one particle

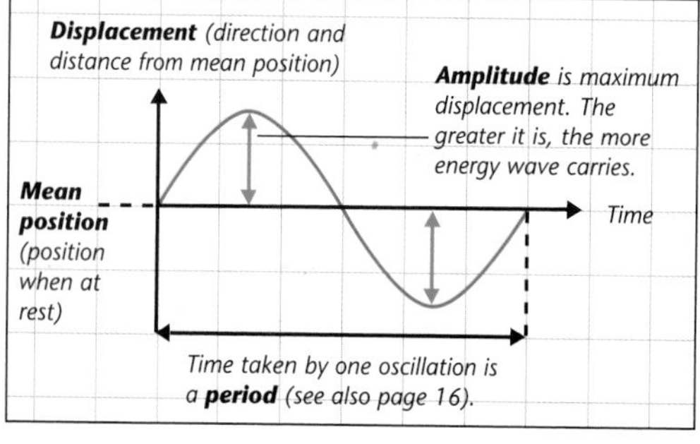
Displacement (direction and distance from mean position)
Amplitude is maximum displacement. The greater it is, the more energy wave carries.
Mean position (position when at rest)
Time
Time taken by one oscillation is a period (see also page 16).

Transverse waves

Waves in which the oscillations are at right angles to the direction of energy (wave) movement, e.g. water waves (oscillation of particles) and all **electromagnetic waves*** (oscillation of fields – see introduction).

Crests or peaks

Points where a wave causes maximum positive displacement of the **medium***. The crests of some waves, e.g. water waves, can be seen as they travel.

Troughs

Points where a wave causes maximum negative displacement of the **medium***. The troughs of some waves, e.g. water waves, can be seen as they travel.

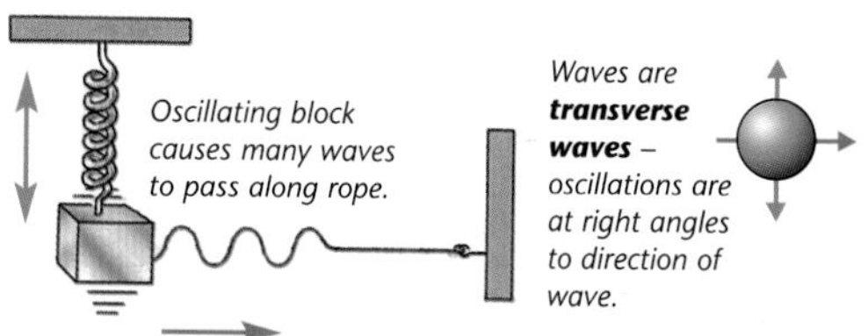
Oscillating block causes many waves to pass along rope.
Waves are transverse waves – oscillations are at right angles to direction of wave.

Displacement/distance graph for particles of section of rope at two "frozen" moments

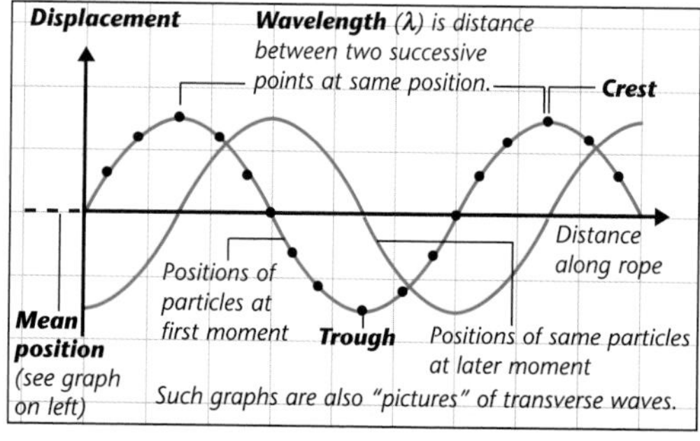
Displacement
Wavelength (λ) is distance between two successive points at same position.
Crest
Distance along rope
Positions of particles at first moment
Trough
Positions of same particles at later moment
Mean position (see graph on left)
Such graphs are also "pictures" of transverse waves.

Wavefront

Any line or section taken through an advancing wave which joins all points that are in the same position in their oscillations. Wavefronts are usually at right angles to the direction of the waves and can have any shape, e.g. **circular** and **straight wavefronts**.

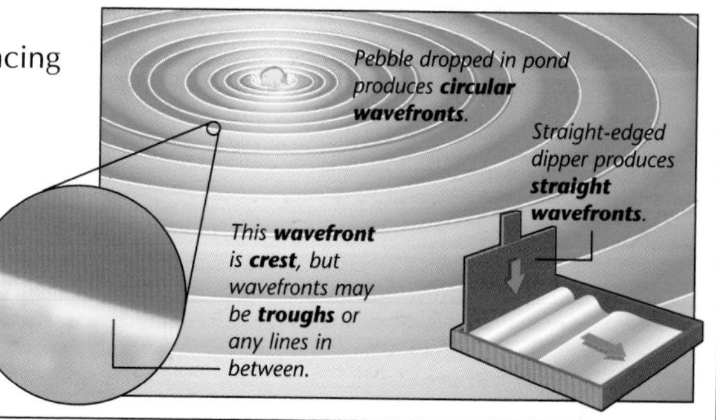
Pebble dropped in pond produces circular wavefronts.
Straight-edged dipper produces straight wavefronts.
This wavefront is crest, but wavefronts may be troughs or any lines in between.

* **Electromagnetic waves**, 44; **Medium**, 115.

Longitudinal waves

Waves in which the oscillations are along the line of the direction of wave movement, e.g. sound waves. They are all **mechanical waves** (see introduction), i.e. it is particles which oscillate.

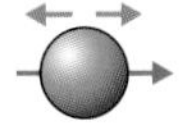

*In **longitudinal waves**, particles oscillate along line of wave direction.*

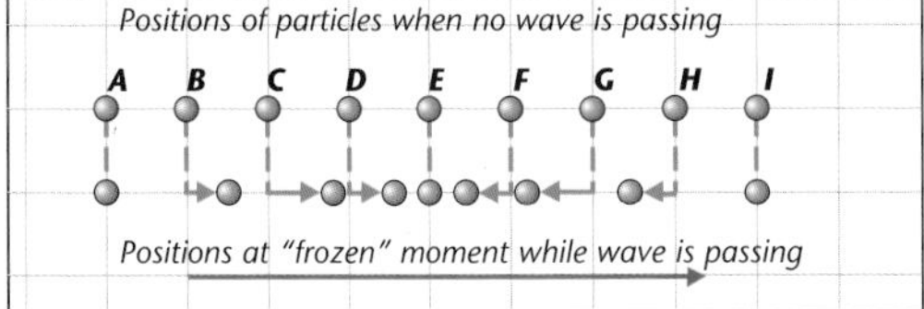
Positions of particles when no wave is passing
A B C D E F G H I
Positions at "frozen" moment while wave is passing

Graph of particles above at "frozen" moment
Graph not in this case "picture" of wave (see second graph, page 34).

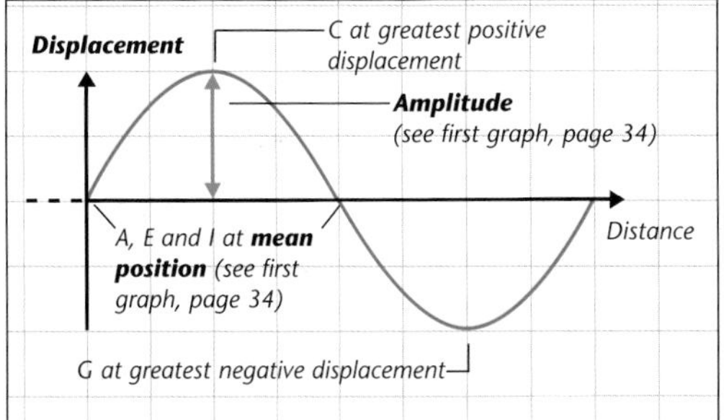
Displacement
C at greatest positive displacement
Amplitude
(see first graph, page 34)
A, E and I at mean position (see first graph, page 34)
Distance
G at greatest negative displacement

Compressions

Regions along a **longitudinal wave** where the pressure and density of the molecules are higher than when no wave is passing.

Rarefactions

Regions along a **longitudinal wave** where the pressure and density of the molecules are lower than when no wave is passing.

Graph of pressure or density versus distance for longitudinal wave shows compressions and rarefactions.

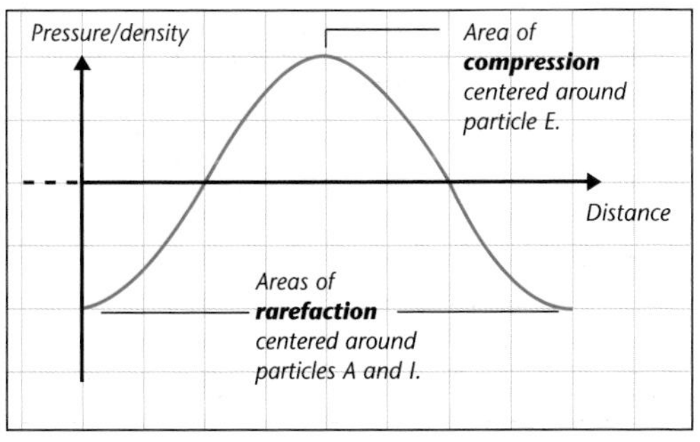
Pressure/density
Area of compression centered around particle E.
Distance
Areas of rarefaction centered around particles A and I.

Wave speed

The distance moved by a wave per unit of time. It depends on the **medium*** through which the wave is traveling.

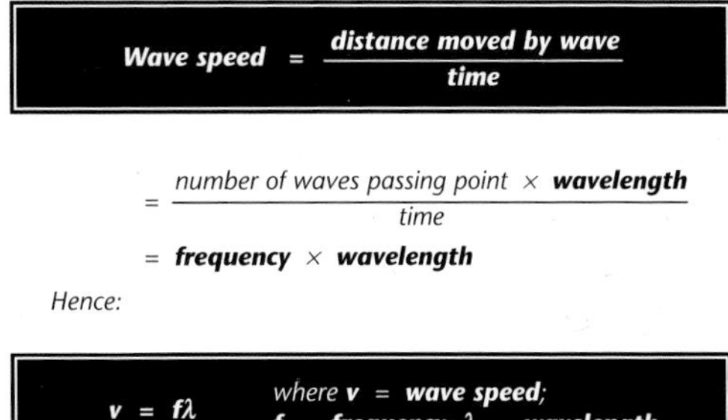
Wave speed = distance moved by wave / time
= number of waves passing point × wavelength / time
= frequency × wavelength
Hence:
v = fλ
where v = wave speed;
f = frequency; λ = wavelength.

Frequency (f)

The number of oscillations which occur in one second when waves pass a given point (see also page 16). It is equal to the number of **wavelengths** (see second graph, page 34) per second.

Attenuation

The gradual decrease in **amplitude** (see first graph, page 34) of a wave as it passes through matter and loses energy. The amplitudes of oscillations occurring further from the source are less than those of oscillations nearer to it. This can be seen as an overall **damping***.

Graph showing attenuated wave

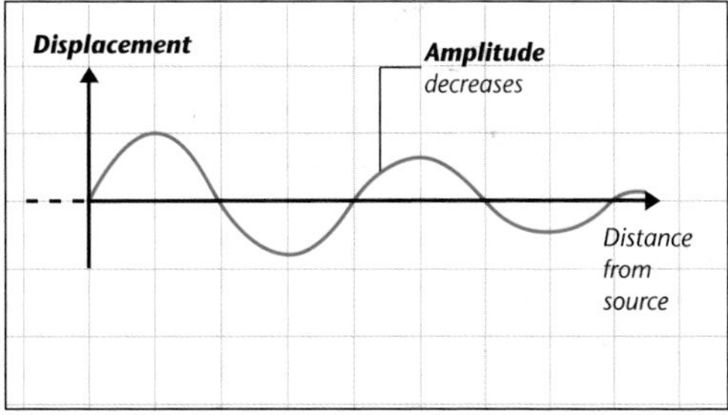
Displacement
Amplitude decreases
Distance from source

Wave intensity

A measurement of the energy carried by a wave. It is worked out as the amount of energy falling on unit area per second. It depends on the **frequency** and **amplitude** of the wave, and also on the **wave speed**.

* **Damping**, 16; **Medium**, 115.

REFLECTION, REFRACTION AND DIFFRACTION

An obstacle or a change of **medium*** causes a wave to undergo **reflection**, **refraction** or **diffraction**. These are different types of change in wave direction and often also result in changes in the shape of the **wavefronts***. For more about the reflection and refraction of light waves, see pages 47-53.

Ripple tank

A tank of water used to demonstrate the properties of water waves (see right).

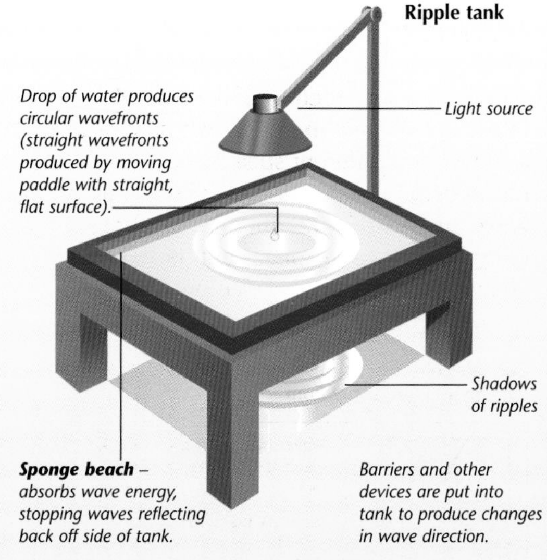
Ripple tank
Drop of water produces circular wavefronts (straight wavefronts produced by moving paddle with straight, flat surface).
Light source
Shadows of ripples
Sponge beach – absorbs wave energy, stopping waves reflecting back off side of tank.
Barriers and other devices are put into tank to produce changes in wave direction.

Reflection

The change in direction of a wave due to its bouncing off a boundary between two **media***. A wave that has undergone reflection is called a **reflected wave**. The shape of its wavefronts depends on the shape of the **incident wavefronts** and the shape of the boundary. For more about the reflection of light waves, see pages 47-49.

Incident wave

A wave that is traveling toward a boundary between two **media***. Its wavefronts are called **incident wavefronts**.

Circular wavefronts hitting concave boundary produce straight wavefronts in this case (i.e. with ship at this distance).

Ship's horn produces sound waves.

*Circular wavefronts (**incident waves**)*

*Straight wavefronts (**reflected waves**)*

Examples of reflected wave shapes

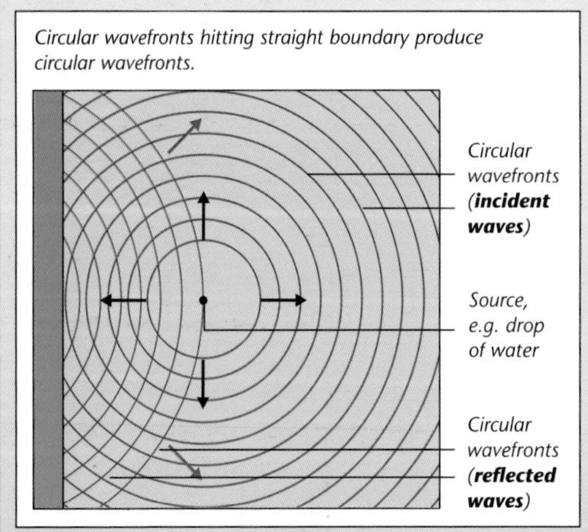
Circular wavefronts hitting straight boundary produce circular wavefronts.
Circular wavefronts (incident waves)
Source, e.g. drop of water
Circular wavefronts (reflected waves)

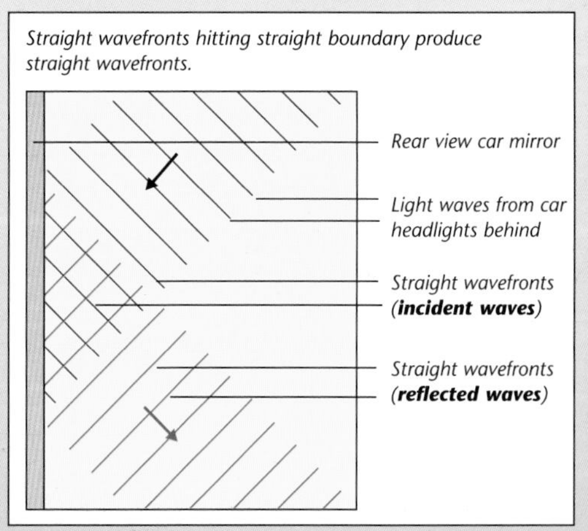
Straight wavefronts hitting straight boundary produce straight wavefronts.
Rear view car mirror
Light waves from car headlights behind
Straight wavefronts (incident waves)
Straight wavefronts (reflected waves)

* **Medium**, 115; **Wavefront**, 34.

Refraction

The change in direction of a wave when it moves into a new **medium*** which causes it to travel at a different speed. A wave which has undergone refraction is called a **refracted wave**. Its **wavelength*** increases or decreases with the change in speed, but there is no change in **frequency***. For more about the refraction of light waves, see pages 50-53.

Examples of refraction of waves in a ripple tank when moving into a new medium

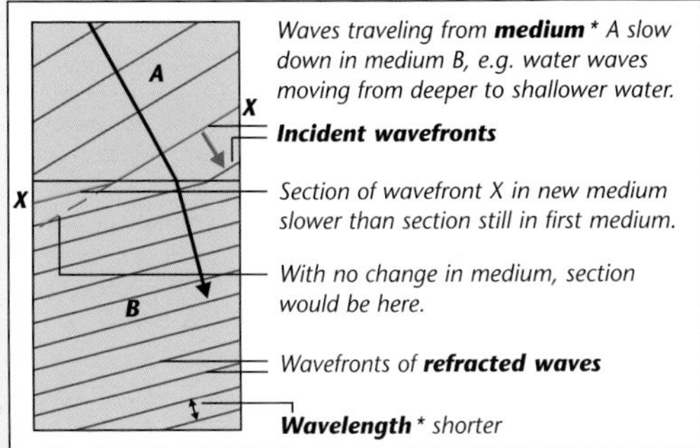
A
X
X
B
Waves traveling from medium * A slow down in medium B, e.g. water waves moving from deeper to shallower water.
Incident wavefronts
Section of wavefront X in new medium slower than section still in first medium.
With no change in medium, section would be here.
Wavefronts of refracted waves
Wavelength * shorter

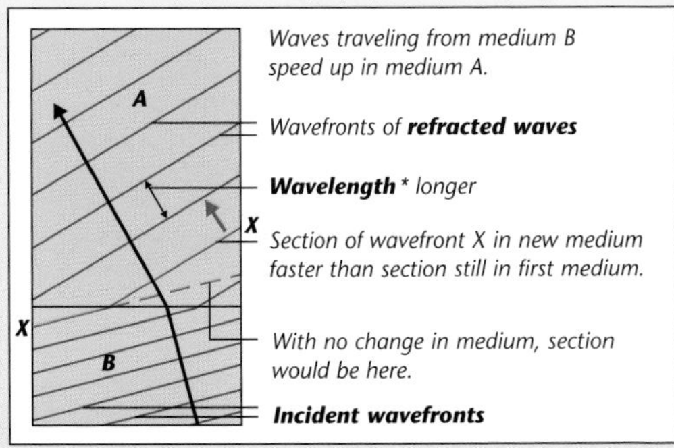
A
X
X
B
Waves traveling from medium B speed up in medium A.
Wavefronts of refracted waves
Wavelength * longer
Section of wavefront X in new medium faster than section still in first medium.
With no change in medium, section would be here.
Incident wavefronts

Other examples:

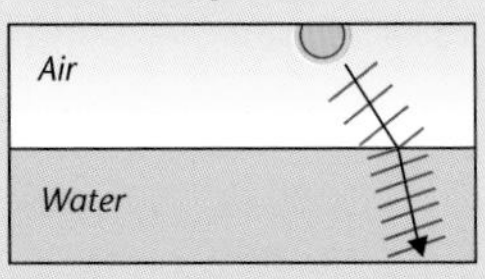
Air
Water

Waves slow down on entering a denser medium.

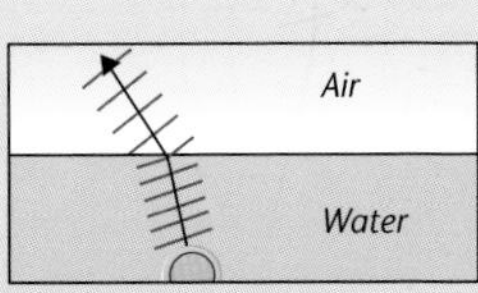
Air
Water

They speed up on entering a less dense medium.

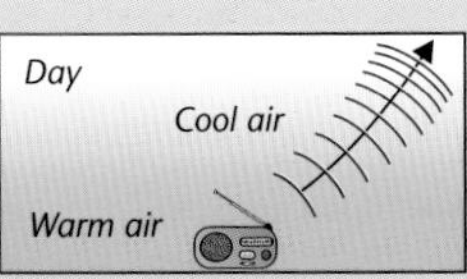
Day
Cool air
Warm air

Sound waves slow down on entering a cooler medium (cooler means denser).

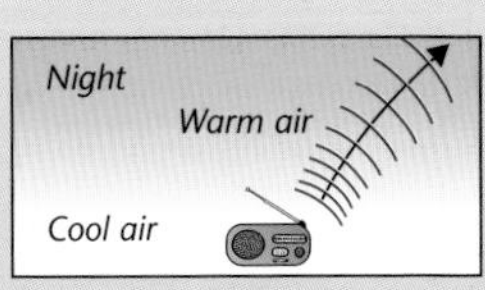
Night
Warm air
Cool air

They speed up on entering a warmer medium (warmer means less dense).

Refractive index (n)

A number which indicates the power of refraction of a given **medium*** relative to a previous medium. It is found by dividing the speed of the **incident wave** in the first medium by the speed of the **refracted wave** in the given medium (subscript numbers are used – see formula). The **absolute refractive index** of a medium is the speed of light in a vacuum (or, generally, in air) divided by the speed of light in that medium†.

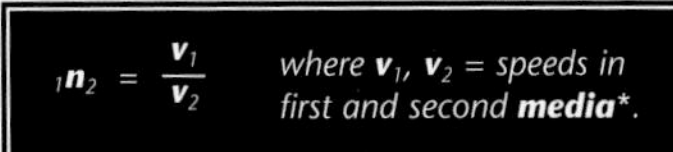
$_1n_2 = \frac{v_1}{v_2}$
where v_1, v_2 = speeds in first and second media*.

*This means **refractive index** of **medium*** 2 relative to medium 1.*

Diffraction

The bending effect which occurs when a wave meets an obstacle or passes through an aperture. The amount the wave bends depends on the size of the obstacle or aperture compared to the **wavelength*** of the wave. The smaller the obstacle or aperture by comparison, the more the wave bends.

Diffraction of waves (sound waves) around obstacle

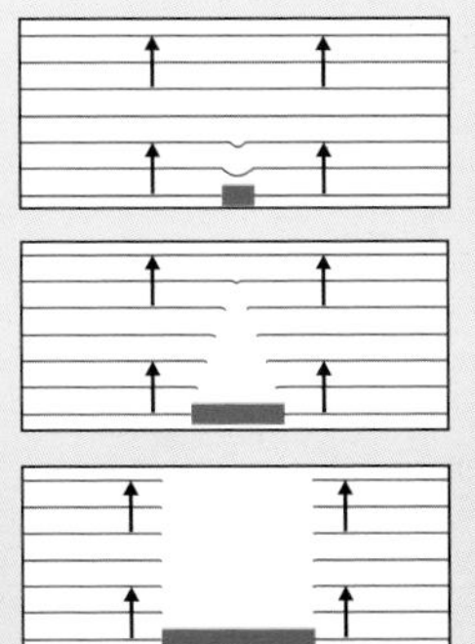

*Obstacle small compared to **wavelength*** (wavelength of sound is about 2m) – a lot of diffraction, so no "shadow" formed.*

Obstacle about same size as wavelength – some diffraction, so small "shadow" formed, i.e. area through which no waves pass.

Obstacle large compared to wavelength – almost no diffraction, so large "shadow" formed.

Diffraction of water waves passing through aperture (slit)

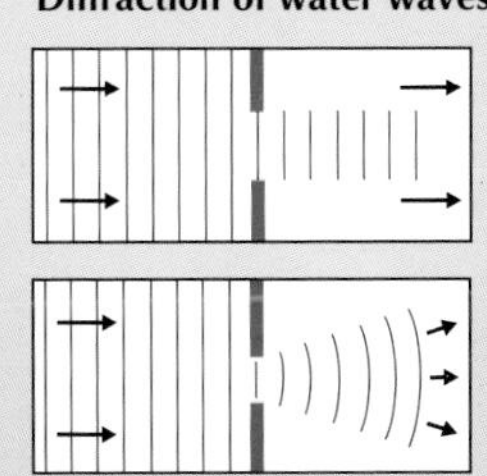

*Aperture wide compared to **wavelength*** – little diffraction.*

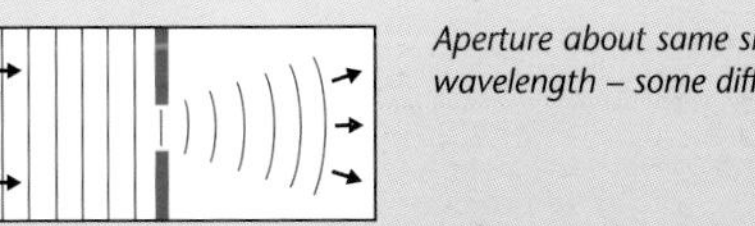

Aperture about same size as wavelength – some diffraction.

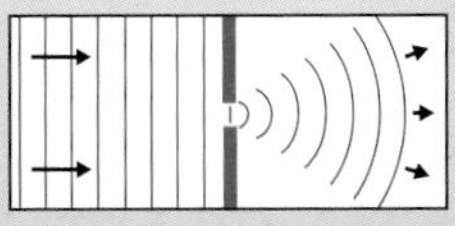

Aperture narrow compared to wavelength – a lot of diffraction.

* **Frequency**, 35; **Medium**, 115; **Wavelength**, 34.
† *For more about **refractive index** and light, see page 50.*

WAVE INTERFERENCE

When two or more waves travel in the same or different directions in a given space, variations in the size of the resulting disturbance occur at points where they meet (see **principle of superposition**). This effect is called **interference**. When interference is demonstrated, e.g. in a **ripple tank***, sources which produce **coherent waves** are always used, i.e. waves with the same wavelength and frequency, and either **in phase** or with a constant **phase difference** (see **phase**). This ensures that the interference produces a regular, identifiable **interference pattern** of disturbance (see picture, page 39). The use of non-coherent waves would result only in a constantly-changing confusion of waves.

Phase

Two waves are **in phase** if they are of the same frequency and corresponding points are at the same place in their oscillations (e.g. both at **crests***) at the same instant. They are **out of phase** if this is not the case, and exactly out of phase if their displacements are exactly opposite (e.g. a crest and a **trough***). The **phase difference** between two waves is the amount, measured as an angle, by which a point on one wave is ahead of or behind the corresponding point on the other. For waves exactly out of phase, the phase difference is 180°; for waves in phase, it is 0°.

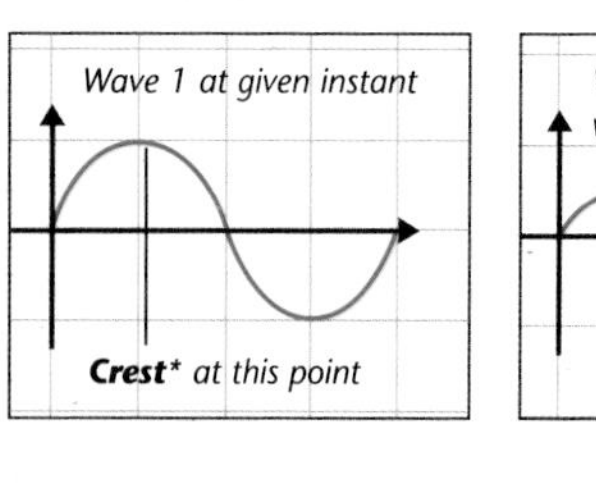

Wave 1 at given instant
Crest* at this point

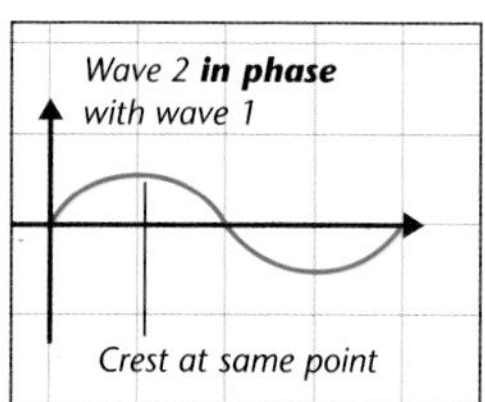

Wave 2 in phase with wave 1
Crest at same point

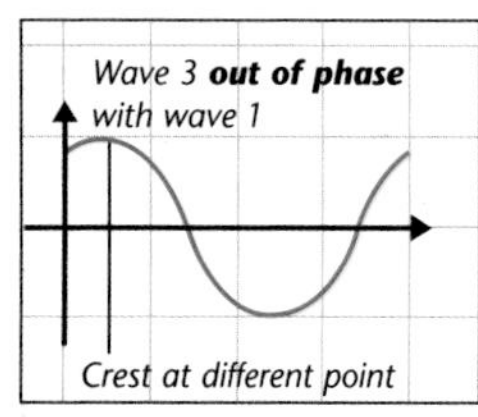

Wave 3 out of phase with wave 1
Crest at different point

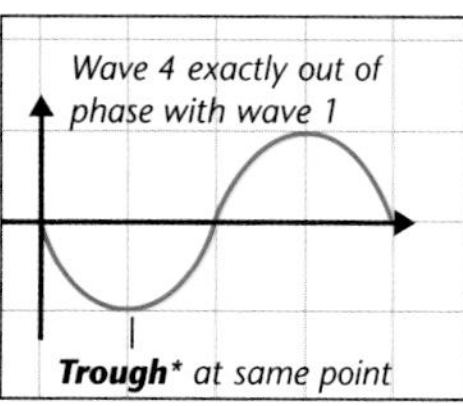

Wave 4 exactly out of phase with wave 1
Trough* at same point

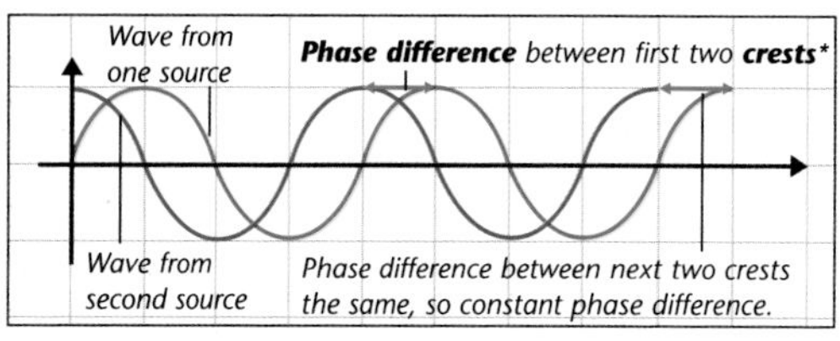

Wave from one source
Phase difference between first two crests*
Wave from second source
Phase difference between next two crests the same, so constant phase difference.

Young's slits

An arrangement of narrow, parallel slits, used to create two sources of **coherent** light (see introduction). They are needed because coherent light waves cannot be produced (for studying interference) as easily as other coherent waves, as light wave emission is usually random. The interference of the light **diffracted*** through the slits is seen on a screen as light and dark bands called **interference fringes**.

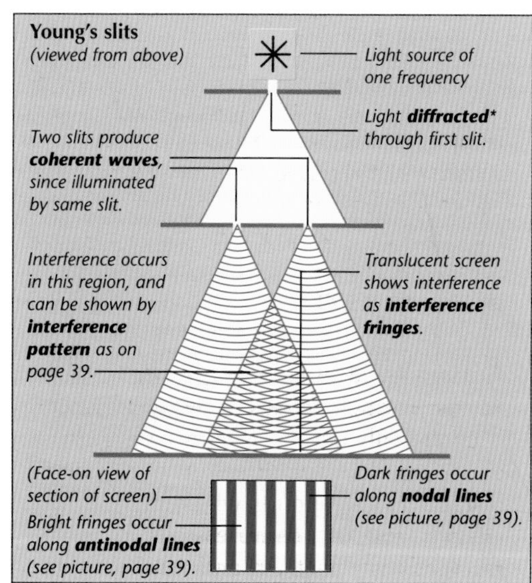

Young's slits
(viewed from above)
Light source of one frequency
Light diffracted* through first slit.
Two slits produce coherent waves, since illuminated by same slit.
Interference occurs in this region, and can be shown by interference pattern as on page 39.
Translucent screen shows interference as interference fringes.
(Face-on view of section of screen)
Bright fringes occur along antinodal lines (see picture, page 39).
Dark fringes occur along nodal lines (see picture, page 39).

Principle of superposition

States that when the **superposition** of two or more waves occurs at a point (i.e. two or more waves come together), the resultant displacement is equal to the sum of the displacements (positive or negative) of the individual waves.

* **Crests**, 34; **Diffraction**, 37; **Ripple tank**, 36; **Troughs**, 34.

Constructive interference

The increase in disturbance (reinforcement) which results from the **superposition** of two waves which are **in phase** (see **phase**).

Constructive interference

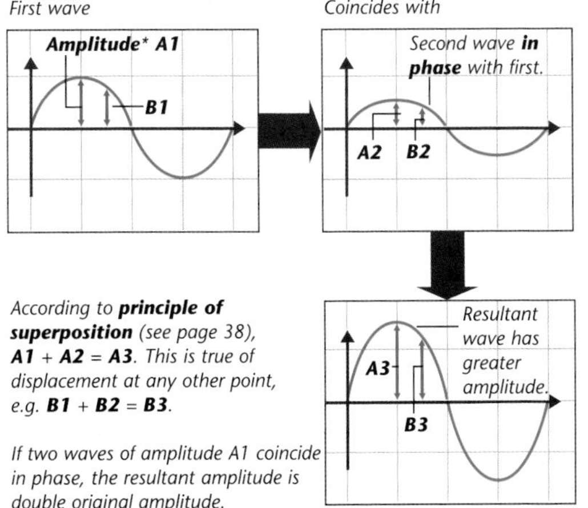

First wave
Coincides with
Amplitude* A1
B1
Second wave in phase with first.
A2
B2
Resultant wave has greater amplitude.
A3
B3

*According to **principle of superposition** (see page 38), **A1** + **A2** = **A3**. This is true of displacement at any other point, e.g. **B1** + **B2** = **B3**.*

If two waves of amplitude A1 coincide in phase, the resultant amplitude is double original amplitude.

Destructive interference

The decrease in disturbance which results from the **superposition** of two waves which are **out of phase**.

Destructive interference

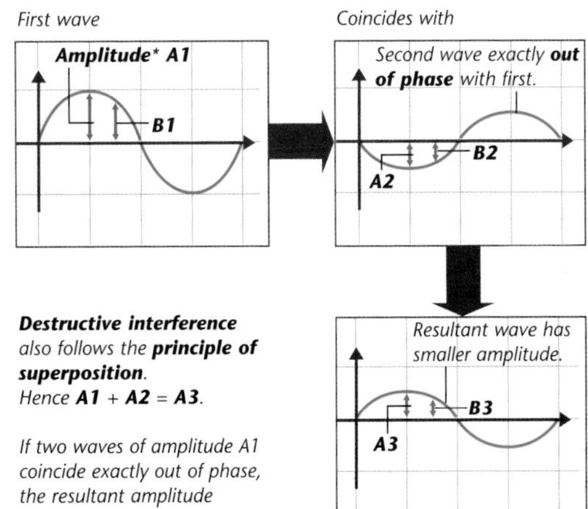

First wave
Coincides with
Amplitude* A1
B1
Second wave exactly out of phase with first.
A2
B2
Resultant wave has smaller amplitude.
A3
B3

***Destructive interference** also follows the **principle of superposition**. Hence **A1** + **A2** = **A3**.*

If two waves of amplitude A1 coincide exactly out of phase, the resultant amplitude is zero.

Nodes or nodal points

Points at which destructive interference is continually occurring, and which are consequently regularly points of minimum disturbance, i.e. points where **crest*** meets **trough*** or **compression*** meets **rarefaction***. A **nodal line** is a line consisting entirely of nodes. Depending on waves, nodal lines may indicate, for example, calm water, soft sound or darkness (see also **Young's slits** picture, page 38).

Antinodes or antinodal points

Points at which **constructive interference** is continually occurring, and which are consequently regularly points of maximum disturbance, i.e. points where two **crests***, **troughs***, **compressions*** or **rarefactions*** meet. An **antinodal line** is a line consisting entirely of antinodes. Depending on waves, antinodal lines may indicate, for example, areas of rough water, loud sound or bright light (see also **Young's slits** picture).

Interference pattern at "frozen" moment
(not all antinodal/nodal lines shown).

*Two sources (**S1** and **S2**) produce **coherent waves**, in this case **in phase**.*

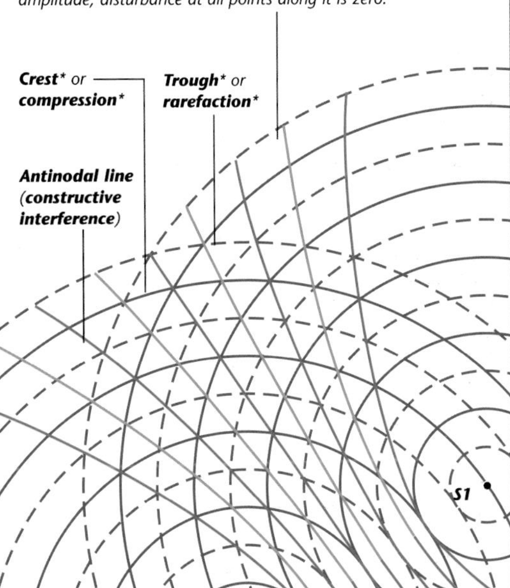

Nodal line (destructive interference). If waves are same amplitude, disturbance at all points along it is zero.
Crest* or compression*
Trough* or rarefaction*
Antinodal line (constructive interference)
S1
S2

* **Amplitude**, 34; **Compressions**, 35; **Crests**, 34; **Rarefactions**, 35; **Troughs**, 34.

SOUND WAVES

Bats emit ***ultrasonic waves*** *to locate objects.*

Sound waves, also called **acoustic waves**, are **longitudinal waves*** – waves which consist of particles oscillating along the same line as the waves travel, creating areas of high and low pressure (**compressions*** and **rarefactions***). They can travel through solids, liquids and gases and have a wide range of **frequencies***. Those with frequencies between about 20 and 20,000 **Hertz*** (the **sonic range**) can be detected by the human ear and are what is commonly referred to as sound (for more about perception of sound, see pages 42-43). Others, with higher and lower frequencies, are known as **ultrasound** and **infrasound**. The study of the behavior of sound waves is called **acoustics**.

Ultrasound

Sound composed of **ultrasonic waves** – waves with **frequencies*** above the range of the human ear, i.e. above 20,000 **Hertz***. Ultrasound has a number of uses.

Ultrasound *is used in* ***ultrasound scanning*** *of the human body (it uses* ***echoes*** *– see page 41).*

Bone, fat and muscle all reflect ***ultrasonic waves*** *differently. Reflected waves (****echoes****), e.g. from an unborn baby, are converted into electrical pulses which form an image (****scan****) on a screen.*

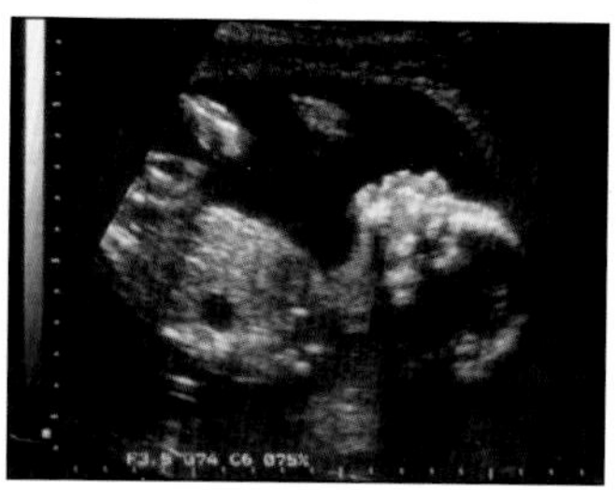

Scan of baby in mother's womb at 20 weeks

Infrasound

Sound composed of **infrasonic waves** – waves with **frequencies*** below the range of the human ear, i.e. below 20 **Hertz***. At present infrasound has few technical uses, as it can cause uncomfortable sensations in humans.

Sonic boom

A loud bang heard when a **shock wave** produced by an aircraft moving at **supersonic speed** passes a listener.

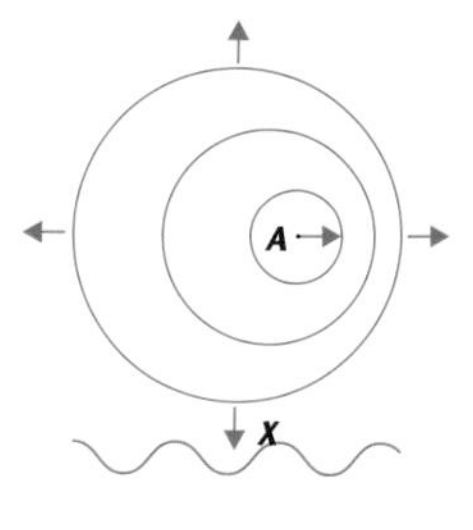
A
X

As aircraft (A) travels forward, it creates ***longitudinal waves**** *in air, i.e. areas of high and low pressure (****compressions**** *and* ***rarefactions****).*

Wavefronts* *can "get away" from aircraft and begin to disperse.*

Listener at X will hear waves as sound (a "whoosh" of air – as well as separate sound of engines).

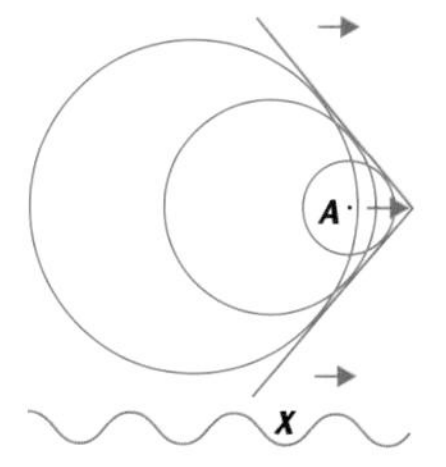
A
X

Supersonic *aircraft (A) overtakes its wavefronts while creating more, so they overlap.*

*Causes large build up of pressure (****shock wave****) pushed in front of aircraft and unable to "get away". It is like bow wave of ship (if ship moving faster than water waves it creates).*

Listener at X will hear wave as sudden loud ***sonic boom****.*

Behavior of sound waves

Speed of sound

The speed at which sound waves move. It depends on the type and temperature of the **medium*** through which the sound waves travel. The speed of sound waves as they travel through dry air at 0°C is 331m s^{-1}, but this increases if the air temperature increases, or decreases if the air temperature goes down.

Subsonic speed

A speed below the **speed of sound** in the same **medium*** and under the same conditions.

Supersonic speed

A speed above the **speed of sound** in the same **medium*** and under the same conditions.

A supersonic passenger jet

* **Compressions**, **Frequency**, 35; **Hertz**, 16 (**Frequency**); **Longitudinal waves**, 35; **Medium**, 115; **Rarefactions**, 35; **Wavefront**, 34.

The **ultrasonic waves** emitted by a bat bounce back, telling it the distance and size of the object. This technique is called **echolocation**.

Echo

A sound wave which has been reflected off a surface, and is heard after the original sound. Echoes, normally those of **ultrasonic waves**, are often used to locate objects and determine their exact position (by measuring the time the echo takes to return to the source). This technique has a number of names, each normally used in a slightly different context, though the distinctions between them are unclear. **Ultrasound scanning** is one example. Others are **echo-sounding** and **sonar**, both of which have marine connotations (echo-sounding normally refers to using echoes to measure the depth of water below a ship, sonar to using them to detect objects under water). **Echolocation** usually describes the way animals use echoes to find prey or avoid obstacles in the dark.

Sonar (derived from **so**und **na**vigation and **r**anging)

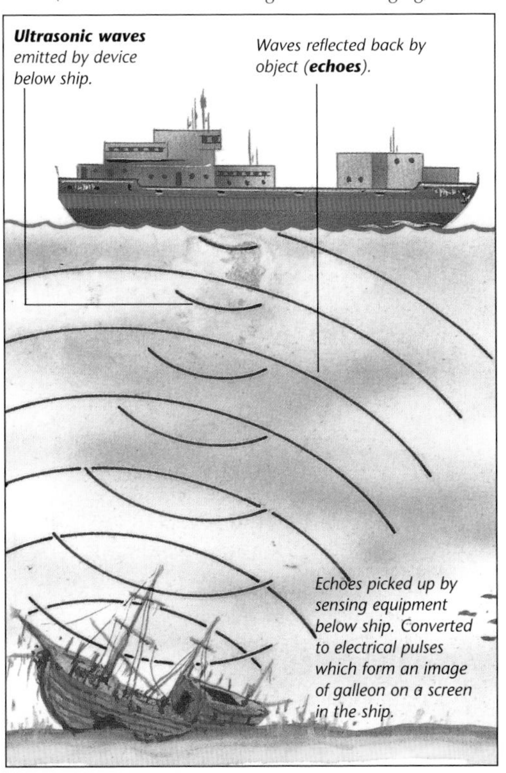
Ultrasonic waves emitted by device below ship.
Waves reflected back by object (**echoes**).
Echoes picked up by sensing equipment below ship. Converted to electrical pulses which form an image of galleon on a screen in the ship.

Reverberation

The effect whereby a sound seems to persist for longer than it actually took to produce. It occurs when the time taken for the **echo** to return to the source is so short that the original and reflected waves cannot be distinguished. If the wave is reflected off many surfaces, then the sound is enhanced further.

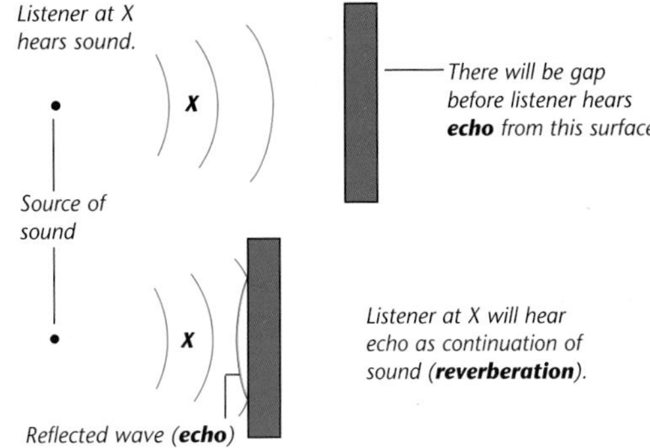
Listener at X hears sound.
X
There will be gap before listener hears **echo** from this surface.
Source of sound
X
Listener at X will hear echo as continuation of sound (**reverberation**).
Reflected wave (**echo**)

Doppler effect

The change in **frequency*** of the sound heard when either the listener or the source moves relative to the other. If the distance between them is decreasing, a higher frequency sound is heard than that actually produced. If it is increasing, a lower frequency sound is heard.

Doppler effect

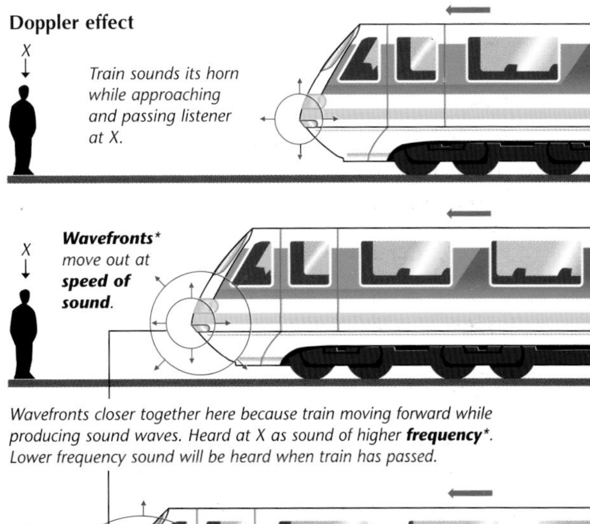
X
Train sounds its horn while approaching and passing listener at X.
X
Wavefronts* move out at **speed of sound.**
Wavefronts closer together here because train moving forward while producing sound waves. Heard at X as sound of higher **frequency***. Lower frequency sound will be heard when train has passed.
X

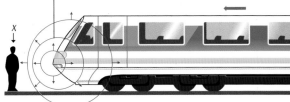

* **Frequency**, 35; **Wavefront**, 34.

PERCEPTION OF SOUND

Sounds heard by the ear can be pleasant or unpleasant. When the waveform of a **sound wave** (see pages 40-41) repeats itself regularly, the sound is usually judged to be pleasant. However, when the waveform is unrepeated and irregular, the sound is thought of as a **noise**. Every sound has a particular **loudness** and **pitch** and many, especially musical sounds, are produced by **stationary waves**.

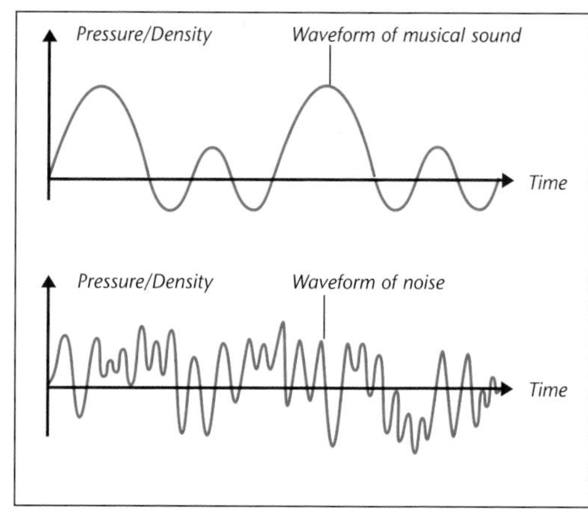
Pressure/Density
Waveform of musical sound
Time
Pressure/Density
Waveform of noise
Time

Loudness

The size of the sensation produced when sound waves fall on the ear. It is subjective, depending on the sensitivity of the ear, but is directly related to the **wave intensity*** of the waves. It is most often measured in **decibels** (**dB**), but also, more accurately, in **phons** (these take into account the fact that the ear is not equally sensitive to sounds of all **frequencies***).

*Aircraft taking off measures 110**dB**.*

Pitch

The perceived **frequency*** of a sound wave, i.e. the frequency heard as sound. A high pitched sound has a high frequency and a low pitched sound has a low frequency.

*The sound of a bird's song is high **pitched**. It has a high **frequency***.*

*A truck's engine has a low-**pitched** hum. It has a low **frequency***.*

Beats

The regular variation in **loudness** with time which is heard when two sounds of slightly different **frequency*** are heard together. This is the result of **interference*** between the two waves. The **beat frequency** is equal to the difference in frequency between the two sounds (see diagram below). The closer together the frequency of the sounds, the slower the beats.

Beat frequency

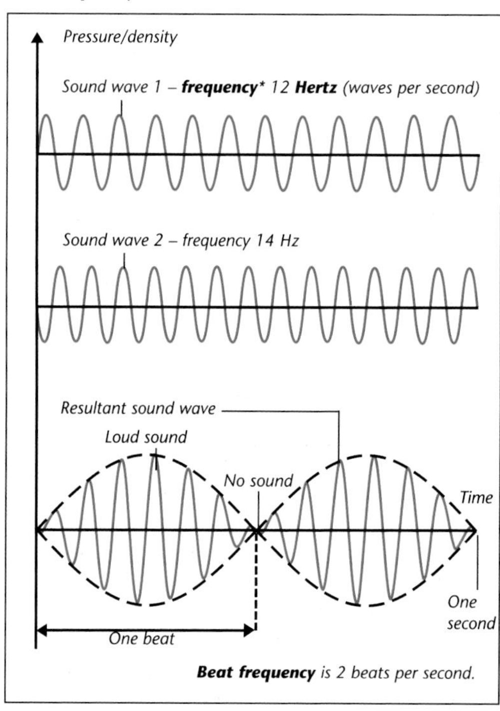
Pressure/density
Sound wave 1 – frequency* 12 Hertz (waves per second)
Sound wave 2 – frequency 14 Hz
Resultant sound wave
Loud sound
No sound
Time
One second
One beat
Beat frequency is 2 beats per second.

* **Frequency**, 35; **Interference**, 38; **Wave intensity**, 35.

Stationary or **standing wave**

A wave that does not appear to move. It is not in fact a true wave, but is instead made up of two waves of the same velocity and **frequency*** continuously moving in opposite directions between two fixed points (most commonly the ends of a plucked string or wire). The repeated crossing of the waves results in **interference*** – when the waves are **in phase***, the resultant **amplitude*** is large, and when they are **out of phase***, it is small or zero. At certain points (the **nodes**), it is always zero. The amplitude and frequency of a stationary wave in a string or wire determines those of the sound waves it produces in the air – the length and tension of the string or wire determine the range of frequencies, and hence the pitch of the sound produced.

Sonometer

*Apparatus used to demonstrate **stationary waves**. When plucked, wire vibrates and sound box amplifies sound caused by vibration.*

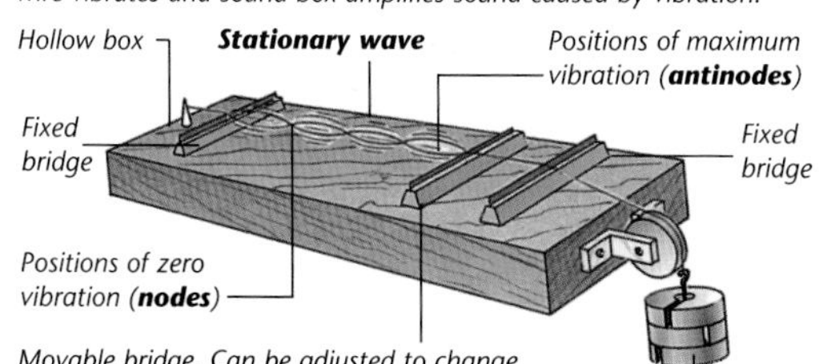
Hollow box
Stationary wave
Positions of maximum vibration (antinodes)
Fixed bridge
Fixed bridge
Positions of zero vibration (nodes)

*Movable bridge. Can be adjusted to change length of wire and so alter **pitch** of note.*

Weights. Can be adjusted to change tension of wire and so alter pitch of note.

Formation of stationary wave

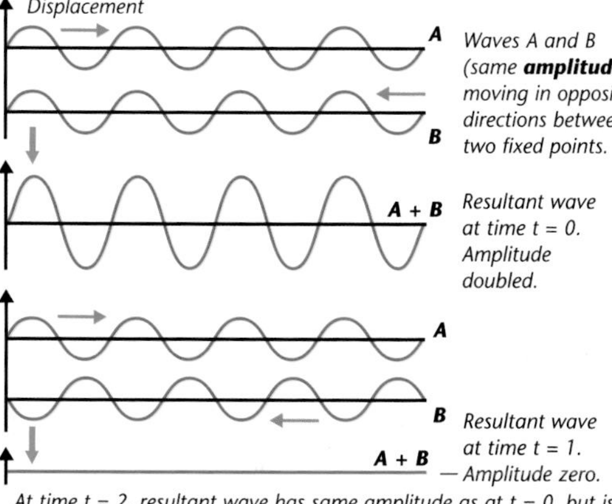
Displacement
A
B
A + B
A
B
A + B

*Waves A and B (same **amplitude***) moving in opposite directions between two fixed points.*

Resultant wave at time t = 0. Amplitude doubled.

Resultant wave at time t = 1. — Amplitude zero.

*At time t = 2, resultant wave has same amplitude as at t = 0, but is transposed, i.e. **crests*** where there were **troughs*** and vice versa.*

Nodes

Antinodes

Resultant wave moves rapidly between position held at t = 0 and that held at t = 2. Wave observed appears stationary.

Musical sounds

All music is based on some kind of **musical scale**. This is a series of **notes** (sounds of specific **pitch**), arranged from low to high pitch with certain **intervals** between them (a musical interval is a spacing in **frequency***, rather than time). The notes are arranged so that pleasant sounds can be obtained. What is regarded as a pleasant sound depends on the culture of the listener.

*Western **musical scale** is based on **diatonic scale** – consists of 8 **notes** (white notes on piano) ranging from lower to upper C.*

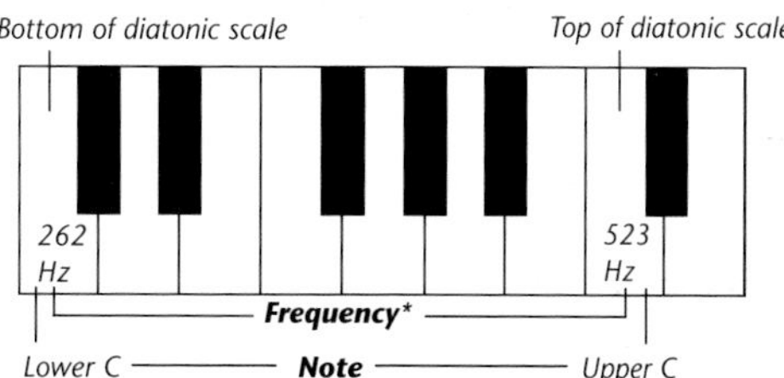
Bottom of diatonic scale
Top of diatonic scale
262 Hz
523 Hz
Frequency*
Lower C
Note
Upper C

*Black notes have **frequencies*** between those of notes on **diatonic scale**. Together with these, they form **chromatic scale**.*

Modes of vibration

The same note played on different instruments, although recognizable as the same, has a distinct sound quality (**timbre**) characteristic to the instrument. This is because, although the strongest vibration is the same for each note whatever the instrument (its **frequency*** is the **fundamental frequency**), vibrations at other frequencies (**overtones**) are produced at the same time. The set of vibrations specific to an instrument are its modes of vibration.

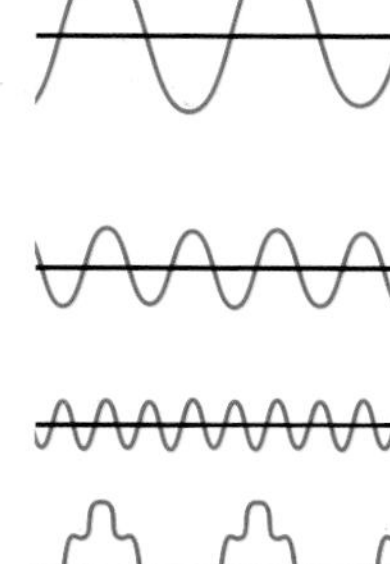

*Lowest **mode of vibration** (**fundamental frequency**) of note on given instrument. If frequencies of **overtones** are simple multiples of fundamental frequency, they are also called **harmonics**.*

1st overtone (2nd harmonic, i.e. frequency doubled. Fundamental frequency is 1st harmonic).

2nd overtone. This is 4th harmonic. In this case there is no 3rd harmonic.

Combined modes of vibration (i.e. all three together). Characteristic waveform of note for this instrument.

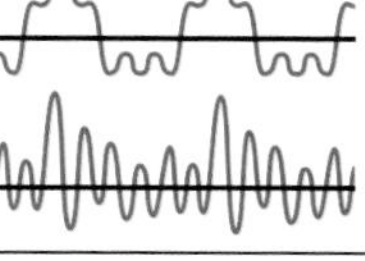

Same note played on different instrument may look like this.

* **Amplitude**, **Crests**, 34; **Frequency**, 35; **In phase**, 38 (**Phase**); **Interference**, 38; **Out of phase**, 38 (**Phase**); **Troughs**, 34.

ELECTROMAGNETIC WAVES

Electromagnetic waves are **transverse waves***, consisting of oscillating **electric** and **magnetic fields***. They have a wide range of **frequencies***, can travel through most **media***, including vacuums, and, when absorbed, cause a rise in temperature (see **infra-red radiation**). **Radio waves** and some **X-rays** are emitted when free **electrons*** are accelerated or decelerated, e.g. as a result of a collision. All other types occur when molecules change energy states (see page 84) and occur as pulses called **photons** (see **quantum theory**, page 84), rather than a continuous stream. For the wavelengths and frequencies of the different types of waves (the **electromagnetic spectrum**), see the table on page 113.

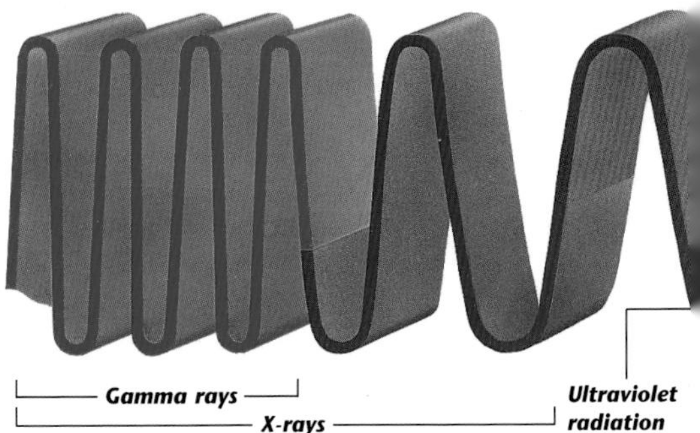

Gamma rays
X-rays
Ultraviolet radiation

Electromagnetic spectrum *(range of electromagnetic waves) shown above. It is made up of **wavebands**, i.e. particular ranges of **frequencies*** and **wavelengths*** within which the waves all have the same characteristic properties.*

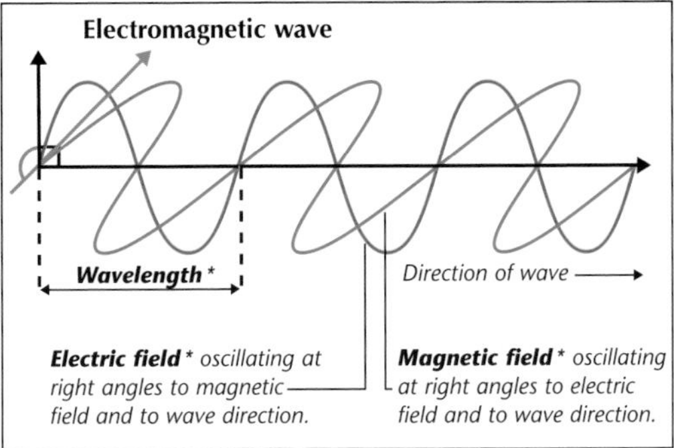

Electromagnetic wave
Wavelength *
Direction of wave
Electric field * oscillating at right angles to magnetic field and to wave direction.
Magnetic field * oscillating at right angles to electric field and to wave direction.

Gamma rays (γ-rays)

Electromagnetic waves emitted by **radioactive*** substances (see also page 86). They are in the same **waveband** and have the same properties as **X-rays**, but are produced in a different way, and are at the top end of the band with regard to energy.

X-rays

Electromagnetic waves which **ionize*** gases they pass through, cause **phosphorescence** and bring about chemical changes on photographic plates. They are produced in **X-ray tubes*** and have many applications.

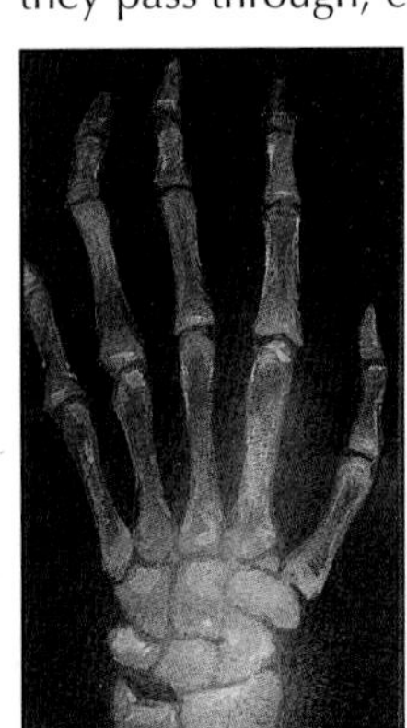

X-radiography *produces pictures (**radiographs**) of inside of body. **X-rays** pass through tissue but are absorbed by denser bones, so bones appear opaque.*

X-rays were passed through this hand to project a clear image of the bones onto a photographic plate.

Ultraviolet radiation (UV radiation)

Electromagnetic waves produced, for example, when an electric current is passed through **ionized*** gas between two **electrodes***. They are also emitted by the Sun, but only small quantities reach the Earth's surface. These small quantities are vital to life, playing the key part in plant photosynthesis, but larger amounts are dangerous. Ultraviolet radiation causes **fluorescence**, e.g. when produced in **fluorescent tubes***, and also a variety of chemical reactions, e.g. tanning of the skin.

Phosphorescence

A phenomenon shown by certain substances (**phosphors**) when they are hit by short **wavelength*** electromagnetic waves, e.g. **gamma rays** or **X-rays**. The phosphors absorb the waves and emit visible light, i.e. waves of longer wavelength. This emission may continue after the gamma or X-rays have stopped. If it only occurs briefly afterwards in rapid flashes, these are called **scintillations** (see also **scintillation counter**, page 90).

* **Electric field**, 58; **Electrode**, 66; **Electrons**, 83; **Fluorescent tube**, 80 (**Discharge tube**); **Frequency**, 35; **Ionization**, 88; **Magnetic field**, 72; **Medium**, 115; **Radioactivity**, 86; **Transverse waves**, **Wavelength**, 34; **X-ray tube**, 80.

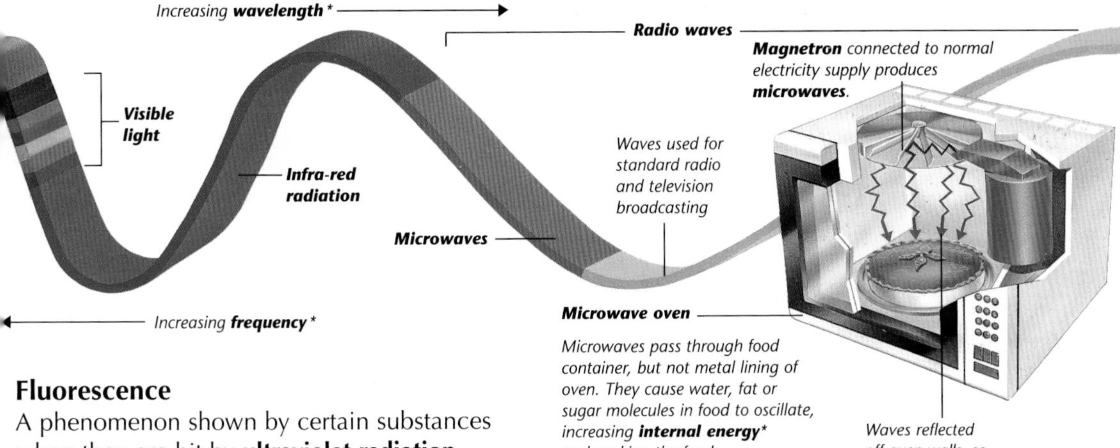
Increasing **wavelength***
Radio waves
Magnetron connected to normal electricity supply produces **microwaves**.
Visible light
Infra-red radiation
Waves used for standard radio and television broadcasting
Microwaves
Increasing **frequency***
Microwave oven
Microwaves pass through food container, but not metal lining of oven. They cause water, fat or sugar molecules in food to oscillate, increasing **internal energy*** and cooking the food.
Waves reflected off oven walls, so food cooks evenly.

Fluorescence

A phenomenon shown by certain substances when they are hit by **ultraviolet radiation**. They absorb the ultraviolet radiation and emit **visible light**, i.e. light waves of a longer **wavelength***. This emission stops as soon as the ultraviolet radiation stops.

Visible light

Electromagnetic waves which the eye can detect. They are produced by the Sun, by **discharge tubes*** and by any substance heated until it glows (emission of light due to heating is called **incandescence**). They cause chemical changes, e.g. on photographic film, and the different **wavelengths*** in the **waveband** are seen as different colors (see page 54).

Infra-red radiation (IR radiation)

The electromagnetic waves most commonly produced by hot objects and therefore those which are most frequently the cause of temperature rises (see introduction and **radiation**, page 29). They can be used to form **thermal images** on special infra-red sensitive film, which is exposed by heat, rather than light.

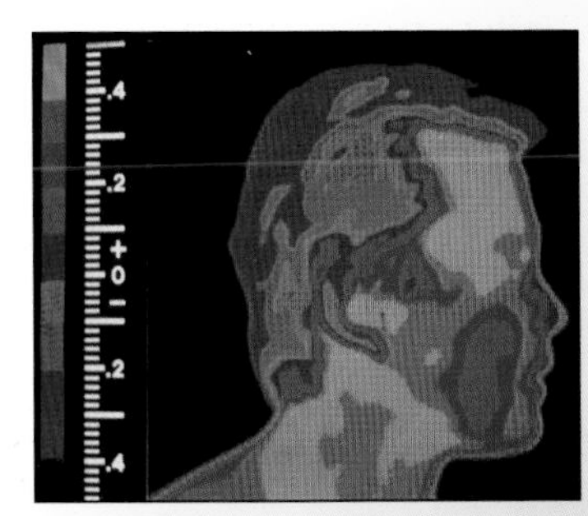
.4
.2
+
0
-
.2
.4

Thermal image *of a man's head*

Each different color represents a temperature difference of 0.1°C (see scale on left of picture).

The blue areas of the head are colder, and the yellow areas are hotter.

Microwaves

Very short **radiowaves** used in **radar** (**ra**dio **d**etection **a**nd **r**anging) to determine the position of an object by the time it takes for a reflected wave to return to the source (see also **sonar**, page 41 (**Echo**)). **Microwave ovens** use microwaves to cook food rapidly.

Radio waves

Electromagnetic waves produced when free **electrons*** in radio antennae are made to oscillate (and are hence accelerated) by an **electric field***. The fact that the frequency of the oscillations is imposed by the field means that the waves occur as a regular stream, rather than randomly.

How radio waves are used to communicate over long distances

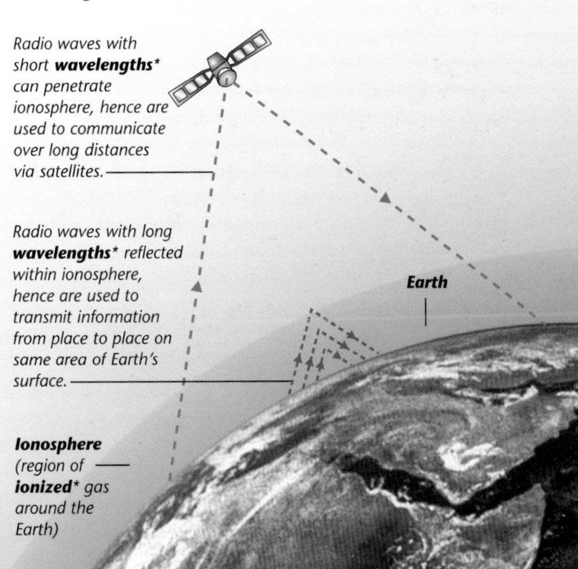
Radio waves with short **wavelengths*** can penetrate ionosphere, hence are used to communicate over long distances via satellites.
Radio waves with long **wavelengths*** reflected within ionosphere, hence are used to transmit information from place to place on same area of Earth's surface.
Earth
Ionosphere (region of **ionized*** gas around the Earth)

* **Discharge tube**, 80; **Electric field**, 58; **Electrons**, 83; **Frequency**, 35; **Internal energy**, 9; **Ionization**, 88; **Nuclear power station**, 94; **Wavelength**, 34.

LIGHT

Light consists of **electromagnetic waves*** of particular **frequencies*** and **wavelengths*** (see pages 44-45), but is commonly referred to and diagrammatically represented as **rays**. Such a ray is actually a line (arrow) which indicates the path taken by the light waves, i.e. the direction in which the energy is being carried.

Shadow

An area which light rays cannot reach due to an obstacle in their path. If the rays come from a point they are stopped by the obstacle, creating a complete shadow called an **umbra**.

Casting an umbra

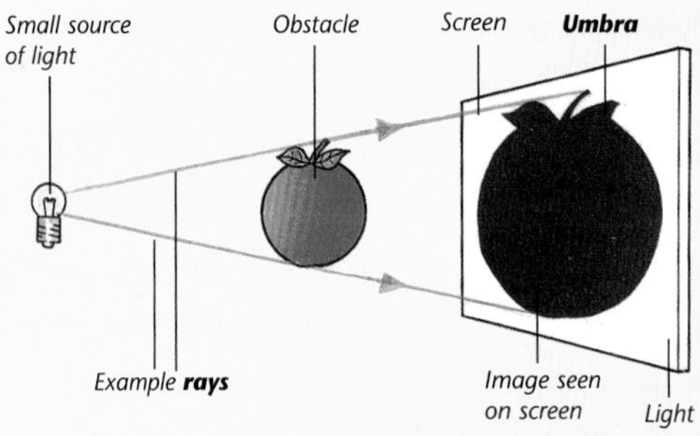

Small source of light
Obstacle
Screen
Umbra
Example rays
Image seen on screen
Light

If the light rays come from an extended source, a semi-shadow area called a **penumbra** is formed around the umbra.

Casting a penumbra

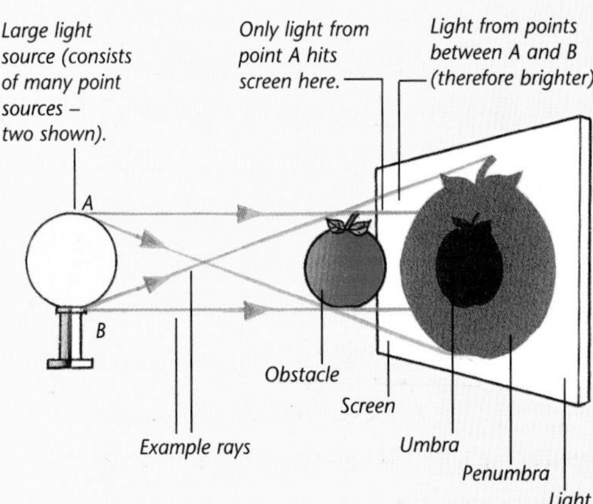

Large light source (consists of many point sources – two shown).
Only light from point A hits screen here.
Light from points between A and B (therefore brighter)
A
B
Obstacle
Screen
Example rays
Umbra
Penumbra
Light

Eclipse

The total or partial "blocking off" of light from a source. This occurs when an object casts a **shadow** by passing between the source and an observer. A **solar eclipse** is seen from the Earth when the Moon passes between the Earth and the Sun, and a **lunar eclipse** is seen when the Earth is between the Sun and the Moon.

Moon blocking out Sun's light in an annular solar eclipse

Solar eclipse

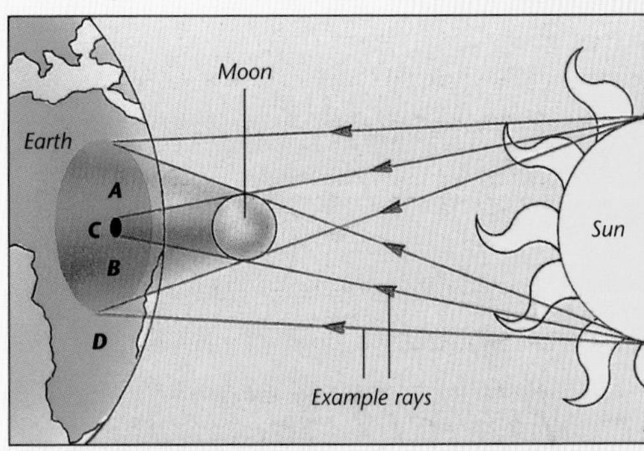

Moon
Earth
A
C
B
D
Sun
Example rays

The eclipse, as seen from positions A, B, C and D.

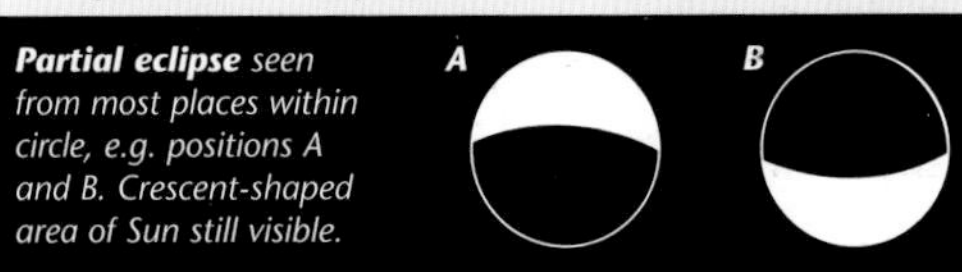

Partial eclipse seen from most places within circle, e.g. positions A and B. Crescent-shaped area of Sun still visible.
A
B

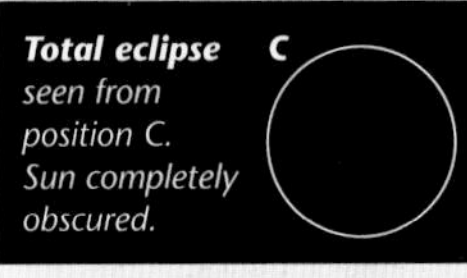

Total eclipse seen from position C. Sun completely obscured.
C

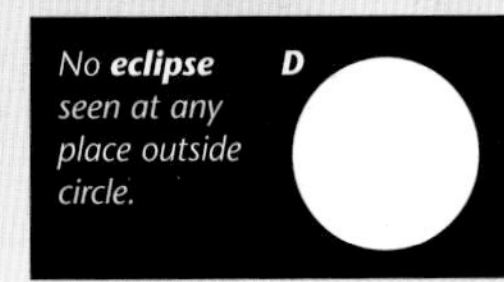

No eclipse seen at any place outside circle.
D

Annular eclipse

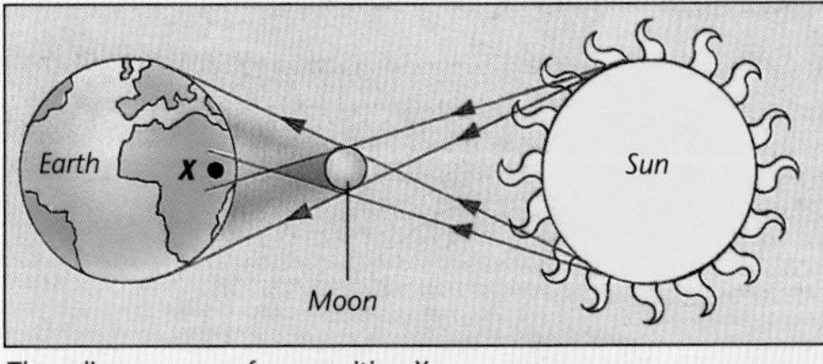

Earth
X
Sun
Moon

The eclipse, as seen from position X.

*An **annular eclipse** is a special **eclipse** which consists of a bright ring around a black area. It occurs when the Moon, Earth and Sun are particular distances apart.*

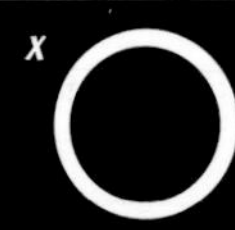

X

* **Electromagnetic waves**, 44; **Frequency**, 35; **Wavelength**, 34.

REFLECTION OF LIGHT

Reflection is the change in direction of a wave when it bounces off a boundary (see page 36). Mirrors are usually used to show the reflection of light (see below and also pages 48-49). It must be noted that when an object and its image are drawn in mirror (and **lens***) diagrams, the object is assumed to be producing light rays itself. In fact the rays come from a source, e.g. the Sun, and are reflected off the object.

Laws of reflection of light

1. The **reflected ray** lies in the same plane as the **incident ray** and the **normal** at the **point of incidence**.
2. The **angle of incidence** (**i**) = the **angle of reflection** (**r**).

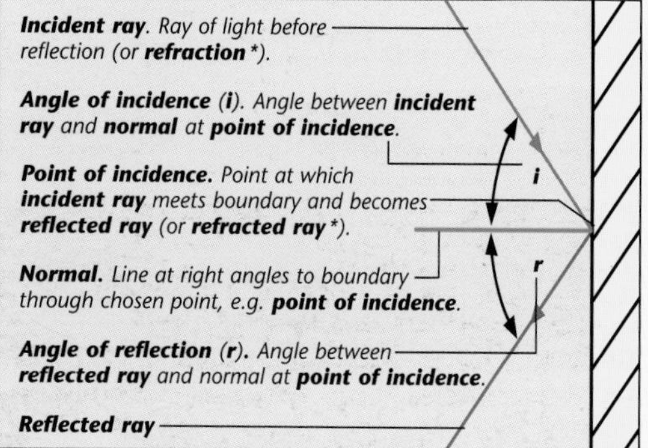
Incident ray. Ray of light before reflection (or refraction*).
Angle of incidence (i). Angle between incident ray and normal at point of incidence.
Point of incidence. Point at which incident ray meets boundary and becomes reflected ray (or refracted ray*).
Normal. Line at right angles to boundary through chosen point, e.g. point of incidence.
Angle of reflection (r). Angle between reflected ray and normal at point of incidence.
Reflected ray
i
r

Regular reflection

The reflection of parallel **incident rays** (see above) off a flat surface such that all the **reflected rays** are also parallel. This occurs when surfaces are very smooth, e.g. highly polished surfaces such as mirrors.

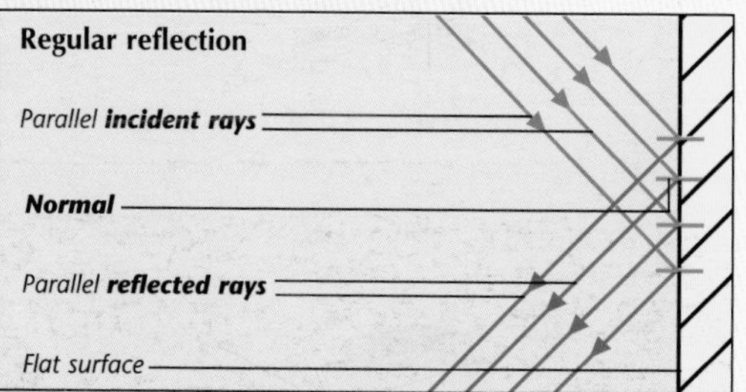
Regular reflection
Parallel incident rays
Normal
Parallel reflected rays
Flat surface

Diffuse reflection

The reflection of parallel **incident rays** (see left) off a rough surface such that the **reflected rays** travel in different directions and the light is scattered. This is the most common type of reflection as most surfaces are irregular when considered on a scale comparable to that of the **wavelength*** of light (see page 113).

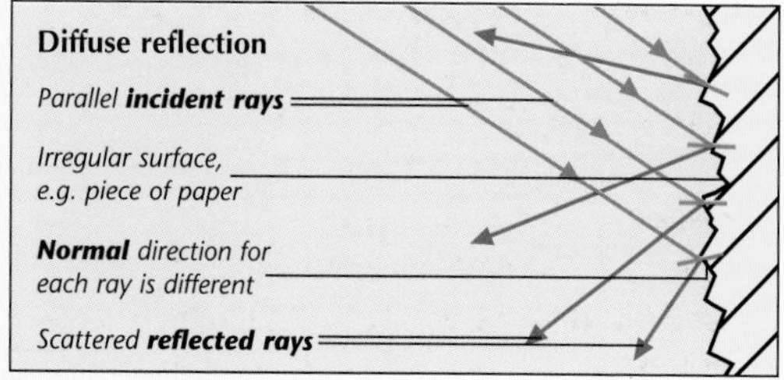
Diffuse reflection
Parallel incident rays
Irregular surface, e.g. piece of paper
Normal direction for each ray is different
Scattered reflected rays

Plane mirror

A mirror with a flat surface (see also **curved mirrors**, pages 48-49). The image it forms is the same size as the object, the same distance behind ("inside") the mirror as the object is in front, and **laterally inverted** (the left and right sides have swapped around).

Reflection in plane mirror

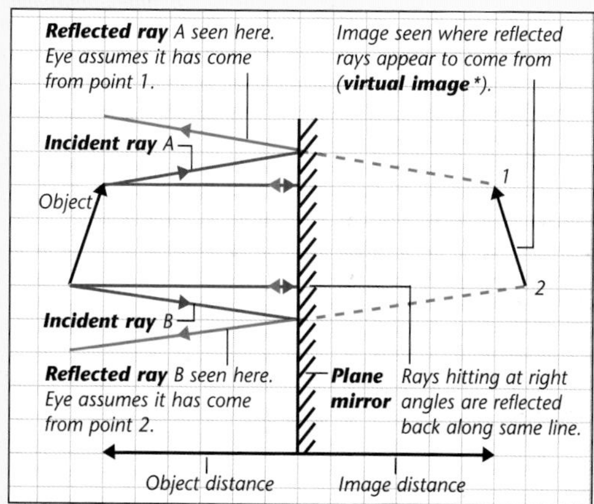
Reflected ray A seen here. Eye assumes it has come from point 1.
Image seen where reflected rays appear to come from (virtual image*).
Incident ray A
Object
1
2
Incident ray B
Reflected ray B seen here. Eye assumes it has come from point 2.
Plane mirror
Rays hitting at right angles are reflected back along same line.
Object distance
Image distance

Parallax

The apparent displacement of an observed object due to the difference between two points of view. For example, an object which is observed first with the left eye, and then with the right eye, appears to have moved. The first point of view is the left eye, and the second is the right eye. (See also **parallax error**, page 102.)

* **Lenses**, 52; **Refracted ray**, **Refraction**, 50; **Virtual image**, 49 (**Image**); **Wavelength**, 34.

Reflection of light (continued)

Light rays are reflected from curved surfaces, as from flat surfaces, according to the **laws of reflection of light** (see page 47). The images formed by reflection from **curved mirrors** are particularly easily observed. There are two types of curved mirror – **concave** and **convex mirrors**. For all diagrams showing reflection of light, the object is assumed to be the source of the light (see **reflection of light**, page 47) and certain points (see below), together with known facts about light rays passing through them, are used to construct the paths of the reflected rays.

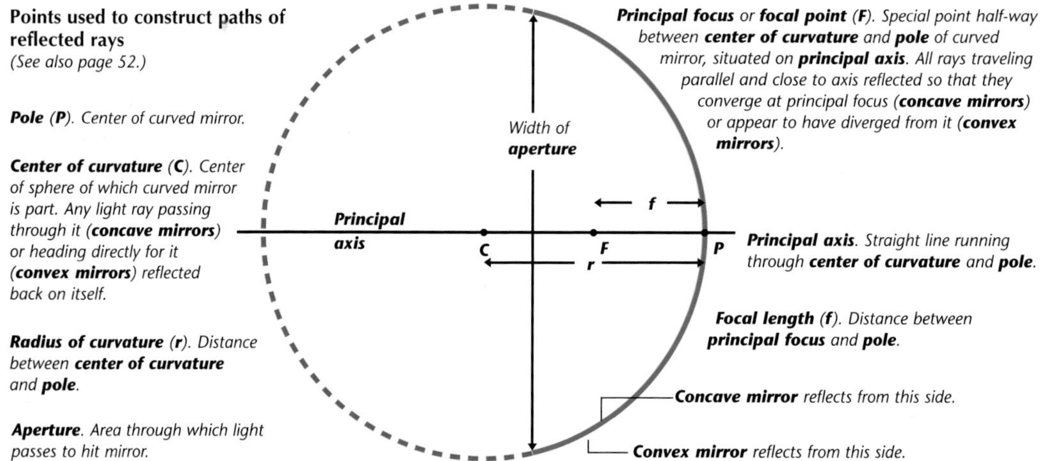

Points used to construct paths of reflected rays
(See also page 52.)
Pole (P). Center of curved mirror.
Center of curvature (C). Center of sphere of which curved mirror is part. Any light ray passing through it (concave mirrors) or heading directly for it (convex mirrors) reflected back on itself.
Radius of curvature (r). Distance between center of curvature and pole.
Aperture. Area through which light passes to hit mirror.
Width of aperture
Principal axis
C
F
P
f
r
Principal focus or focal point (F). Special point half-way between center of curvature and pole of curved mirror, situated on principal axis. All rays traveling parallel and close to axis reflected so that they converge at principal focus (concave mirrors) or appear to have diverged from it (convex mirrors).
Principal axis. Straight line running through center of curvature and pole.
Focal length (f). Distance between principal focus and pole.
Concave mirror reflects from this side.
Convex mirror reflects from this side.

Concave or **converging mirror**

A mirror with a reflecting surface which curves inward (part of the inside of a sphere). When light rays parallel to the **principal axis** fall on such a mirror, they are reflected so that they converge at the **principal focus** in front of the mirror. The size, position and type of **image** formed depends on how far the object is from the mirror.

Concave mirror

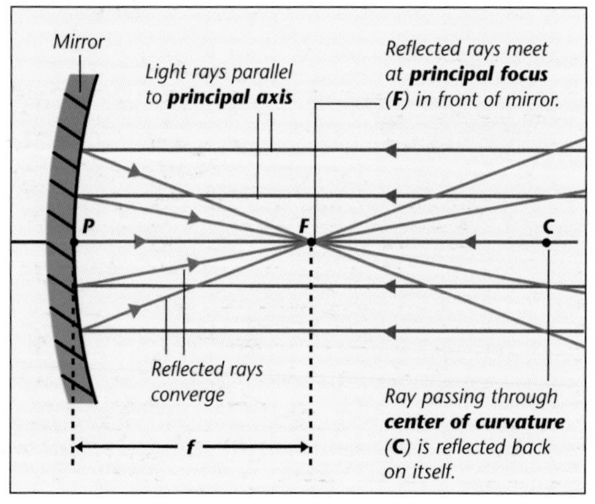

Mirror
Light rays parallel to principal axis
Reflected rays meet at principal focus (F) in front of mirror.
P
F
C
Reflected rays converge
Ray passing through center of curvature (C) is reflected back on itself.
f

Convex or **diverging mirror**

A mirror with a reflecting surface which curves outwards (part of the outside of a sphere). When light rays parallel to the **principal axis** fall on such a mirror, they are reflected so that they appear to diverge from the **principal focus** behind ("inside") the mirror. The **images** formed are always upright and reduced, and **virtual images** (see **image**).

Convex mirror

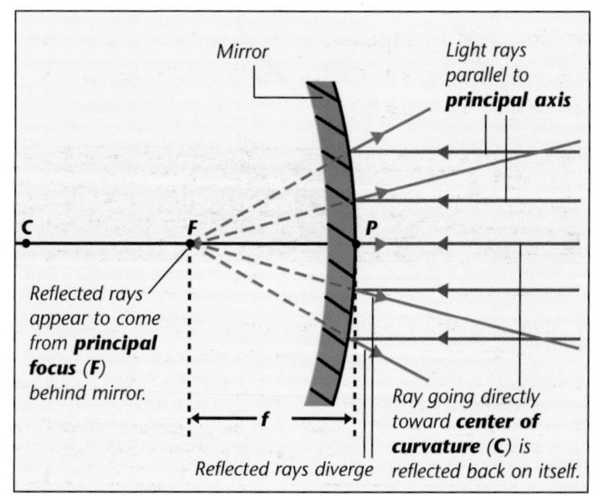

Mirror
Light rays parallel to principal axis
C
F
P
Reflected rays appear to come from principal focus (F) behind mirror.
f
Reflected rays diverge
Ray going directly toward center of curvature (C) is reflected back on itself.

Image

A view of an object as seen in a mirror. Just as an object is only seen because of light rays coming from it (see **reflection of light**, page 47), so too an image is seen where reflected rays (originally from the object) actually diverge from (**real image**), or appear to diverge from (**virtual image**).

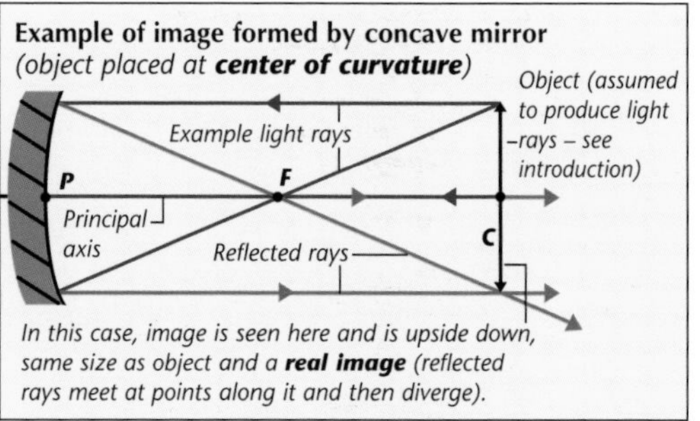
Example of image formed by concave mirror
(object placed at center of curvature)
Object (assumed to produce light rays – see introduction)
Example light rays
P
F
Principal axis
Reflected rays
C
In this case, image is seen here and is upside down, same size as object and a real image (reflected rays meet at points along it and then diverge).

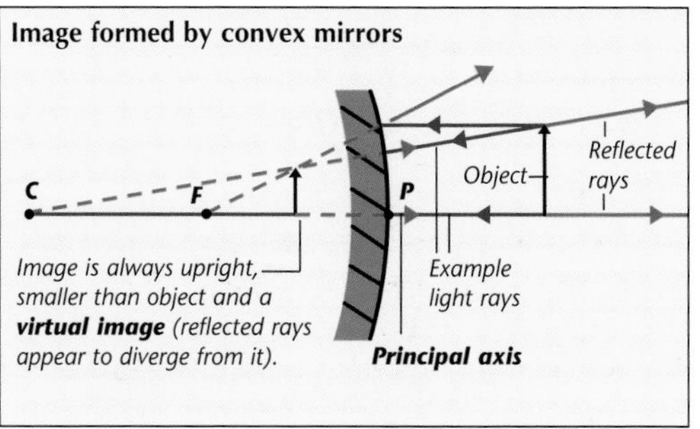
Image formed by convex mirrors
C
F
P
Object
Reflected rays
Image is always upright, smaller than object and a virtual image (reflected rays appear to diverge from it).
Example light rays
Principal axis

Mirror or lens formula

Gives the relationship between the distance of an object from the center of a curved mirror or **lens***, the distance of its **image** from the same point and the **focal length** of the mirror or lens. An image may be formed either side of a mirror or lens, so a **sign convention*** is used to give position.

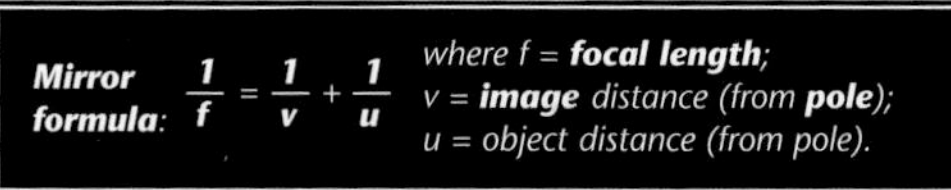
Mirror formula: $\frac{1}{f} = \frac{1}{v} + \frac{1}{u}$
where f = focal length;
v = image distance (from pole);
u = object distance (from pole).

Real is positive sign convention for mirrors and lenses

1. All distances are measured from the mirror as origin.
*2. Distances of objects and **real images** are positive.*
*3. Distances of **virtual images** are negative.*
*4. The **focal lengths** of **convex mirrors** and **lenses*** are positive. The focal lengths of **concave mirrors** and lenses are negative.*

Linear magnification

The ratio of the height of the image formed by a mirror or **lens*** to the object height.

Linear magnification = $\frac{\text{height of image}}{\text{height of object}}$

Example of linear magnification

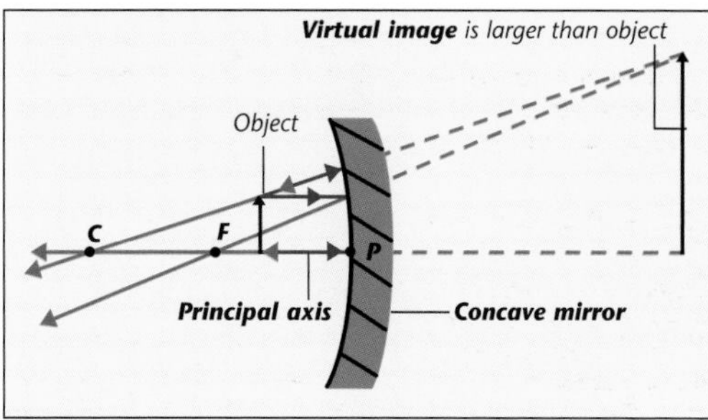
Virtual image is larger than object
Object
C
F
P
Principal axis
Concave mirror

Principle of reversibility of light

States that, for a ray of light on a given path due to reflection, **refraction*** or **diffraction***, a ray of light in the opposite direction in the same conditions will follow the same path. Light rays parallel to the **principal axis**, for example, are reflected by a **concave mirror** to meet at the **principal focus**. If a point source of light is placed at the principal focus, the rays are reflected parallel to the axis.

Spherical aberration

An effect seen when rays parallel to the **principal axis** (and different distances from it), hit a curved mirror and are reflected so that they intersect at different points along the axis, forming a **caustic curve**. The larger the **aperture**, the more this effect is seen. It is also seen in **lenses*** with large apertures.

Spherical aberration

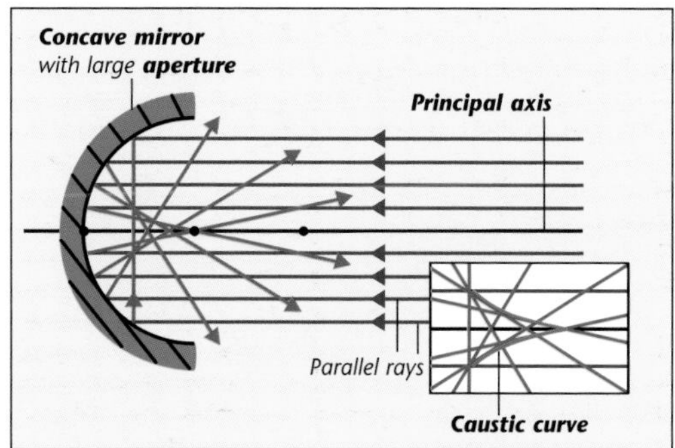
Concave mirror with large aperture
Principal axis
Parallel rays
Caustic curve

* **Diffraction**, 37; **Lens**, 52; **Refraction**, 37; **Sign convention**, 11.

REFRACTION OF LIGHT

Refraction is the change in direction of any wave as a result of its velocity changing when it moves from one **medium*** into another (see also page 37). When light rays (see page 46) move into a new medium, they are refracted according to the **laws of refraction of light**. The direction in which they are refracted depends on whether they move into a denser or less dense medium and are consequently slowed down or speeded up (see diagram below).

***Refraction** makes the end of this straw appear bent in the drink.*

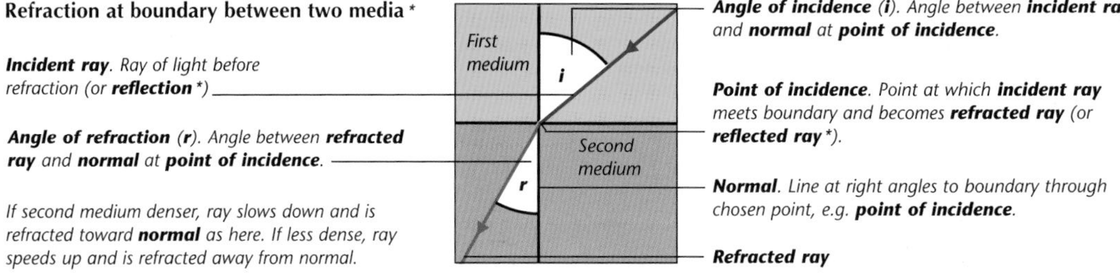
Refraction at boundary between two media *
***Incident ray**. Ray of light before refraction (or **reflection** *)*
***Angle of refraction** (**r**). Angle between **refracted ray** and **normal** at **point of incidence**.*
*If second medium denser, ray slows down and is refracted toward **normal** as here. If less dense, ray speeds up and is refracted away from normal.*
First medium
i
Second medium
r
***Angle of incidence** (**i**). Angle between **incident ray** and **normal** at **point of incidence**.*
***Point of incidence**. Point at which **incident ray** meets boundary and becomes **refracted ray** (or **reflected ray** *).*
***Normal**. Line at right angles to boundary through chosen point, e.g. **point of incidence**.*
Refracted ray

Laws of refraction of light

1. The **refracted ray** lies in the same plane as the **incident ray** and **normal** at the **point of incidence**.

2. (**Snell's law**). The ratio of the **sine*** of the **angle of incidence** to the sine of the **angle of refraction** is a constant for two given **media***.

This constant is the **refractive index** (**n** – see page 37). When referring to light, this is also known as the **optical density** and, as with refractive index in other cases, can also be calculated by dividing the velocity of light in one medium by its velocity in the second medium. See also **apparent depth** picture.

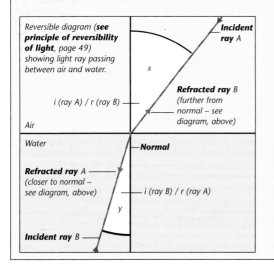

*Reversible diagram (**see principle of reversibility of light**, page 49) showing light ray passing between air and water.*

Air | Water | x | y

***Incident ray** A*

***Refracted ray** B (further from normal – see diagram, above)*

i (ray A) / r (ray B)

Normal

***Refracted ray** A (closer to normal – see diagram, above)*

i (ray B) / r (ray A)

***Incident ray** B*

*For either direction, **refractive index** * of second **medium** * relative to first is written $_1n_2$.*

*According to **Snell's law**:*

$$_1n_2 = \frac{\sin i}{\sin r}$$

Media may also be specified by subscript letters – $_an_w$ means refractive index of water relative to air and $_wn_a$ means that of air relative to water.

$$_an_w = \frac{\sin i \text{ (ray A)}}{\sin r \text{ (ray B)}} = \frac{\sin x}{\sin y}$$

$$_wn_a = \frac{\sin i \text{ (ray B)}}{\sin r \text{ (ray B)}} = \frac{\sin y}{\sin x}$$

$$\text{Thus } _an_w = \frac{1}{_wn_a}$$

*If no subscripts are given, the value is the **absolute refractive index** *.*

* **Absolute refractive index**, 37 (**Refractive index**); **Medium**, 115; **Reflected ray**, **Reflection**, 47; **Sine**, 115.

Apparent depth

The position at which an object in one **medium*** appears to be when viewed from another medium. The brain assumes the light rays have traveled in a straight line, but in fact they have changed direction as a result of refraction. Hence the object is not actually where it appears to be.

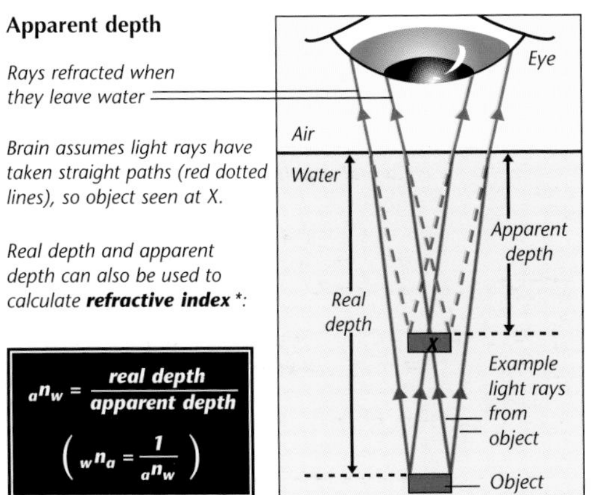

Apparent depth
Rays refracted when they leave water
Brain assumes light rays have taken straight paths (red dotted lines), so object seen at X.
Real depth and apparent depth can also be used to calculate refractive index *:
Eye
Air
Water
Apparent depth
Real depth
X
Example light rays from object
Object

$$_an_w = \frac{\text{real depth}}{\text{apparent depth}}$$

$$\left({_wn_a} = \frac{1}{_an_w} \right)$$

Critical angle (c)

The particular **angle of incidence** of a ray hitting a less dense **medium*** which results in it being refracted at 90° to the **normal**. This means that the refracted ray (**critical ray**) travels along the boundary, and does not enter the second medium.

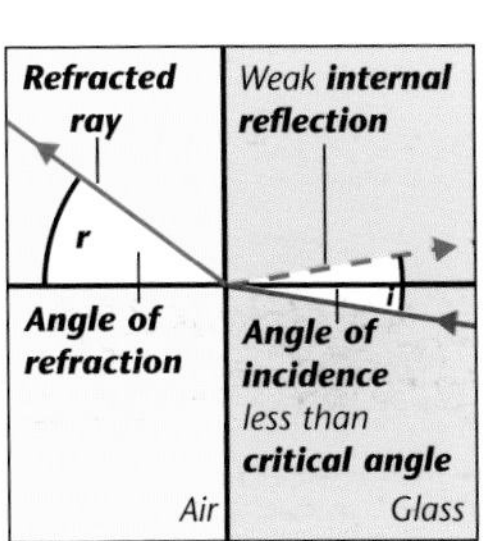

Refracted ray
Weak internal reflection
r
i
Angle of refraction
Angle of incidence less than critical angle
Air
Glass

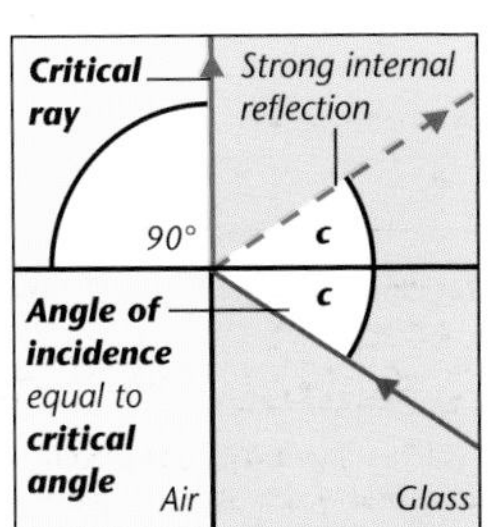

Critical ray
Strong internal reflection
90°
c
c
Angle of incidence equal to critical angle
Air
Glass

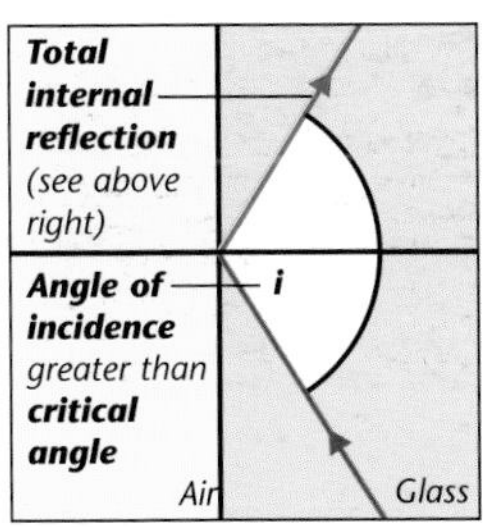

Total internal reflection (see above right)
Angle of incidence greater than critical angle
i
Air
Glass

Critical angle *can also be used to calculate* ***refractive index*** **:*

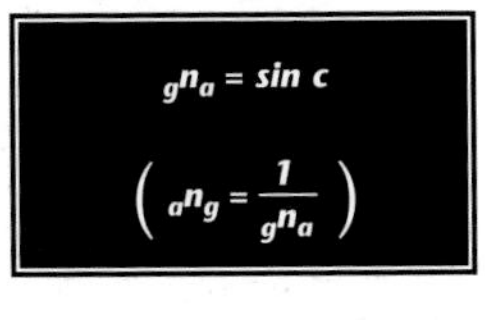

$$_gn_a = \sin c$$

$$\left({_an_g} = \frac{1}{_gn_a} \right)$$

(Note: sine of 90° is 1.)

Rainbows form when light is ***refracted*** *through tiny drops of rain present in the air after rain. Each drop acts like a* ***prism****,* ***dispersing**** *light into the colors of the* ***visible light spectrum*****.*

Total internal reflection

When light traveling from a dense to a less dense **medium*** hits the boundary between them, some degree of reflection back into the denser medium always accompanies refraction. When the **angle of incidence** is greater than the **critical angle**, total internal reflection occurs, i.e. all the light is internally reflected.

Optical fibers *transmit light by* ***total internal reflection****. Bundles of such fibers have a number of uses, e.g. in communications and in medicine (e.g. in* ***endoscopes****, used by doctors to see inside the body).*

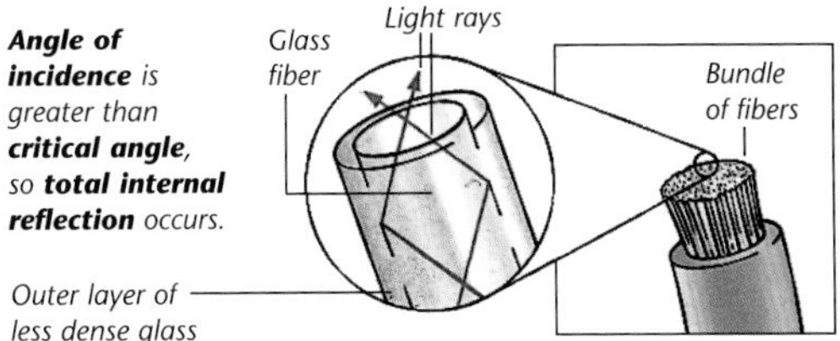

Angle of incidence is greater than critical angle, so total internal reflection occurs.
Glass fiber
Light rays
Bundle of fibers
Outer layer of less dense glass

Prism

A transparent solid which has two plane refracting surfaces at an angle to each other. Prisms are used to produce **dispersion*** and change the path of light by refraction and **total internal reflection.**

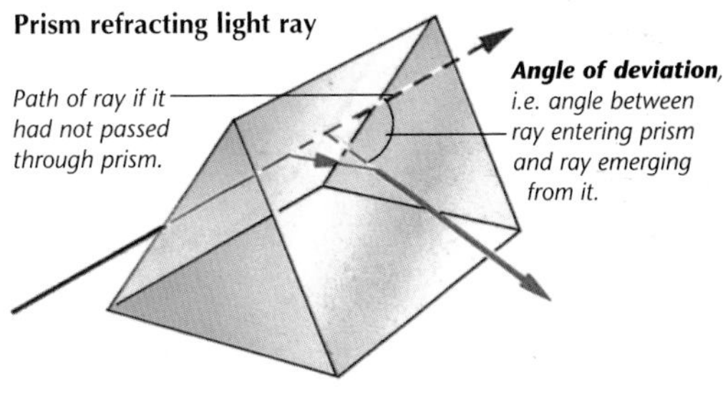

Prism refracting light ray
Path of ray if it had not passed through prism.
Angle of deviation, i.e. angle between ray entering prism and ray emerging from it.

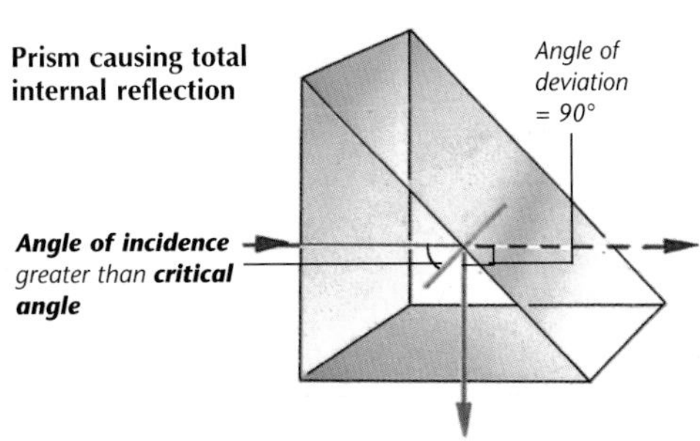

Prism causing total internal reflection
Angle of deviation = 90°
Angle of incidence greater than critical angle

* **Dispersion**, 54 (**Color**); **Medium**, 115; **Refractive index**, 37; **Visible light spectrum**, 54.

Refraction of light (continued)

A magnifying glass is a **converging lens** used so that objects are made to look bigger than they really are.

Light rays are refracted at curved surfaces, e.g. **lenses**, as at flat surfaces, according to the **laws of refraction of light** (see page 50). Unlike with flat surfaces, though, images are formed. There are two basic types of lens, **concave** and **convex lenses**, which can act as **diverging** or **converging lenses** depending on their **refractive index*** relative to the surrounding **medium***. For all diagrams showing image production by refraction, the object is assumed to be the light source (see **reflection of light**, page 47), and certain points (see below), together with known facts about light rays passing through them, are used to construct the paths of the refracted rays. The positions of objects and images can be determined using the **mirror** (**lens**) **formula***.

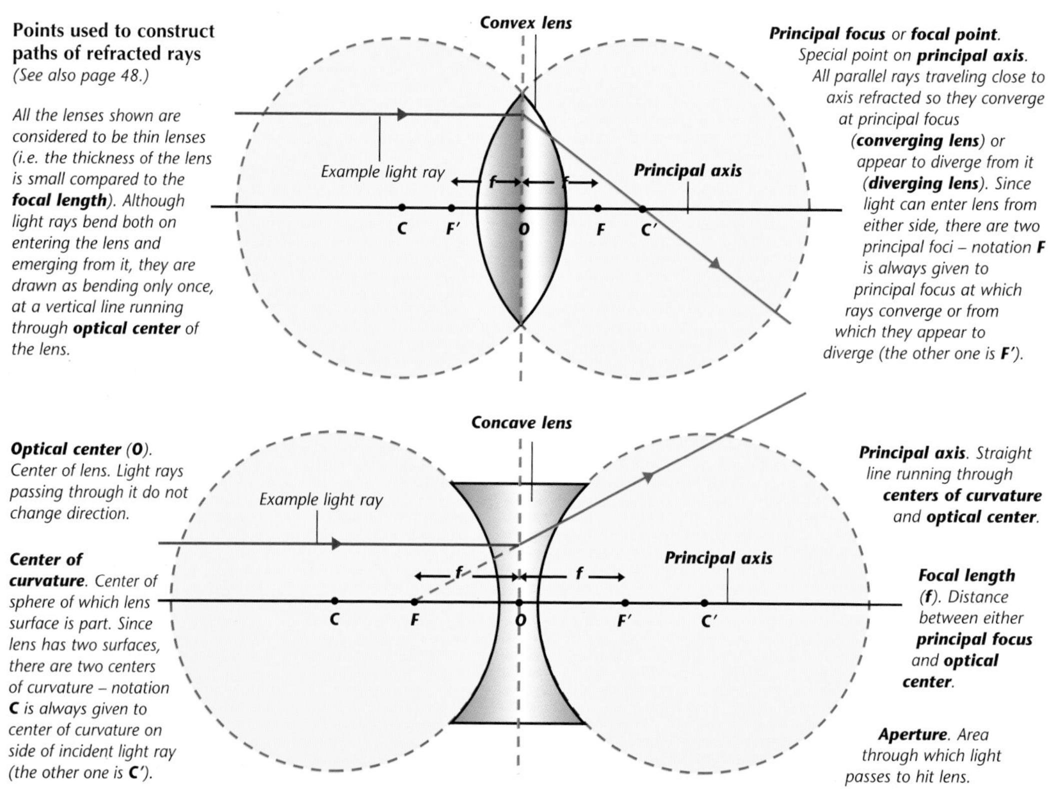
Points used to construct paths of refracted rays
(See also page 48.)
*All the lenses shown are considered to be thin lenses (i.e. the thickness of the lens is small compared to the **focal length**). Although light rays bend both on entering the lens and emerging from it, they are drawn as bending only once, at a vertical line running through **optical center** of the lens.*
Convex lens
Example light ray
f
f
Principal axis
C
F′
O
F
C′
Principal focus or focal point. Special point on principal axis. All parallel rays traveling close to axis refracted so they converge at principal focus (converging lens) or appear to diverge from it (diverging lens). Since light can enter lens from either side, there are two principal foci – notation F is always given to principal focus at which rays converge or from which they appear to diverge (the other one is F′).
Concave lens
Example light ray
f
f
Principal axis
C
F
O
F′
C′
Optical center (O). Center of lens. Light rays passing through it do not change direction.
Center of curvature. Center of sphere of which lens surface is part. Since lens has two surfaces, there are two centers of curvature – notation C is always given to center of curvature on side of incident light ray (the other one is C′).
Principal axis. Straight line running through centers of curvature and optical center.
Focal length (f). Distance between either principal focus and optical center.
Aperture. Area through which light passes to hit lens.

Converging lens

A lens which causes parallel rays falling on it to converge on the **principal focus** on the other side of the lens. Both **concave** and **convex lenses** can act as **converging lenses**, depending on the **refractive index*** of the lens relative to the surrounding **medium***. A glass convex lens in air acts as a converging lens, as shown in the diagram on the right.

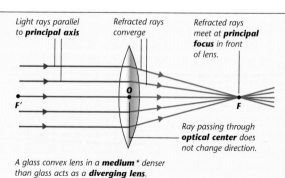

*Light rays parallel to **principal axis***

Refracted rays converge

*Refracted rays meet at **principal focus** in front of lens.*

O

F′

F

*Ray passing through **optical center** does not change direction.*

*A glass convex lens in a **medium*** denser than glass acts as a **diverging lens**.*

* **Medium**, 115; **Mirror formula**, 49; **Refractive index**, 37.

Power (P)

A measure of the ability of a lens to converge or diverge light rays, given in **diopters** (when **focal length** is measured in meters). The shorter the focal length, the more powerful the lens.

$$P = \frac{1}{f}$$ *where P =* ***power*** *of lens; f =* ***focal length****.*

Convex lens

A lens with at least one surface curving outwards. A lens with one surface curving inwards and one outwards is convex if its middle is thicker than its outer edges (it is a **convex meniscus**). A glass convex lens in air acts as a **converging lens**. The size, position and type of image it forms (**real*** or **virtual***) depends on how far it is from the object.

Types of convex lens

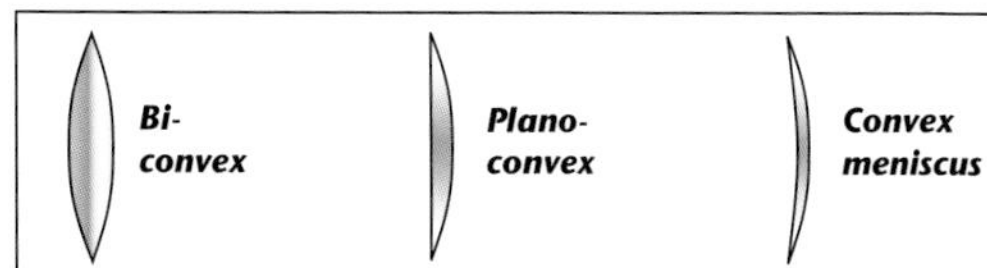

Bi-convex
Plano-convex
Convex meniscus

Convex lens

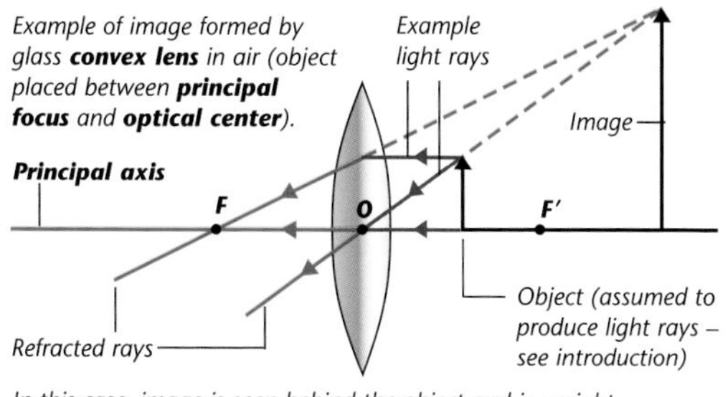

Example of image formed by glass **convex lens** in air (object placed between **principal focus** and **optical center**).
Example light rays
Image
Principal axis
F
O
F′
Refracted rays
Object (assumed to produce light rays – see introduction)

In this case, image is seen behind the object and is upright, larger than object and a ***virtual image****.

Binoculars use lenses to magnify objects.

Concave lens

A lens which has at least one surface curving inwards. A lens with one surface curving inwards and one outwards is concave if its middle is thinner than its outer edges (it is a **concave meniscus**). A glass concave lens in air acts as a **diverging lens**. The position of the object in relation to the lens may vary, but the image is always of the same type.

Types of concave lens

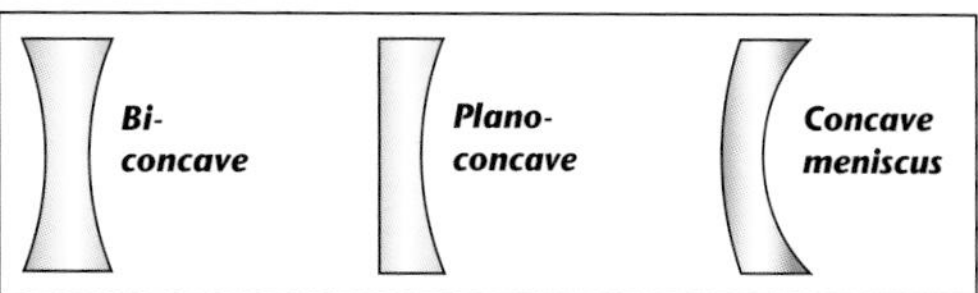

Bi-concave
Plano-concave
Concave meniscus

Concave lens

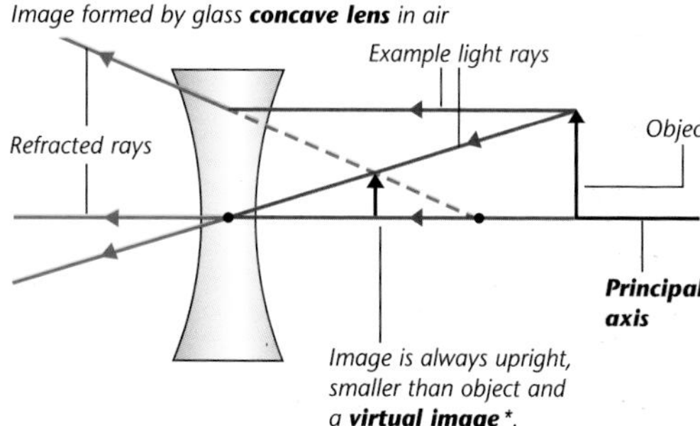

Image formed by glass **concave lens** in air
Example light rays
Refracted rays
Object
Principal axis
Image is always upright, smaller than object and a **virtual image***.

Diverging lens

A lens which causes parallel rays falling on it to diverge so that they appear to have come from the **principal focus** on the same side as the rays enter. Both **concave** and **convex lenses** can act as diverging lenses, depending on the **refractive index*** of the lens relative to the surrounding **medium***. A glass concave lens in air acts as a diverging lens, as shown in the diagram on the right.

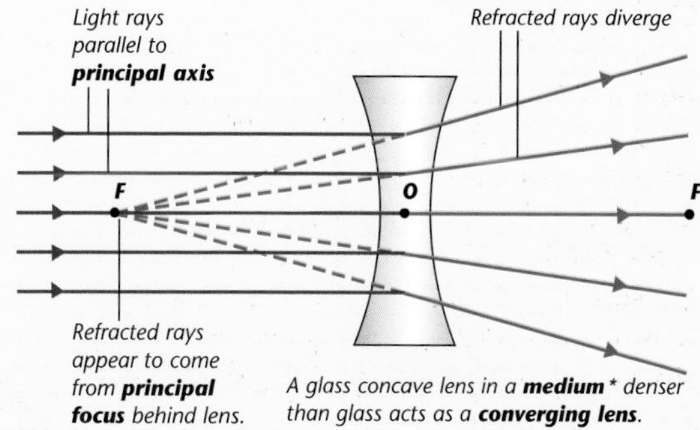

Light rays parallel to **principal axis**
Refracted rays diverge
F
O
F′
Refracted rays appear to come from **principal focus** behind lens.

A glass concave lens in a ***medium**** *denser than glass acts as a* ***converging lens****.

* **Medium**, 115; **Real image**, 49 (**Image**); **Refractive index**, 37; **Virtual image**, 49 (**Image**).

OPTICAL INSTRUMENTS

An **optical instrument** is one which acts on light, using one or more **lenses*** or **curved mirrors*** to produce a required type of image. Listed below are some of the more common optical instruments.

Camera

An optical instrument that is used to form and record an image of an object on film. The image is inverted and a **real image***.

Camera (reflex)

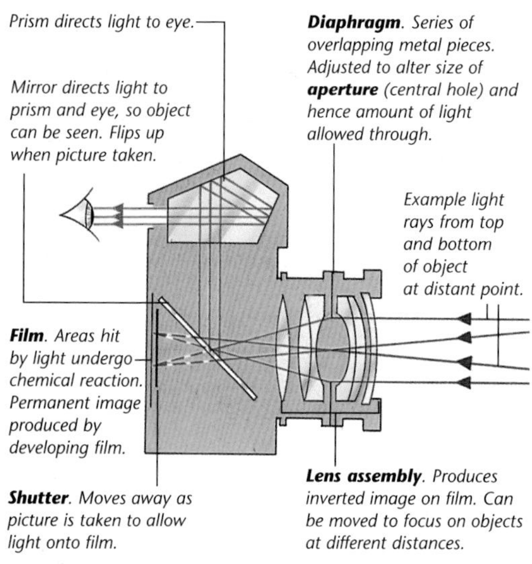
Prism directs light to eye.
Mirror directs light to prism and eye, so object can be seen. Flips up when picture taken.
Diaphragm. Series of overlapping metal pieces. Adjusted to alter size of **aperture** (central hole) and hence amount of light allowed through.
Example light rays from top and bottom of object at distant point.
Film. Areas hit by light undergo chemical reaction. Permanent image produced by developing film.
Shutter. Moves away as picture is taken to allow light onto film.
Lens assembly. Produces inverted image on film. Can be moved to focus on objects at different distances.

As before (see page 52), refraction by lenses shown as one change of direction only, this time on line through optical center of whole lens assembly.

Microscope

An optical instrument which magnifies very small objects. If it has only one **lens***, it is a **simple microscope** or **magnifying glass**. If it has more, it is a **compound microscope**.

Compound microscope

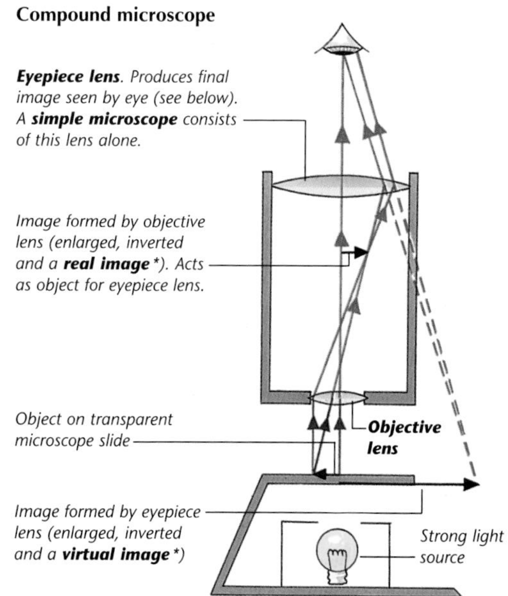
Eyepiece lens. Produces final image seen by eye (see below). A **simple microscope** consists of this lens alone.
Image formed by objective lens (enlarged, inverted and a **real image***). Acts as object for eyepiece lens.
Object on transparent microscope slide
Objective lens
Image formed by eyepiece lens (enlarged, inverted and a **virtual image***)
Strong light source

Color

When all the different **wavelengths*** of **visible light** (see page 45) fall on the eye at the same time, white light is seen. However, white light can also undergo **dispersion**, whereby it is split into the **visible light spectrum** (i.e. its different wavelengths) by **refraction***. This may occur accidentally (see **chromatic aberration**), or it may be produced on purpose, e.g. with a **spectrometer**.

Inside a spectrometer

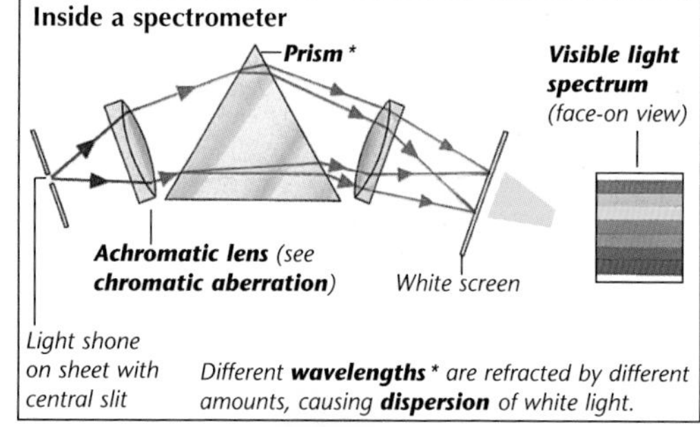
Prism *
Visible light spectrum (face-on view)
Achromatic lens (see **chromatic aberration**)
White screen
Light shone on sheet with central slit

*Different **wavelengths*** are refracted by different amounts, causing **dispersion** of white light.*

Visible light spectrum

A display of the colors that make up a beam of white light. Each color band represents a very small range of **wavelengths*** – see **visible light**, page 45.

White light enters **prism***.

*Light **refracted** by **prism*** to form a color spectrum.*

Slide projector

An optical instrument which produces a magnified image of a slide.

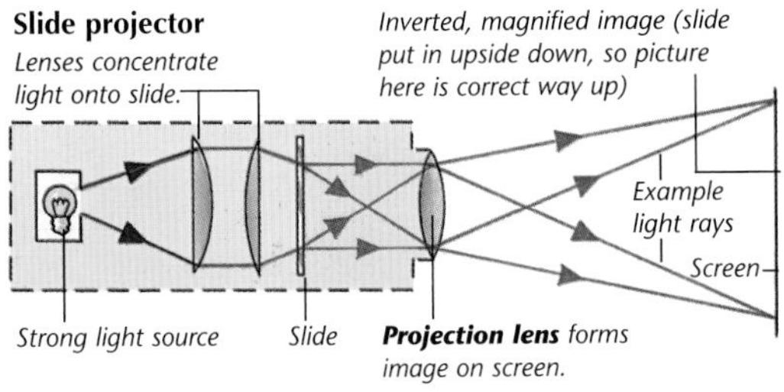
Slide projector
Lenses concentrate light onto slide.
Inverted, magnified image (slide put in upside down, so picture here is correct way up)
Example light rays
Screen
Strong light source
Slide
Projection lens forms image on screen.

Telescope

An optical instrument used to make very distant (and therefore apparently very small) objects appear larger.

Telescope

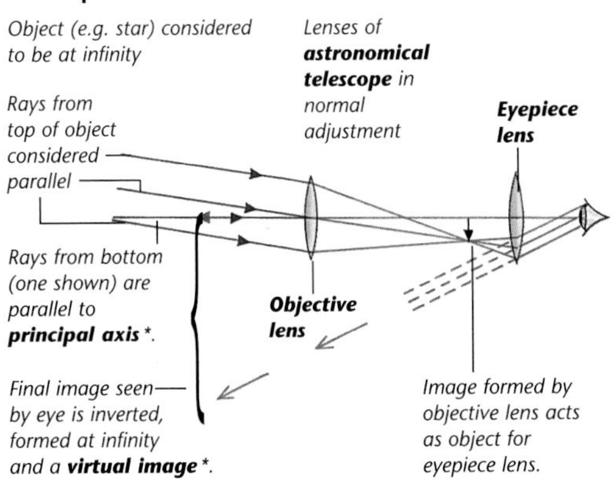
Object (e.g. star) considered to be at infinity
Lenses of **astronomical telescope** in normal adjustment
Rays from top of object considered parallel
Eyepiece lens
Rays from bottom (one shown) are parallel to **principal axis***.
Objective lens
Final image seen by eye is inverted, formed at infinity and a **virtual image***.
Image formed by objective lens acts as object for eyepiece lens.

Visual angle

The angle, at the eye, of the rays coming from the top and bottom of an object or its image. The greater it is, the larger the object or image appears. Optical instruments which produce magnification, e.g. **microscopes**, do so by creating an image whose visual angle is greater than that of the object seen by the unaided eye. The **angular magnification** or **magnifying power** (see below) of such an instrument is a measurement of the amount by which it does so.

$$\textit{Angular magnification} = \frac{\textit{visual angle of image}}{\textit{visual angle of object}}$$

Chromatic aberration or chromatism

The halo of colors (the **visible light spectrum** – see below, left) sometimes seen around images viewed through lenses. It results from **dispersion** (see **color**). To avoid this, good quality optical instruments contain one or more **achromatic lenses** – each consisting of two lenses combined so that any dispersion produced by one is corrected by the other.

***Achromatic lenses** in **compound microscopes** minimize **chromatic aberration**.*

Primary colors

Red, blue and green light – colors that cannot be made by combining other colored light. Mixed equally, they give white light. By mixing them in the right proportions, every color in the **visible light spectrum** can be produced. Note that these are the pure primary colors – those referred to in art (red, blue and yellow) only act as primary colors because the paints are impure.

Primary colors

Green
Blue
Red
△Cyan
△Yellow
△Magenta

***Complementary** colors are any two that produce white light when mixed, e.g. red and cyan.*

*△ = **secondary colors** (combinations of primary colors)*

Color mixing

If white light is shone onto a pure colored filter, only light of the same color (range of **wavelengths***) as the filter passes through (the other colors are absorbed). This is **subtractive mixing** or **color mixing by subtraction**. If light of two different colors, filtered out in this way, is shone onto a white surface, a third color (a mixture of the two) is seen by the eye. This is **additive mixing** or **color mixing by addition**.

This light bulb looks blue because it only lets through blue light (all other colors have been absorbed by the blue coating).

* **Curved mirrors**, 48; **Lenses**, **Principal axis**, 52; **Prism**, 51; **Real image**, 49 (**Image**); **Refraction**, 50; **Virtual image**, 49 (**Image**); **Wavelength**, 34.

STATIC ELECTRICITY

Electricity is the phenomenon caused by the presence or movement of charges (**electrons*** or **ions***) which exert an **electric force***. A material is said to have a negative electric charge if it has a surplus of electrons, and a positive electric charge if it has a deficit of electrons. An electric **current** (see page 60) is the movement of a charge through materials. (In a metal it is the electrons that move.) This can be contrasted with **static electricity**, which can be said to be electricity "held" by a material with electric charge.

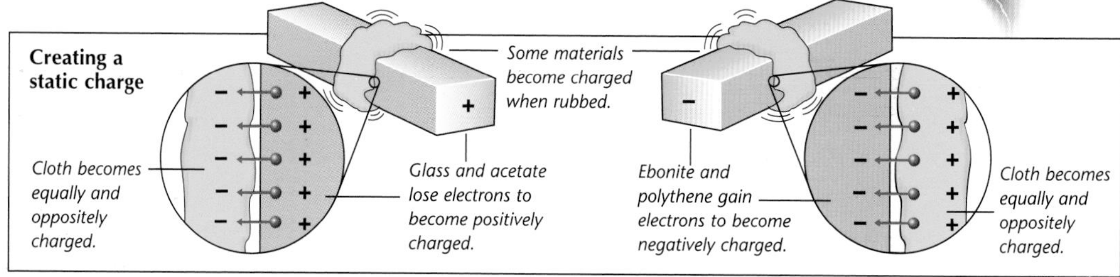
Creating a static charge
Some materials become charged when rubbed.
Cloth becomes equally and oppositely charged.
Glass and acetate lose electrons to become positively charged.
Ebonite and polythene gain electrons to become negatively charged.
Cloth becomes equally and oppositely charged.

First law of electrostatics

Like charges repel each other and unlike charges attract. A charged particle always attracts an uncharged **conductor** by **induction**.

Attraction and repulsion

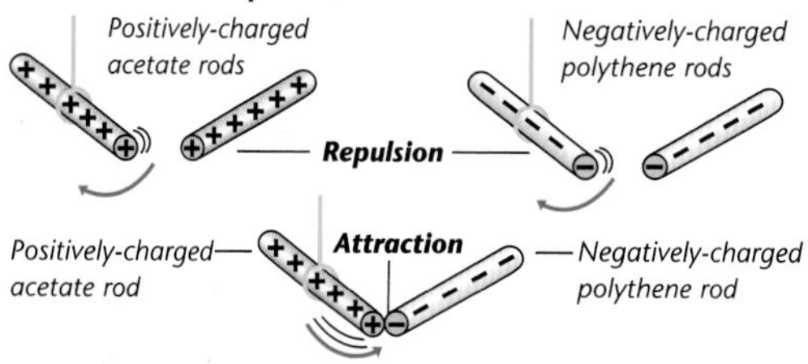
Positively-charged acetate rods
Negatively-charged polythene rods
Repulsion
Positively-charged acetate rod
Attraction
Negatively-charged polythene rod

Conductor

A material containing a large number of charges (e.g. electrons) which are free to move (see also **conductivity**, page 63). It can therefore **conduct** electricity (carry an electric **current** – see introduction). Metals, e.g. copper, aluminum and gold, are good conductors because they contain large numbers of electrons which are free to move.

Insulator

A material with very few or no charges (e.g. electrons) free to move (i.e. a bad **conductor**). Some insulators become electrically charged when rubbed. This is because electrons from the surface atoms are transferred from one substance to the next, but the charge remains on the surface.

Electroscope

An instrument for detecting small amounts of electric charge. A **gold leaf electroscope** is the most common type. When the leaf and rod become charged, they repel and the leaf diverges from the rod. The greater the charges, the larger the divergence of the leaf. A **condensing electroscope** contains a **capacitor*** between the cap and the case which increases the sensitivity.

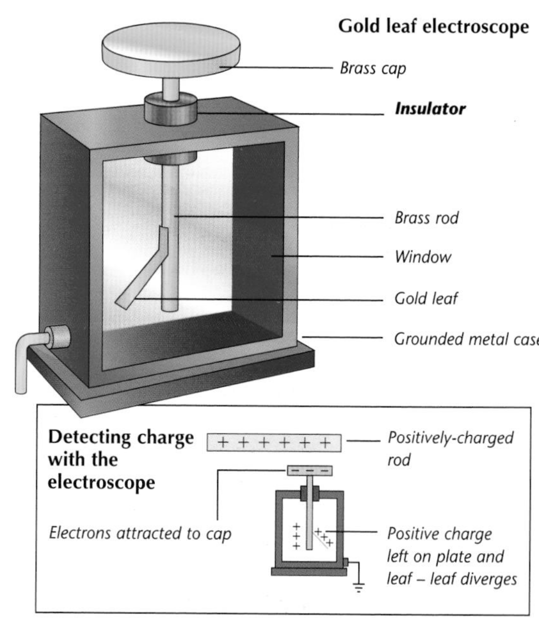
Gold leaf electroscope
Brass cap
Insulator
Brass rod
Window
Gold leaf
Grounded metal case
Detecting charge with the electroscope
Positively-charged rod
Electrons attracted to cap
Positive charge left on plate and leaf – leaf diverges

* **Capacitor**, 59; **Electric force**, 6; **Electrons**, 83; **Ions**, 88 (**Ionization**).

Induction or **electrostatic induction**

A process by which a **conductor** becomes charged with the use of another charge but without contact. Generally charges are induced in different parts of an object because of repulsion and attraction. By removing one type of charge the object is left permanently charged.

Charging a conductor by induction

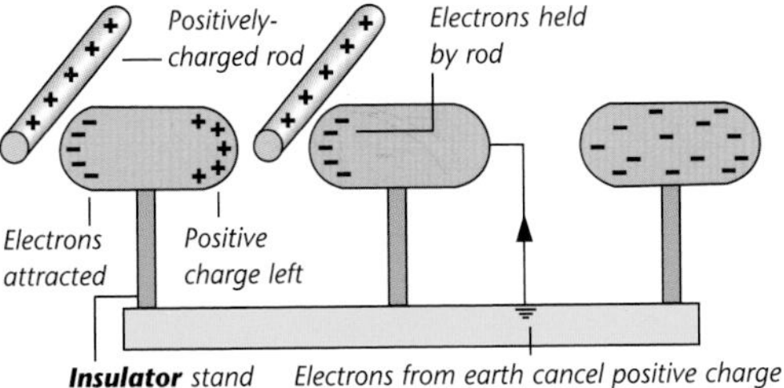

Positively-charged rod
Electrons held by rod
Electrons attracted
Positive charge left
Insulator stand
Electrons from earth cancel positive charge

Proof plane

A small disk made of a **conductor** mounted on a handle made of an **insulator**. It is used to transfer charge between objects.

Surface density of charge

The amount of charge per unit area on the surface of an object. It is greater where the surface is more curved, which leads to charge being concentrated at sharp points (see **point action**). Only a sphere has constant surface density of charge.

Variations in surface density of charge

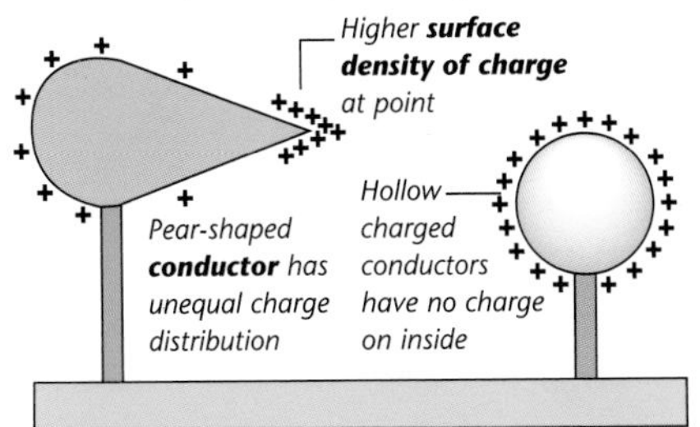

Higher surface density of charge at point
Hollow charged conductors have no charge on inside
Pear-shaped conductor has unequal charge distribution

Point action

The action which occurs around a sharp point on the surface of a positively-charged object. Positive ions in the air are repelled by the large charge at the point (see **surface density of charge**). These collide with air molecules and knock off electrons to produce more positive ions which are also repelled. The result is an **electric wind** of air molecules.

Lightning

The sudden flow of electricity from a cloud which has become charged due to the rubbing together of different particles, e.g. water droplets. A **lightning conductor** is used to help cancel the charge on the cloud by **point action** and to conduct the electricity down to earth so that it does not flow through buildings. The lightning strike is like the effect in a **discharge tube***.

Action of lightning conductor

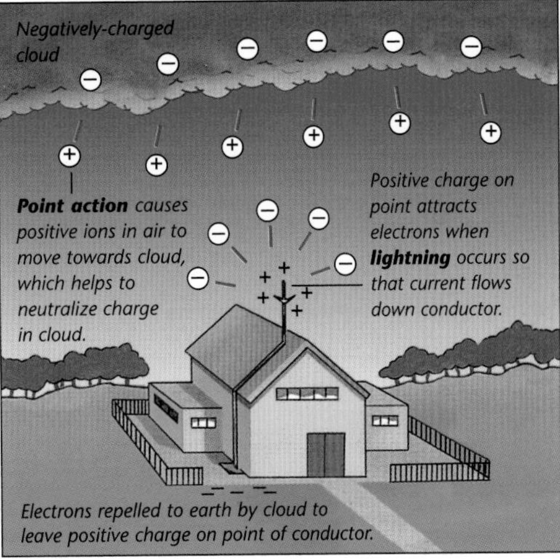

Negatively-charged cloud
Point action causes positive ions in air to move towards cloud, which helps to neutralize charge in cloud.
Positive charge on point attracts electrons when lightning occurs so that current flows down conductor.
Electrons repelled to earth by cloud to leave positive charge on point of conductor.

Van de Graaff generator

A machine in which positive charge from a point is transferred (by **point action**) to a moving band, collected by another point and deposited on a sphere-shaped conductor.

Van de Graaff generator

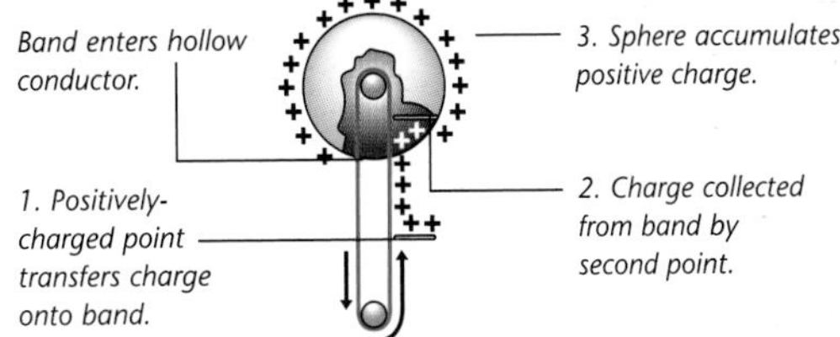

Band enters hollow conductor.
3. Sphere accumulates positive charge.
1. Positively-charged point transfers charge onto band.
2. Charge collected from band by second point.

Electrophorus

An instrument consisting of a negatively-charged **insulator** and a brass plate attached to an insulating handle. It is used to produce a number of positive charges from one negative charge.

* **Discharge tube**, 80; **Mechanical energy**, 9.

POTENTIAL AND CAPACITANCE

A charge or collection of charges causes an **electric field**, i.e. a **force field*** in which charged particles experience an **electric force***. The intensity of an electric field at a point is the force per unit positive charge at that point, and the direction is the direction of the force on a positive charge at that point (see also pages 104-107). Charged objects in an electric field have **potential energy*** because of their charge and position. **Potential** itself is a property of the field (see below).

— Lines of force —

***Electric field** of two opposite charges*

***Electric field** of a single point charge*

$$F \propto \frac{q_1 q_2}{d^2}$$

*where F = **electric force***;*
q_1, q_2 = size of charges;
d = separation.

d

q_1 q_2

Electric force*

Potential

The **potential energy*** per unit charge at a point in an electric field, i.e. the work done in moving a unit positive charge to this point. The potential energy of a charge depends on the potential of its position and on its size. A positive charge tends to move towards points of lower potential. This is moving down the **potential gradient**. Potential cannot be measured, but the **potential difference** between two points can.

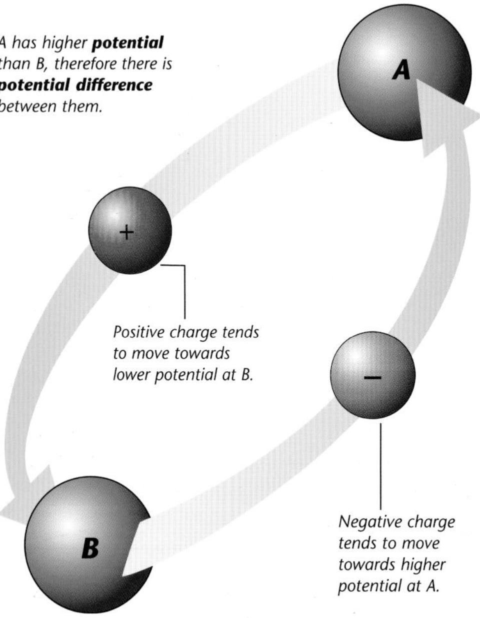
A has higher **potential** than B, therefore there is **potential difference** between them.
A
+
Positive charge tends to move towards lower potential at B.
–
Negative charge tends to move towards higher potential at A.
B

Potential difference

A difference in **potential** between two points, equal to the energy change when a unit positive charge moves from one place to another in an electric field. The unit of potential difference is the **volt** (potential difference is sometimes called **voltage**). There is an energy change of one joule if a charge of one **coulomb*** moves through one volt. A reference point (usually a connection to earth) is chosen and given a potential of zero.

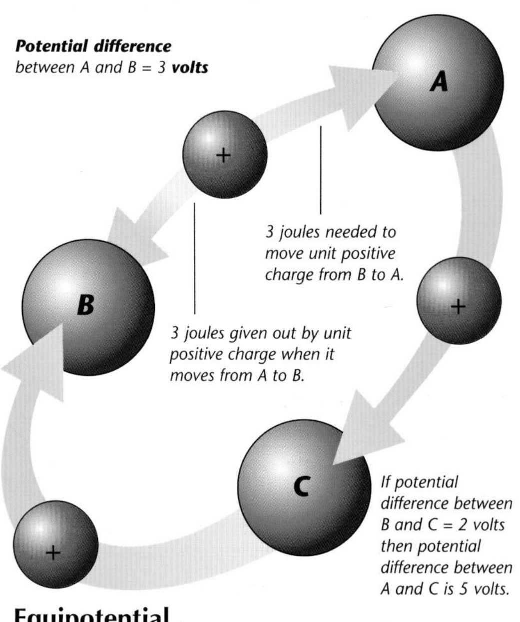
Potential difference between A and B = 3 **volts**
A
+
3 joules needed to move unit positive charge from B to A.
B
3 joules given out by unit positive charge when it moves from A to B.
+
C
If potential difference between B and C = 2 volts then potential difference between A and C is 5 volts.
+

Equipotential

A surface over which the **potential** is constant.

* **Coulomb**, 60; **Electric force**, **Force field**, 6; **Potential energy**, 8.

Capacitance

When a **conductor*** is given a charge it undergoes a change in **potential**. **Capacitance** is the ratio of the charge gained by an object to its increase in potential. An object with a higher capacitance requires a larger charge to change its potential by the same amount as an object with a smaller capacitance.

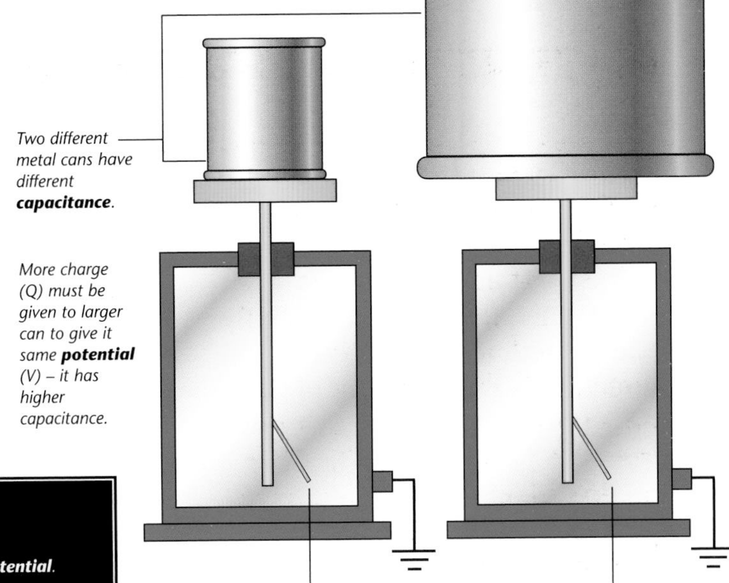

Two different metal cans have different **capacitance**.
More charge (Q) must be given to larger can to give it same **potential** (V) – it has higher capacitance.

Same leaf divergence shows same potential.

$$C = \frac{Q}{V}$$

*where C = **capacitance**; Q = charge; V = **potential**.*

Farad

The unit of capacitance. It is the capacitance of an object whose **potential** is increased by one **volt** when given a charge of one **coulomb***.

Capacitor

A device for storing electric charge, consisting of two parallel metal plates separated by an insulating material called a **dielectric**. The capacitance of a capacitor depends on the dielectric used, so a dielectric is chosen to suit the capacitance needed and the physical size required.

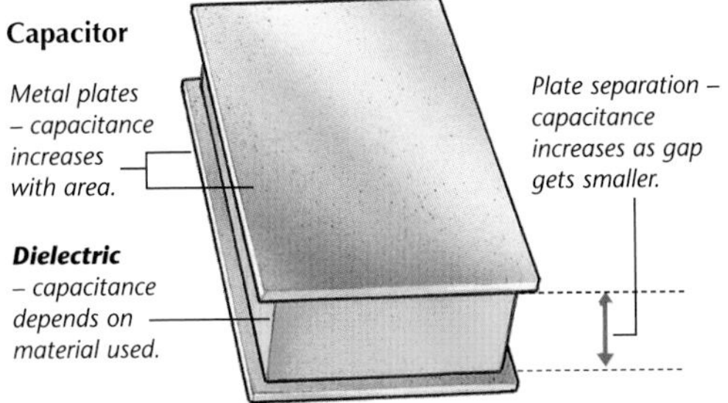

Capacitor
Metal plates – capacitance increases with area.
Dielectric – capacitance depends on material used.
Plate separation – capacitance increases as gap gets smaller.

Dielectric constant

The ratio of the capacitance of a **capacitor** with a given **dielectric** to the capacitance of the same capacitor with a vacuum between the plates. The value is thus the factor by which the capacitance is increased by using the given dielectric instead of a vacuum. (Note that measuring the dielectric against air would produce a very similar result.)

Electrolytic capacitor

A **capacitor** with a paste or jelly **dielectric** which gives it a very high capacitance in a small volume. Due to the nature of the dielectric, it must be connected correctly to the electricity supply.

Variable capacitor

A **capacitor** consisting of two sets of interlocking vanes, often with an air **dielectric**. The size of the interlocking area is altered to change the capacitance.

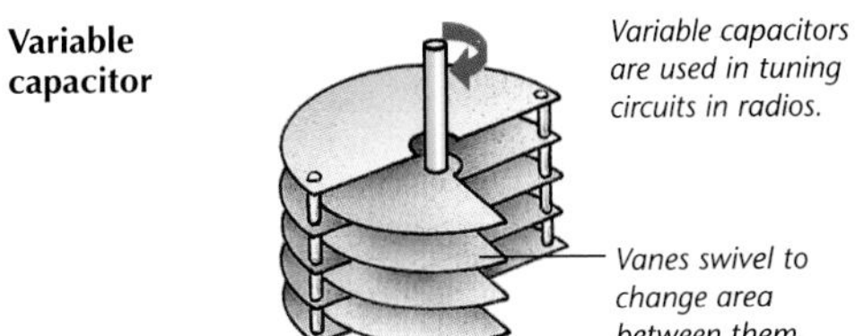

Variable capacitor
Variable capacitors are used in tuning circuits in radios.
Vanes swivel to change area between them.

Leyden jar

A **capacitor** consisting of a glass jar with foil linings inside and out. It was one of the first capacitors invented.

Paper capacitor

A **capacitor** made with two long foil plates separated by a thin waxed paper **dielectric**. **Polyester capacitors** are made in a similar way.

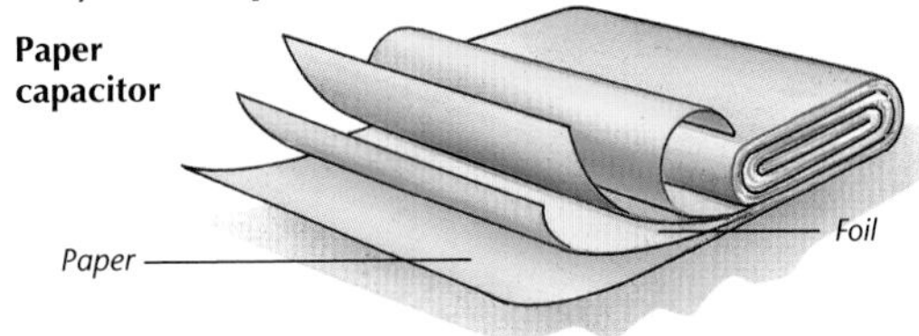

Paper capacitor
Paper
Foil

* **Conductor**, 56; **Coulomb**, 60.

ELECTRIC CURRENT

An electric **current** (**I**) is the rate of flow of electric charge. In metal conductors, the charge which flows consists of electrons (negatively charged particles – see page 83), and these flow because in an **electric field*** there is a difference in **potential*** between two places. Therefore a **potential difference*** is needed to produce an electric current. A **circuit** is a closed loop, consisting of a source of potential difference and one or more components, around which the current flows.

This battery (current source), wires and light bulb form a circuit.

Electromotive force (e.m.f.)

The **potential difference*** produced by a **cell***, **battery*** or **generator***, which causes current to flow in a circuit. A source of e.m.f. has two **terminals** (where wires are connected), between which it maintains a potential difference. A **back e.m.f.** is an e.m.f. produced by a component in the circuit which opposes the main e.m.f.

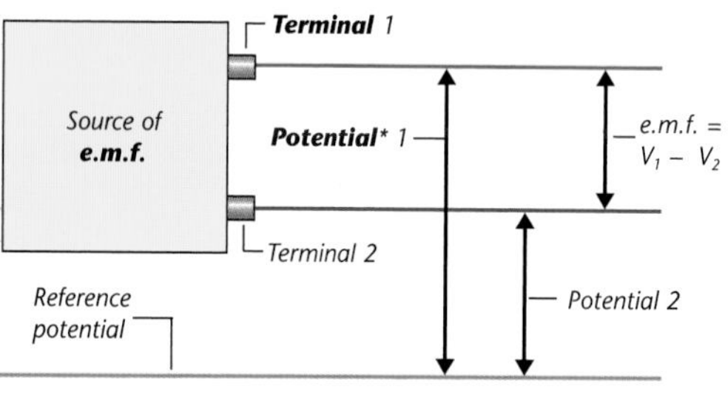
Terminal 1
Source of e.m.f.
Potential* 1
e.m.f. = $V_1 - V_2$
Terminal 2
Potential 2
Reference potential

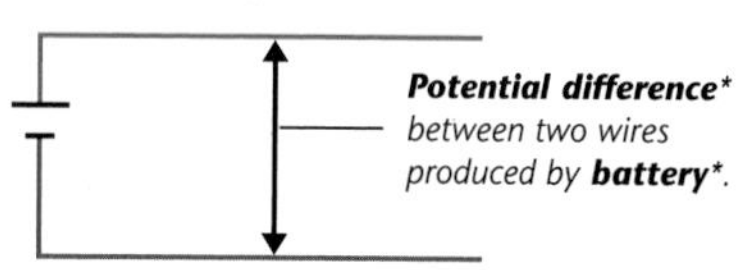
Potential difference* between two wires produced by battery*.

*One **terminal** connected to reference **potential****

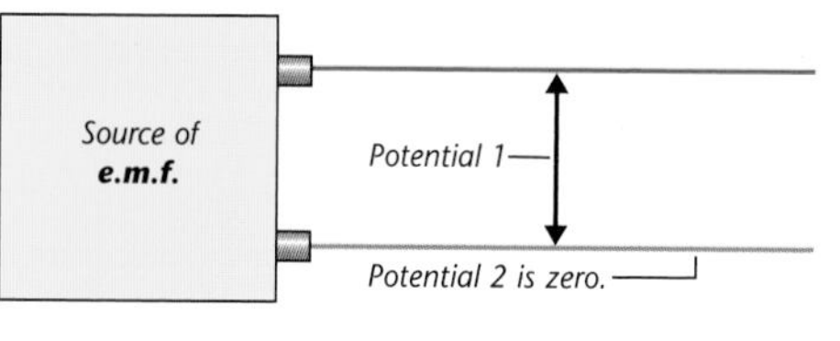
Source of e.m.f.
Potential 1
Potential 2 is zero.

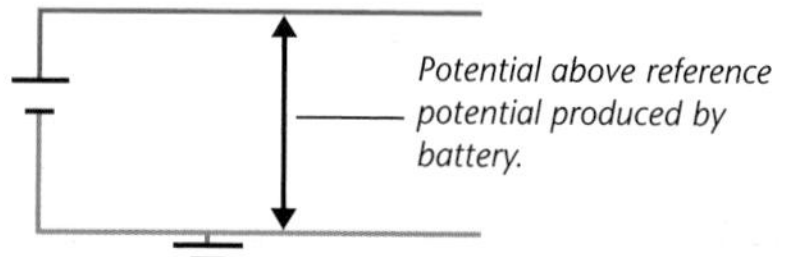
Potential above reference potential produced by battery.

Ampere or amp (A)

The **SI unit*** of current (see also page 96). One ampere is the current which, when flowing through two infinitely long wires one meter apart in a vacuum, produces a force of 2×10^{-7} newtons per meter of wire. Current is accurately measured by a **current balance**, which, by adapting the theory above, measures the force between two coils of wire through which current is flowing. **Ammeters*** are **calibrated*** using current balances.

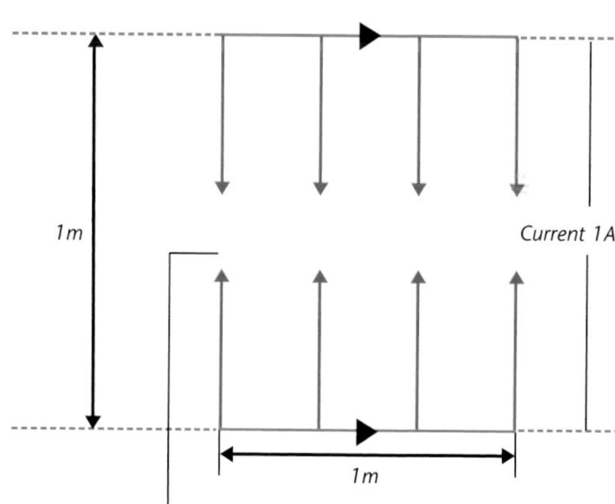
1m
Current 1A
1m

Force between each meter of wire = 2×10^{-7}N

Coulomb

The **SI unit*** of electric charge. It is equal to the amount of charge which passes a point in a conductor if one **ampere** flows through the conductor for one second.

$$Q = I \times t$$

*where Q = charge past a point in **coulombs**; I = current; t = time.*

*** **Ammeter**, 77; **Battery**, 68; **Calibration**, 115; **Cell**, 68; **Electric field**, 58; **Generator**, 78; **Potential**, **Potential difference**, 58; **SI units**, 96.

Direct current (d.c.)

Current which flows in one direction only. Originally current was assumed to flow from a point with higher **potential*** to a point with lower potential. Electrons actually flow the other way, but the convention has been kept.

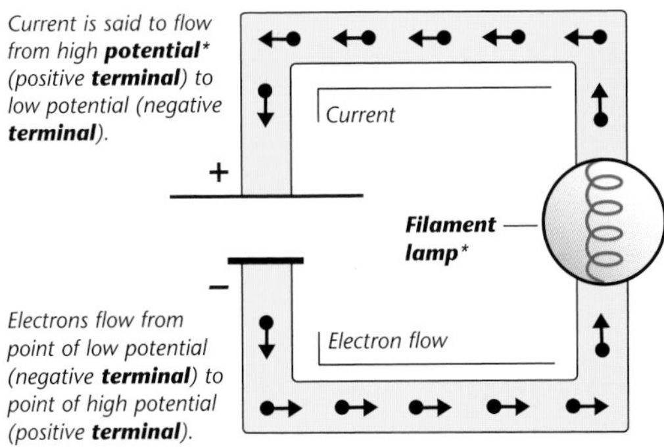

Current is said to flow from high **potential*** (positive **terminal**) to low potential (negative **terminal**).
+
–
Current
Filament lamp*
Electrons flow from point of low potential (negative **terminal**) to point of high potential (positive **terminal**).
Electron flow

Alternating current (a.c.)

Current whose direction in a circuit changes at regular intervals. It is caused by an alternating **electromotive force**. Plotting a graph of current versus time gives the waveform of the current. Alternating currents and electromotive forces are generally expressed as their **root mean square** values (see picture, below).

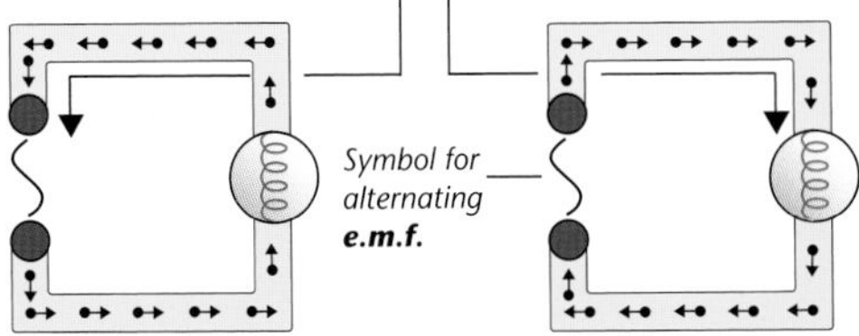

Electrons flow alternately one way then the other.
Symbol for alternating **e.m.f.**

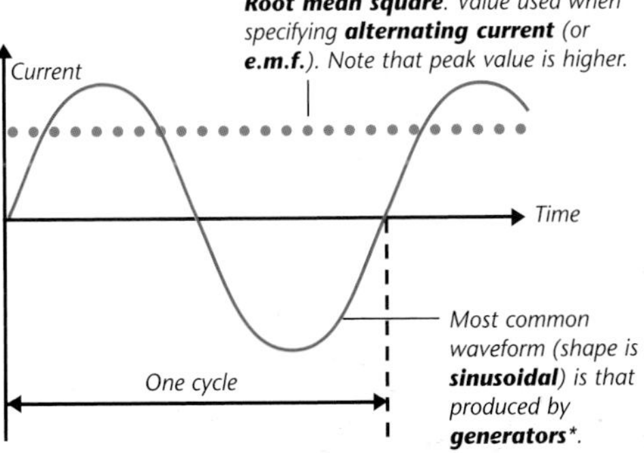

Graph of current versus time
Root mean square. Value used when specifying **alternating current** (or **e.m.f.**). Note that peak value is higher.
Current
Time
One cycle
Most common waveform (shape is **sinusoidal**) is that produced by **generators***.

Electricity supply

Electricity for domestic and industrial use is produced at power stations by large **generators***. These produce **alternating current** at a frequency of 60Hz. Alternating current, unlike **direct current**, can be easily transformed (see **transformer**, page 79) to produce larger or smaller **potential differences***. This means that high voltages and thus low currents can be used for transmission, which considerably reduces power losses in the transmission cables.

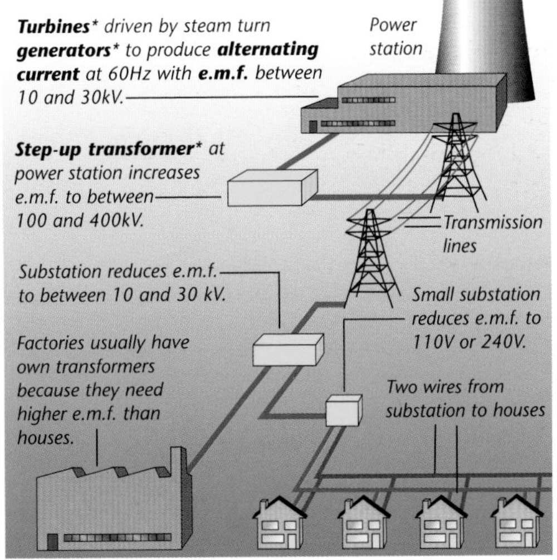

Turbines* driven by steam turn **generators*** to produce **alternating current** at 60Hz with **e.m.f.** between 10 and 30kV.
Power station
Step-up transformer* at power station increases e.m.f. to between 100 and 400kV.
Transmission lines
Substation reduces e.m.f. to between 10 and 30 kV.
Small substation reduces e.m.f. to 110V or 240V.
Factories usually have own transformers because they need higher e.m.f. than houses.
Two wires from substation to houses

All domestic electricity supplies consist of at least two wires from a substation along which **alternating current** flows. In some cases, one of the wires is connected to ground so that the **potential*** of the other alternates above and below ground. In some countries there is an additional wire connected to ground as a safety measure.

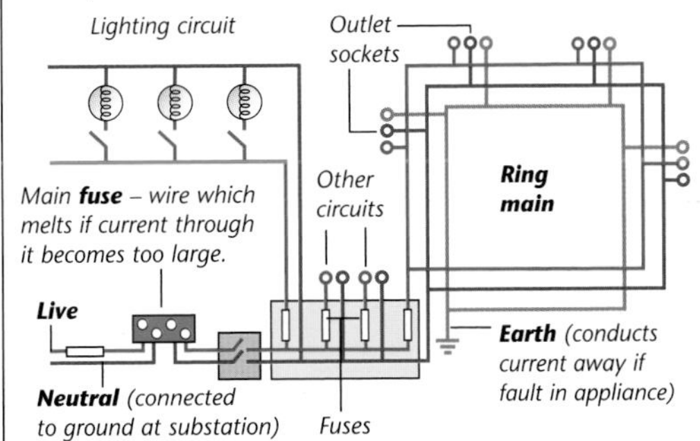

Lighting circuit
Outlet sockets
Ring main
Other circuits
Main **fuse** – wire which melts if current through it becomes too large.
Live
Neutral (connected to ground at substation)
Fuses
Earth (conducts current away if fault in appliance)

* **Filament lamp**, 64; **Generator**, 78; **Potential**, 58; **Potential difference**, 58; **Step-up transformer**, 79; **Turbine**, 115.

CONTROLLING CURRENT

The strength of a current flowing in a circuit depends on the nature of the components in the circuit as well as the **electromotive force***. The **resistance** of the components and the magnetic and electric fields they set up all affect the current in them.

Ohm's law

The current in an object at constant temperature is proportional to the **potential difference*** across its ends. The ratio of the potential difference to the current is the **resistance** of the object. The object must be at constant temperature for the law to apply since a current will heat it up and this will change its resistance (see also **filament lamp**, page 64). Ohm's law does not apply to some materials, e.g. **semiconductors***.

Ohm's law *states:*

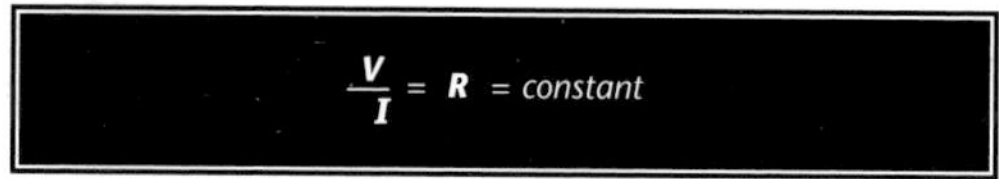

$$\frac{V}{I} = R = \text{constant}$$

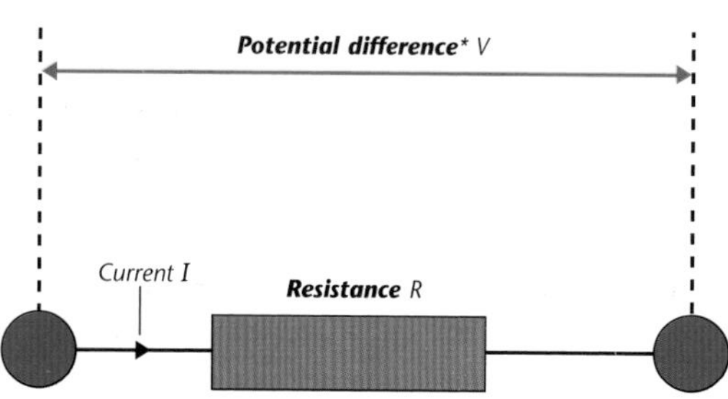

Potential difference* V
Current I
Resistance R

Example:

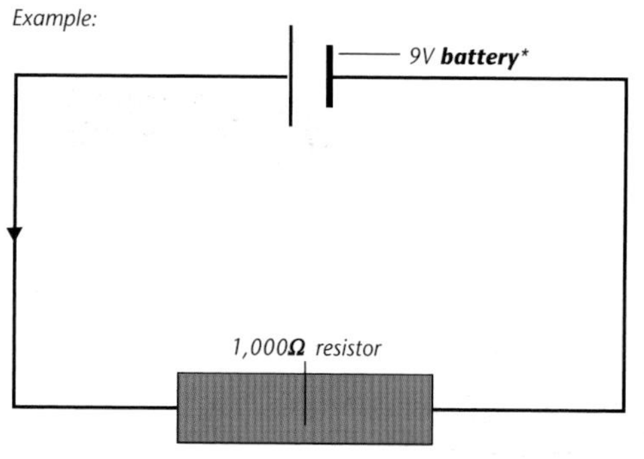

9V battery*
1,000Ω resistor

Current I through **resistor** $R = \frac{V}{R} = \frac{9}{1{,}000} = 0.009A = 9mA$

Resistance (R)

The ability of an object to resist the flow of current. The value depends on the **resistivity** of the substance from which the object is made, its shape and its size. The unit of resistance is the **ohm** (**Ω**). Electrons moving in the object hit atoms and give them energy, heating the object and using up energy from the source of **electromotive force***.

The rate at which electrical energy is changed, because of ***resistance****, to heat energy (i.e. the* ***power*****) can be calculated thus:*

$$\text{Power} = IV = I^2R$$

*where I = current; V = **potential difference*** across resistance; R = resistance.*

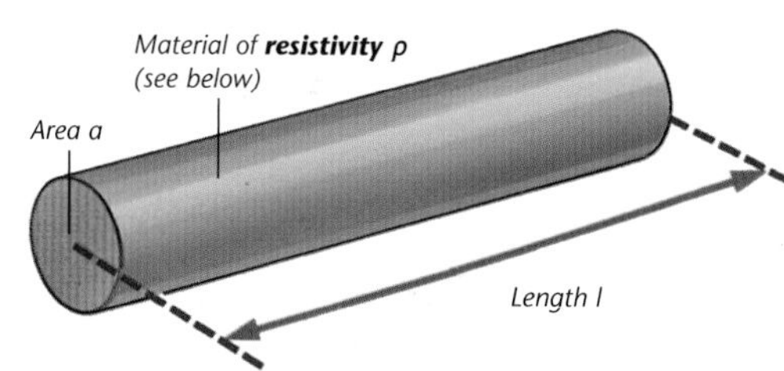

Material of resistivity ρ (see below)
Area a
Length l

Resistance *is inversely proportional to area and proportional to length.*

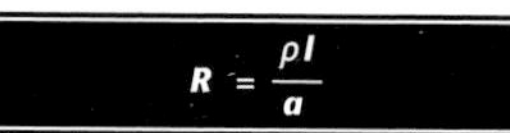

$$R = \frac{\rho l}{a}$$

Resistivity (ρ)

The ability of a substance to resist current. Good **conductors*** have a low resistivity and **insulators*** have a high resistivity. It is the **reciprocal*** of the **conductivity** of the substance and depends on temperature. See also page 112.

Resistor

A device with a particular **resistance** value. Resistors can have values from less than one **ohm** up to many millions of ohms. The most common type is the **carbon resistor**, made from compressed carbon of known **resistivity**.

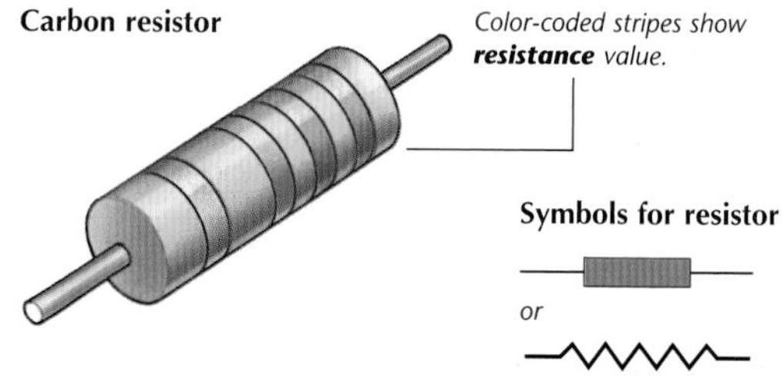

Carbon resistor
Color-coded stripes show resistance value.
Symbols for resistor
or

* **Battery**, 68; **Conductor**, 56; **Electromotive force** (**e.m.f.**), 60; **Insulator**, 56; **Potential difference**, 58; **Power**, 9; **Reciprocal**, 115; **Semiconductors**, 65.

Conductivity

The ability of a substance to allow the flow of current (see also **conductor** and **insulator**, page 56). It is the inverse of the **resistivity**.

Internal resistance (r)

The **resistance** of a **cell*** or **battery*** to the current it causes. It is the resistance of the connections in the cell and some chemical effects (e.g. **polarization***). The current in a circuit may therefore be less than expected.

***Internal resistance** is part of **resistance** of circuit.*

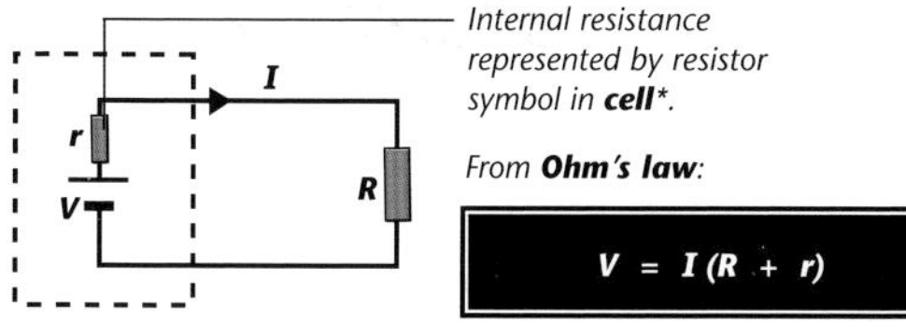

I
r
V
R
Internal resistance represented by resistor symbol in cell*.
From Ohm's law:

$$V = I(R + r)$$

Variable resistor

A device whose **resistance** can be changed mechanically. It is either a coil of wire of a particular **resistivity** around a drum along which a contact moves (for high currents) or a carbon track with a moving contact. A variable resistor can be used as a **potential divider** if an extra contact is added. It is then a **potentiometer**.

Types of variable resistor

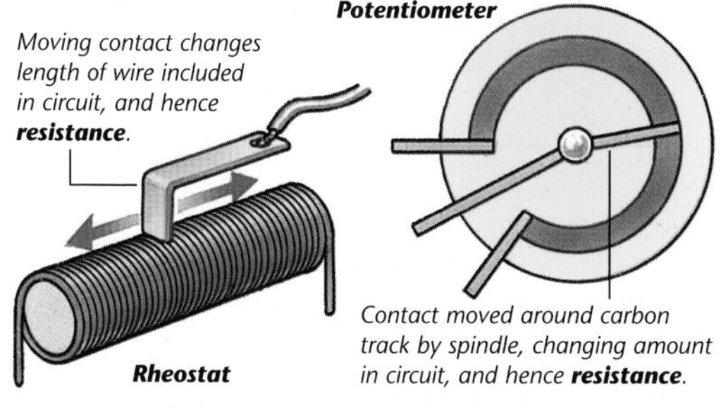

Potentiometer
Moving contact changes length of wire included in circuit, and hence resistance.
Rheostat
Contact moved around carbon track by spindle, changing amount in circuit, and hence resistance.

Potential divider or voltage divider

A device used to produce a **potential difference*** from another, higher potential difference.

Circuit diagram of potential divider

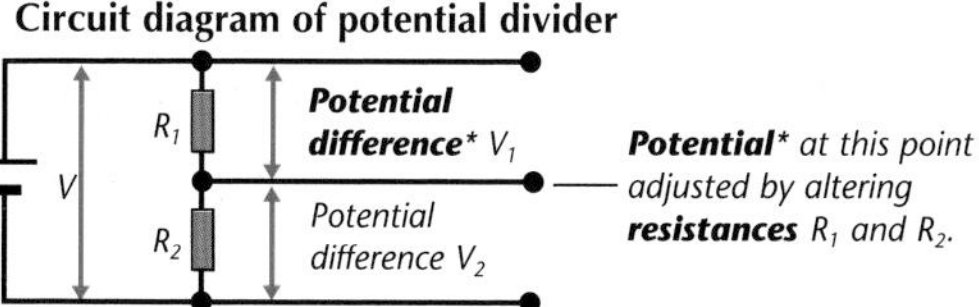

V
R1
R2
Potential difference* V1
Potential difference V2
Potential* at this point adjusted by altering resistances R1 and R2.

Wheatstone bridge

A circuit used to measure an unknown **resistance** (see diagram). When the **galvanometer*** indicates no current, the unknown value of one **resistor** can be calculated from the other three. The **meter bridge** is a version of the wheatstone bridge in which two of the resistors are replaced by a meter of wire with a high resistance. The position of the contact from the galvanometer on the wire gives the ratio R_3/R_4 in the circuit shown below.

Wheatstone bridge

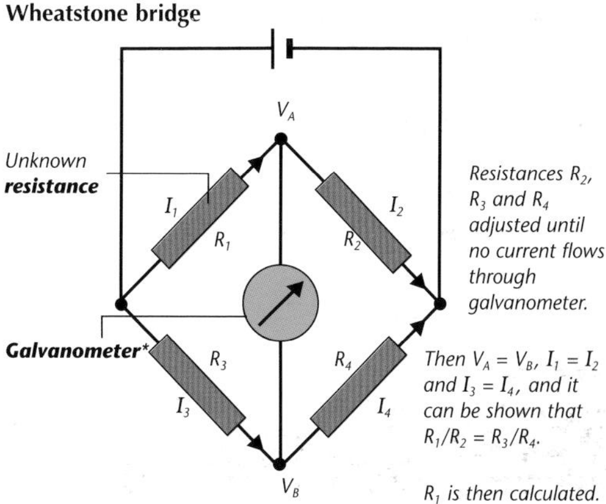

VA
VB
Unknown resistance
Galvanometer*
I1
I2
I3
I4
R1
R2
R3
R4
Resistances R2, R3 and R4 adjusted until no current flows through galvanometer.
Then VA = VB, I1 = I2 and I3 = I4, and it can be shown that R1/R2 = R3/R4.
R1 is then calculated.

Kirchhoff's laws

Two laws which summarize conditions for the flow of current at an instant. The first states that the total current flowing towards a junction is equal to the total current flowing away from the junction. The second states that the sum of the **potential differences*** around a circuit, which for each **resistor** is the product of the current and the **resistance**, is equal to the **electromotive force*** applied to the circuit.

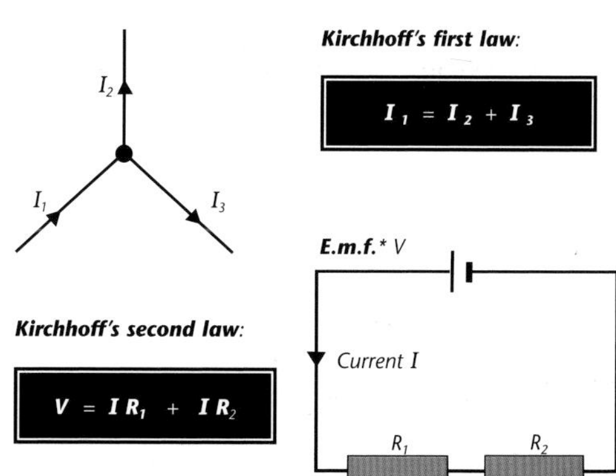

I1
I2
I3
Kirchhoff's first law:
E.m.f.* V
Current I
R1
R2
Kirchhoff's second law:

$$I_1 = I_2 + I_3$$

$$V = IR_1 + IR_2$$

*Battery, Cell, 68; Electromotive force (e.m.f.), 60; Galvanometer, 77; Polarization, 68; Potential, Potential difference, 58.

Controlling current (continued)

Series

An arrangement of components in which all of the current passes through them one after the other.

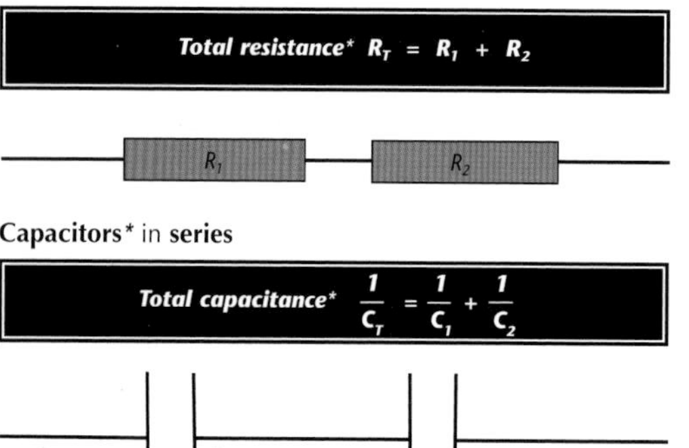

Resistors* in series
Total resistance* $R_T = R_1 + R_2$
R_1
R_2
Capacitors* in series
Total capacitance* $\frac{1}{C_T} = \frac{1}{C_1} + \frac{1}{C_2}$
C_1
C_2

Parallel

An arrangement of components in which current divides to pass through all at once.

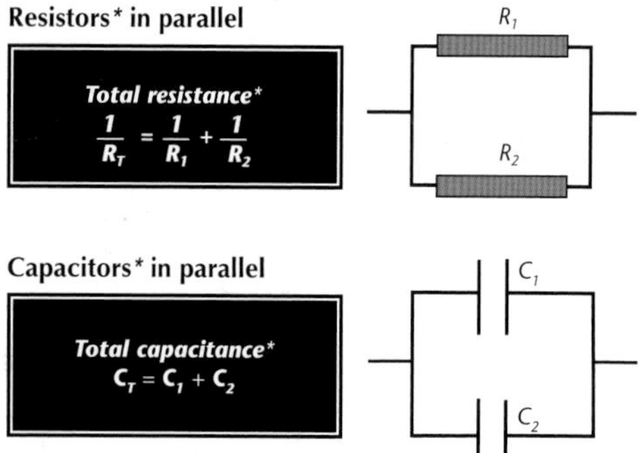

Resistors* in parallel
Total resistance* $\frac{1}{R_T} = \frac{1}{R_1} + \frac{1}{R_2}$
R_1
R_2
Capacitors* in parallel
Total capacitance* $C_T = C_1 + C_2$
C_1
C_2

Filament lamp

A lamp consisting of a coil of tungsten wire (the **filament**) inside a glass bulb containing argon or nitrogen gas at low pressure. When current flows through the coil, it heats up rapidly and gives out light. Tungsten is used because it has a very high melting point and the bulb is gas-filled to reduce evaporation of the tungsten.

Filament lamp
Close-up of coiled filament
Low pressure gas
Contacts for current under base of bulb

Switch

A device, normally mechanical (but see also **transistor**), which is used to make or break a circuit. A **relay*** is used when a small current is required to switch a larger current on and off.

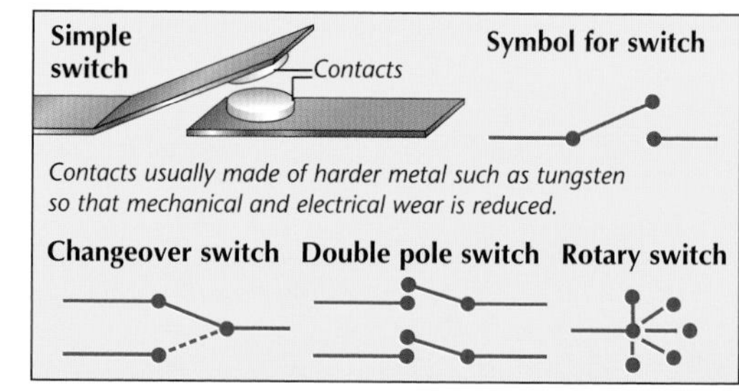

Simple switch
Contacts
Symbol for switch
Contacts usually made of harder metal such as tungsten so that mechanical and electrical wear is reduced.
Changeover switch
Double pole switch
Rotary switch

Impedance

The ratio of the **potential difference*** applied to a circuit to the **alternating current*** which flows in it. It is due to two things, the **resistance*** of the circuit and the **reactance**. The effect of impedance is that the **e.m.f.*** and current can be out of phase.

Reactance

The "active" part of **impedance** to **alternating current***. It is caused by **capacitance*** and **inductance** in a circuit which alter the **electromotive forces*** as the current changes.

Inductance

The part of the **impedance** of a circuit due to changing current affecting the **e.m.f.*** (see also **electromagnetic induction**, page 78). This happens in a device called an **inductor**.

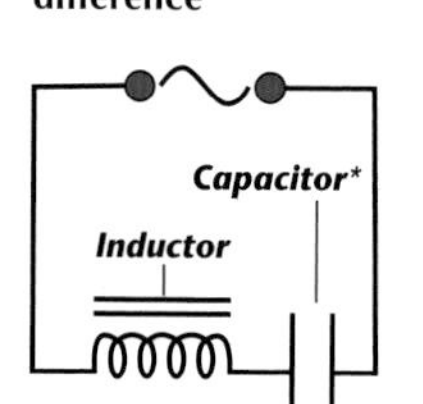

Alternating potential difference*
Capacitor*
Inductor

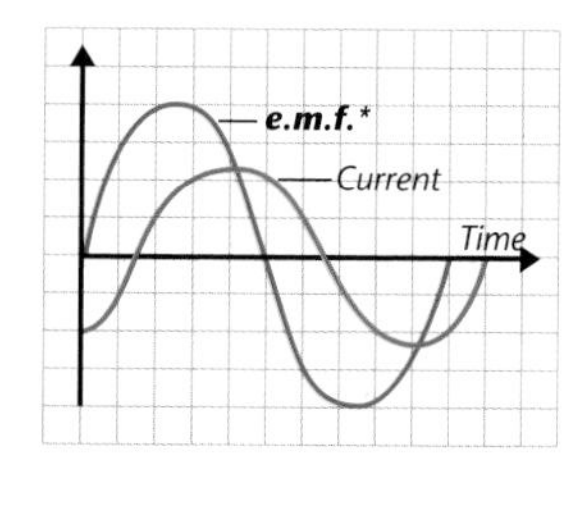

e.m.f.*
Current
Time

* **Alternating current**, 61; **Capacitance**, **Capacitor**, 59; **Electromotive force** (**e.m.f.**), 60; **Potential difference**, 58; **Relay**, 75; **Resistance**, **Resistor**, 62.

SEMICONDUCTORS

Semiconductors are materials whose **resistivity*** is between that of a **conductor** and an **insulator** (see page 56) and decreases with increasing temperature or increasing amounts of impurities (see **doping**, below). They are widely used in electronic circuits (see also page 111).

Doping

The introduction of a small amount of impurity into a semiconductor. Depending on the impurity used, the semiconductor is known as either a **p-type** or **n-type**. Combinations of these types are used to make **diodes** and **transistors**.

Diode

A device made from one piece of **p-type** semiconductor (see **doping**) and one piece of **n-type** semiconductor joined together. It has a very low **resistance*** in one direction (when it is said to be **forward biased**) and a very high resistance in the other direction (**reverse biased**).

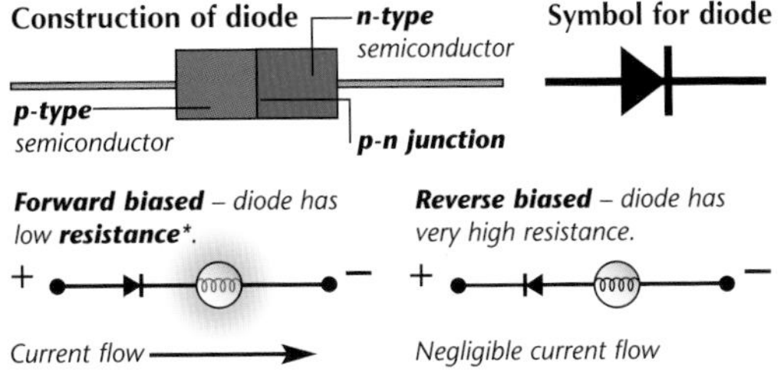
Construction of diode
n-type semiconductor
p-type semiconductor
p-n junction
Symbol for diode
Forward biased – diode has low resistance*.
+
–
Current flow
Reverse biased – diode has very high resistance.
+
–
Negligible current flow

Half-wave rectification

The use of a **diode** to remove all the current flowing in one direction from **alternating current***. Current only flows one way around the circuit.

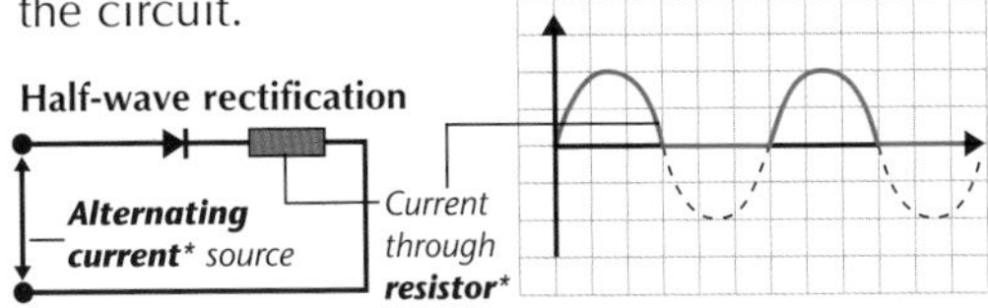
Half-wave rectification
Alternating current* source
Current through resistor*

Full-wave rectification

The conversion of **alternating current*** to **direct current***. It is used when direct current is required from alternating current.

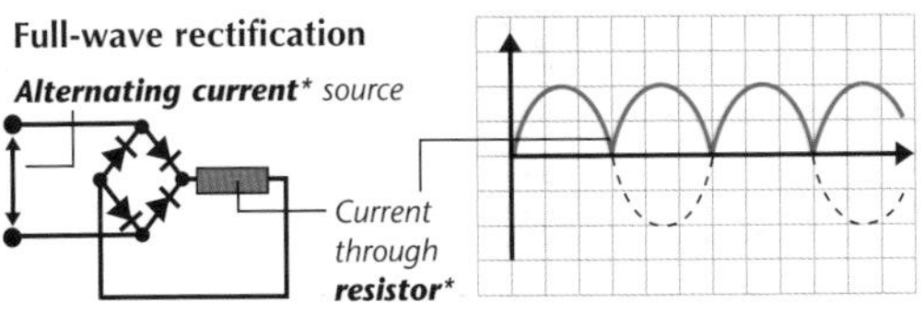
Full-wave rectification
Alternating current* source
Current through resistor*

Light emitting diode (LED)

A **diode** with a higher **resistance*** than normal, in which light is produced instead of heat.

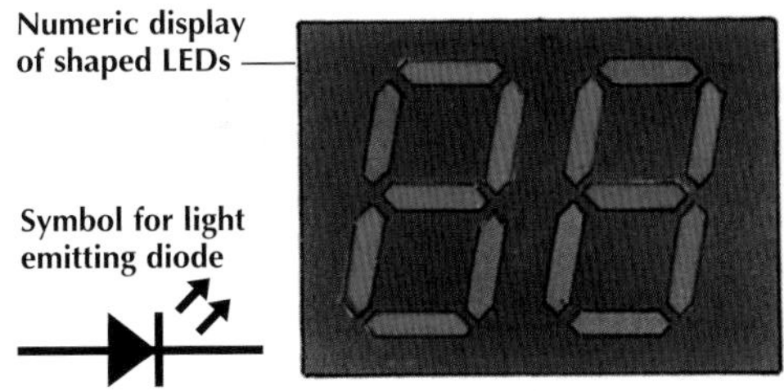
Numeric display of shaped LEDs
Symbol for light emitting diode

Thermistor

A semiconductor device whose **resistance*** varies with temperature, used in electronic circuits to detect temperature changes.

Transistor

A semiconductor, normally made from a combination of the two types of semiconductor. There are three connections, the **base**, **collector** and **emitter** (see diagrams below). The **resistance*** between the collector and emitter changes from very high to very low when a small current flows into the base. This small base current can therefore be used to control a much larger collector to emitter current.

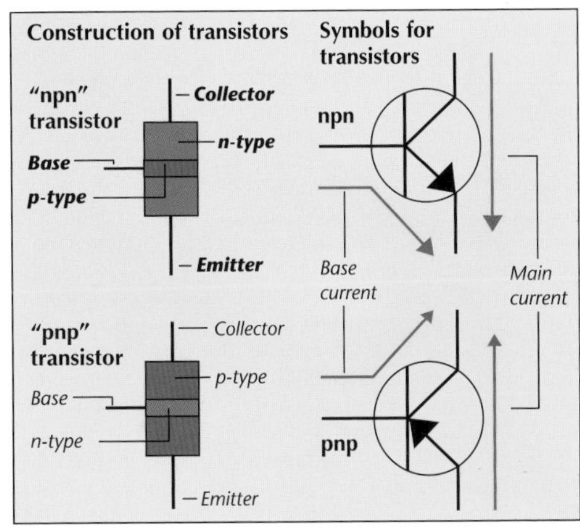
Construction of transistors
"npn" transistor
Collector
n-type
Base
p-type
Emitter
"pnp" transistor
Collector
p-type
Base
n-type
Emitter
Symbols for transistors
npn
pnp
Base current
Main current

* **Alternating current**, 61; **Direct current**, 61; **Resistance**, **Resistivity**, **Resistor**, 62.

ELECTROLYSIS

Electrolysis is the process whereby electric current flows through a liquid containing **ions*** (atoms which have gained or lost an **electron*** to become charged) and the liquid is broken down as a result. The current is conducted by the movement of ions in the liquid, and chemicals are deposited at the points where the current enters or leaves the liquid. There are a number of industrial applications.

Electrolyte

A compound which conducts electricity when either molten or dissolved in water. All compounds made from ions or which split into ions when dissolved (**ionization***) are electrolytes. The concentration of ions in an electrolyte determines how well it conducts electricity.

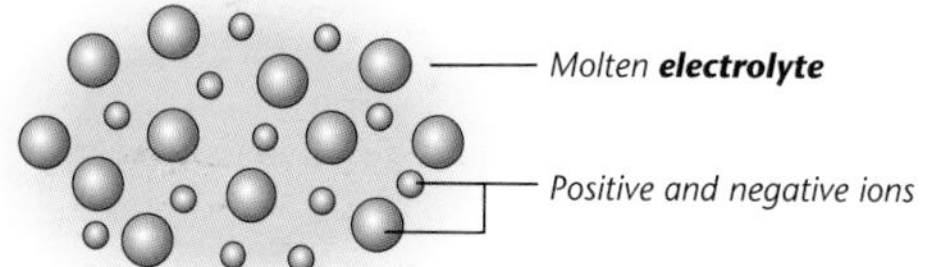
Molten electrolyte
Positive and negative ions

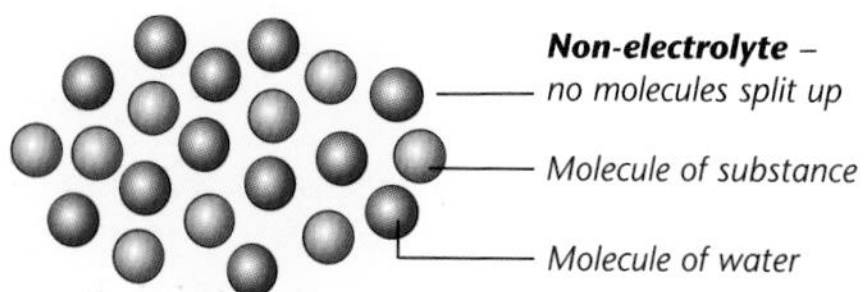
Non-electrolyte – no molecules split up
Molecule of substance
Molecule of water

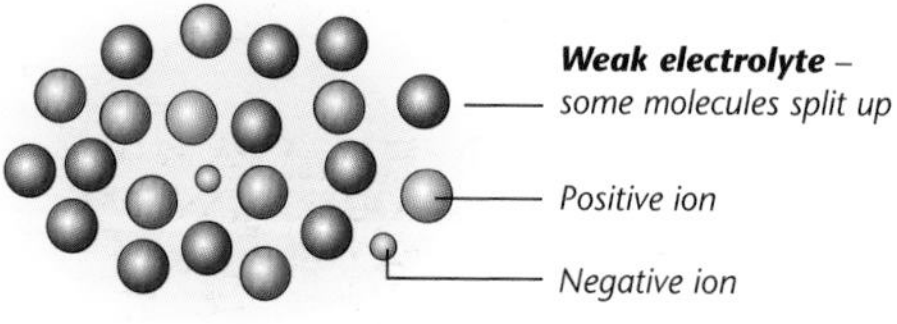
Weak electrolyte – some molecules split up
Positive ion
Negative ion

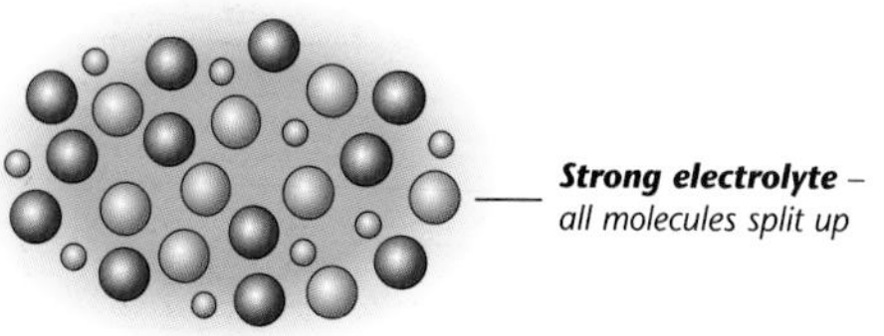
Strong electrolyte – all molecules split up

Electrode

A piece of metal or carbon placed in an **electrolyte** through which electric current enters or leaves during electrolysis. Two are needed – the **anode** (positive electrode) and the **cathode** (negative electrode). An **active electrode** is one which is chemically changed by electrolysis; an **inert electrode** is one which is not changed.

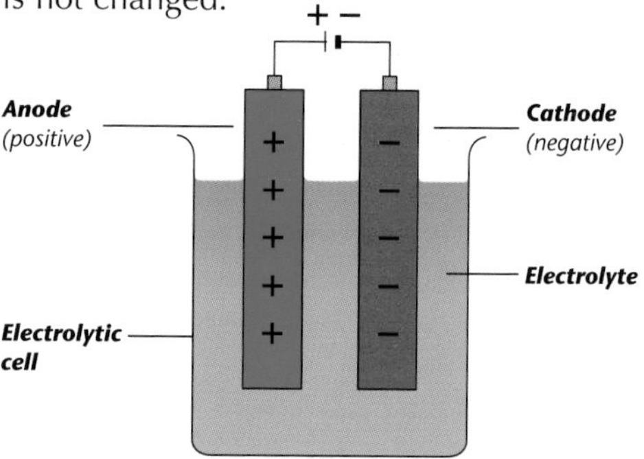
+ –
Anode (positive)
Cathode (negative)
Electrolyte
Electrolytic cell

Electrolytic cell

A vessel in which electrolysis takes place. It contains the **electrolyte** and the **electrodes**.

Ionic theory of electrolysis

A theory which attempts to explain what happens in the **electrolyte** and at the **electrodes** during electrolysis. It states that the **cations** (positive ions) are attracted towards the **cathode** and the **anions** (negative ions) towards the **anode**. There they gain or lose electrons respectively to form atoms (they are then said to be **discharged**). If there are two or more different anions, then one of them will be discharged in preference to the others. This is called **preferential discharge**.

Electrolysis of copper sulfate solution

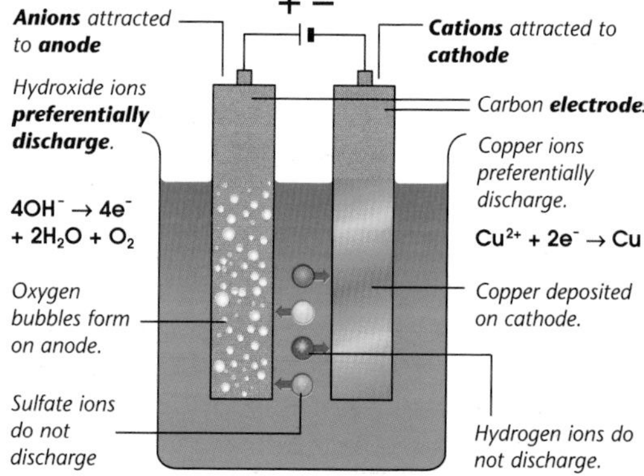
+ –
Anions attracted to anode
Cations attracted to cathode
Hydroxide ions preferentially discharge.
Carbon electrodes
Copper ions preferentially discharge.
$4OH^- \rightarrow 4e^- + 2H_2O + O_2$
$Cu^{2+} + 2e^- \rightarrow Cu$
Oxygen bubbles form on anode.
Copper deposited on cathode.
Sulfate ions do not discharge
Hydrogen ions do not discharge.

* **Electrons**, 83; **Ions**, 88 (**Ionization**).

Faraday's laws of electrolysis

Two laws which relate the quantity of electricity which passes through an **electrolyte** to the masses of the substances which are deposited. **Faraday's first law** states that the mass of the substance deposited is proportional to the quantity of electricity (the **electrochemical equivalent** of a substance is the mass liberated by one ampere flowing for one second). **Faraday's second law** states that the mass of the substance deposited is inversely proportional to the size of the charge on its ion.

Electrolysis of copper sulfate solution with copper electrodes (copper voltameter)

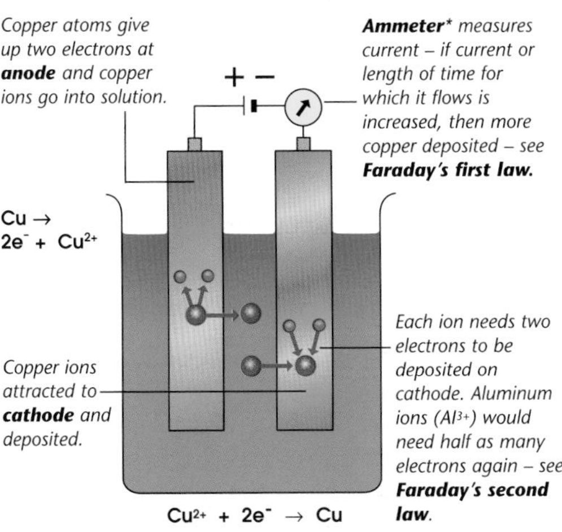

Copper atoms give up two electrons at ***anode*** *and copper ions go into solution.*
+ –
Ammeter* *measures current – if current or length of time for which it flows is increased, then more copper deposited – see* ***Faraday's first law.***
$Cu \rightarrow 2e^- + Cu^{2+}$
Copper ions attracted to ***cathode*** *and deposited.*
Each ion needs two electrons to be deposited on cathode. Aluminum ions (Al^{3+}) would need half as many electrons again – see ***Faraday's second law.***
$Cu^{2+} + 2e^- \rightarrow Cu$

Voltameter or coulometer

An **electrolytic cell** used for investigating the relationships between the amount of substance produced at the **electrodes** and the current which passes through the cell. For example, the **copper voltameter** (see below left) contains copper sulfate and copper electrodes.

Hoffmann voltameter

A type of **voltameter** used for collecting and measuring the volumes (and hence the masses) of gases liberated during electrolysis. For example, electrolysis of acidified water produces hydrogen and oxygen in a two to one ratio (note that this also indicates the chemical composition of water, i.e. H_2O).

Hoffmann voltameter

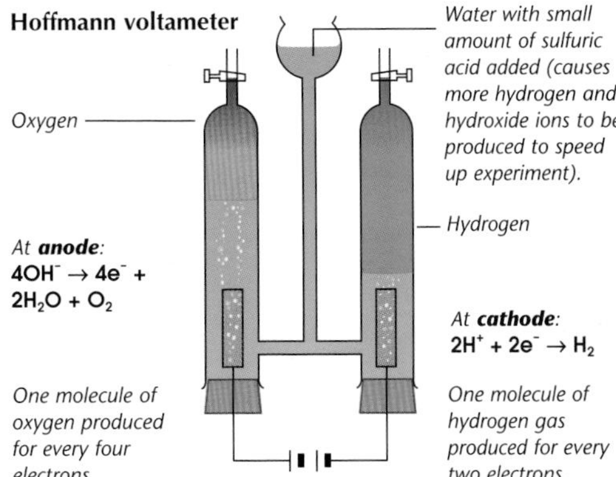

Water with small amount of sulfuric acid added (causes more hydrogen and hydroxide ions to be produced to speed up experiment).
Oxygen
Hydrogen
At ***anode****:* $4OH^- \rightarrow 4e^- + 2H_2O + O_2$
At ***cathode****:* $2H^+ + 2e^- \rightarrow H_2$
One molecule of oxygen produced for every four electrons.
One molecule of hydrogen gas produced for every two electrons.

Uses of electrolysis

Electroplating or electrodeposition

The coating of a metal object with a thin layer of another metal by electrolysis. The object forms the **cathode**, and ions of the coating metal are in the **electrolyte**.

Steel is cheap but corrodes easily, so steel food cans are plated with a very fine layer of tin (which is less reactive) to prevent corrosion.

Electro-refining

A method of purifying metals by electrolysis. Impure metal forms the **anode**, from which metal ions move to the **cathode** and form pure metal. The impurities fall to the bottom of the vessel.

Metal extraction

A process which produces metals from their molten ores by electrolysis. Very reactive metals are obtained by this process, e.g. sodium and aluminum.

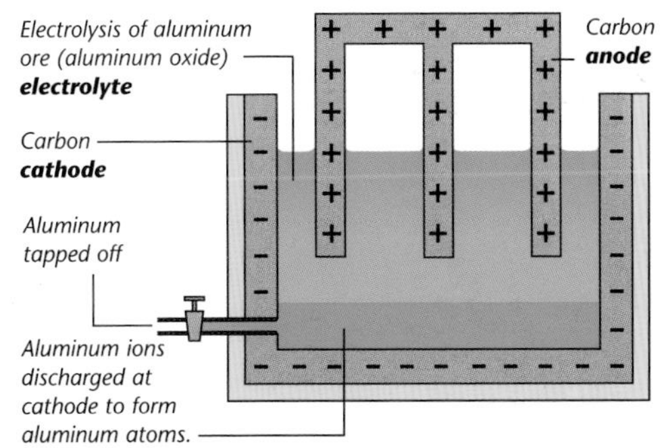

Electrolysis of aluminum ore (aluminum oxide) ***electrolyte***
Carbon ***anode***
Carbon ***cathode***
Aluminum tapped off
Aluminum ions discharged at cathode to form aluminum atoms.

* **Ammeter**, 77.

CELLS AND BATTERIES

The Italian scientist Volta first showed that a **potential difference*** exists between two different metals when they are placed in certain liquids (**electrolytes***) and therefore that a **direct current*** can be produced from chemical energy. This arrangement is called a **cell**, **electrochemical** or **voltaic cell**. The potential difference (caused by chemical changes in the cell) is called an **electromotive force*** and its size depends on the metals used. A **battery** is two or more connected cells.

Engraving showing an experiment with frog's legs

Early experiments showed that fluids in a dead frog act as an ***electrolyte**** *and carry current between two pieces of metal.*

Voltaic pile

The first battery made, consisting of a pile of silver and zinc disks separated by cardboard or cloth soaked in salt water. This arrangement is the same as a number of **simple cells** linked together.

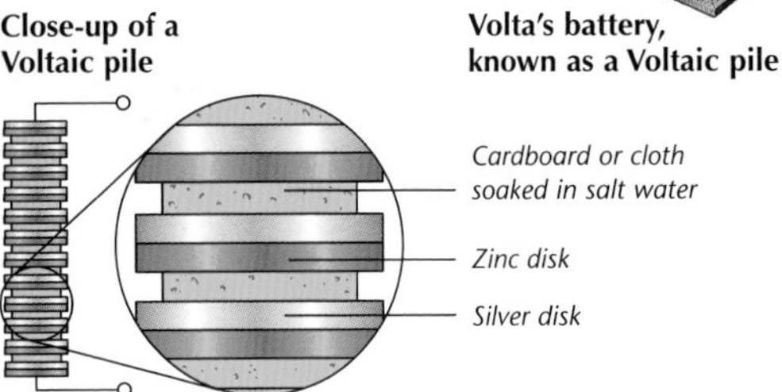
Cardboard or cloth soaked in salt water
Zinc disk
Silver disk

Close-up of a Voltaic pile

Volta's battery, known as a Voltaic pile

Simple cell

Two plates of different metals separated by a salt or acid solution **electrolyte*** (normally copper and zinc plates and dilute sulfuric acid). The simple cell only produces an **electromotive force*** for a short time before **polarization** and **local action** have an effect.

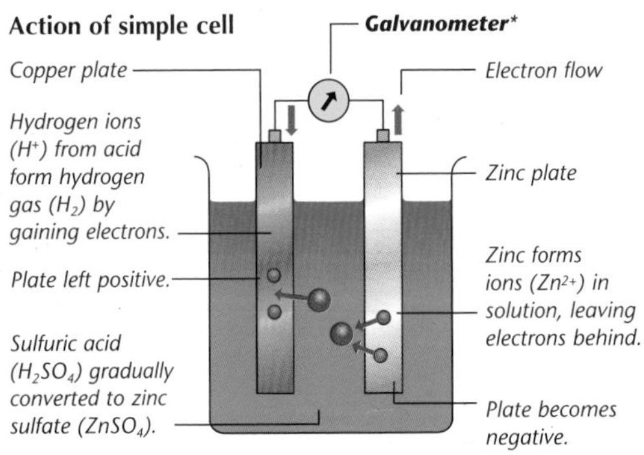
Galvanometer*
Copper plate
Electron flow
Hydrogen ions (H^+) from acid form hydrogen gas (H_2) by gaining electrons.
Zinc plate
Plate left positive.
Zinc forms ions (Zn^{2+}) in solution, leaving electrons behind.
Sulfuric acid (H_2SO_4) gradually converted to zinc sulfate ($ZnSO_4$).
Plate becomes negative.

Action of simple cell

Polarization

The formation of bubbles of hydrogen on the copper plate in a **simple cell**. This reduces the **electromotive force*** of the cell, both because the bubbles insulate the plate and also because a **back e.m.f.*** is set up. Polarization can be eliminated by adding a **depolarizing agent**, which reacts with the hydrogen to form water.

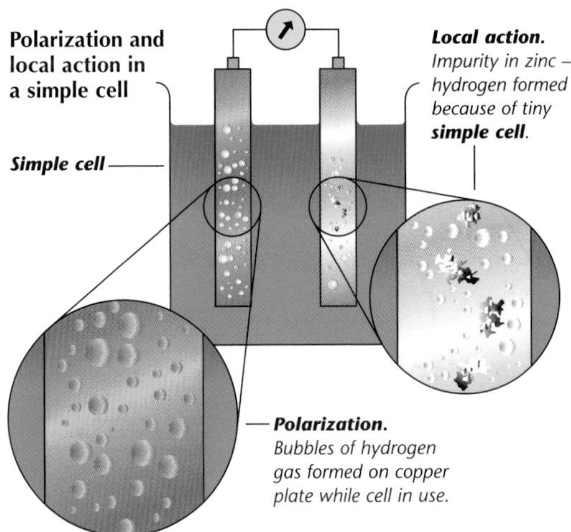
Simple cell
Local action. Impurity in zinc – hydrogen formed because of tiny simple cell.
Polarization. Bubbles of hydrogen gas formed on copper plate while cell in use.

Polarization and local action in a simple cell

Local action

The production of hydrogen at the zinc plate in a **simple cell**. Impurities (traces of other metals) in the zinc plate mean that tiny simple cells are formed which produce hydrogen due to **polarization**. Hydrogen is also produced as the zinc dissolves in the acid (even when the cell is not working). Local action can be prevented by coating the plate with an **amalgam***.

* **Amalgam**, 115; **Back e.m.f.**, 60 (**Electromotive force**); **Direct current**, 61; **Electrolyte**, 66; **Galvanometer**, 77; **Potential difference**, 58.

Capacity

The ability of a cell to produce current over a period of time. It is measured in **ampere hours**. For example, a 10 ampere-hour cell should produce one ampere for 10 hours.

Leclanché cell

A cell in which **polarization** is overcome by manganese dioxide (a **depolarizing agent**). This removes hydrogen more slowly than it is formed, but continues working to remove excess hydrogen when the cell is not in use. The cell provides an **electromotive force*** of 1.5V.

Leclanché cell

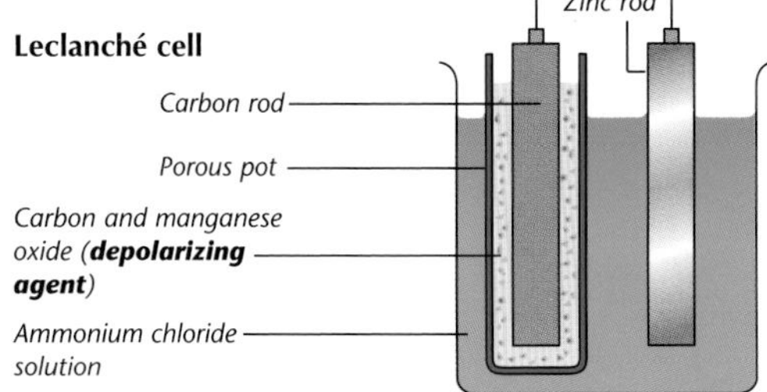
Zinc rod
Carbon rod
Porous pot
Carbon and manganese oxide (**depolarizing agent**)
Ammonium chloride solution

Standard cell

A cell which produces an accurately known and constant **electromotive force***. It is used in laboratories for experimental work.

Primary cell

Any cell which has a limited life because the chemicals inside it are eventually used up and cannot be replaced easily.

Dry cell

A version of the **Leclanché cell** in which the ammonium chloride solution is replaced by paste containing ammonium chloride, meaning that it is portable. The cell provides an **electromotive force*** of 1.5V. Dry cells deteriorate slowly due to **local action**, but still have a life of many months.

Dry cell

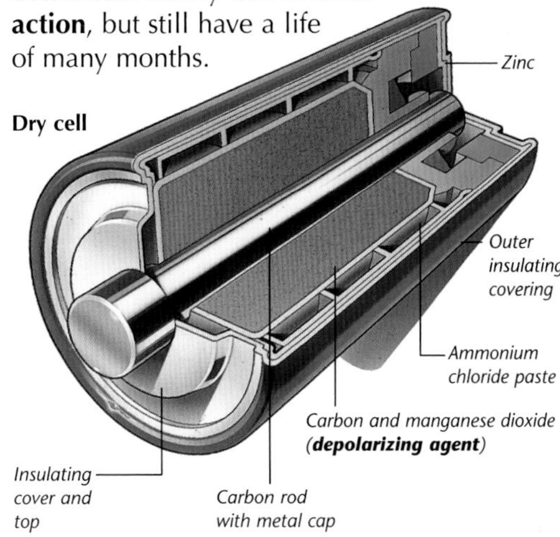
Zinc
Outer insulating covering
Ammonium chloride paste
Carbon and manganese dioxide (**depolarizing agent**)
Insulating cover and top
Carbon rod with metal cap

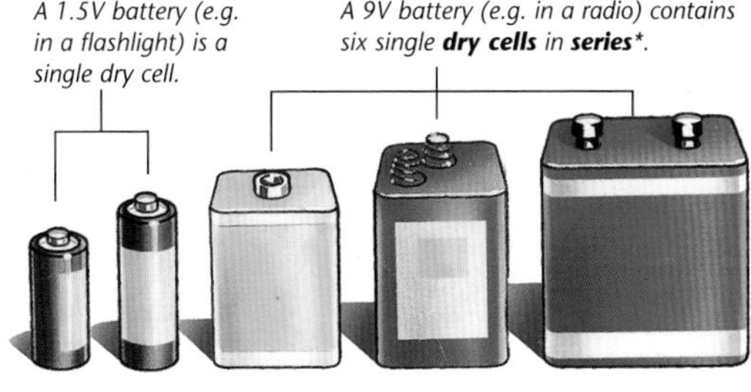
A 1.5V battery (e.g. in a flashlight) is a single dry cell.
A 9V battery (e.g. in a radio) contains six single **dry cells** in **series***.

Secondary cell

Also known as an **accumulator** or **storage cell**. A cell which can be recharged by connection to another source of electricity. The main types are the **lead-acid accumulator** and the **nickel-cadmiun alkaline cell**.

Alkaline cell

A secondary cell containing an **electrolyte*** of potassium hydroxide solution. The plates are normally made of nickel and cadmium compounds (it is then called a **nickel-cadmium cell**). Alkaline cells may be left for months in a discharged condition without ill-effect.

Lead-acid accumulator

A **secondary cell** containing a dilute sulphuric acid **electrolyte***, and plates made from lead and lead compounds. The cell can give out a very large current because it has a low **internal resistance***. It is mainly used in vehicles for starting and lighting.

Battery consisting of lead-acid accumulators

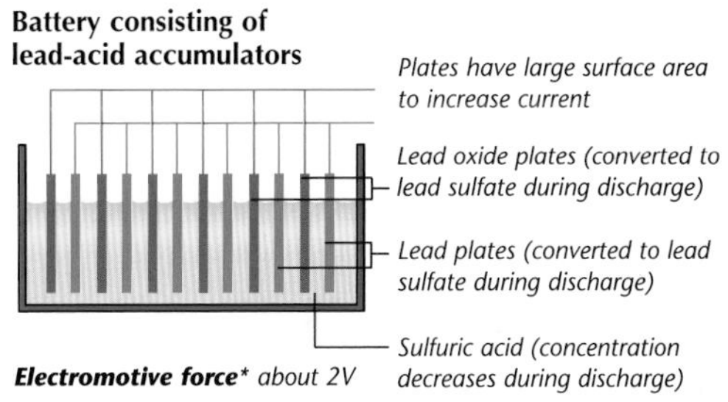
Plates have large surface area to increase current
Lead oxide plates (converted to lead sulfate during discharge)
Lead plates (converted to lead sulfate during discharge)
Sulfuric acid (concentration decreases during discharge)
Electromotive force* about 2V

* **Electromotive force (e.m.f.)**, 60; **Electrolyte**, 66; **Internal resistance**, 63; **Series**, 64.

MAGNETS

All **magnets** have a **magnetic field*** around them, and a **magnetic force*** exists between two magnets due to the interaction of their fields. Any material which is capable of being **magnetized** (can become a magnet) is described as **magnetic** (see **ferromagnetic**, below) and becomes magnetized when placed in a magnetic field. The movement of charge (normally **electrons***) also causes a magnetic field (see **electromagnetism**, pages 74-76).

*These paper clips have been temporarily **magnetized**.*

Pole

A point in a magnet at which its **magnetic force*** appears to be concentrated. There are two types of pole – the **north** or **north seeking pole** and the **south** or **south seeking pole** (identified by allowing the magnet to line up with the Earth's **magnetic field***). All magnets have an equal number of each type of pole. The **first law of magnetism** states that unlike poles attract and like poles repel.

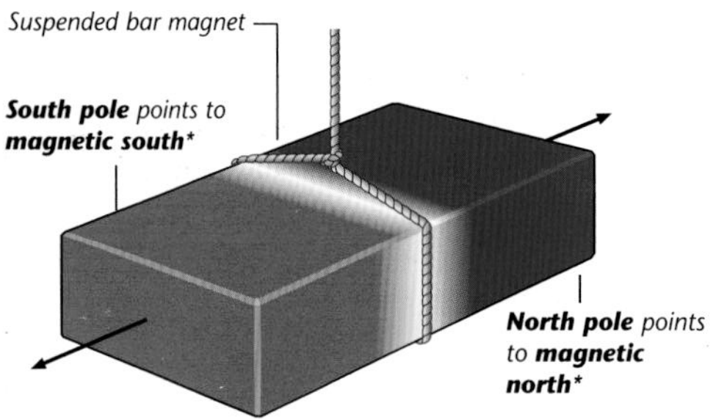
Suspended bar magnet
South pole points to magnetic south*
North pole points to magnetic north*

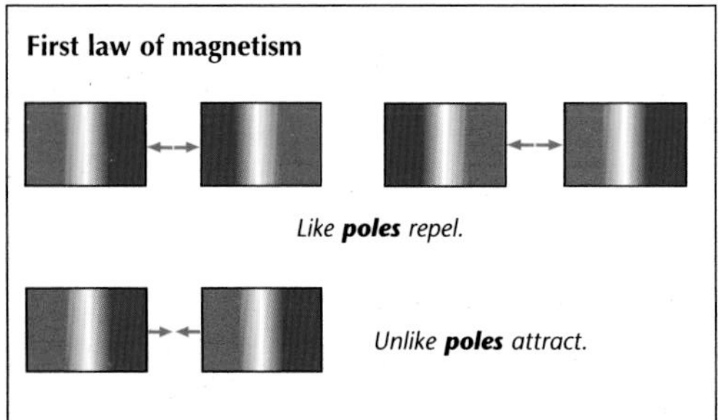
First law of magnetism
Like poles repel.
Unlike poles attract.

Magnetic axis

An imaginary line about which the **magnetic field*** of a magnet is symmetrical.

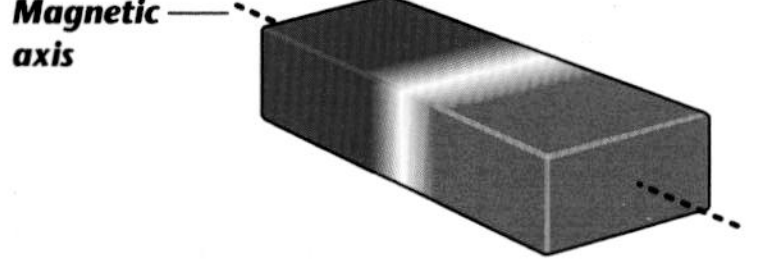
Magnetic axis

Ferromagnetic

Describes a material which is strongly magnetic (i.e. is magnetized easily). Iron, nickel, cobalt and alloys of these are ferromagnetic, and are described as either **hard** or **soft**. **Sintered** materials (made by converting various mixtures of powders of the above metals into solids by heat and pressure) can be made magnetically very hard or soft by changing the metals used.

Hard

Describes a **ferromagnetic** material which does not easily lose its magnetism after being magnetized, e.g. steel. Magnets made from these materials are called **permanent magnets**.

***Hard ferromagnetic** materials are used as **permanent magnets**, e.g. as compass needles.*

Soft

Describes a **ferromagnetic** material which does not retain its magnetism after being magnetized, e.g. iron. Magnets made from these materials are called **temporary magnets**. **Residual magnetism** is the small amount of magnetism which can be left in magnetically soft materials.

Soft ferromagnetic** materials are used as **cores in **electromagnets***.*

Susceptibility

A measurement of the ability of a substance to become magnetized. **Ferromagnetic** materials have a high susceptibility.

* **Core**, **Electromagnet**, 74; **Electrons**, 83; **Magnetic field**, 72; **Magnetic force**, 6; **Magnetic north**, **Magnetic south**, 73.

Domain theory of magnetism

States that **ferromagnetic** materials consist of **dipoles** or **molecular magnets**, which interact with each other. These are all arranged in areas called **domains**, in which they all point in the same direction. A ferromagnetic material becomes magnetized when the domains become **ordered** (i.e. aligned).

*In a non-magnetized state, **domains** are jumbled. The overall effect is that the domains cancel each other out.*

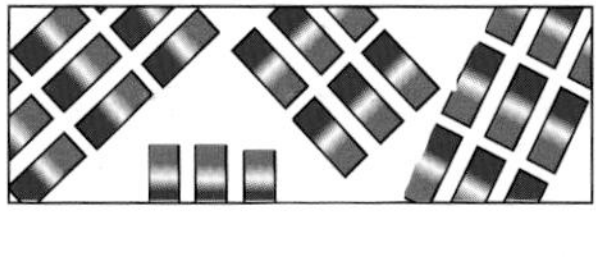

*In a magnetized state, **domains** are ordered. If ordered completely (as here) magnet is **saturated** – cannot become stronger.*

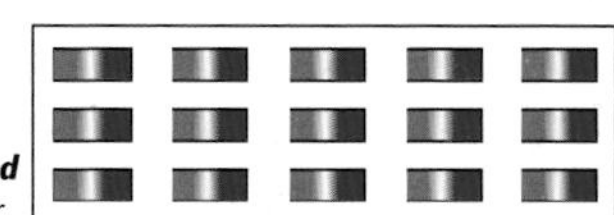

Magnetization

When an object is magnetized, all the **dipoles** become aligned (see **domain theory**). This only happens when an object is in a **magnetic field*** and is called **induced magnetism**.

Induced magnetism

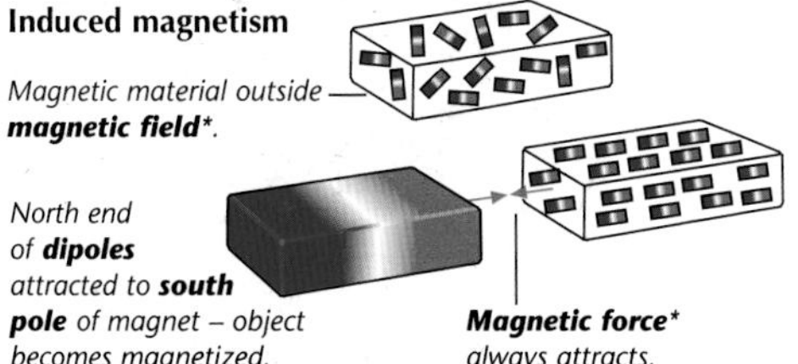
*Magnetic material outside **magnetic field****.
*North end of **dipoles** attracted to **south pole** of magnet – object becomes magnetized.*
Magnetic force* *always attracts.*

Single touch

A method of magnetizing an object by stroking it repeatedly with the **pole** of a **permanent magnet** (see **hard**). Magnetism is induced in the object from the **magnetic field*** of the magnet.

Magnetism induced by single touch

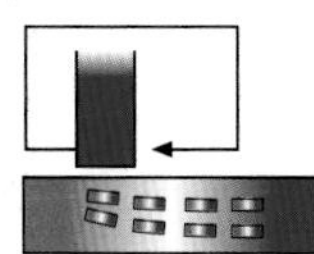

Divided touch

A method of magnetizing an object by stroking it repeatedly from the center out with the opposite **poles** of two **permanent magnets** (see **hard**). Magnetism is induced in the object from the **magnetic field*** of the magnets.

Magnetism induced by divided touch

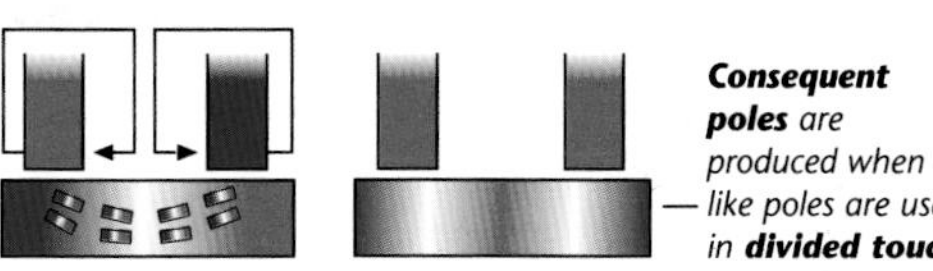
Consequent poles** are produced when like poles are used in **divided touch.

Demagnetization

The removal of magnetism from an object. This can be achieved by placing the object in a changing **magnetic field***, such as that created by a coil carrying **alternating current***. Alternatively, the **dipoles** (see **domain theory**, above) can be excited to point in random directions by hammering randomly or by heating above 700°C.

Self-demagnetization

Loss of magnetism by a magnet because of the attraction of the **dipoles** (see **domain theory**) for the opposite **poles** of the magnet. It is reduced using pieces of soft iron (called **keepers**) arranged to form a closed loop of poles.

Self-demagnetization of bar magnet

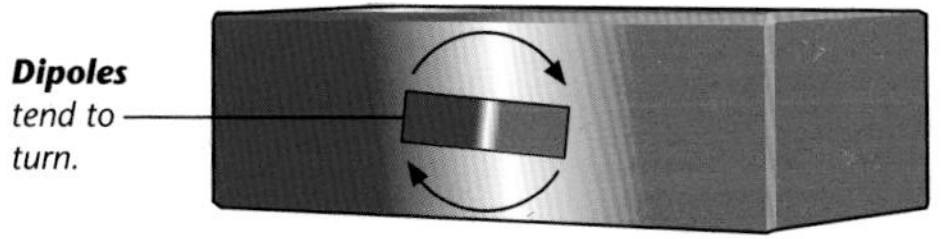
***Dipoles** tend to turn.*

Reducing self-demagnetization

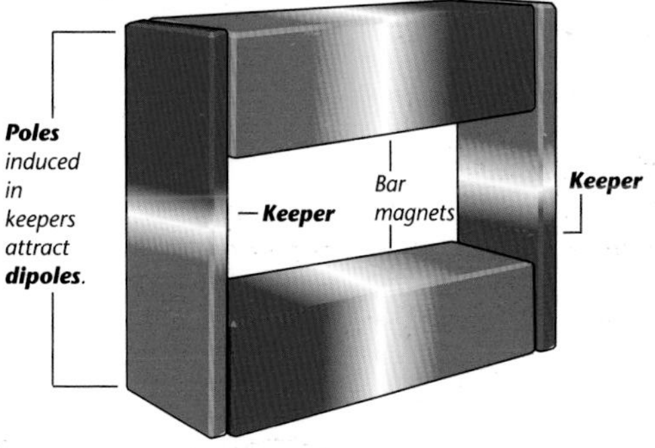
***Poles** induced in keepers attract **dipoles**.*
Keeper
Bar magnets
Keeper

* **Alternating current**, 61; **Magnetic field**, 72; **Magnetic force**, 6.

MAGNETIC FIELDS

A **magnetic field** is a region around a **magnet** (see page 70) in which objects are affected by the **magnetic force***. The strength and direction of the magnetic field are shown by **magnetic field lines**.

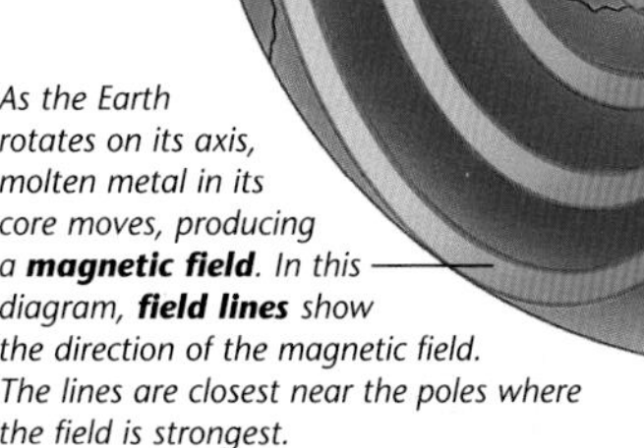

*As the Earth rotates on its axis, molten metal in its core moves, producing a **magnetic field**. In this diagram, **field lines** show the direction of the magnetic field. The lines are closest near the poles where the field is strongest.*

Magnetic field lines or flux lines

Lines which indicate the direction of the magnetic field around a magnet. They also show the strength of the field (see **magnetic flux density**, below). The direction of the field is the direction of the force on a **north pole***. Magnetic field lines are plotted by sprinkling iron filings around a magnet or by recording the direction of a **plotting compass** (a small compass with no directions marked on it) at various points.

Result of sprinkling iron filings around a magnet

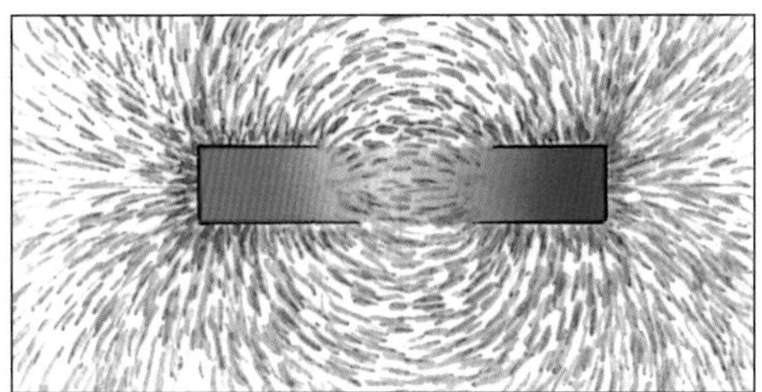

*Iron filings line up due to **induced magnetism***.*

Plotting the magnetic field lines around a bar magnet

Plotting compass

Previous recordings

S N

Complete plot of magnetic field lines *(Arrows indicate direction)*

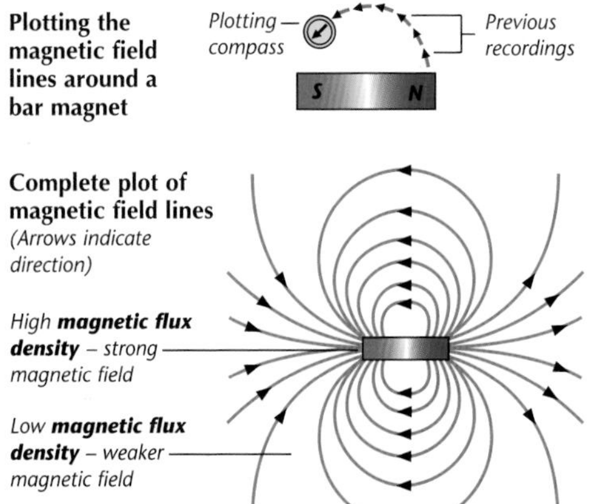
*High **magnetic flux density** – strong magnetic field*
*Low **magnetic flux density** – weaker magnetic field*

Magnetic flux density

A measurement of the strength of a magnetic field at a point. This is shown by the closeness of the **magnetic field lines** to each other. Magnetic flux density is normally highest around the **poles***.

Neutral point

A point of zero magnetism (the **magnetic flux density** is zero). It occurs where two or more magnetic fields interact with an equal but opposite effect. A bar magnet positioned along the **magnetic meridian**, with the **south pole*** pointing to the north, has two neutral points in line with its **magnetic axis***.

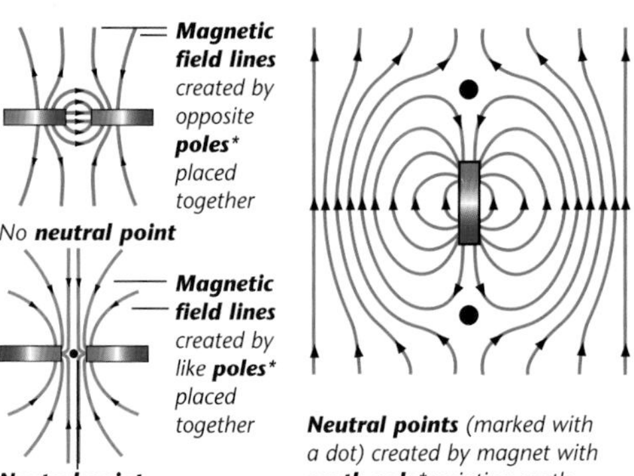
Magnetic field lines created by opposite poles placed together*
No neutral point
Magnetic field lines created by like poles placed together*
Neutral point

Neutral points** (marked with a dot) created by magnet with **south pole pointing north*

Diamagnetism

Magnetism displayed by some substances when placed in a strong magnetic field. A piece of diamagnetic material tends to spread **magnetic field lines** out and lines up with its long side perpendicular to them.

Paramagnetism

Magnetism displayed by some substances when placed in a strong magnetic field. A piece of paramagnetic material tends to concentrate **magnetic field lines** through it and lines up with its long side parallel to them. It is caused by **dipoles*** moving slightly towards alignment.

* **Dipole**, 71 (**Domain theory of magnetism**); **Electrons**, 83; **Induced magnetism**, 71; **Magnetic force**, 6; **Magnetic axis**, **Pole**, 70.

The Earth's magnetism

The Earth has a magnetic field which acts as though there were a giant bar magnet in its center, lined up approximately between its geographic north and south poles, although the angle is constantly changing. The north pole of a compass points towards a point called **magnetic north**, its south pole to **magnetic south**.

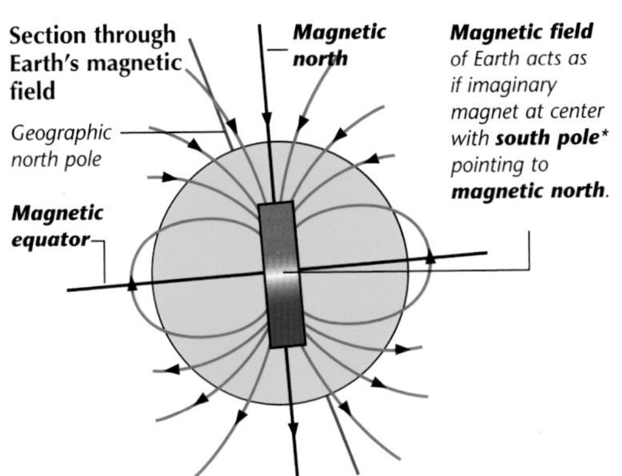
Section through Earth's magnetic field
Geographic north pole
Magnetic equator
Magnetic north
Magnetic field** of Earth acts as if imaginary magnet at center with **south pole pointing to **magnetic north**.*

Magnetic meridian
The vertical plane containing the **magnetic axis*** of a magnet suspended in the Earth's magnetic field (i.e. with its **north pole*** pointing to **magnetic north**).

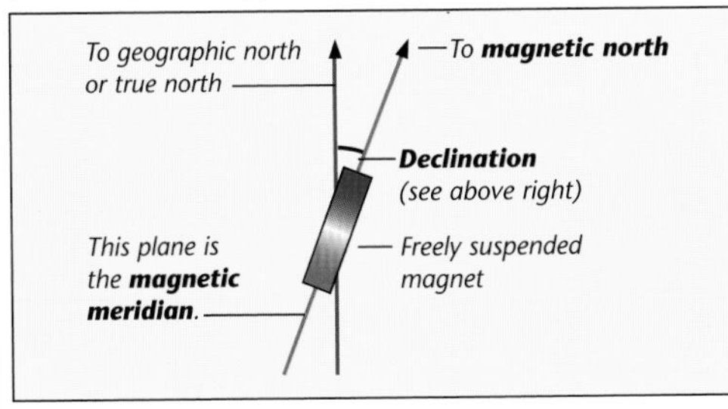
To geographic north or true north
*To **magnetic north***
***Declination** (see above right)*
*This plane is the **magnetic meridian**.*
Freely suspended magnet

Declination
The angle between a line taken to true north (the geographic north pole) and one taken along the **magnetic meridian** (towards **magnetic north**) at a point. The position of magnetic north is gradually changing and so the declination alters slowly with time.

This migrating tern may use the Earth's magnetic field to guide it.

Isogonal lines
Lines joining places with equal **declination**. These are redrawn from time to time because of the changing direction of the Earth's magnetic field.

Inclination or dip
The angle between a horizontal line on the Earth's surface and the direction of the Earth's magnetic field at a point. It is measured using a **dip circle** (see picture, below).

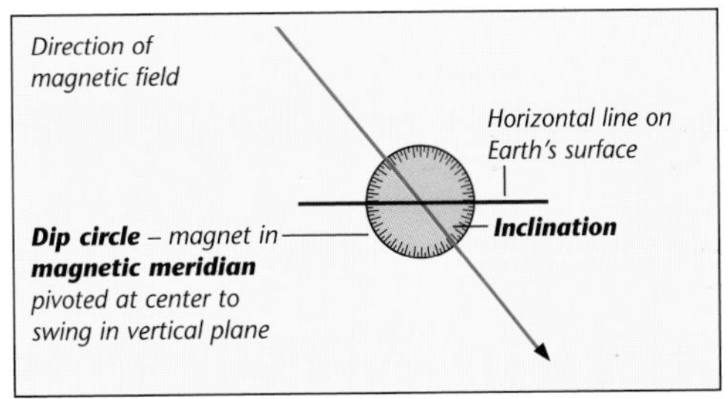
Direction of magnetic field
Horizontal line on Earth's surface
Inclination
***Dip circle** – magnet in **magnetic meridian** pivoted at center to swing in vertical plane*

Isoclinal line
A line linking places with the same **inclination**.

Permeability
A measure of the ability of a substance to "conduct" a magnetic field. Soft iron is much more permeable than air, so the magnetic field tends to be concentrated through it.

*Soft iron has a higher **permeability** than air.*

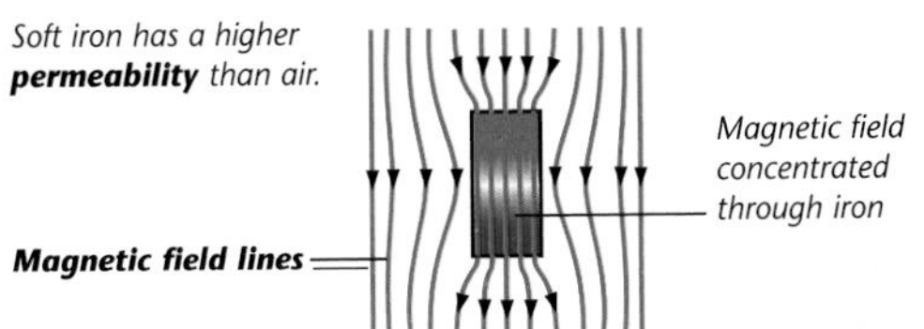
Magnetic field concentrated through iron
Magnetic field lines

Shielding or screening
The use of soft magnetic material to stop a magnetic field from reaching a point, effectively by "conducting" the field away. This is used in sensitive instruments, e.g. oscilloscopes.

*Oscilloscope beams are **shielded** from unwanted magnetic fields by **mumetal**, a special alloy with a very high **permeability**.*

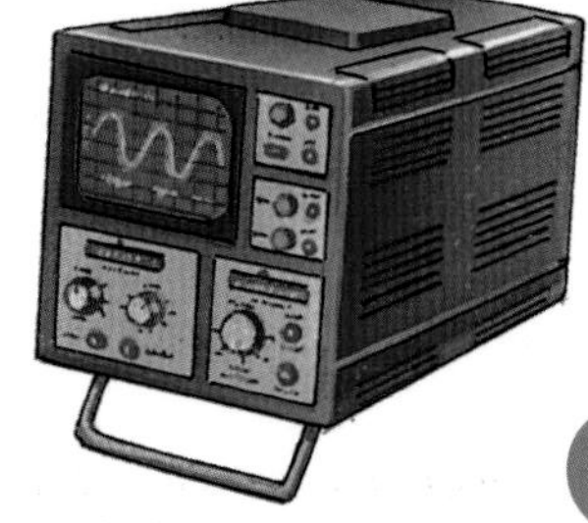

* **Magnetic axis**, **Pole**, 70.

ELECTROMAGNETISM

An electric current flowing through a wire produces a **magnetic field** (see pages 72-73) around the wire, the shape of which depends on the shape of the wire and the current flowing. These magnetic fields can be plotted in the same way as for **permanent magnets***. This effect, called **electromagnetism**, is used in very powerful magnets and also to produce motion from an electric current.

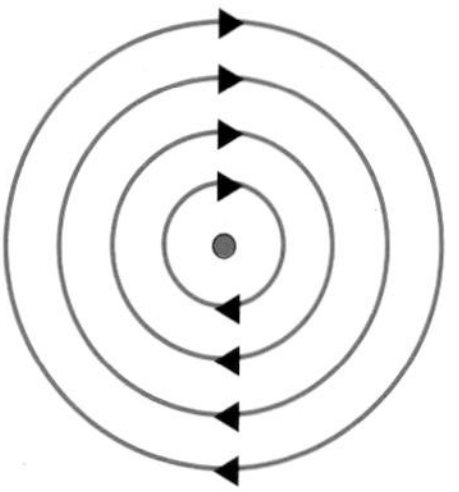

*Cross-section of the **magnetic field** which would exist if there was a wire (shown in green) carrying current directly into the page.*

Maxwell's screw rule

States that the direction of the magnetic field around a current-carrying wire is the way a screw turns when being screwed in the direction of the current.

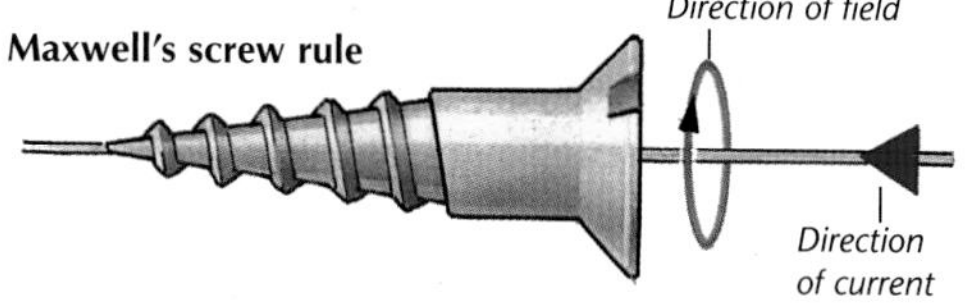

Maxwell's screw rule
Direction of field
Direction of current

Right-hand grip rule

States that the direction of a magnetic field around a wire is that from the base to the tips of the fingers if the wire is gripped by the right hand with the thumb pointing in the direction of the current.

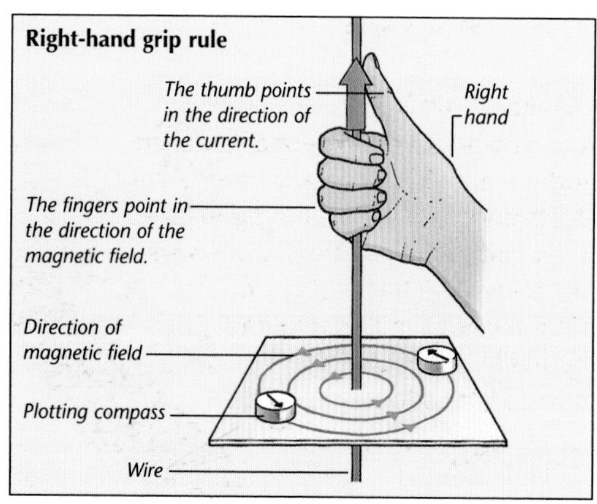

Right-hand grip rule
The thumb points in the direction of the current.
Right hand
The fingers point in the direction of the magnetic field.
Direction of magnetic field
Plotting compass
Wire

Coil

A number of turns of current-carrying wire, produced by wrapping the wire around a shaped piece of material (a **former**). Examples are a **flat coil** and a **solenoid**.

Flat coil or plane coil

A **coil** of wire whose length is small in comparison with its diameter.

Solenoid

A **coil** whose length is large in comparison with its diameter. The magnetic field produced by a solenoid is similar to that produced by a bar magnet. The position of the **poles*** depends on the current direction.

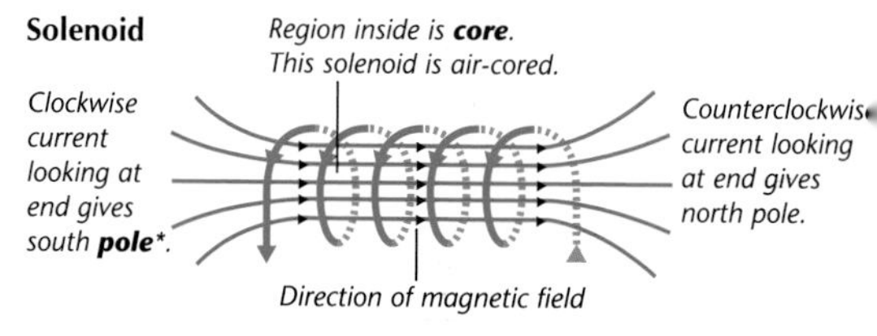

Solenoid
Region inside is **core**. This solenoid is air-cored.
Clockwise current looking at end gives south **pole***.
Counterclockwise current looking at end gives north pole.
Direction of magnetic field

S

Arrowheads on an S point in a clockwise direction (clockwise current = south pole).

Arrowheads on an N point in an counterclockwise direction (counterclockwise current = north pole).

Core

The material in the center of a **coil** which dictates the strength of the field. Soft **ferromagnetic*** materials, most commonly soft iron, create the strongest magnetic field and are used in **electromagnets**.

Electromagnet

A **solenoid** with a **core** of soft, strongly **ferromagnetic*** material. This forms a magnet which can be switched on and off simply by turning the current on and off. Practical electromagnets are constructed so that two opposite **poles*** are close to each other, producing a strong magnetic field.

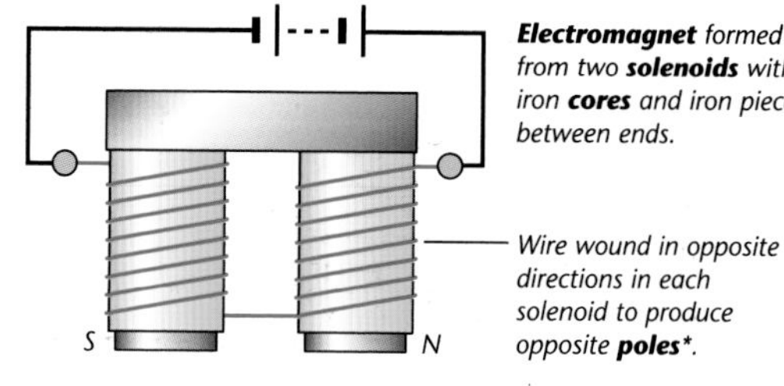

S
N
Wire wound in opposite directions in each solenoid to produce opposite **poles***.

***Electromagnet** formed from two **solenoids** with iron **cores** and iron piece between ends.*

* **Ferromagnetic**, 70; **Permanent magnets**, 70 (**Hard**); **Pole**, 70.

Applications of electromagnets

Electromagnets have a large number of applications, all of which use the fact that they attract metals when they are switched on and therefore convert **electric energy*** to **mechanical energy***. In two of the following examples, sound energy is produced from the mechanical energy.

Electric buzzer

A device which produces a buzzing noise from **direct current***. A metal arm is attracted by an **electromagnet**, moves towards it, and in doing so breaks the circuit carrying current to the electromagnet. The arm is thus released and the process is repeated. The resulting vibration of the arm produces a buzzing noise. In the **electric bell**, a hammer attached to the arm repeatedly strikes a bell.

Electric bell

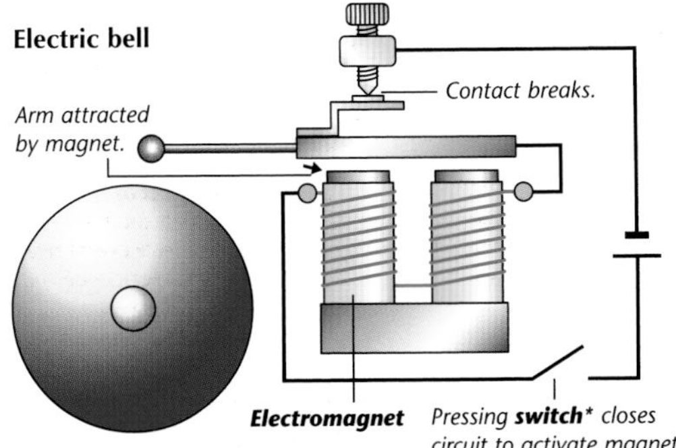
Contact breaks.
Arm attracted by magnet.
Electromagnet
Pressing switch* closes circuit to activate magnet.

Earphone

A device used to transform electrical signals to sound waves. The **permanent magnet*** attracts the metal diaphragm, but the strength of this attraction is changed as changing current (the incoming signals) flows through the coils of the **electromagnet**. The diaphragm thus vibrates to produce sound waves.

Earphone

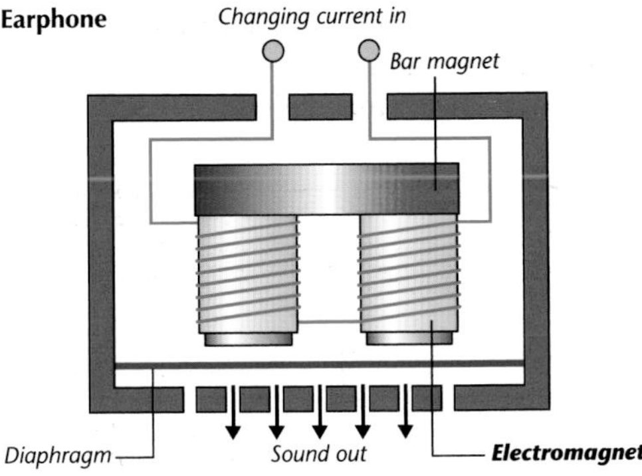
Changing current in
Bar magnet
Diaphragm
Sound out
Electromagnet

Lifting magnets

Large **electromagnets** which are used in steelworks to lift heavy loads. The activated electromagnet attracts steel, enabling it to be moved. The load is released when the current is switched off.

***Lifting magnet** used to move scrap metal from one place to another.*

Relay

A device in which a **switch*** is closed by the action of an **electromagnet**. A relatively small current in the **coil** of the electromagnet can be used to switch on a large current without the circuits being electrically linked.

Relay

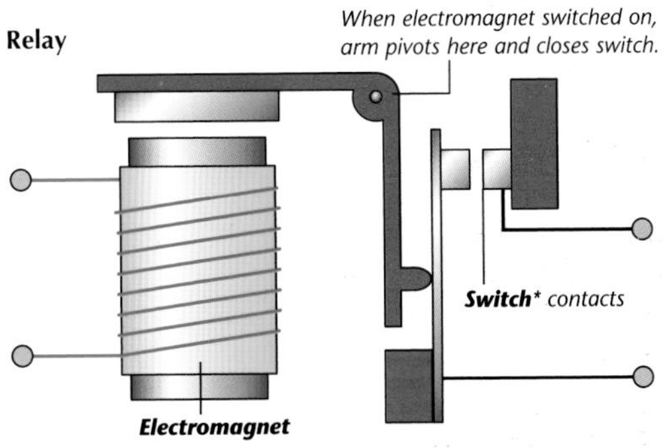
When electromagnet switched on, arm pivots here and closes switch.
Switch* contacts
Electromagnet

"Maglev" train

A train with **electromagnets** attached underneath, which runs on tracks with electromagnets on them. The magnets repel each other, so the train hovers just above the track. The reduced friction between the train and the track means that the train can travel faster.

Japanese "maglev" train

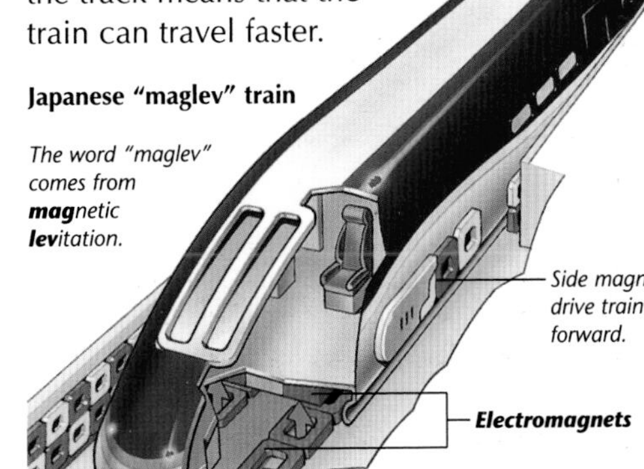
Side magnets drive train forward.
Electromagnets

*The word "maglev" comes from **mag**netic **lev**itation.*

* **Direct current**, 61; **Electric energy**, 9; **Ferromagnetic**, 70; **Mechanical energy**, 9; **Permanent magnets**, 70 (**Hard**); **Pole**, 70; **Switch**, 64.

Electromagnets continued – the Lorentz force

The **Lorentz force** occurs when a current-carrying wire goes through a magnetic field. A force acts on the wire which can produce movement. This effect is used in **electric motors**, where **mechanical energy*** is produced from **electric energy***. The effect can also be used to measure current (see page 77), since the force depends on its magnitude.

Exploded view of a powerful electric motor

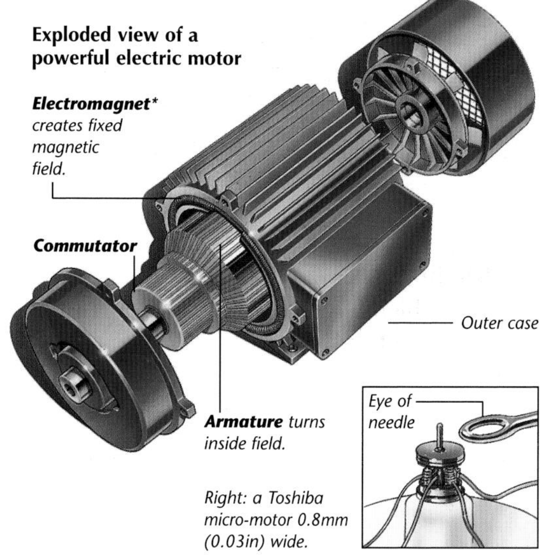

Electromagnet* creates fixed magnetic field.
Commutator
Outer case
Armature turns inside field.
Eye of needle

Right: a Toshiba micro-motor 0.8mm (0.03in) wide.

Fleming's left-hand rule.

See diagram, right. A right-hand rule can also be used. The thumb indicates force, but the meaning of the index and first fingers is reversed.

Fleming's left-hand rule

Points in direction of force

Points in direction of field

Points in direction of current

Electric motor

A device which uses the **Lorentz force** to transform **electric energy*** to **mechanical energy***. The simplest motor consists of a current-carrying, square-shaped **flat coil***, free to rotate in a magnetic field (see diagram below). Motors produce a **back e.m.f.*** opposing the e.m.f. which drives them. This is produced because once the motor starts, it acts as a **generator*** (i.e. the movement of the coil in the field produces an opposing current).

Simple electric motor

Commutator*. A ring split into two or more pieces, via which current enters and leaves the **coil*** of an **electric motor**. It ensures that the current enters the coil in the correct direction to make the motor rotate in one direction continuously.*

Brushes*. Contacts, normally made of carbon, through which current enters the **commutator** in an **electric motor**.*

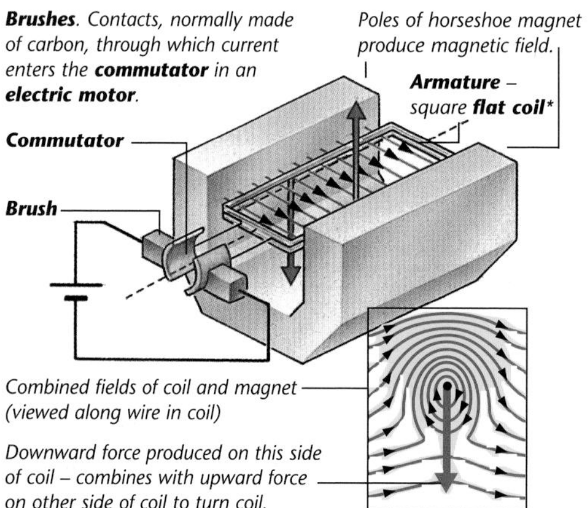

Poles of horseshoe magnet produce magnetic field.
Armature – square flat coil*
Commutator
Brush
Combined fields of coil and magnet (viewed along wire in coil)
Downward force produced on this side of coil – combines with upward force on other side of coil to turn coil.

Field windings

Sets of **coils*** around the outside of an **electric motor**, which take the place of a permanent magnet to produce a stronger magnetic field. This increases the power of the motor.

Loudspeaker

A device which uses the **Lorentz force** to transform electrical signals into **sound waves***. It consists of a **coil*** in a **radial magnetic field** (the direction of the field at any point is along a radius of this coil). As the current changes, the coil, which is attached to a paper cone, moves in and out of the field (see diagram). The paper cone vibrates the air, producing sound waves which depend on the strength and frequency of the current.

Loudspeaker

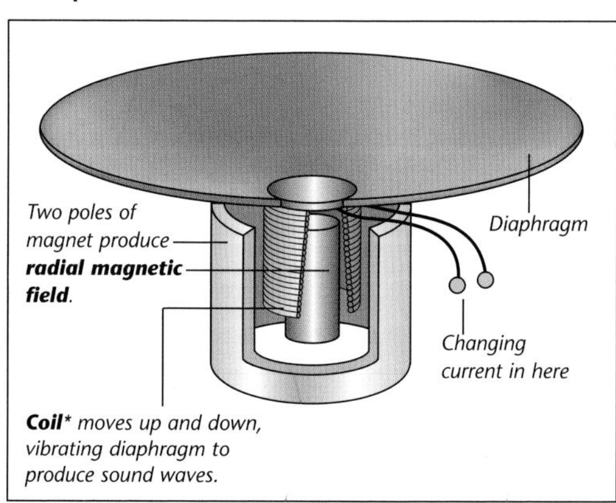

Two poles of magnet produce radial magnetic field.
Diaphragm
Changing current in here
Coil* moves up and down, vibrating diaphragm to produce sound waves.

* **Back e.m.f.**, 60 (**Electromotive force**); **Coil**, 74; **Electric energy**, 9; **Electromagnet**, **Flat coil**, 74; **Generator**, 78; **Mechanical energy**, 9; **Sound waves**, 40.

ELECTRIC METERS

Current can be detected by placing a suspended magnet near a wire and observing its deflection. This idea can be extended to produce a device (a **meter**) in which the deflection indicates on a scale the strength of the current. The current measuring device can then be adapted to measure **potential difference***.

Galvanometer

Any device used to detect a **direct current*** by registering its magnetic effect. The simplest is a compass placed near a wire to show whether a current is present. The **moving coil galvanometer** uses the **Lorentz force** to show a deflection on a scale (see diagram).

Moving coil galvanometer

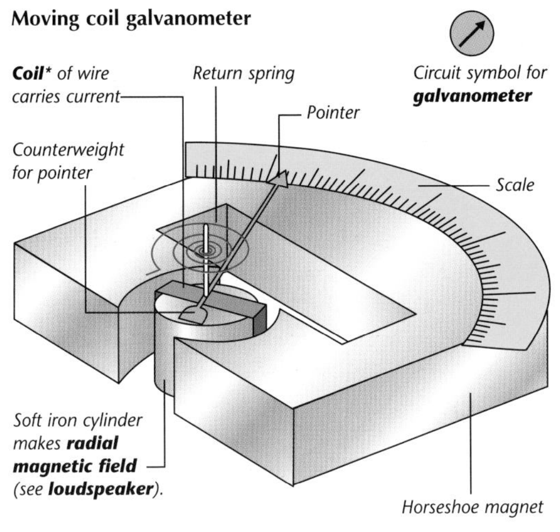

Circuit symbol for **galvanometer**
Coil* of wire carries current
Return spring
Pointer
Counterweight for pointer
Scale
Soft iron cylinder makes **radial magnetic field** (see **loudspeaker**).
Horseshoe magnet

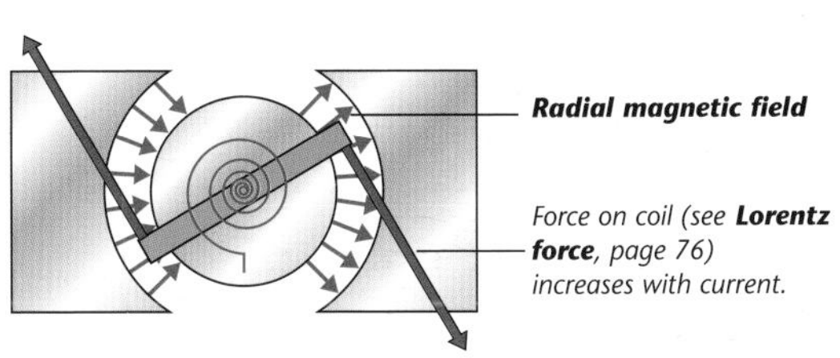

Radial magnetic field
Force on coil (see **Lorentz force**, page 76) increases with current.

Moving iron meter

A **meter** in which the current to be measured induces magnetism in two pieces of iron which attract or repel each other to produce a deflection.

Ammeter

A device used to measure current. It is a version of the **moving coil galvanometer**, designed so that a certain current produces a **full scale deflection**, i.e. the pointer moves to its maximum position. To measure higher currents, a **shunt** is added (see diagram below). A larger current now produces full scale deflection on the new scale.

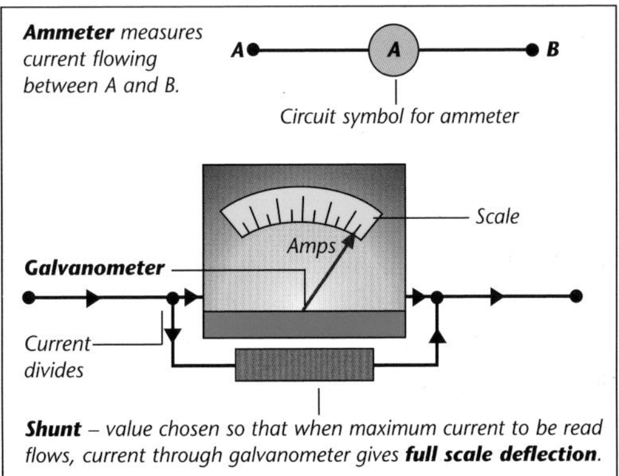

Ammeter measures current flowing between A and B.
A
A
B
Circuit symbol for ammeter
Amps
Scale
Galvanometer
Current divides
Shunt – value chosen so that when maximum current to be read flows, current through galvanometer gives **full scale deflection**.

Voltmeter

A device used to measure the **potential difference*** between two points. It is a **galvanometer** between the two points with a high **resistance*** in **series***. A certain potential difference produces the current for a **full scale deflection** (see **ammeter**). To measure higher potential differences, a **multiplier** is added (see diagram below).

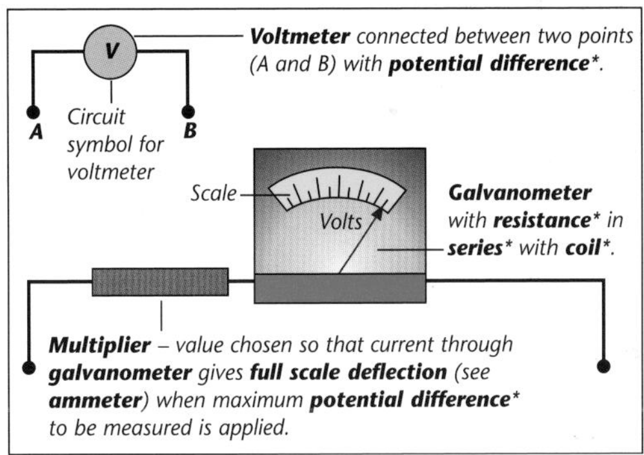

V
Voltmeter connected between two points (A and B) with **potential difference***.
A
B
Circuit symbol for voltmeter
Scale
Volts
Galvanometer with **resistance*** in **series*** with **coil***.
Multiplier – value chosen so that current through **galvanometer** gives **full scale deflection** (see **ammeter**) when maximum **potential difference*** to be measured is applied.

Multimeter

A **galvanometer** combined with the **shunts** (see **ammeter**) and **multipliers** (see **voltmeter**) necessary to measure currents and **potential differences***.

* **Coil**, 74; **Direct current**, 61; **Potential difference**, 58; **Resistance**, 62; **Series**, 64.

ELECTROMAGNETIC INDUCTION

Michael Faraday found that, as well as a current passing through a magnetic field producing movement (see **motor effect**, page 76), movement of a **conductor*** in a magnetic field produces an **electromotive force*** in the conductor. This effect, called **electromagnetic induction**, happens whenever a conductor is placed in a changing magnetic field.

*Faraday induced an electromotive force by rotating a disk (the **conductor***) near a magnet, using this device called a disk **dynamo**.*

Faraday's law of induction

States that the size of an induced electromotive force in a **conductor*** is proportional to the rate at which the magnetic field changes.

Lenz's law

States that an induced electromotive force always acts to oppose the cause of it, e.g. in an **electric motor***, the e.m.f. produced because it acts as a **generator** opposes the e.m.f. driving the motor.

Fleming's right-hand rule or dynamo rule

The direction of an induced current can be worked out from the direction of the magnetic field and the movement by using the right hand (see diagram).

Fleming's right-hand rule

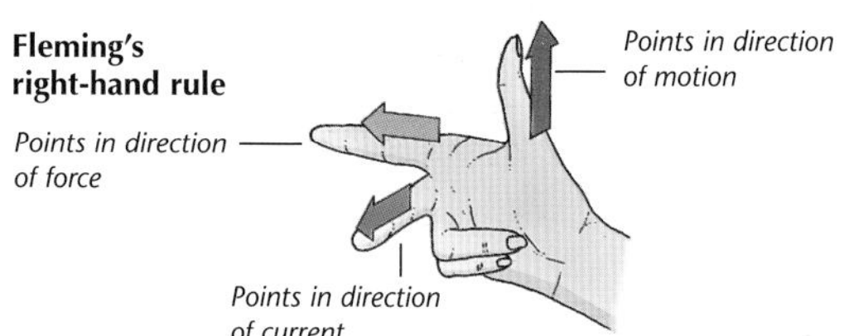
Points in direction of motion
Points in direction of force
Points in direction of current

Generator or dynamo

A device used to produce electric current from **mechanical energy***. In the simplest generator (see diagram, right), an alternating electromotive force is induced in a **coil*** as it rotates in a magnetic field. A generator for **direct currents*** has a **commutator***, as on an **electric motor***, which means the current always flows in the same direction.

Simple generator

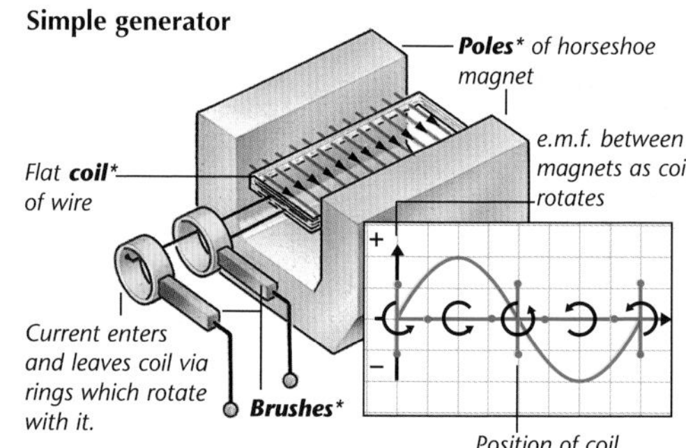
Poles* of horseshoe magnet
e.m.f. between magnets as coil rotates
Flat coil* of wire
+
–
Current enters and leaves coil via rings which rotate with it.
Brushes*
Position of coil

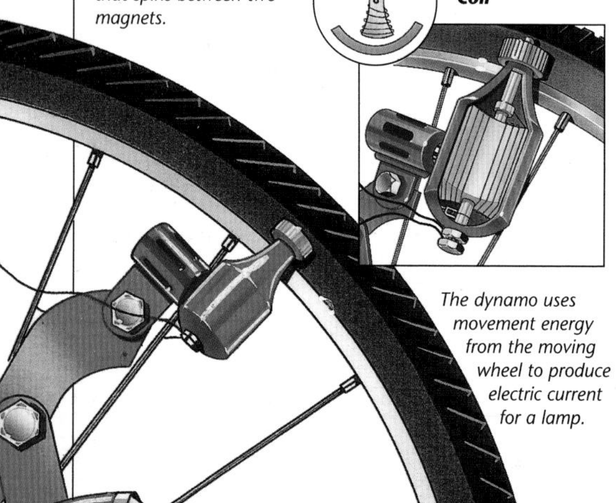
Fixed magnet
Coil*

*A bicycle **dynamo** contains a **coil*** of wire that spins between two magnets.*

The dynamo uses movement energy from the moving wheel to produce electric current for a lamp.

Mutual induction

The induction of an electromotive force in a **coil*** of wire by changing the current in a different coil. The changing current produces a changing magnetic field which induces a current in any other coil in the field. This was first demonstrated with **Faraday's iron ring**.

Faraday's iron ring

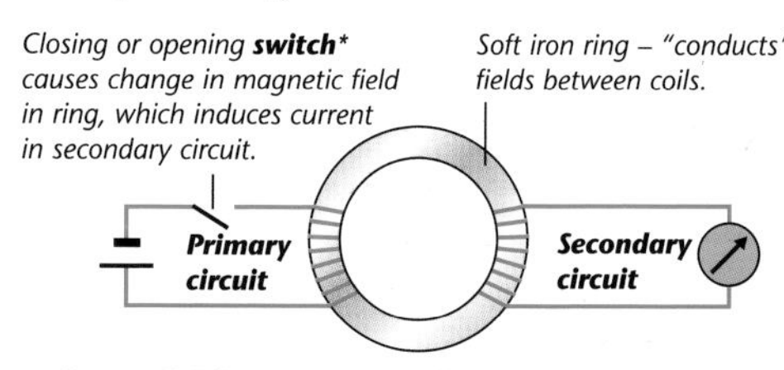
Closing or opening switch* causes change in magnetic field in ring, which induces current in secondary circuit.
Soft iron ring – "conducts" fields between coils.
Primary circuit
Secondary circuit

* **Brushes**, 76; **Coil**, 74; **Commutator**, 76; **Conductor**, 56; **Direct current**, 61; **Electric motor**, 76; **Electromotive force** (**e.m.f.**), 60; **Mechanical energy**, 9; **Pole**, 70; **Switch**, 64.

Self-induction

The induction of an electromotive force in a **coil*** of wire due to the current inside it changing. For example, if the current in a coil is switched off, the resulting change in the magnetic field produces an electromotive force across the coil, in some cases much higher than that of the original.

Eddy current

A current set up in a piece of metal when a magnetic field around it changes, even though the metal may not be part of a circuit. Eddy currents can cause unwanted heat energy, e.g. in the iron core of a **transformer**. This can be prevented by laminating the iron core (see **transformers**, below).

Transformers

A **transformer** consists of two **coils*** of wire wound onto the same **core*** of soft **ferromagnetic*** material. It is used to change an alternating electromotive force in one of the coils to a different e.m.f. in the other coil, e.g. in electricity supply, see page 61. Hardly any energy is lost between the two circuits in a well-designed transformer.

Simple transformer

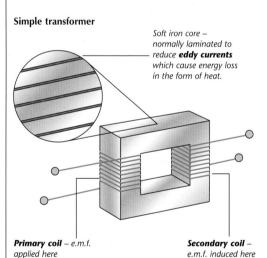

*Soft iron core – normally laminated to reduce **eddy currents** which cause energy loss in the form of heat.*

***Primary coil** – e.m.f. applied here*

***Secondary coil** – e.m.f. induced here*

Turns ratio

The ratio of the number of turns in the **secondary coil** in a **transformer** to the number of turns in the **primary coil**. The turns ratio is also the ratio of the electromotive force in the secondary coil to that in the primary coil.

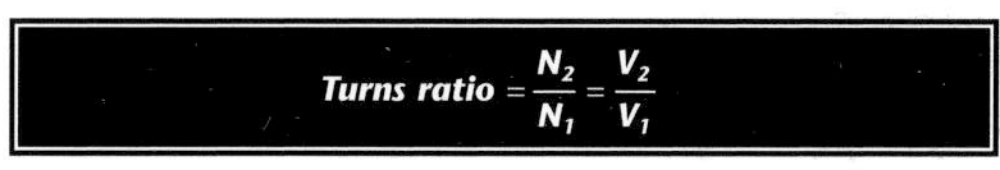

Turns ratio $= \frac{N_2}{N_1} = \frac{V_2}{V_1}$

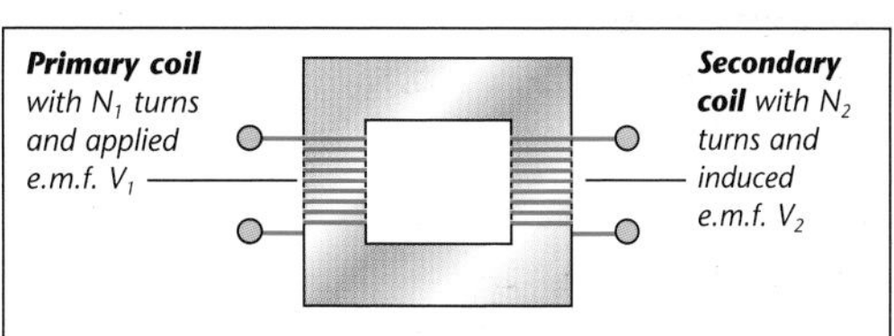

Primary coil with N_1 turns and applied e.m.f. V_1
Secondary coil with N_2 turns and induced e.m.f. V_2

Step-up transformer

A **transformer** in which the electromotive force in the **secondary coil** is greater than that in the **primary coil**. The **turns ratio** is greater than one.

Step-up transformer

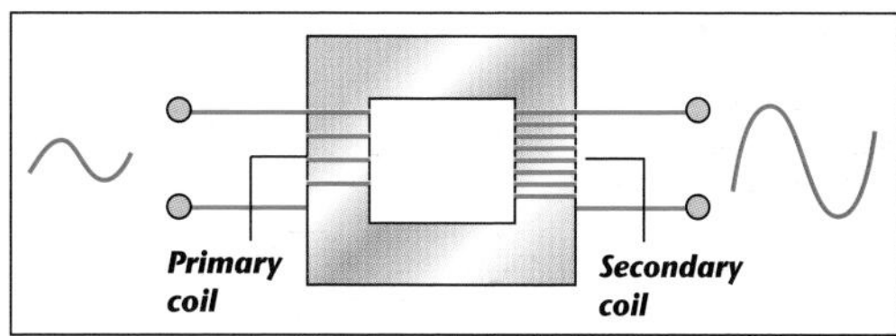

Primary coil
Secondary coil

Primary coil

The **coil*** in a transformer to which an alternating electromotive force is applied in order to produce an electromotive force in the **secondary coil**.

Step-down transformer

A **transformer** in which the electromotive force in the **secondary coil** is less than that in the **primary coil**. The **turns ratio** is less than one.

Step-down transformer

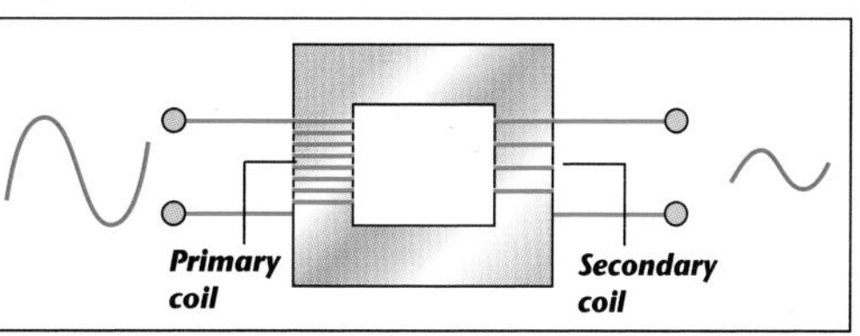

Primary coil
Secondary coil

Secondary coil

The **coil*** in a transformer in which an alternating electromotive force is induced by the electromotive force applied to the **primary coil**. Some transformers have two or more secondary coils.

* **Coil**, **Core**, 74; **Ferromagnetic**, 70.

CATHODE RAYS

A **cathode ray** is a continuous stream of **electrons** (negatively-charged particles – see page 83) traveling through a low pressure gas or a vacuum. It is produced when electrons are freed from a metal **cathode*** and attracted to an **anode***. Cathode rays have a number of applications, from the production of **X-rays*** to **television**. All of these involve the use of a shaped glass tube (called an **electron tube**) containing a low pressure gas or a vacuum for the rays to travel in. The rays are normally produced by an **electron gun**, which forms part of the tube.

Electron gun

A device which produces a continuous stream of electrons (a cathode ray). It consists of a heated **cathode*** which gives off electrons (this is called **thermionic emission**) and an **anode*** which attracts them to form a stream.

Typical experimental electron tube

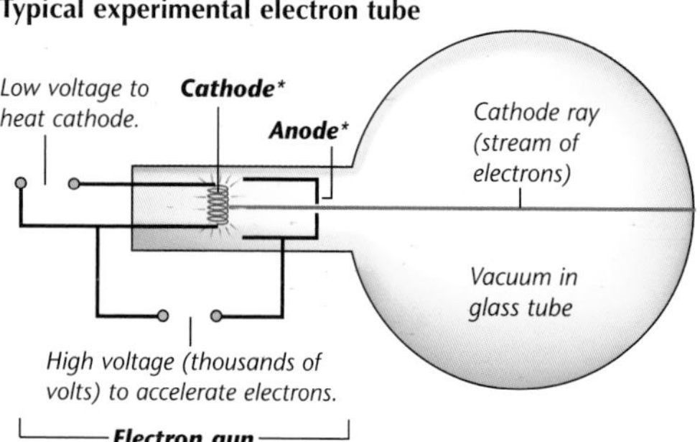

Low voltage to heat cathode.
Cathode*
Anode*
Cathode ray (stream of electrons)
Vacuum in glass tube
High voltage (thousands of volts) to accelerate electrons.
Electron gun

Maltese cross tube

An **electron tube** in which the cathode ray is interrupted by a cross which casts a "shadow" on a **fluorescent*** screen at the end of the tube. This shows that the electrons are moving in straight lines.

Maltese cross tube

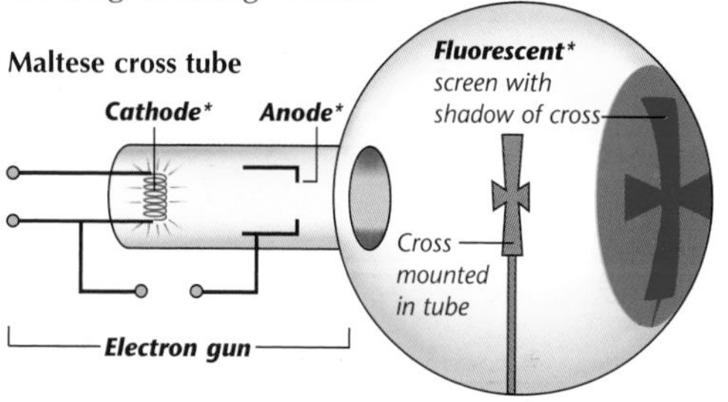

Cathode*
Anode*
Fluorescent* screen with shadow of cross
Cross mounted in tube
Electron gun

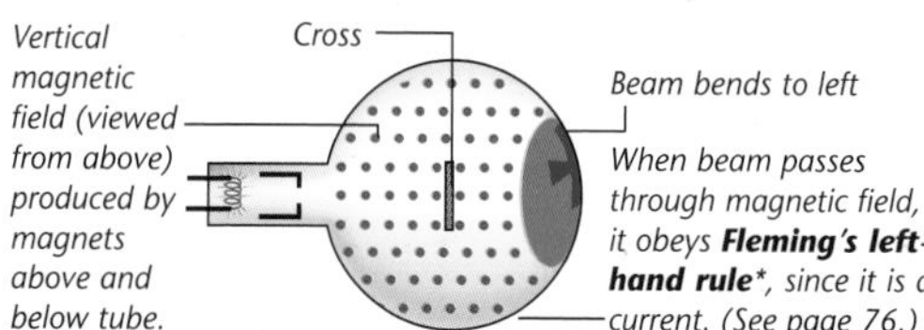

Vertical magnetic field (viewed from above) produced by magnets above and below tube.
Cross
Beam bends to left
When beam passes through magnetic field, it obeys Fleming's left-hand rule*, since it is a current. (See page 76.)

Discharge tube

A gas-filled glass tube in which **ions*** and electrons are attracted by the **electrodes*** and move towards them at high speed. As they do so, they collide with gas atoms, causing these atoms to split into more ions and electrons, and emit light at the same time. The color of the light depends on the gas used, e.g. neon produces orange light (used in advertising displays) and mercury vapor produces blue-green light (used for street lighting). Discharge tubes use up to five times less electricity than other lighting. A **fluorescent tube** is a discharge tube filled with mercury vapor, which emits **ultraviolet radiation***. This hits the inside of the tube, causing its coating of special powder to give out **visible light*** (see **fluorescence**, page 45).

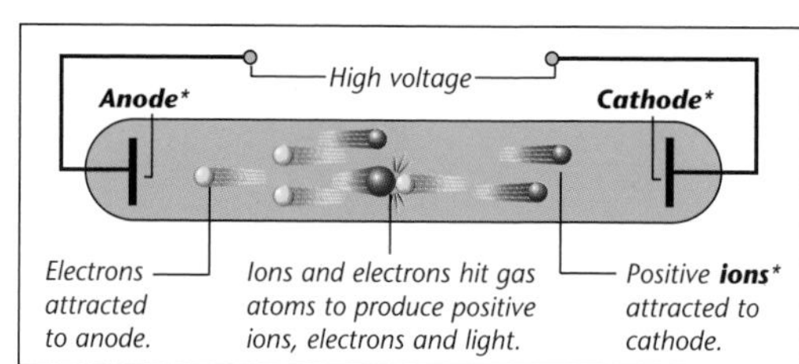

High voltage
Anode*
Cathode*
Electrons attracted to anode.
Ions and electrons hit gas atoms to produce positive ions, electrons and light.
Positive ions* attracted to cathode.

X-ray tube

A special electron tube used to produce a beam of **X-rays***. A cathode ray hits a tungsten target which stops the electrons suddenly. This causes X-rays to be emitted.

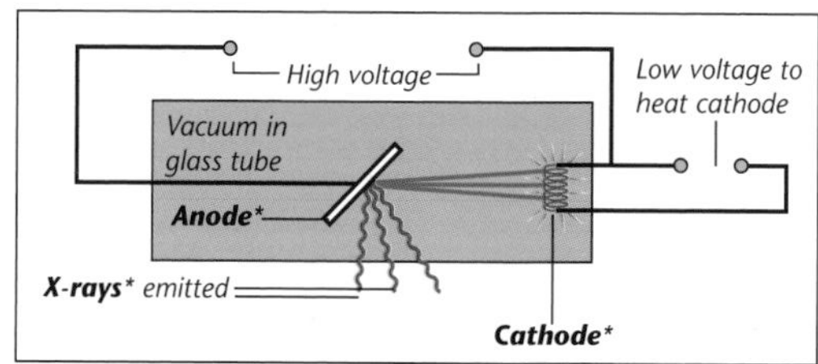

High voltage
Low voltage to heat cathode
Vacuum in glass tube
Anode*
X-rays* emitted
Cathode*

* **Anode**, **Cathode**, 66 (**Electrode**); **Fleming's left-hand rule** 76; **Fluorescence**, 45; **Ions**, 88 (**Ionization**); **Ultraviolet radiation**, 44; **Visible light**, 45; **X-rays**, 44.

The cathode ray oscilloscope

The **cathode ray oscilloscope** (**CRO**) is an instrument used to study currents and **potential differences***. A cathode ray from an **electron gun** produces a spot on a **fluorescent*** screen. In normal use, the ray is repeatedly swept across the back of the screen at a selected speed and so produces a visible trace across the front. If a signal is fed into the oscilloscope, the vertical position of the beam will change according to the strength of the signal, and the trace on the screen then shows this change over time.

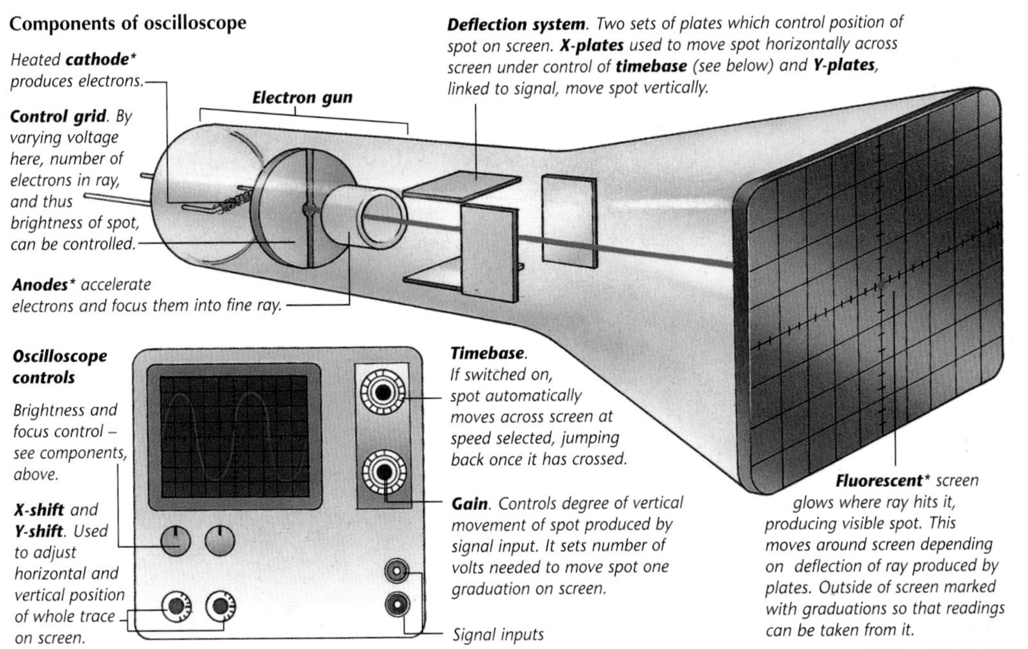
Components of oscilloscope
Heated **cathode*** produces electrons.
Control grid. By varying voltage here, number of electrons in ray, and thus brightness of spot, can be controlled.
Anodes* accelerate electrons and focus them into fine ray.
Electron gun
Deflection system. Two sets of plates which control position of spot on screen. **X-plates** used to move spot horizontally across screen under control of **timebase** (see below) and **Y-plates**, linked to signal, move spot vertically.
Oscilloscope controls
Brightness and focus control – see components, above.
X-shift and **Y-shift**. Used to adjust horizontal and vertical position of whole trace on screen.
Timebase. If switched on, spot automatically moves across screen at speed selected, jumping back once it has crossed.
Gain. Controls degree of vertical movement of spot produced by signal input. It sets number of volts needed to move spot one graduation on screen.
Signal inputs
Fluorescent* screen glows where ray hits it, producing visible spot. This moves around screen depending on deflection of ray produced by plates. Outside of screen marked with graduations so that readings can be taken from it.

Television

Television pictures are reproduced by using an **electron tube** in which the cathode ray scans across the screen varying in strength according to the signal. Different levels of light, according to the strength of the ray, are given off from different parts of the screen to produce a picture (see diagram on right).

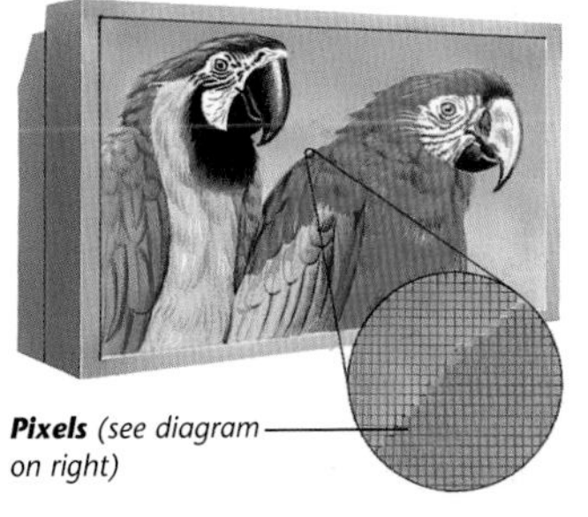
Pixels (see diagram on right)

Extra large high-definition televisions (HTDVs) have more **pixels** than ordinary TVs (see right), so the picture is sharper.

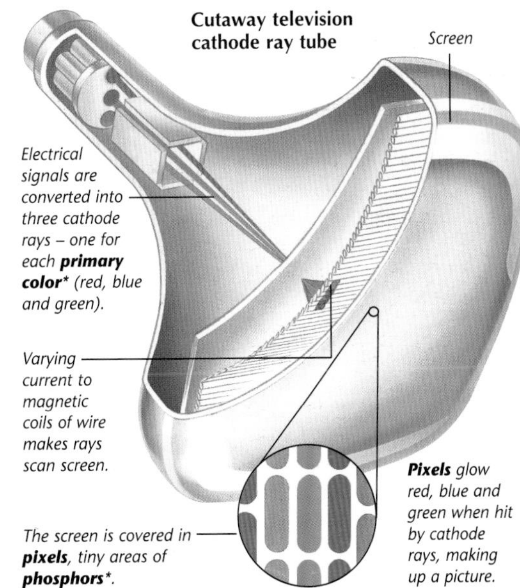
Cutaway television cathode ray tube
Screen
Electrical signals are converted into three cathode rays – one for each **primary color*** (red, blue and green).
Varying current to magnetic coils of wire makes rays scan screen.
The screen is covered in **pixels**, tiny areas of **phosphors***.
Pixels glow red, blue and green when hit by cathode rays, making up a picture.

* **Anode**, **Cathode**, 66 (**Electrode**); **Fluorescence**, 45; **Phosphors**, 44 (**Phosphorescence**); **Potential difference**, 58; **Primary colors**, 55.

ATOMIC STRUCTURE

A great deal has been learned about the physical nature of atoms (see also page 4) since Greek philosophers first proposed that all matter was made of basic indivisible "building blocks". It is now known that an atom is not indivisible, but has a complex internal structure, consisting of many different smaller particles (**subatomic particles**) and a lot of empty space.

Orbital *model of an atom (see page 83)*

Rutherford-Bohr atom

A "solar system" representation of an atom, devised by Ernest Rutherford and Niels Bohr in 1911. It is now known to be incorrect (**electrons** have no regular "orbits" – see **electron shells**).

Rutherford-Bohr atom model

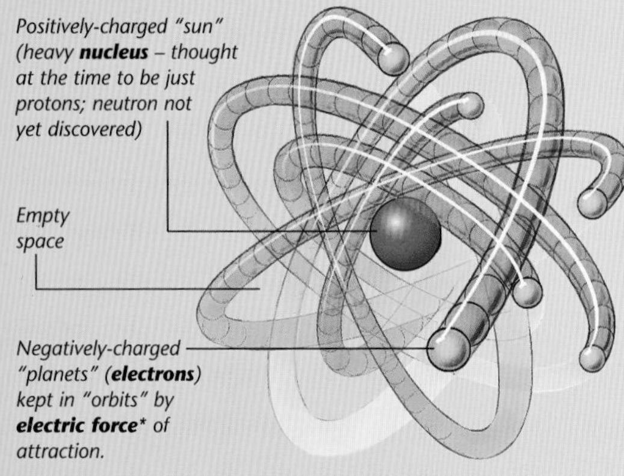
Positively-charged "sun" (heavy nucleus – thought at the time to be just protons; neutron not yet discovered)
Empty space
Negatively-charged "planets" (electrons) kept in "orbits" by electric force* of attraction.

Nucleus (pl. nuclei) or atomic nucleus

The central core of an atom, consisting of closely-packed **nucleons** (**protons** and **neutrons**).

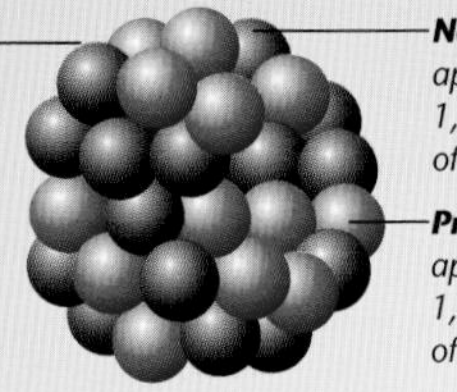
Nucleus – (almost all the mass of the atom, but very tiny – its radius is approximately 1/10,000th that of the atom)
Neutron (mass approximately 1,840 times that of an electron)
Proton (mass approximately 1,836 times that of an electron)

Protons

Positively-charged particles in the **nucleus**. The number of protons (**atomic number**) identifies the element and equals the number of **electrons**, so atoms are electrically neutral.

Neutrons

Electrically neutral particles in the **nucleus**. The number of neutrons in atoms of the same element can vary (see **isotope**).

Mass number (A)

The number of **protons** and **neutrons** (**nucleons**) in a **nucleus**. It is the whole number nearest to the **relative atomic mass** of the atom, and is important in identifying **isotopes**.

Atomic number (Z)

The number of **protons** in a **nucleus** (hence also the number of **electrons** around it). All atoms with the same atomic number are of the same element (see also **isotope**).

Neutron number (N)

The number of **neutrons** in a **nucleus**, calculated by subtracting the atomic number from the mass number. See also graph, page 87.

*The **mass** and **atomic numbers** are often written with the symbol of an element:*

$^{12}_{6}C$

Mass number (A) *shows nucleus has 12* ***nucleons****.*

Atomic number (Z) *shows that six of these are* ***protons****.*

Neutron number (N) *= A – Z*
So N = 6

$^{23}_{11}Na$

Mass number (A) *shows nucleus has 23* ***nucleons****.*

Atomic number (Z) *shows that 11 of these are* ***protons****.*

Neutron number (N) *= A – Z*
So N = 12

* **Electric force**, 6.

Electrons

Particles with a negative charge and very small mass. They move around the **nucleus** in **electron shells**. See also **protons**.

Electron shells

Regions of space around a **nucleus** containing moving **electrons**. An atom can have up to seven (from the inside, called the **K**, **L**, **M**, **N**, **O**, **P** and **Q shells**). Each can hold up to a certain number of electrons (the first four, from the inside, can take up to 2, 8, 18 and 32 electrons respectively).

The further away the shell is from the nucleus, the higher the energy of its electrons (the shell has a given **energy level**). The **outer shell** is the last shell with electrons in it. If this is full or has an **octet** (8 electrons), the atom is very stable (see page 85).

The positions of electrons in their shells cannot be exactly determined at any one time, but each shell consists of **orbitals**, or **probability clouds**. Each of these is a region in which one or two electrons are likely to be found at any time (see also illustration on page 82).

Modern model (simplified), carbon-12 isotope

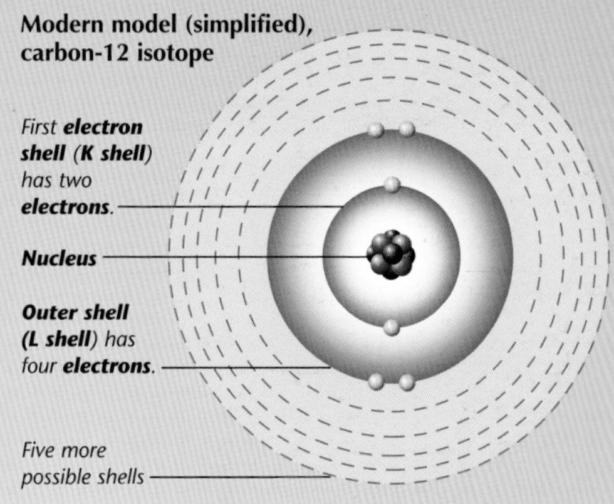
*First **electron shell (K shell)** has two **electrons**.*
Nucleus
***Outer shell (L shell)** has four **electrons**.*
Five more possible shells

Modern model (complex), carbon-12 isotope

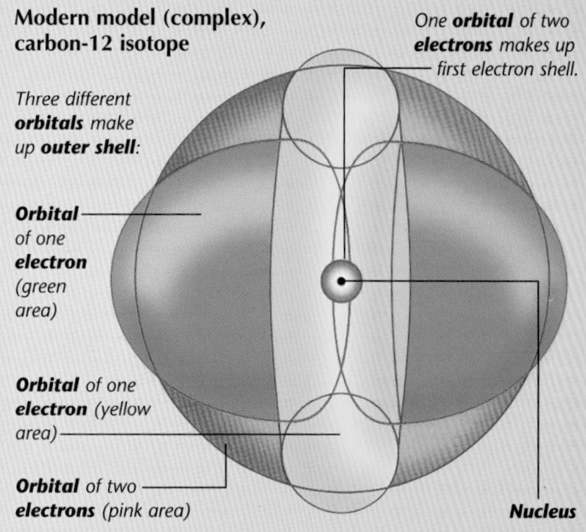
*One **orbital** of two **electrons** makes up first electron shell.*
*Three different **orbitals** make up **outer shell**:*
***Orbital** of one **electron** (green area)*
***Orbital** of one **electron** (yellow area)*
***Orbital** of two **electrons** (pink area)*
Nucleus

Isotopes

Different forms of the same element, with the same atomic number, but different **neutron numbers** and hence different **mass numbers**. There are isotopes of every element, since even if only one natural form exists (i.e. the element is **monoisotopic**), others can be made artificially (see **radioisotope**, page 86).

***Mass numbers** are used with names or symbols when **isotopes** are being specified:*

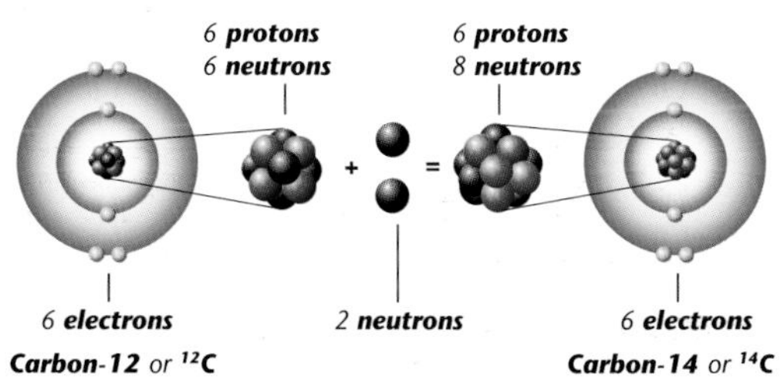
*6 **protons***
*6 **neutrons***
*6 **protons***
*8 **neutrons***
+
=
*6 **electrons***
*2 **neutrons***
*6 **electrons***
Carbon-12** or ^{12}**C
Carbon-14** or ^{14}**C

Relative atomic mass

Also called **atomic mass** or **atomic weight**. The mass of an atom in **unified atomic mass units** (**u**). Each of these is equal to $^1/_{12}$ of the mass of a carbon-12 atom (**isotope**). The relative atomic mass of a carbon-12 atom is thus 12u, but no other values are whole numbers, e.g. the relative atomic mass of aluminum is 26.9815u.

The relative atomic mass takes into account the various isotopes of the element, if these occur in a natural sample. Natural chlorine, for example, has three chlorine-35 atoms to every one of chlorine-37, and the relative atomic mass of chlorine (35.453u) is a proportional average of the two different masses of these isotopes.

ATOMIC AND NUCLEAR ENERGY

All things, whether large objects or minute particles, have a particular **energy state**, or level of **potential energy*** ("stored" energy). Moreover, they will always try to find their lowest possible energy state, called the **ground state**, which is the state of the greatest stability. In most cases, this involves recombining in some way, i.e. adding or losing constituents. In all cases it results in the release of the "excess" energy – in large amounts if the particles are atoms, and vast amounts if they are nuclei. The greater the **binding energy** of an atom or nucleus, the greater its stability, i.e. the less likely it is to undergo any change.

Binding energy (B.E.)

The energy input needed to split a given atom or nucleus into its constituent parts (see pages 82-83). The **potential energy*** of an atom or nucleus is less than the total potential energy of its parts when these are apart. This is because, when they came together, the parts found a lower (collective) **energy state** (see introduction and **nuclear force**), and so lost energy. The binding energy is a measure of this difference in potential energy – it is the energy needed to "go back the other way" – so the greater it is, the lower the potential energy of an atom or nucleus and the greater its stability. Binding energy varies from atom to atom and nucleus to nucleus.

Nuclear force

The strong force which holds the parts of a nucleus (**nucleons***) together and overcomes the **electric force*** of repulsion between the **protons***. Its effect varies according to the size of the nucleus (see graph, opposite) as the force only acts between immediately adjacent nucleons. The greater the attractive effect of the nuclear force, the higher the **binding energy** of the nucleus (i.e. the more energy was lost when the parts came together).

Quantum theory

States that energy takes the form of minute, separate pulses called **quanta** (sing. **quantum**), rather than a steady stream. The theory was originally limited to energy emitted by bodies (i.e. **electromagnetic wave*** energy), though all other kinds of energy (see pages 8-9) are now generally included. Electromagnetic quanta are now specified as **photons**. The theory further states that the amount of energy carried by a photon is proportional to the **frequency*** of the emitted electromagnetic radiation (see pages 44-45).

*Energy carried by **quantum** (**photon**):*

$$E = hf$$

*where E = energy in joules; h = **Planck's constant** (6.63×10^{-34} J s^{-1}); f = **frequency*** in Hertz.*

Electron volt** (**eV**). Unit of atomic energy, equal to energy gained by one electron moved through **potential difference of 1V.*

$$1eV = 1.6 \times 10^{-19} J$$

***Megaelectron volt** (**MeV**). Unit of nuclear energy, equal to 1 million eV.*

$$1MeV = 1.6 \times 10^{-13} J$$

Mass defect

The mass of an atom or nucleus is less than the sum of the masses of its parts when these are apart. The difference is the mass defect. It is the mass of the **potential energy*** lost when the parts came together (see **binding energy**, above, and formula, right).

*Einstein showed that energy has mass. Hence any loss of **potential energy*** also results in a loss of mass – the mass of the energy itself. **Einstein's mass-energy formula**:*

$$E = mc^2$$

where E = energy in joules; m = mass in kilograms; c = 3×10^8 (numerical value of speed of light in m s^{-1}).

* **Electric force**, 6; **Electromagnetic waves**, 44; **Frequency**, 35; **Nucleons**, 82 (**Nucleus**); **Potential difference**, 58; **Potential energy**, 8; **Protons**, 82.

Levels of nuclear stability

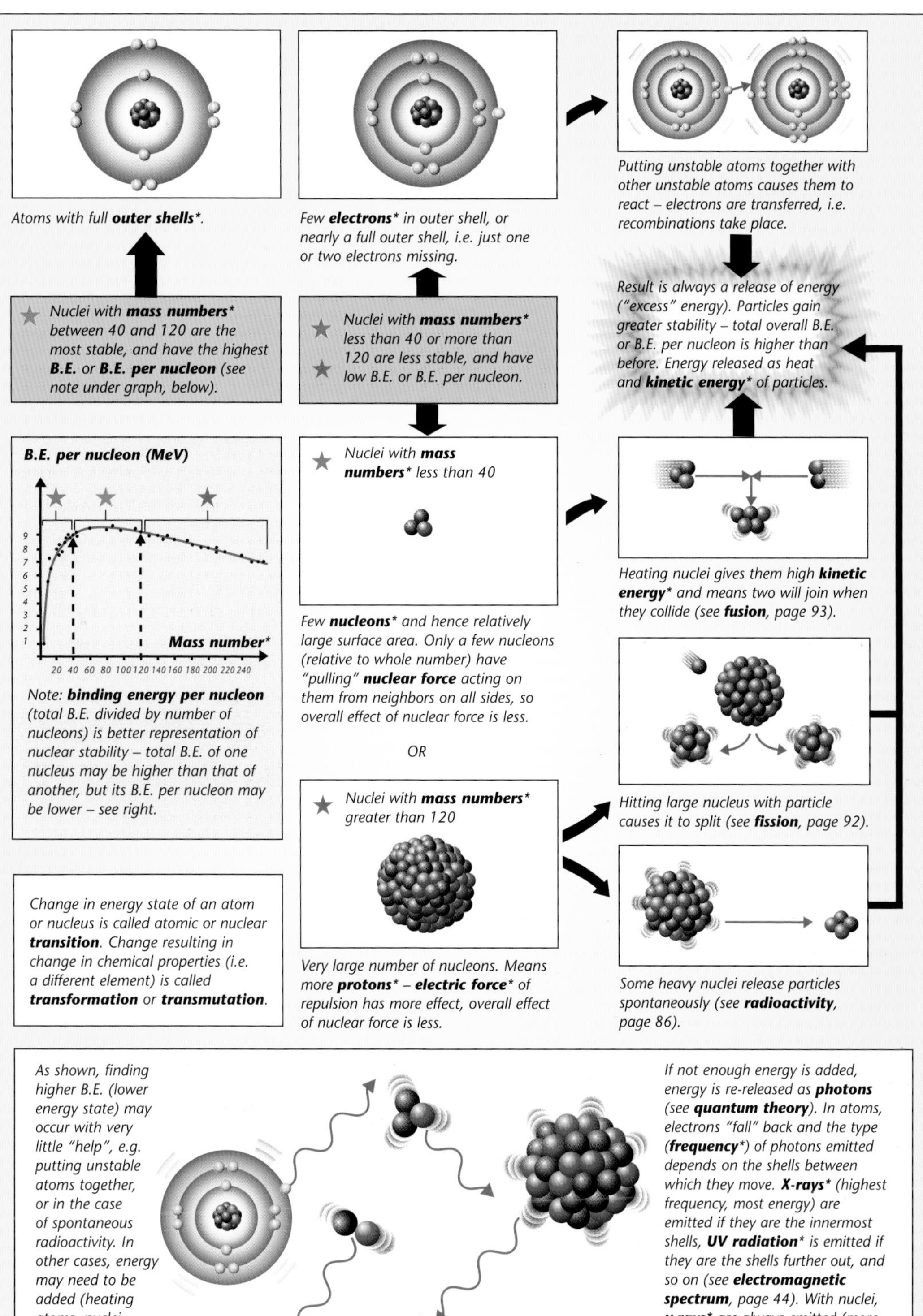
Atoms with full **outer shells***.
Few **electrons*** in outer shell, or nearly a full outer shell, i.e. just one or two electrons missing.
Putting unstable atoms together with other unstable atoms causes them to react – electrons are transferred, i.e. recombinations take place.
Result is always a release of energy ("excess" energy). Particles gain greater stability – total overall B.E. or B.E. per nucleon is higher than before. Energy released as heat and **kinetic energy*** of particles.
Nuclei with **mass numbers*** between 40 and 120 are the most stable, and have the highest **B.E.** or **B.E. per nucleon** (see note under graph, below).
Nuclei with **mass numbers*** less than 40 or more than 120 are less stable, and have low B.E. or B.E. per nucleon.
B.E. per nucleon (MeV)
9
8
7
6
5
4
3
2
1
Mass number*
20 40 60 80 100 120 140 160 180 200 220 240
Note: **binding energy per nucleon** (total B.E. divided by number of nucleons) is better representation of nuclear stability – total B.E. of one nucleus may be higher than that of another, but its B.E. per nucleon may be lower – see right.
Nuclei with **mass numbers*** less than 40
Few **nucleons*** and hence relatively large surface area. Only a few nucleons (relative to whole number) have "pulling" **nuclear force** acting on them from neighbors on all sides, so overall effect of nuclear force is less.
OR
Nuclei with **mass numbers*** greater than 120
Very large number of nucleons. Means more **protons*** – **electric force*** of repulsion has more effect, overall effect of nuclear force is less.
Heating nuclei gives them high **kinetic energy*** and means two will join when they collide (see **fusion**, page 93).
Hitting large nucleus with particle causes it to split (see **fission**, page 92).
Some heavy nuclei release particles spontaneously (see **radioactivity**, page 86).
Change in energy state of an atom or nucleus is called atomic or nuclear **transition**. Change resulting in change in chemical properties (i.e. a different element) is called **transformation** or **transmutation**.
As shown, finding higher B.E. (lower energy state) may occur with very little "help", e.g. putting unstable atoms together, or in the case of spontaneous radioactivity. In other cases, energy may need to be added (heating atoms, nuclei or particles).
If not enough energy is added, energy is re-released as **photons** (see **quantum theory**). In atoms, electrons "fall" back and the type (**frequency***) of photons emitted depends on the shells between which they move. **X-rays*** (highest frequency, most energy) are emitted if they are the innermost shells, **UV radiation*** is emitted if they are the shells further out, and so on (see **electromagnetic spectrum**, page 44). With nuclei, **γ-rays*** are always emitted (more energy is involved).

* **Electric force**, 6; **Electrons**, 83; **Frequency**, 35; **Kinetic energy**, 9; **Mass number**, 82; **Nucleons**, 82 (**Nucleus**); **Outer shell**, 83 (**Electron shells**); **Protons**, 82; **Ultraviolet** (**UV**) **radiation**, **X-rays**, 44; **Gamma** (γ) **rays**, 44, 86.

RADIOACTIVITY

Radioactivity is a property of some unstable **nuclei** (see pages 82 and 84), whereby they break up spontaneously into nuclei of other elements and emit **radiation***, a process known as **radioactive decay**. There are three types of radiation emitted by radioactive elements: streams of **alpha particles** (called **alpha rays**); streams of **beta particles** (**beta rays**) and **gamma rays**. For more about the detection and uses of radiation, see pages 88-91.

Radioisotope or radioactive isotope

Any radioactive substance (all substances are effectively isotopes – see page 83). There are several naturally-occurring radioisotopes, most of which still exist because they have very long **half-lives** (e.g. uranium-238), though one, carbon-14, is continually produced by **cosmic rays** (see **background radiation**, page 88). Other radioisotopes are produced by **nuclear fission***, and more still are produced in research centers, where nuclei are hit by fast particles (e.g. **protons*** and **neutrons***). These are speeded up in **particle accelerators**, e.g. **cyclotrons** (see picture below).

Cut-away diagram of vacuum chamber (central part of cyclotron)

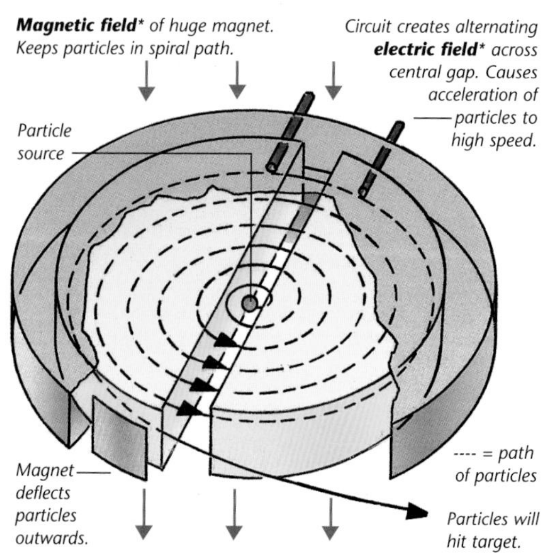
*Magnetic field** of huge magnet. Keeps particles in spiral path.*
*Circuit creates alternating **electric field*** across central gap. Causes acceleration of particles to high speed.*
Particle source
Magnet deflects particles outwards.
---- = path of particles
Particles will hit target.

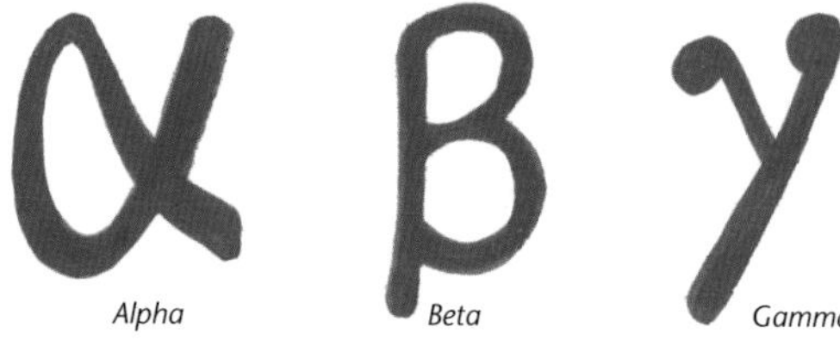
Alpha
Beta
Gamma

The Greek letters used for the three types of radiation*

Alpha particles (α-particles)

Positively-charged particles ejected from some radioactive nuclei (see **alpha decay**). They are relatively heavy (two **protons*** and two **neutrons***), move relatively slowly and have a low penetrating power.

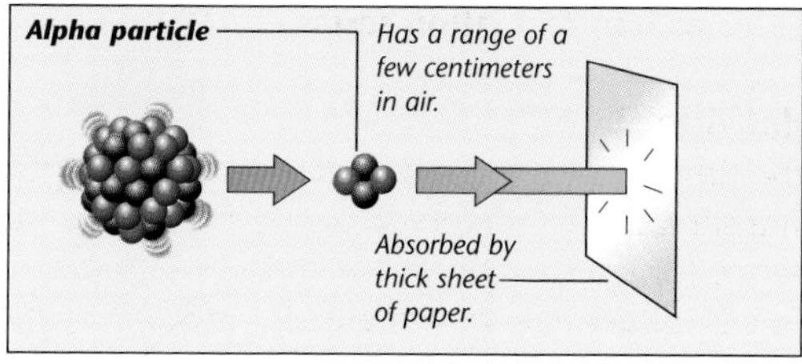
Alpha particle
Has a range of a few centimeters in air.
Absorbed by thick sheet of paper.

Beta particles (β-particles)

Particles ejected from some radioactive nuclei at about the speed of light. There are two types – **electrons*** and **positrons**, which have the same mass as electrons, but a positive charge. See **beta decay**, page 87.

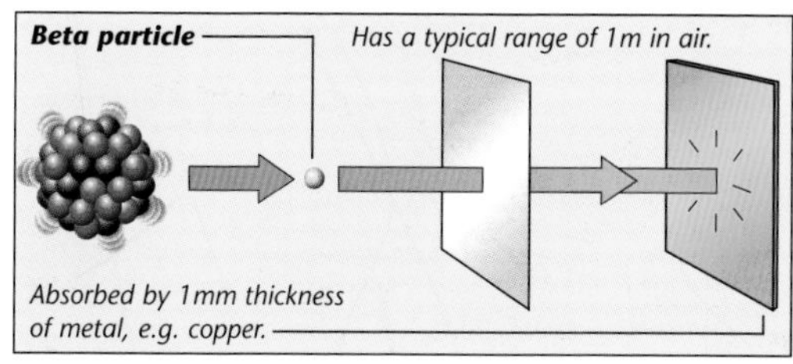
Beta particle
Has a typical range of 1m in air.
Absorbed by 1mm thickness of metal, e.g. copper.

Gamma rays (γ-rays)

Invisible **electromagnetic waves** (see also page 44). They have the highest penetrating power and are generally, though not always, emitted from a radioactive nucleus after an **alpha** or **beta particle**.

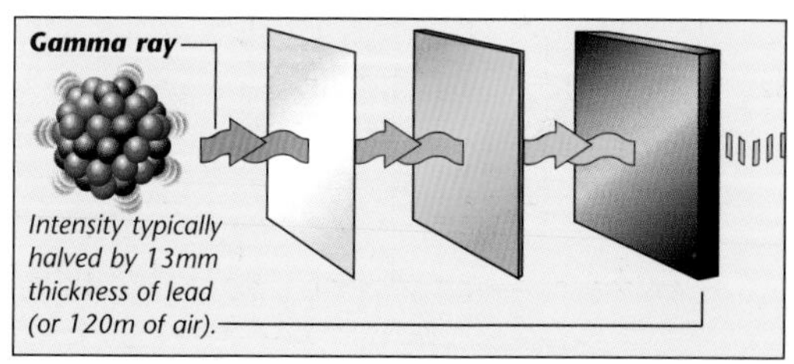
Gamma ray
Intensity typically halved by 13mm thickness of lead (or 120m of air).

* **Electric field**, 58; **Electrons**, 83; **Magnetic field**, 72; **Neutrons**, 82; **Nuclear fission**, 92; **Protons**, 82; **Radiation**, 9.

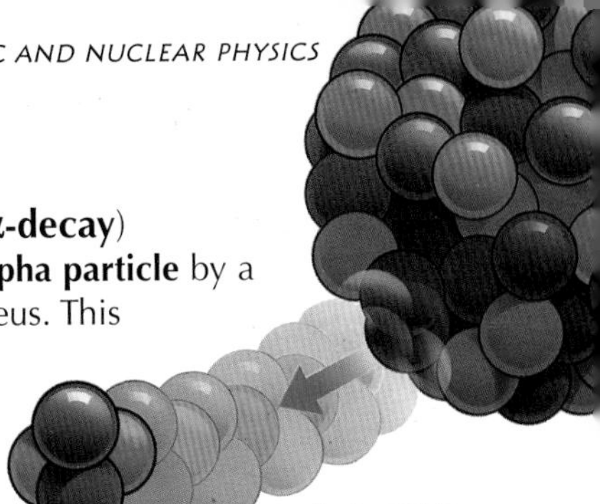

Radioactive decay

The spontaneous splitting up of a radioactive nucleus, which results in the ejection of **alpha** or **beta particles**, often followed by **gamma rays**. When a nucleus ejects such a particle, i.e. undergoes a nuclear **disintegration**, energy is released (see page 84), and a different nucleus (and atom) is formed. If this is also radioactive, the decay process continues until a stable (non-radioactive) atom is reached. Such a series of disintegrations is called a **decay series, decay chain, radioactive series** or **transformation series**.

Half-life (T½)

The time it takes for half the atoms on average in a sample to undergo **radioactive decay**, and hence for the radiation emitted to be halved. This is all that can be accurately predicted – it is impossible to predict the decay of any single atom, since they decay individually and randomly. The range of half-lives is vast, e.g. the half-life of strontium-90 is 28 years; that of uranium-238 is 4.5×10^9 years.

Alpha decay (α-decay)

The loss of an **alpha particle** by a radioactive nucleus. This decreases the **atomic number*** by two and the **mass number*** by four, and so a new nucleus is formed.

*An **α-particle** is identical to the nucleus of a helium atom.*

Beta decay (β-decay)

The loss of either kind of **beta particle** by a radioactive nucleus. The electron (**β⁻** or **e⁻**) is ejected (with another particle called an **antineutrino**) when a **neutron*** decays into a **proton***. The positron (**β⁺** or **e⁺**) is ejected (with another particle called a **neutrino**) when a proton decays into a neutron. Beta decay thus increases or decreases the **atomic number*** by one (the **mass number*** stays the same).

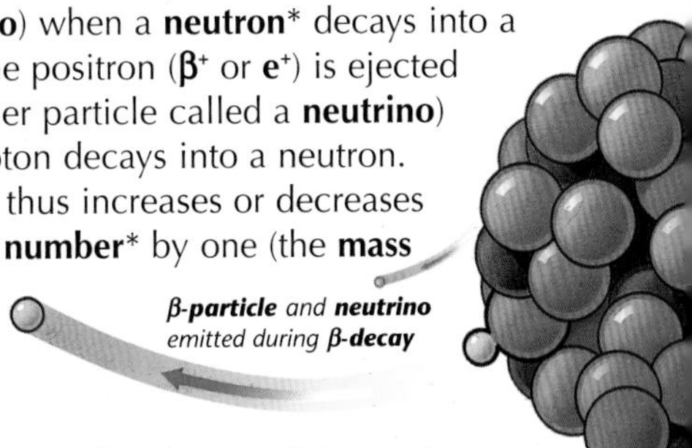

β-particle** and **neutrino** emitted during **β-decay

*The rate of **radioactive decay** is measured in **becquerels** (**Bq**). One becquerel equals one **disintegration** per second. An older unit, the **curie**, equals 3.7×10^{10} becquerels.*

Decay series, showing radioactive decay of thorium-232 to stable lead-208

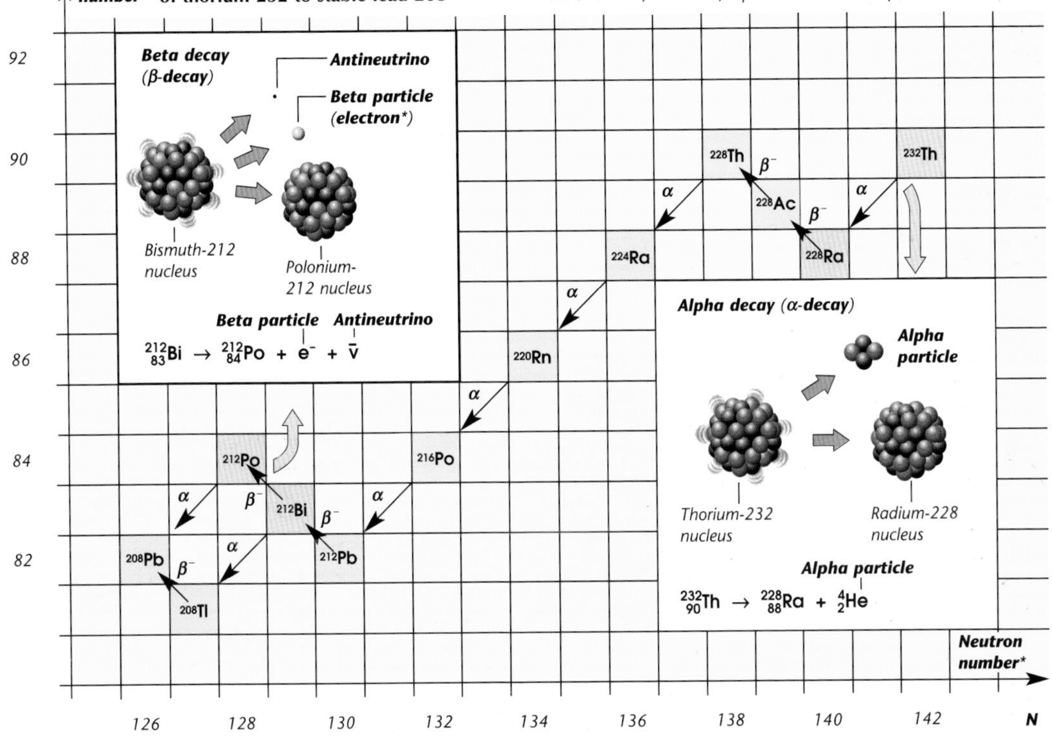

Z Atomic number*; N Neutron number*

Beta decay (β-decay)

Antineutrino; Beta particle (electron*); Bismuth-212 nucleus; Polonium-212 nucleus

$$^{212}_{83}\text{Bi} \rightarrow {}^{212}_{84}\text{Po} + e^- + \bar{\nu}$$

(Beta particle; Antineutrino)

Alpha decay (α-decay)

Alpha particle; Thorium-232 nucleus; Radium-228 nucleus

$$^{232}_{90}\text{Th} \rightarrow {}^{228}_{88}\text{Ra} + {}^{4}_{2}\text{He}$$

(Alpha particle)

* **Atomic number**, 82; **Electrons**, 83; **Mass number**, **Neutron number**, **Neutrons**, **Protons**, 82.

DETECTING AND MEASURING RADIOACTIVITY

There are a number of devices which detect and measure the radiation emitted by radioactive substances (**radioisotopes***). Some are used mainly in laboratories (to study artificially produced radioisotopes); others have a wider range of uses (e.g. as monitoring devices for safety purposes) and can also be used to detect **background radiation**. Most of the devices detect and measure the radiation by monitoring the **ionization** it causes – see **Geiger counter** and **pulse electroscope**, right, and **cloud** and **bubble chambers**, page 90.

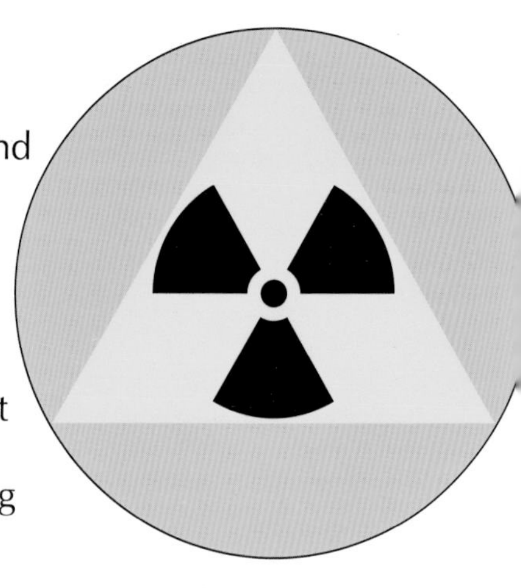

*Radioactive substances (**radioisotopes***) have special hazard warning labels.*

Background radiation

Radiation present on Earth (in relatively small amounts), originating both from natural and unnatural sources. One notable natural source is carbon-14, which is taken in by plants and animals. This is constantly being produced from stable nitrogen-14 due to bombardment by **cosmic rays** (**cosmic radiation**) entering the atmosphere from outer space. These are streams of particles of enormously high energy. Unnatural sources of radiation include industry, medicine and weapons testing. The **background count** is a measure of the background radiation.

Plants, rocks and animals contain carbon-14, a natural source of radiation.

*A **Geiger counter**, used for measuring the **background count**.*

Ionization

The creation of **ions** (electrically-charged particles), which occurs when atoms (which are electrically neutral) lose or gain **electrons***, creating **cations** (positive ions) or **anions** (negative ions) respectively.

Ionization

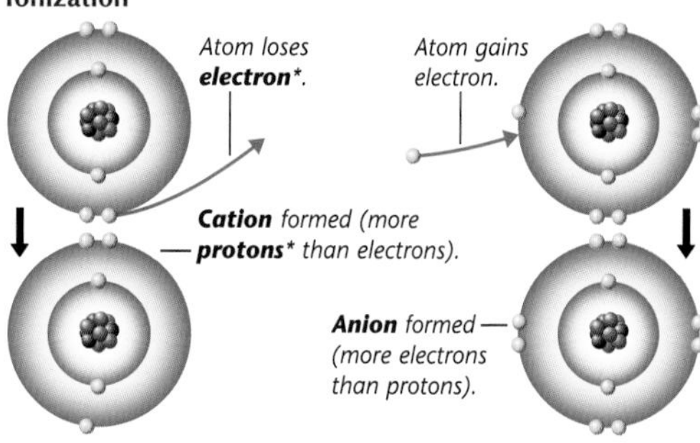
Atom loses electron*.
Atom gains electron.
Cation formed (more protons* than electrons).
Anion formed (more electrons than protons).

In the case of radiation, **alpha** and **beta particles*** ionize the atoms of substances they pass through, usually creating cations. This is because their energy is so high that they cause one or more electrons to be "knocked out" of the atoms. **Gamma rays*** can also ionize atoms.

Ionization due to radiation

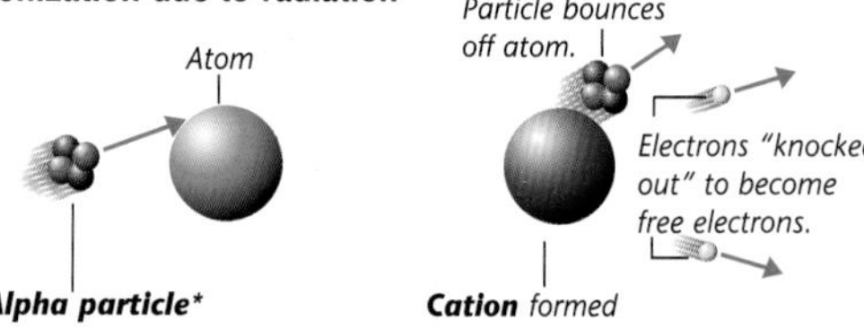
Particle bounces off atom.
Atom
Electrons "knocked out" to become free electrons.
Alpha particle*
Cation formed

* **Alpha particles**, **Beta particles**, 86; **Electrons**, 83; **Gamma rays**, 86; **Protons**, 82; **Radioisotope**, 86.

Detection devices

Dosimeter or film badge

A device worn by all who work with radioactive material. It contains photographic film (which radiation will darken). This is developed regularly and the amount of darkening shows the **dose** of radiation the wearer has been exposed to.

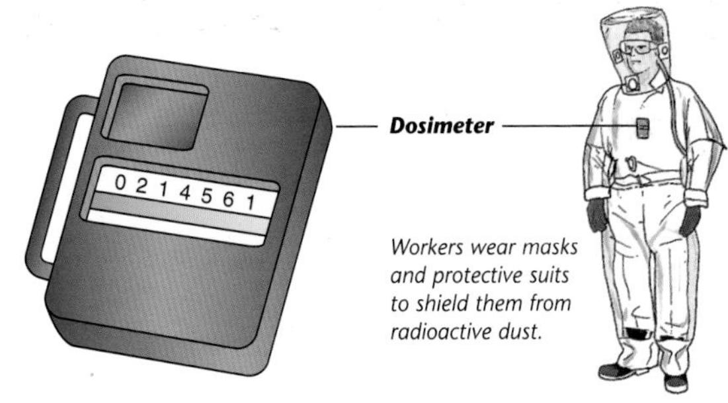
0 2 1 4 5 6 1
Dosimeter
Workers wear masks and protective suits to shield them from radioactive dust.

Geiger counter

A piece of apparatus (see picture, page 88) consisting of a **Geiger-Müller tube**, a **scaler** and/or **ratemeter** and often a loudspeaker. The tube is a gas-filled cylinder with two **electrodes*** – its walls act as the **cathode***, and it has a central wire **anode***. The whole apparatus indicates the presence of radiation by registering pulses of current between the electrodes. These pulses result from the **ionization** the radiation causes in the gas (normally low pressure argon, plus a trace of bromine). A scaler is an electronic counter which counts the pulses and a ratemeter measures the count rate – the average rate of pulses in counts per second.

Geiger counter

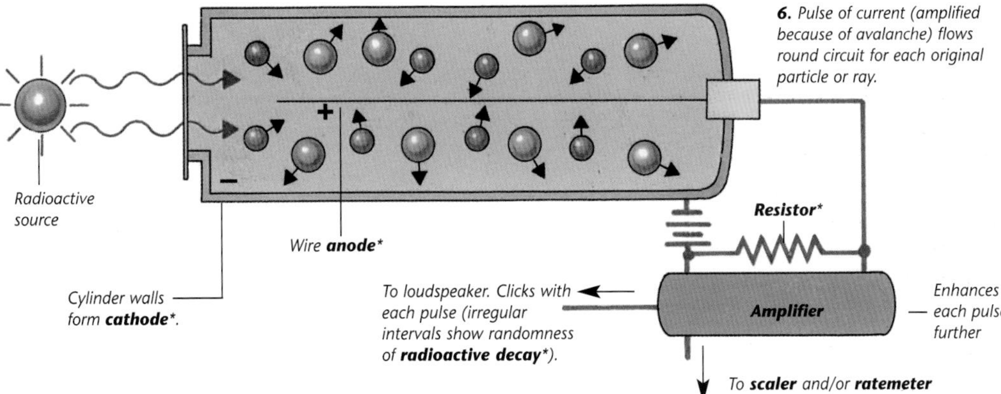
1. Radiation enters via thin window.
2. Each particle or ray ionizes several gas atoms.
3. Ions attracted to cathode, electrons* to anode.
4. Other atoms are hit on the way, creating avalanche of more ions and electrons.
5. Electrons taken in at anode and "pulled" from cathode (to turn ions back into atoms).
6. Pulse of current (amplified because of avalanche) flows round circuit for each original particle or ray.
+
–
Radioactive source
Wire anode*
Cylinder walls form cathode*.
Resistor*
To loudspeaker. Clicks with each pulse (irregular intervals show randomness of radioactive decay*).
Amplifier
Enhances each pulse further
To scaler and/or ratemeter

Pulse (Wulf) electroscope

A type of **gold-leaf electroscope***. The walls of a chamber of air around the cap form the **cathode***, and a side **anode*** is placed close to the leaf. This attracts **electrons*** down from the cap, leaving it positively charged (the leaf moves away from the rod, as they are both negatively charged, but not enough to touch the anode before the radioactive source is introduced). The leaf indicates the presence of radiation by beating forward and back for each **ionization** it causes.

Pulse (Wulf) electroscope

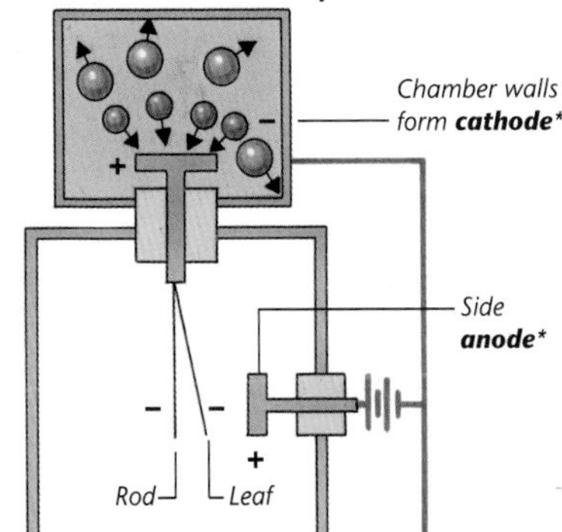
Chamber walls form cathode*.
Side anode*
Rod
Leaf
+
–

1. Radiation from radioactive source **ionizes** air in chamber.

2. **Avalanche** of ions and **electrons*** formed (see **Geiger counter**).

3. Ions move to cathode, electrons enter cap and are pulled down leaf by anode.

4. Leaf moves over to touch anode and pulse of current flows (see **Geiger counter**).

5. Leaf becomes neutral and moves back to rod, aided by spring. Process starts again.

* **Anode**, **Cathode**, 66 (**Electrode**); **Electrons**, 83;
Gold-leaf electroscope, 56 (**Electroscope**); **Radioactive decay**, 87; **Resistor**, 62.

Detection devices (continued)

Cloud chamber

A device in which the paths taken by **alpha** and **beta particles*** show up as tracks. This happens when the vapor in the chamber (alcohol or water vapor) is turned into **supersaturated** vapor by cooling (in one of two different ways – see below). A supersaturated vapor is vapor below the temperature at which it should condense, but which does not condense because there are no dust or other particles present for droplets to form around.

Wilson cloud chamber
Vapor cooled by sudden increase in volume (withdrawal of piston).

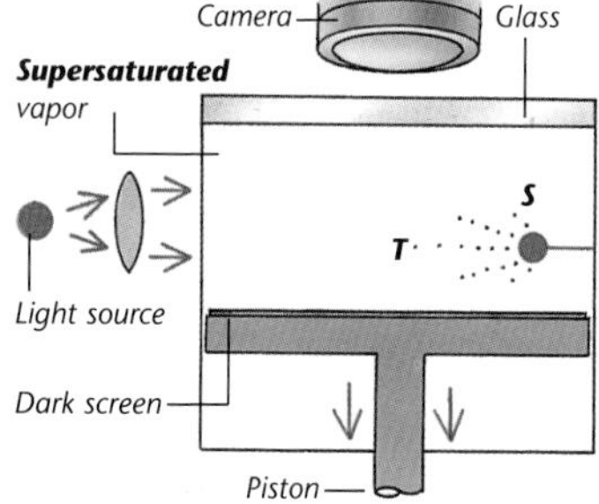

Camera
Glass
Supersaturated vapor
S
T
Light source
Dark screen
Piston

*1. Radiation from source (**S**) causes **ionization*** of vapor.*

2. Ions formed act like dust particles, i.e. vapor condenses on them.

*3. Tracks of liquid droplets (**T**) left where vapor has condensed (visible long enough to be photographed).*

Diffusion cloud chamber
*Vapor cooled by a base of dry ice (solid carbon dioxide). Vapor **diffuses*** downwards.*

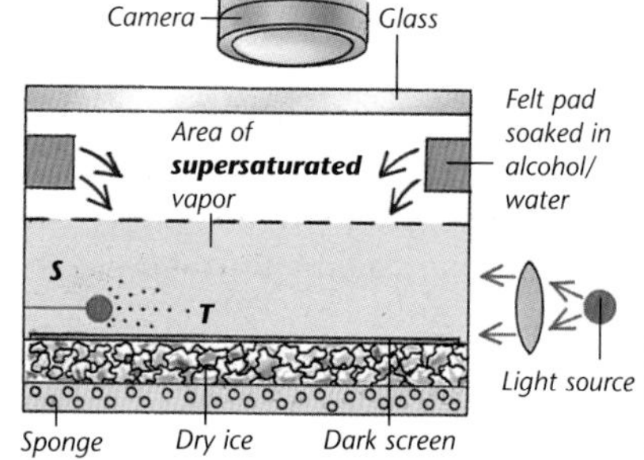

Camera
Glass
Area of supersaturated vapor
Felt pad soaked in alcohol/ water
S
T
Light source
Sponge
Dry ice
Dark screen

Cloud chamber** tracks (right) are produced at irregular intervals, showing random nature of **radioactive decay.*

*Tracks made by heavy α-**particles*** are short, straight and thick.*

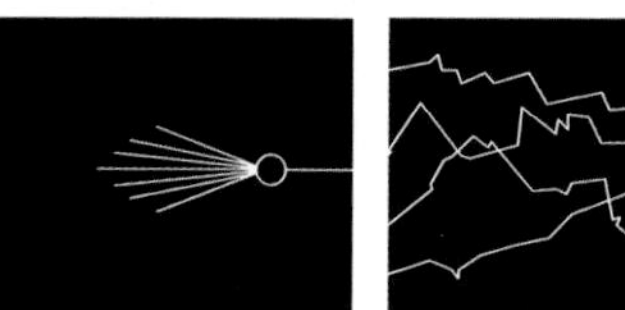

*Tracks made by light β-**particles*** are long, straggly and thin.*

Gamma rays do not create tracks themselves, but can knock **electrons*** out of single atoms. These then speed away and create tracks like β-particle tracks (see left).*

Bubble chamber

A device which, like a cloud chamber, shows particle tracks. It contains **superheated** liquid (usually hydrogen or helium) – liquid heated to above its boiling point, but not actually boiling because it is under pressure. After the pressure is suddenly lowered, nuclear particles entering the chamber cause **ionization*** of the liquid atoms. Wherever this occurs, the energy released makes the liquid boil, producing tracks of bubbles.

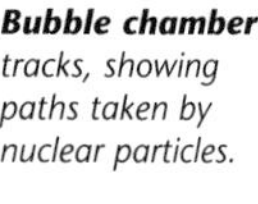

***Bubble chamber** tracks, showing paths taken by nuclear particles.*

Bubble tracks are generally curved, because a magnetic field is set up to deflect particles. (This leads to better identification.)

Scintillation counter

A device which detects **gamma rays***. It consists of a **scintillation crystal** and a **photomultiplier** tube. The crystal is made of a **phosphor*** (e.g. sodium iodide). Phosphors emit light flashes (**scintillations**) when hit by radiation.

Scintillation counter

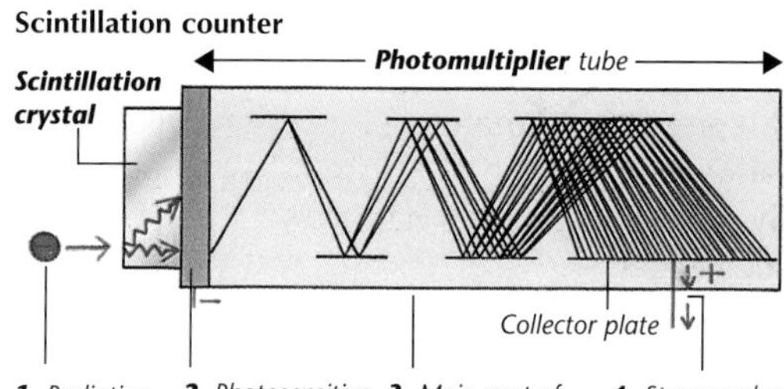

Photomultiplier tube
Scintillation crystal
Collector plate

1. Radiation from source makes crystal emit light

*2. Photosensitive material with negative charge. Emits **electrons*** when hit by light flashes.*

*3. Main part of tube (**electron multiplier**). Electrons accelerated to far end by electric field, hitting metal plates and releasing more electrons.*

*4. Strong pulse of current hence produced for each original **gamma ray***. This is shown on **scaler** and/or **ratemeter** (see **Geiger counter**, page 89).*

* **Alpha particles**, **Beta particles**, 86; **Diffusion**, 5; **Electrons**, 83; **Gamma rays**, 86; **Ionization**, 88; **Phosphors**, 44 (**Phosphorescence**); **Radioactive decay**, 87.

USES OF RADIOACTIVITY

The radiation emitted by **radioisotopes*** (radioactive substances) can be put to a wide variety of uses, particularly in the fields of medicine, industry and archaeological research.

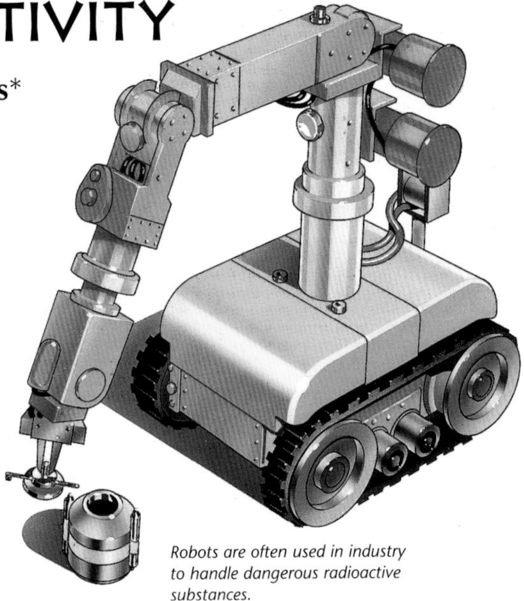

Robots are often used in industry to handle dangerous radioactive substances.

Radiology

The study of radioactivity and **X-rays***, especially with regard to their use in medicine.

Radiotherapy

The use of the radiation emitted by **radioisotopes*** to treat disease. All living cells are susceptible to radiation, so it is possible to destroy malignant (cancer) cells by using carefully controlled doses of radiation.

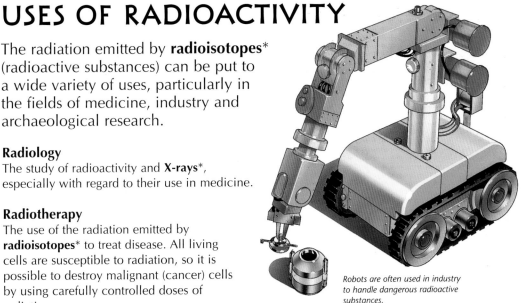

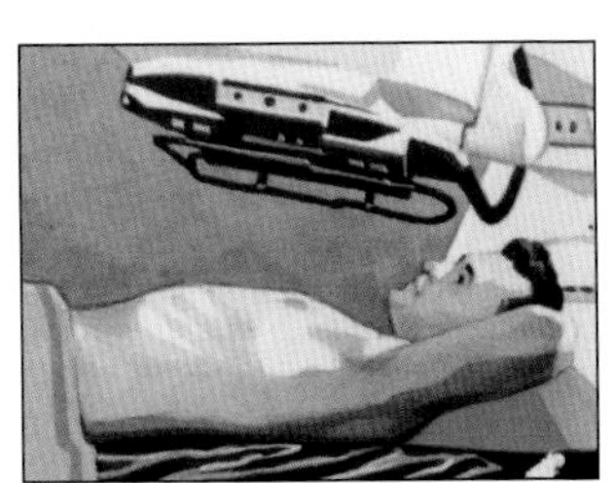

*This patient is undergoing **external beam radiotherapy**, where the radiation is emitted from a machine outside the body. Some types of cancer can be treated by **radioactive implants** inserted into the body.*

Radioactive tracing

A method of following the path of a substance through an object, and detecting its concentration as it moves. This is done by introducing a **radioisotope*** into the substance and tracking the radiation it emits. The radioisotope used is called a **tracer**, and the substance is said to be **labeled**. In medical diagnosis, for example, high levels of the radioisotope in an organ may indicate the presence of malignant (cancer) cells. The radioisotopes used always have short **half-lives*** and decay into harmless substances.

Irradiation

Food, such as fruit and meat can be **irradiated** with **gamma rays***. The radiation delays ripening in fruit and vegetables, and destroys bacteria in meat, enabling it to keep fresh for longer.

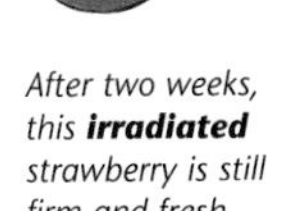

*After two weeks, this **irradiated** strawberry is still firm and fresh.*

Gamma radiography (γ-radiography)

The production of a **radiograph** (similar to a photograph) by the use of **gamma rays*** (see also **X-radiography**, page 44). This has many uses, including quality control in industry.

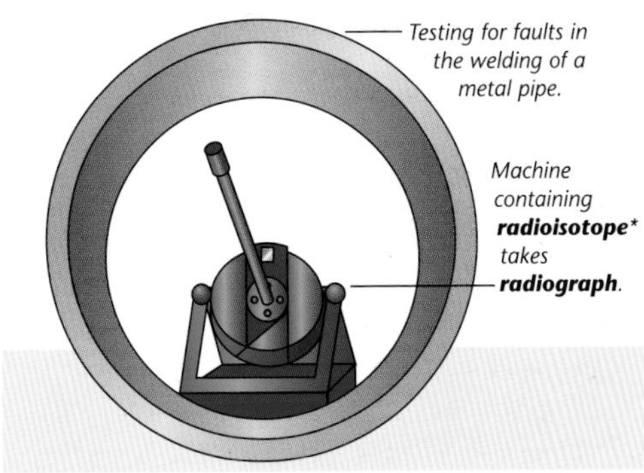
Testing for faults in the welding of a metal pipe.
Machine containing ***radioisotope**** takes ***radiograph***.

Radiocarbon dating or carbon dating

A way of calculating the time elapsed since living matter died. All living things contain a small amount of carbon-14 (a **radioisotope*** absorbed from the atmosphere), which continues to emit radiation after death. This emission gradually decreases (carbon-14 has a **half-life*** of 5,700 years), so the age of the remains can be calculated from its strength.

__Radiocarbon dating__ showed that this insect trapped in amber is 5,000 years old.

* **Gamma rays**, 86; **Half-life**, 87; **Radioisotope**, 86; **X-rays**, 44.

NUCLEAR FISSION AND FUSION

The central **nucleus** of an atom (see page 82) holds vast amounts of "stored" energy (see pages 84-85). **Nuclear fission** and **nuclear fusion** are both ways in which this energy can be released. They are both **nuclear reactions** (reactions which bring about a change in the nucleus).

Mushroom-shaped cloud from the explosion of a ***fission bomb***.

Nuclear fission

The process in which a heavy, unstable nucleus splits into two (or more) lighter nuclei, roughly equal in size, with the release of two or three **neutrons*** (**fission neutrons**) and a large amount of energy (see also page 84). The two lighter nuclei are called **fission products** or **fission fragments** and many of them are **radioactive***. Fission is made to happen (see **induced fission**) in **fission reactors*** to produce heat energy. It does not often occur naturally (**spontaneous fission**).

Induced fission of uranium-235

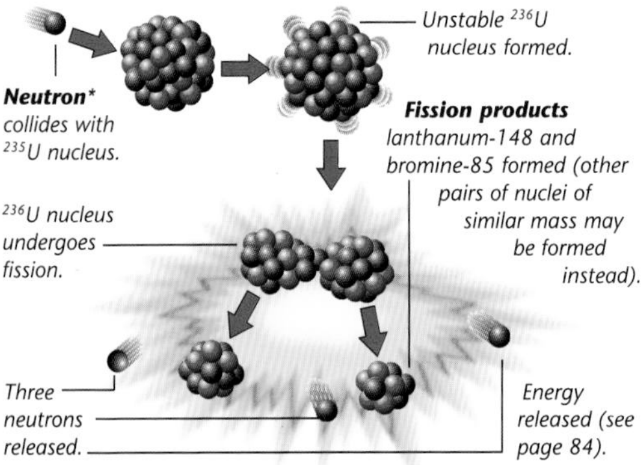
Unstable ^{236}U nucleus formed.
Neutron* collides with ^{235}U nucleus.
Fission products lanthanum-148 and bromine-85 formed (other pairs of nuclei of similar mass may be formed instead).
^{236}U nucleus undergoes fission.
Three neutrons released.
Energy released (see page 84).

Nuclear equation *for reaction, above (see* ***mass*** *and* ***atomic numbers****, page 82):*

$$^{235}_{92}U + ^{1}_{0}n \rightarrow ^{236}_{92}U \rightarrow ^{148}_{57}La + ^{85}_{35}Br + 3^{1}_{0}n + \text{energy}$$

Spontaneous fission

Nuclear fission which occurs naturally, i.e. without assistance from an outside agency. This may happen to a nucleus of a heavy element, e.g. the **isotope*** uranium-238, but the probability is very low compared to that of a simpler process like **alpha decay*** occurring instead.

Induced fission

Nuclear fission of a nucleus made unstable by artificial means, i.e. by being hit by a particle (often a **neutron***), which it then absorbs. Not all nuclei can be induced to fission in this way; those which can, e.g. those of the **isotopes*** uranium-235 and plutonium-239, are described as **fissile**. If there are lots of fissile nuclei in a substance (see also **thermal** and **fast reactor**, page 95), the neutrons released by induced fissions will cause more fissions (and neutrons), and so on. This is known as a **chain reaction**. A well-controlled chain reaction is allowed to occur in a **fission reactor***, but that occurring in a **fission bomb** is uncontrolled and extremely explosive.

Induced fission causing a chain reaction

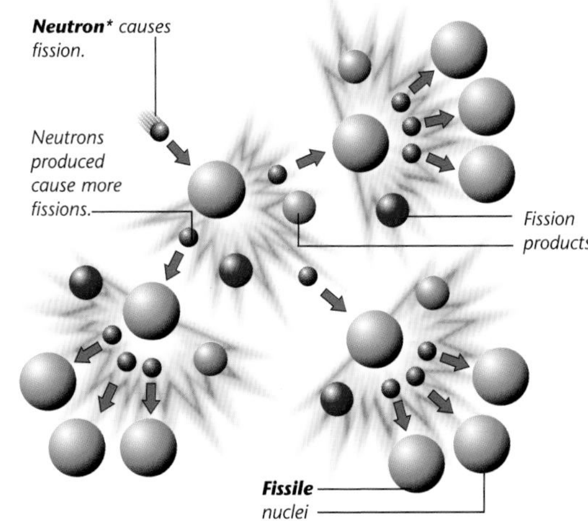
Neutron* causes fission.
Neutrons produced cause more fissions.
Fission products
Fissile nuclei

* **Alpha decay**, 87; **Fission reactor**, 94; **Isotopes**, 83; **Neutrons**, 82; **Radioactivity**, 86.

Critical mass

The minimum mass of a **fissile** substance needed to sustain a **chain reaction** (see **induced fission**). In smaller **subcritical masses**, the surface area to volume ratio is too high, and too many of the **neutrons*** produced by the first fissions escape into the atmosphere. Nuclear fuel is kept in subcritical masses.

Fission bomb or atom bomb (A-bomb)

A bomb in which two **subcritical masses** (see above) are brought together by a trigger explosion. The resulting **chain reaction** (see **induced fission**) releases huge amounts of energy.

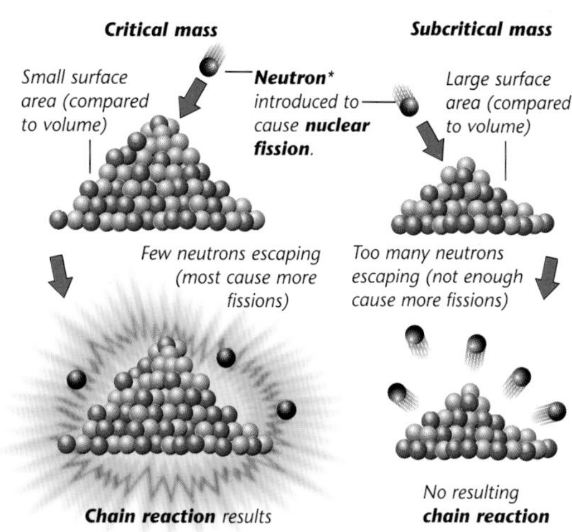
Critical mass
Subcritical mass
Small surface area (compared to volume)
Neutron* introduced to cause nuclear fission.
Large surface area (compared to volume)
Few neutrons escaping (most cause more fissions)
Too many neutrons escaping (not enough cause more fissions)
Chain reaction results
No resulting chain reaction

Nuclear fusion

The collision and combination of two light nuclei to form a heavier, more stable nucleus, with the release of large amounts of energy (see also page 84). Unlike **nuclear fission**, it does not leave **radioactive*** products. Nuclear fusion requires temperatures of millions of degrees Celsius, to give the nuclei enough **kinetic energy*** for them to fuse when they collide. (Because of the high temperatures, fusion reactions are also called **thermonuclear reactions**.) It therefore only occurs naturally in the Sun (and stars like it), but research is being carried out with the aim of achieving controlled, induced fusion in **fusion reactors***.

Example of nuclear fusion
(***D-T reaction*** – *see also* ***fusion reactor****, page 94.)*

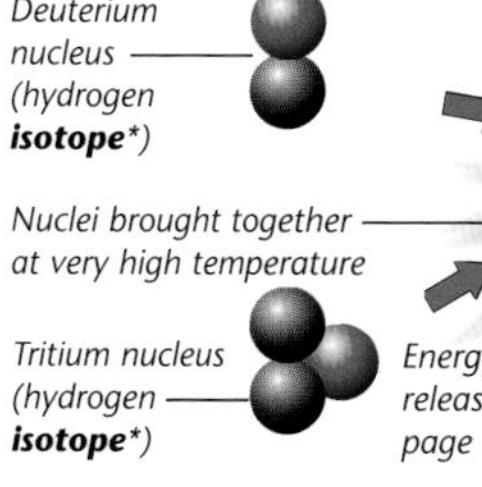
Deuterium nucleus (hydrogen isotope*)
Nuclei brought together at very high temperature
Tritium nucleus (hydrogen isotope*)
Energy released (see page 84).
Fusion produces helium nucleus.
Single neutron* released.

Nuclear equation *for reaction above (see* ***mass and atomic numbers****, page 82):*

$$ {}^{2}_{1}\mathrm{H} + {}^{3}_{1}\mathrm{H} \rightarrow {}^{4}_{2}\mathrm{He} + {}^{1}_{0}\mathrm{n} + \text{energy} $$

Fusion bomb or hydrogen bomb (H-bomb)

A bomb in which uncontrolled **nuclear fusion** occurs in a mixture of tritium and deuterium (hydrogen **isotopes***). A trigger **fission bomb** creates the high temperature needed (fusion bombs are also called **fission-fusion bombs**). The energy released is about 30 times that released from a fission bomb of the same size.

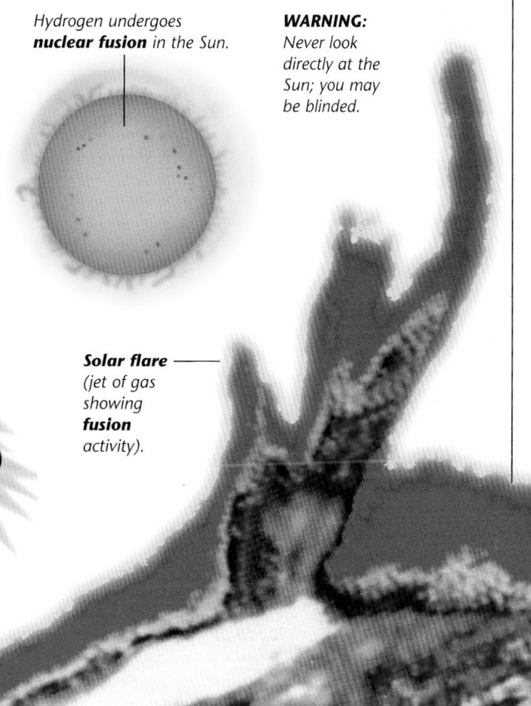
Hydrogen undergoes nuclear fusion in the Sun.
WARNING: Never look directly at the Sun; you may be blinded.
Solar flare (jet of gas showing fusion activity).

* **Fusion reactor**, 94; **Isotopes**, 83; **Kinetic energy**, 9; **Neutrons**, 82; **Radioactivity**, 86.

POWER FROM NUCLEAR REACTIONS

A **nuclear reactor** is a structure inside which nuclear reactions produce vast amounts of heat. There are potentially two main types of reactor – **fission reactors** and **fusion reactors**, though the latter are still being researched. All present-day **nuclear power stations** are built around a central fission reactor and each generates, per unit mass of fuel, far larger amounts of power (electricity) than any other type of power station.

Fission reactor

A **nuclear reactor** in which the heat is produced by **nuclear fission***. There are two main types in use in nuclear power stations – **thermal reactors** and **fast reactors** or **fast breeder reactors** (see page opposite), both of which use uranium as their main fuel.

The uranium is held in long cylinders packed in the **core** (center of the reactor). The rate of the **chain reaction*** (and hence the rate of power production) is closely controlled by **control rods**. The diagram below shows how a fission reactor can be used to generate power.

Schematic diagram of fission reactor and power station complex

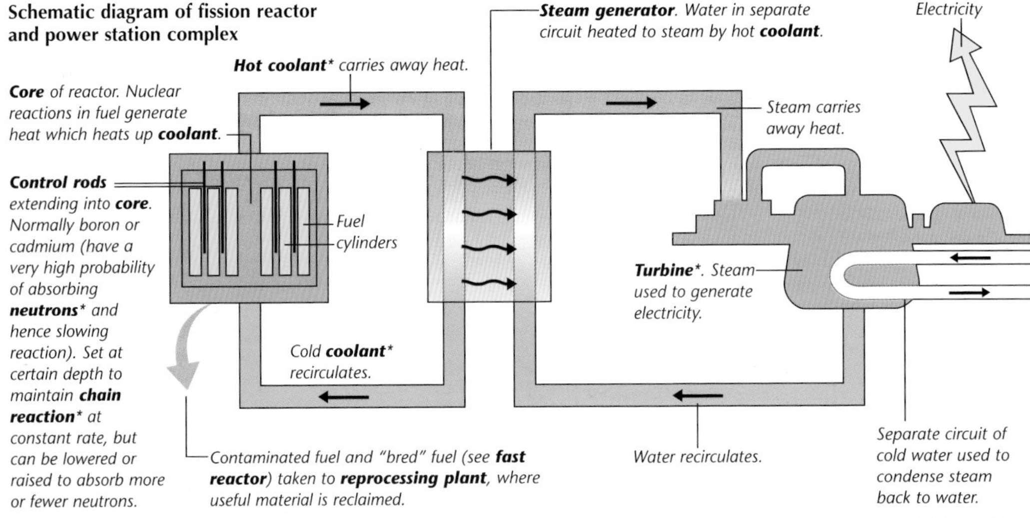

Hot coolant* carries away heat.
Core of reactor. Nuclear reactions in fuel generate heat which heats up **coolant**.
Control rods extending into **core**. Normally boron or cadmium (have a very high probability of absorbing **neutrons*** and hence slowing reaction). Set at certain depth to maintain **chain reaction*** at constant rate, but can be lowered or raised to absorb more or fewer neutrons.
Fuel cylinders
Cold **coolant*** recirculates.
Contaminated fuel and "bred" fuel (see **fast reactor**) taken to **reprocessing plant**, where useful material is reclaimed.
Steam generator. Water in separate circuit heated to steam by hot **coolant**.
Electricity
Steam carries away heat.
Turbine*. Steam used to generate electricity.
Water recirculates.
Separate circuit of cold water used to condense steam back to water.

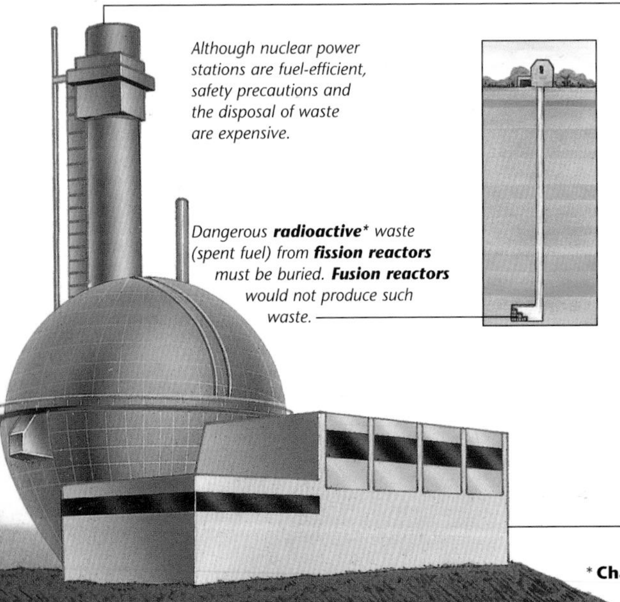

Although nuclear power stations are fuel-efficient, safety precautions and the disposal of waste are expensive.
Dangerous **radioactive*** waste (spent fuel) from **fission reactors** must be buried. **Fusion reactors** would not produce such waste.

Fusion reactor

A type of **nuclear reactor**, being researched but as yet undeveloped, in which the heat would be produced by **nuclear fusion***. This would probably be the fusion of the nuclei of the hydrogen **isotopes*** deuterium and tritium – known as the **D-T reaction** (see picture, page 93). There are several major problems to be overcome before a fusion reactor becomes a reality, but it would produce about four times as much energy per unit mass of fuel as a **fission reactor**. Also, hydrogen is abundant, whereas uranium is scarce, and dangerous and expensive to mine.

* **Chain reaction**, 92 (**Induced fission**); **Coolant**, 115; **Isotopes**, 83; **Neutrons**, 82; **Nuclear fission**, 92; **Nuclear fusion**, 93; **Radioactivity**, 86; **Turbine**, 115.

Types of fission reactor

Thermal reactor

A **fission reactor** containing a **moderator** around the fuel cylinders. This is a substance with light nuclei, such as graphite or water. It is used to slow down the fast **neutrons*** produced by the first fissions in the uranium fuel – the neutrons bounce off the light nuclei (which themselves are unlikely to absorb neutrons) and eventually slow down to about 2,200m s^{-1}. Slowing the neutrons improves their chances of causing further fissions (and continuing the **chain reaction***). Faster neutrons are likely to be "captured" by the most abundant nuclei – those of the **isotope*** uranium-238 (see **fast reactor**), whereas slow neutrons can travel on until they find uranium-235 nuclei. These will undergo fission when hit by neutrons of any speed, but make up a smaller percentage of the fuel (despite the fact that it is now often enriched with extra atoms of ^{235}U).

Types of thermal reactor

Pressurized water reactor (PWR)

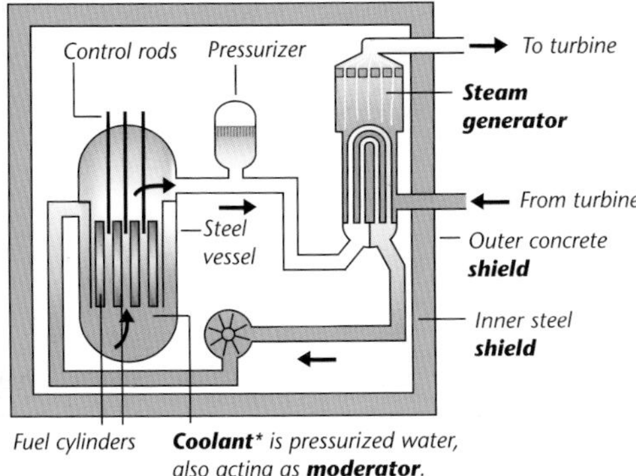
Control rods
Pressurizer
To turbine
Steam generator
From turbine
Steel vessel
Outer concrete shield
Inner steel shield
Fuel cylinders
Coolant* is pressurized water, also acting as moderator.

Advanced gas-cooled reactor (AGR)

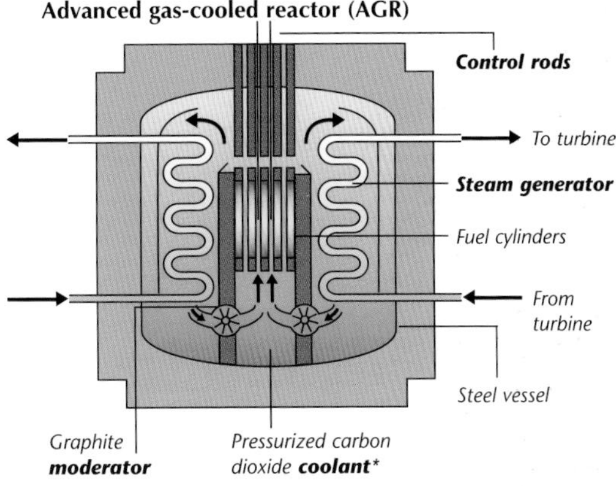
Control rods
To turbine
Steam generator
Fuel cylinders
From turbine
Steel vessel
Graphite moderator
Pressurized carbon dioxide coolant*

Fast reactor or fast breeder reactor (FBR)

A **fission reactor**, inside which the **neutrons*** which cause the fission are allowed to remain as fast neutrons (traveling at about 2×10^7m s^{-1}). The fuel used is always enriched with extra nuclei of uranium-235 (see **thermal reactor**) and plutonium-239. Both of these will fission easily when hit by fast neutrons, unlike uranium-238, which is far more likely to "capture" the neutrons (becoming ^{239}U) and undergo **radioactive decay***. The final product of this decay, however, is ^{239}Pu. Fast reactors are also called "breeders" because this decay process of ^{239}U to ^{239}Pu is allowed to happen in a blanket of ^{238}U around the main fuel. Hence more fuel is created and can be stored. Fast reactors have a more compact core and run at higher temperatures than thermal reactors. They are also more efficient, using up a much greater proportion of their fuel before it becomes contaminated.

Fast reactor

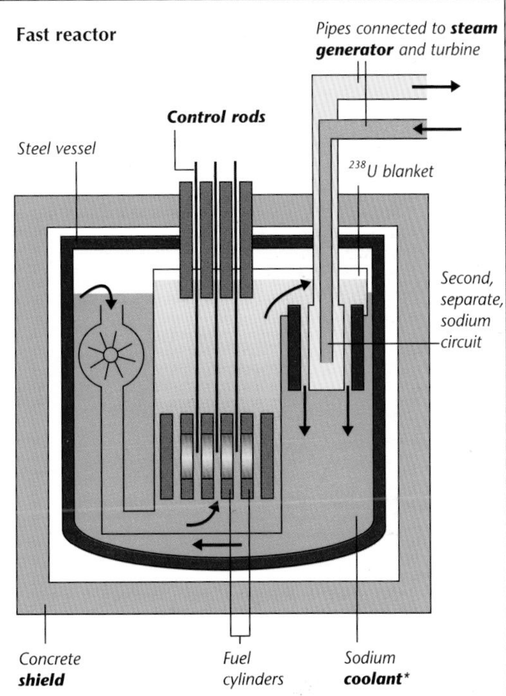
Pipes connected to steam generator and turbine
Control rods
Steel vessel
238U blanket
Second, separate, sodium circuit
Concrete shield
Fuel cylinders
Sodium coolant*

* **Chain reaction**, 92 (**Induced fission**); **Coolant**, 115; **Isotopes**, 83; **Neutrons**, 82; **Radioactive decay**, 87.

QUANTITIES AND UNITS

Physical quantities are such things as **mass***, **force*** and **current***, which are used in the physical sciences. They all have to be measured in some way and each therefore has its own **unit**. These are chosen by international agreement and are called **International System** or **SI units** – abbreviated from the French Système International d'Unités. All quantities are classified as either **basic quantities** or **derived quantities**.

Basic quantities

A set of quantities from which all other quantities (see **derived quantities**) can be defined (see table, below). Each basic quantity has its **basic SI unit**, in terms of which any other SI unit can be defined.

Basic quantity	Symbol	Basic SI unit	Abbreviation
Mass	*m*	*kilogram*	*kg*
Time	*t*	*second*	*s*
Length	*l*	*meter*	*m*
Current	*I*	*ampere*	*A*
Temperature	*T*	*kelvin*	*K*
Quantity of substance	–	*mole*	*mol*
Luminous intensity	–	*candela*	*cd*

Prefixes

A given SI unit may sometimes be too large or small for convenience, e.g. the meter is too large for measuring the thickness of a piece of paper. Standard fractions and multiples of the SI units are therefore used and written by placing a prefix before the unit (see table below). For example, the millimeter (mm) is equal to one thousandth of a meter.

Fractions and multiples in use

Fraction or multiple	Prefix	Symbol
10^{-9}	*nano-*	*n*
10^{-6}	*micro-*	*μ*
10^{-3}	*milli-*	*m*
10^{-2}	*centi-*	*c*
10^{-1}	*deci-*	*d*
10^{1}	*deca-*	*dc*
10^{2}	*hecto-*	*h*
10^{3}	*kilo-*	*k*
10^{6}	*mega-*	*M*
10^{9}	*giga-*	*G*

Basic SI units

Kilogram (kg)

The SI unit of mass. It is equal to the mass of an international prototype metal cylinder kept at Sèvres, near Paris.

Second (s)

The SI unit of time. It is equal to the duration of 9,192,631,770 **periods*** of a certain type of radiation emitted by the cesium-133 atom.

Meter (m)

The SI unit of length. It is equal to the distance light travels in a vacuum in $^{1}/_{299,792,458}$ of a second.

Ampere (A)

The SI unit of electric current (see also page 60). It is equal to the size of a current flowing through parallel, infinitely long, straight wires in a vacuum that produces a force between the wires of 2 x 10^{-7}N every meter.

Kelvin (K)

The SI unit of temperature. It is equal to $^{1}/_{273.16}$ of the temperature of the **triple point** of water (the point at which ice, water and steam can all exist at the same time) on the **absolute temperature scale***.

Mole (mol)

The SI unit of the quantity of a substance (note that this is different from mass because it is the number of particles of a substance). It is equal to the amount of substance which contains 6.023 x 10^{23} (this is **Avogadro's number**) particles (e.g. atoms or molecules).

Candela (cd)

The SI unit of intensity of light. It is equal to the strength of light from $^{1}/_{600,000}$ square meters of a **black body*** at the temperature of freezing platinum and at a pressure of 101,325N m^{-2}.

* **Absolute temperature scale**, 27; **Black body**, 29 (**Leslie's cube**); **Current**, 60; **Force**, 6; **Mass**, 12; **Period**, 16.

Derived quantities

Quantities other than **basic quantities** which are defined in terms of these or in terms of other derived quantities. The derived quantities have **derived SI units** which are defined in terms of the **basic SI units** or other derived units. They are determined from the defining equation for the quantity and are sometimes given special names.

Derived quantity	Symbol	Defining equation	Derived SI unit	Name of unit	Abbreviation
Velocity	v	$v = \frac{\text{change in displacement}}{\text{time}}$	$m\ s^{-1}$	–	–
Acceleration	a	$a = \frac{\text{change in velocity}}{\text{time}}$	$m\ s^{-2}$	–	–
Force	F	$F = \text{mass} \times \text{acceleration}$	$kg\ m\ s^{-2}$	newton	N
Work	W	$W = \text{force} \times \text{distance}$	N m	joule	J
Energy	E	Capacity to do work	J	–	–
Power	P	$P = \frac{\text{work done}}{\text{time}}$	$J\ s^{-1}$	watt	W
Area	A	Depends on shape (see page 101)	m^2	–	–
Volume	V	Depends on shape (see page 101)	m^3	–	–
Density	ρ	$\rho = \frac{\text{mass}}{\text{volume}}$	$kg\ m^{-3}$	–	–
Pressure	P	$P = \frac{\text{force}}{\text{area}}$	$N\ m^{-2}$	pascal	Pa
Period	T	Time for one cycle	s	–	–
Frequency	f	Number of cycles per second	s^{-1}	hertz	Hz
Impulse	–	Impulse = force × time	N s	–	–
Momentum	–	Momentum = mass × velocity	$kg\ m\ s^{-1}$	–	–
Electric charge	Q	$Q = \text{current} \times \text{time}$	A s	coulomb	C
Potential difference	V	$V = \frac{\text{energy transferred}}{\text{charge}}$	$J\ C^{-1}$	volt	V
Capacitance	C	$C = \frac{\text{charge}}{\text{potential difference}}$	$C\ V^{-1}$	farad	F
Resistance	R	$R = \frac{\text{potential difference}}{\text{current}}$	$V\ A^{-1}$	ohm	Ω

EQUATIONS, SYMBOLS AND GRAPHS

All **physical quantities** (see pages 96-97) and their units can be represented by **symbols** and are normally dependent in some way on other quantities. There is therefore a relationship between them which can be expressed as an **equation** and shown on a **graph**.

Equations

An **equation** represents the relationship between two or more physical quantities. This relationship can be expressed as a **word equation** or as an equation relating **symbols** which represent the quantities. The latter is used when a number of quantities are involved, since it is then easier to manipulate. Note that the meaning of the symbols must be stated.

Word equation

$$\text{Density} = \frac{\text{mass}}{\text{volume}}$$

Symbol equation

$$Q = m \times c \times (t_2 - t_1) \text{ or } Q = mc(t_2 - t_1)$$

where Q = heat energy lost or gained; m = mass; c = specific heat capacity; t_1 and t_2 = temperatures.

Graphs

A **graph** is a visual representation of the relationship between two quantities. It shows how one quantity depends on another. Points on a graph are plotted using the values for the quantities obtained during an experiment or by using the equation for the relationship if it is known. The two quantities plotted are called the **variables**.

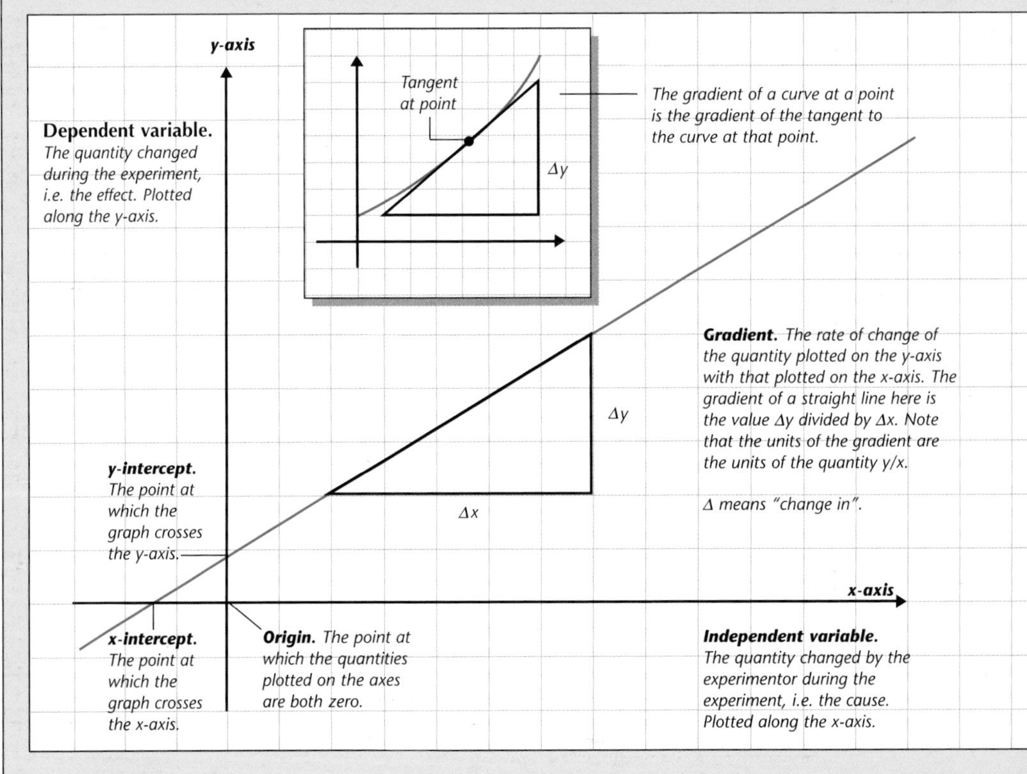
y-axis
Tangent at point
The gradient of a curve at a point is the gradient of the tangent to the curve at that point.
Δy
Dependent variable. The quantity changed during the experiment, i.e. the effect. Plotted along the y-axis.
Gradient. The rate of change of the quantity plotted on the y-axis with that plotted on the x-axis. The gradient of a straight line here is the value Δy divided by Δx. Note that the units of the gradient are the units of the quantity y/x.
Δ means "change in".
Δy
Δx
y-intercept. The point at which the graph crosses the y-axis.
x-axis
x-intercept. The point at which the graph crosses the x-axis.
Origin. The point at which the quantities plotted on the axes are both zero.
Independent variable. The quantity changed by the experimentor during the experiment, i.e. the cause. Plotted along the x-axis.

Symbols

Symbols are used to represent **physical quantities**. The value of a physical quantity consists of a numerical value and its unit. Therefore any symbol represents both a number and a unit.

Symbols represent number and unit, e.g. m = 2.1kg, or s = 400J kg^{-1} K^{-1}.

"Current through resistor = I" (i.e. it is not necessary to say I amps since the unit is included).

Note that a symbol divided by a unit is a pure number, e.g. m = 2.1kg means that m/kg = 2.1.

This notation is used in tables and to label graph axes.

Any number in this column is a length in meters.

Any number in this column is a time squared measured in seconds squared.

l/m	t^2/s^2
0.9	3.6
1.0	4.0
1.1	4.4
1.2	4.8

Any number on this scale is a force in newtons.

Any number on this scale is a length in millimeters.

F/N

l/mm

Plotting graphs

1. The quantity controlled during an experiment should be plotted along the x-axis, and the quantity which changes as a result along the y-axis.

2. Scales on the axes should have values that are easy to find. (Avoid squares representing multiples of three.)

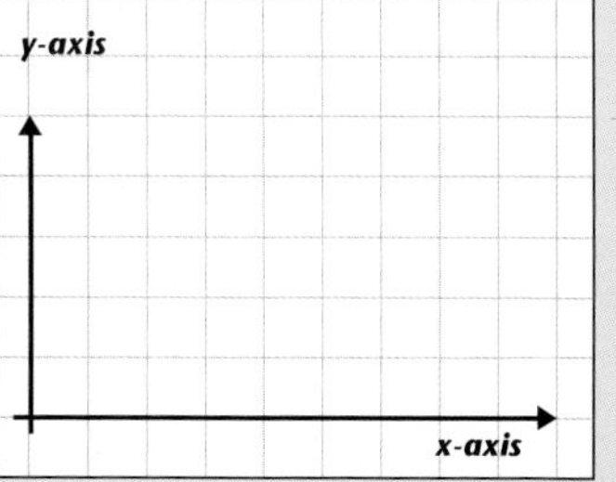
y-axis
x-axis

3. The axes should be labeled by the symbol representing the quantity (or name of the quantity) and its unit, e.g. length/mm.

4. Points on the graph should be marked in pencil with a × or a ⊙.

Velocity/m s^{-1}

Time/s

5. A smooth curve or straight line should be drawn which best fits the points (this is because physical quantities are normally related in some definite way). Note that joining the points up will not often produce a smooth curve. This is due to experimental errors.

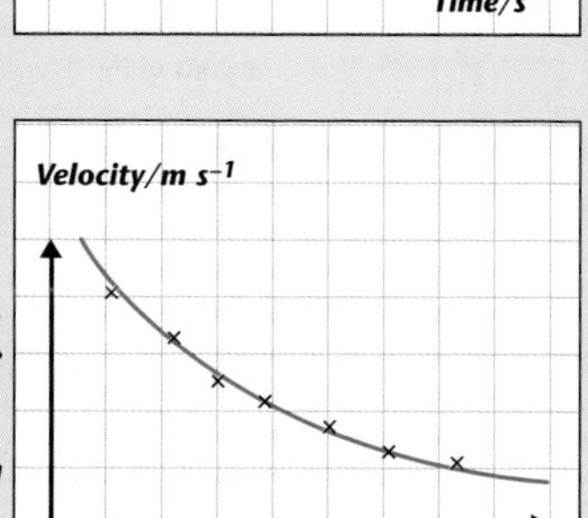
Velocity/m s⁻¹
Time/s

Information from graphs

A straight line graph which passes through the origin shows that the quantities plotted on the axes are proportional to each other (i.e. if one is doubled then so is the other).

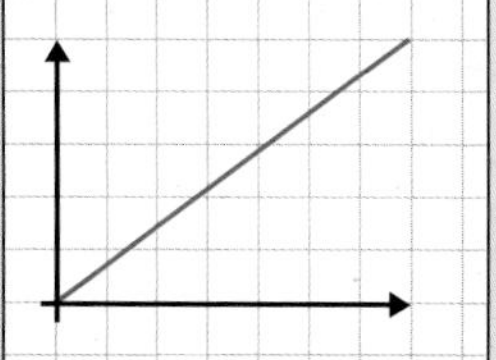

A straight line portion of a graph shows the region in which the relationship between two quantities is linear (i.e. one always changes by the same amount for a fixed change in the other).

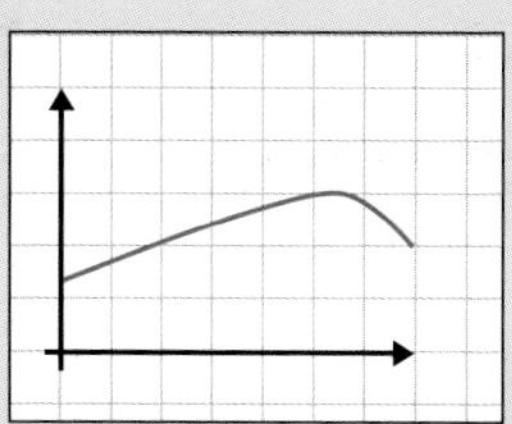

The amount of scatter of the points about the smooth curve gives an indication of the errors in the data due to inaccuracies in the procedure, the equipment and the measuring (this happens in any experiment).

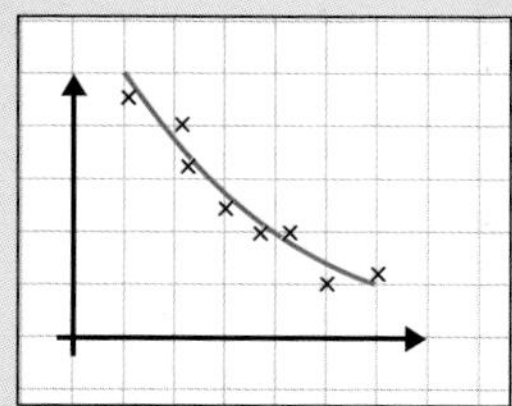

Individual points a long way from the curve are probably due to an error in measuring that piece of data in the experiment. However, the point should not be ignored – it should be checked and remeasured if possible.

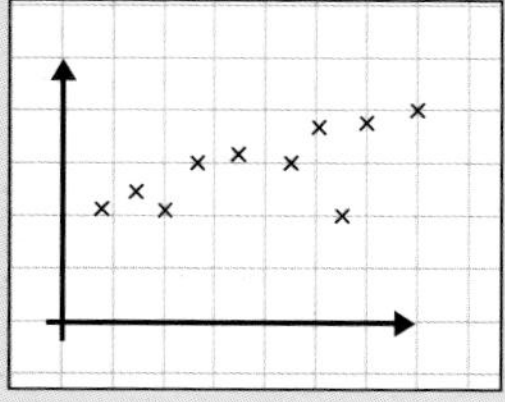

MEASUREMENTS

Measurement of length

The method used to measure a length depends on the magnitude of the length. A meter ruler is used for lengths of 50mm or more. The smallest division is normally 1mm and so lengths can be estimated to the nearest 0.5mm. For lengths less than 50mm, the error involved would be unacceptable (see also **reading error**, page 103). A **vernier scale** is therefore used. For the measurement of very small lengths (to 0.01mm) a **micrometer screw gauge** is used (see opposite).

Vernier scale

A short scale which slides along a fixed scale. The position on the fixed scale of the zero line of the vernier scale can be found accurately. It is used in measuring devices such as the **vernier slide callipers**.

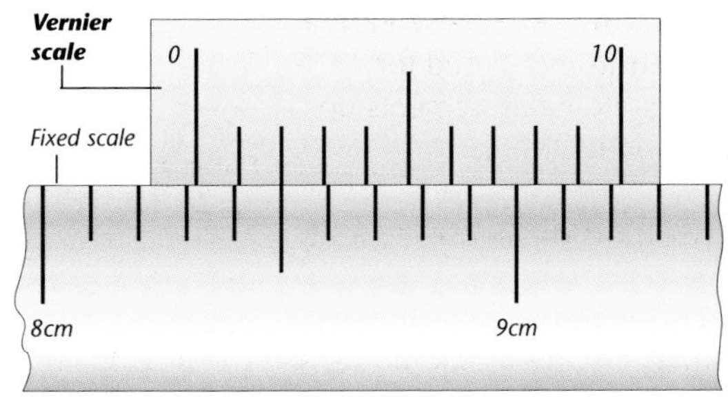

Vernier scale
0
10
Fixed scale
8cm
9cm

Method of reading position of zero line on vernier scale:

1. Read the position of the zero line approximately – in this case 8.3cm.

2. Find the position on the vernier scale where the marks coincide – in this case 2.

3. Add this to the previous figure – the accurate reading is 8.32cm.

Vernier slide callipers

An instrument containing a **vernier scale**, used to measure lengths in the range 10 to 100mm.

Method of measurement:

1. Close the jaws and check that the zero on the **vernier scale** coincides with the zero on the fixed scale. If not, note the reading (this is the **zero error***).

2. Close or open the jaws onto the object to be measured.

3. Lock the sliding jaw into position.

4. Record the reading on the scale.

5. Add or subtract the zero error (see 1) to get the correct reading.

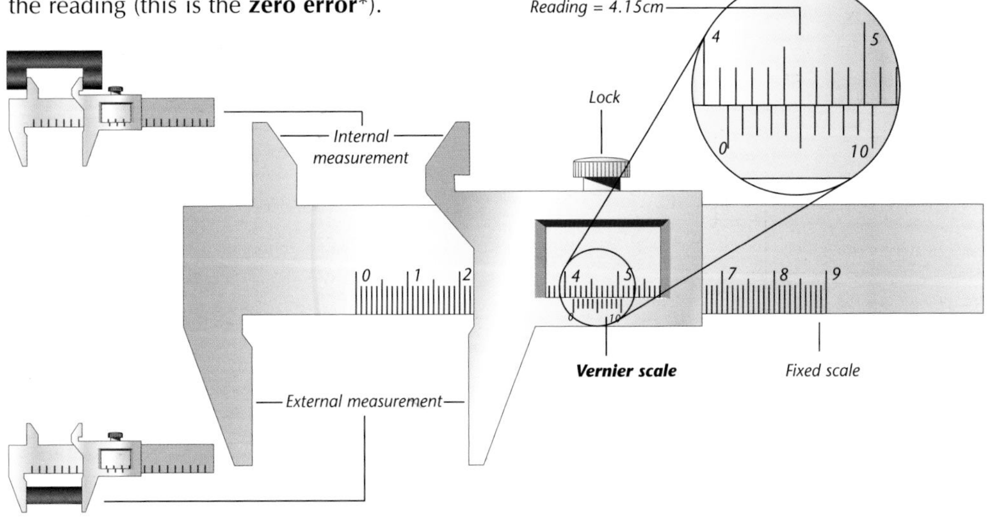

Reading = 4.15cm
4
5
0
10
Lock
Internal measurement
External measurement
0
1
2
4
5
7
8
9
Vernier scale
Fixed scale

* **Zero error**, 102.

Micrometer screw gauge

An instrument used for accurate measurements up to about 30mm.

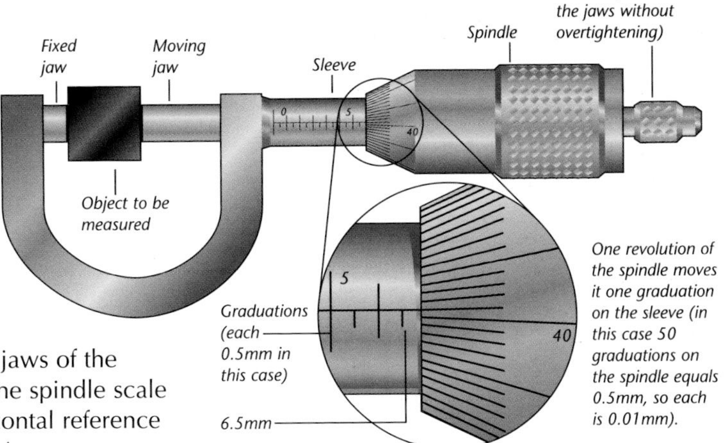
Fixed jaw
Moving jaw
Sleeve
Spindle
Ratchet (used to close the jaws without overtightening)
Object to be measured
0
5
40
Graduations (each 0.5mm in this case)
6.5mm
One revolution of the spindle moves it one graduation on the sleeve (in this case 50 graduations on the spindle equals 0.5mm, so each is 0.01mm).

Method of measurement:

1. Determine the value of a division on the spindle scale (see diagram).

2. Using the ratchet, close the jaws of the instrument fully. The zero on the spindle scale should coincide with the horizontal reference line. If not, note the **zero error***.

3. Using the ratchet, close the jaws on the object to be measured until it is gripped.

4. Note the reading of the highest visible mark on the sleeve scale (in this case 6.5mm).

5. Note the division on the spindle scale which coincides with the horizontal reference line (in this case 0.41mm).

6. Add the two readings and add or subtract the zero error (see 2) to get the correct reading (in this case 6.91mm).

Measurement of area and volume

The volume of a liquid is calculated from the space it takes up in its containing vessel. The internal volume of the containing vessel is called its **capacity**. The **SI unit*** of capacity is the **liter** (**l**), equal to $10^{-3}m^3$. Note that $1ml = 1cm^3$. The volume of a liquid is measured using a graduated vessel.

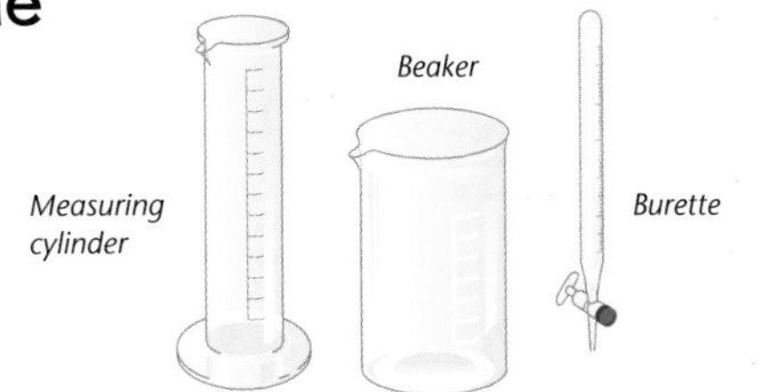
Measuring cylinder
Beaker
Burette

Examples of graduated vessels for measuring volume

The surface area and volume of a solid of regular shape are calculated from length measurements of the object (see below).

For solids of irregular shape, see **eureka can**, page 24.

Regular shaped solid	*Rectangular bar*	*Sphere*	*Cylinder*
	h, *w*, *l*	*r*	*r*, *l*
Measurements made using ***vernier slide callipers*** *or* ***micrometer screw gauge***	*h = height* *w = width* *l = length*	*r = radius*	*r = radius* *l = length*
Volume V of solid calculated from	$V = lwh$	$V = \frac{4}{3}\pi r^3$	$V = \pi r^2 l$
Surface area A calculated from	$A = 2wl + 2hl + 2hw$ *Top Sides Ends*	$A = 4\pi r^2$	$A = 2\pi rl + 2\pi r^2$ *Curved surface Ends*

* **SI units**, 96; **Zero error**, 102.

ACCURACY AND ERRORS

All experimental measurements are subject to some errors, other than those caused by carelessness (like misreading a scale). The most common errors which occur are **parallax errors**, **zero errors** and **reading errors**. When stating a reading, therefore, a number of **significant figures** should be quoted which give an estimate of the accuracy of the readings.

Parallax error

The error which occurs when the eye is not placed directly opposite a scale when a reading is being taken.

Parallax error reading a meter ruler

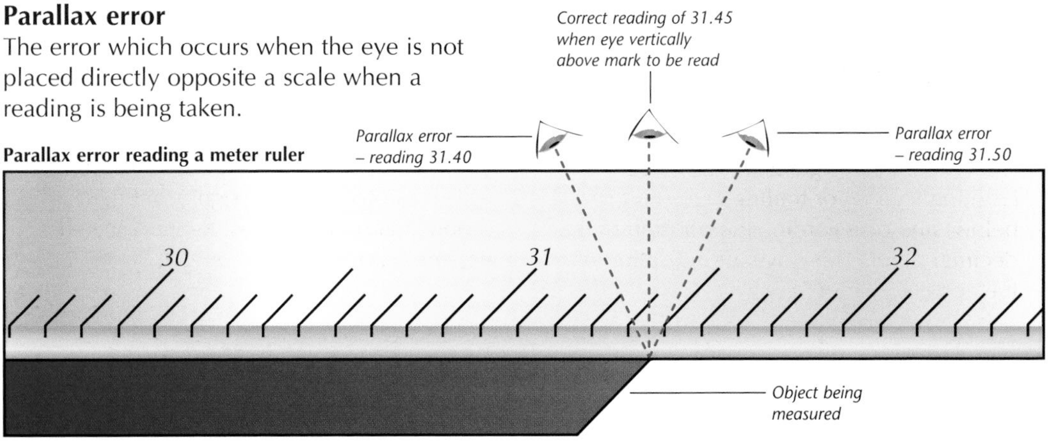

Correct reading of 31.45 when eye vertically above mark to be read

Parallax error – reading 31.40

Parallax error – reading 31.50

30 31 32

Object being measured

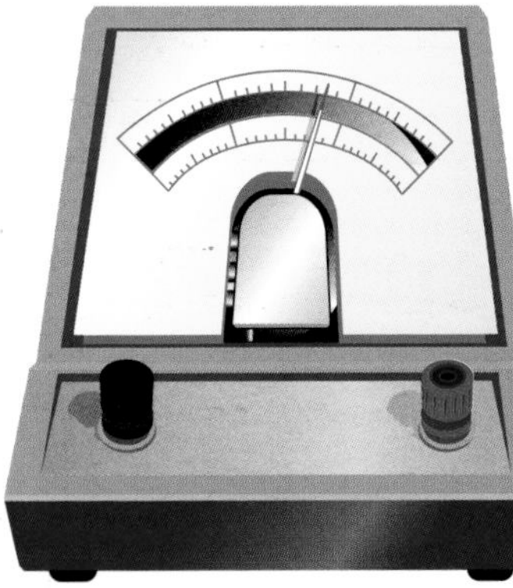

Some scales with pointers have a mirror behind the pointer. The correct reading is obtained by placing the eye so that the reflection of the pointer is hidden behind it.

To avoid parallax errors, readings of liquid levels must be taken with the eye lined up with the top or bottom of the ***meniscus*****.*

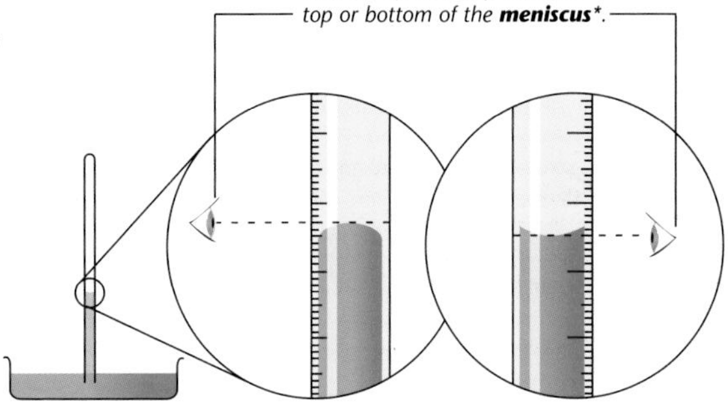

Zero error

The error which occurs when a measuring instrument does not indicate zero when it should. If this happens, the instrument should either be adjusted to read zero or the inaccurate "zero reading" should be taken and should be added to or subtracted from any other reading taken.

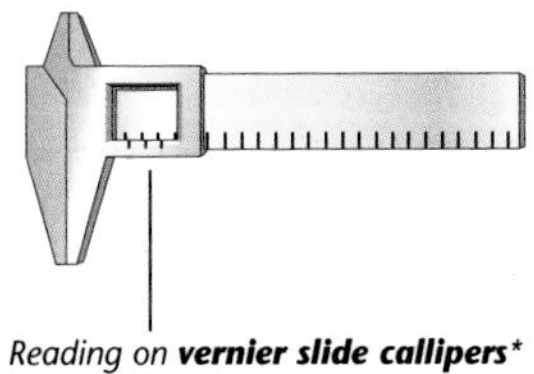

Reading on ***vernier slide callipers***** when closed (i.e. should read zero) is 0.2mm. This is* ***zero error****.*

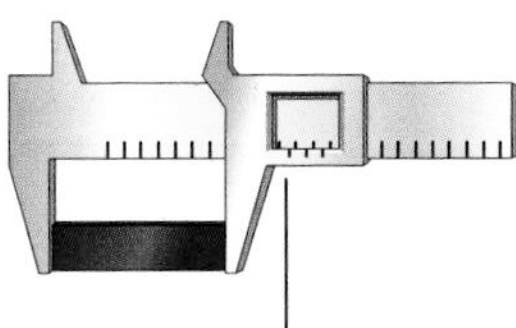

0.2mm must be subtracted from any reading (in this case, apparent reading is 53.9 but actual length is 53.9 – 0.2, i.e. 53.7mm).

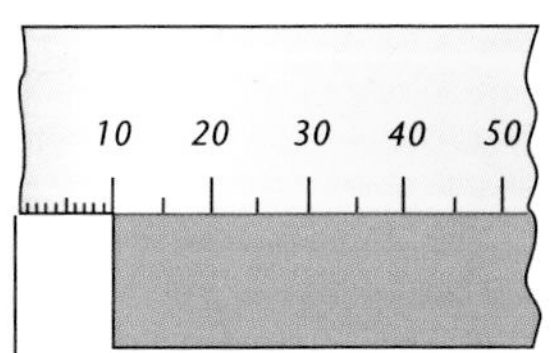
10 20 30 40 50

Zero error on meter ruler may be due to worn end. Should be solved by measuring from 10mm line and subtracting 10mm from all readings.

* **Meniscus**, 115; **Vernier slide callipers**, 100.

Reading error
The error due to the guesswork involved in taking a reading from a scale when the reading lies between the scale divisions.

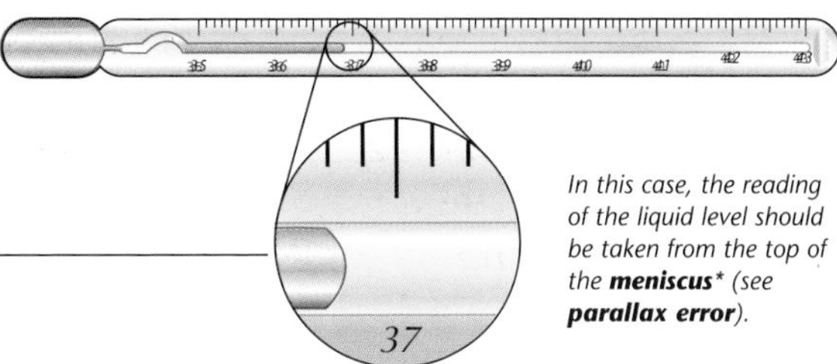
35
36
37
38
39
40
41
42
43
37

Reading on thermometer is between 36.8°C and 36.9°C. Best estimate of next figure is half a division to give a reading of 36.85°C.

*In this case, the reading of the liquid level should be taken from the top of the **meniscus*** (see **parallax error**).*

Significant figures

The number of **significant figures** in a value is the number of figures in that value ignoring leading or trailing zeros (but see below) and disregarding the position of the decimal point. They give an indication of the accuracy of a reading.

*A reading of 3704mm has four **significant figures**. It can be written as:*

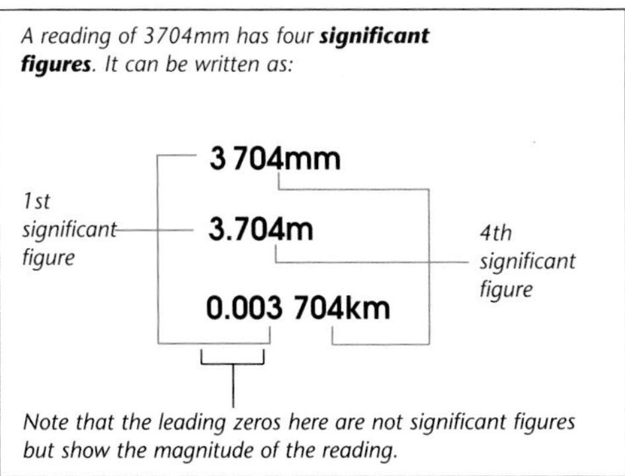
3 704mm
1st significant figure
3.704m
4th significant figure
0.003 704km

Note that the leading zeros here are not significant figures but show the magnitude of the reading.

The number of significant figures quoted is an indication of the accuracy of a reading or result.

Smallest division on ammeter scale = 0.1A

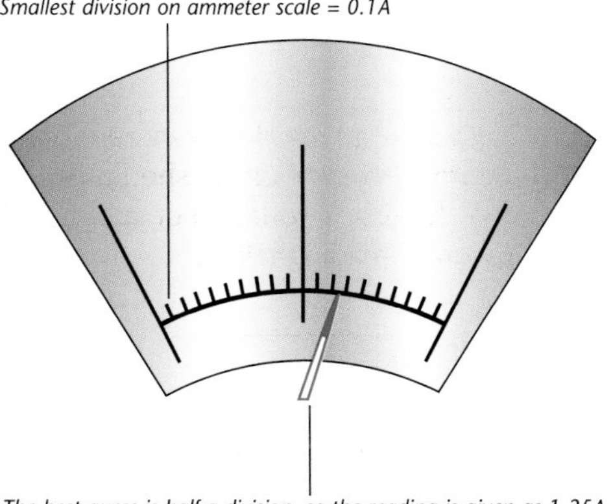

The best guess is half a division, so the reading is given as 1.25A. Three significant figures indicate that the reading is accurate to about 0.05A.

A reading with more figures, e.g. 1.2518A, implies more accuracy than is possible on this scale.

Rounding
The process of reducing the number of figures quoted. The last significant figure is dropped and the new last figure changed depending on the one dropped.

7.3925	*(quoted to 5 significant figures)*
= 7.393	*(rounded to 4 significant figures)*
= 7.39	*(rounded to 3 significant figures)*
= 7.4	*(rounded to 2 significant figures)*
= 7	*(rounded to 1 significant figure)*

0.08873	*(quoted to 4 significant figures)*
= 0.0887	*(rounded to 3 significant figures)*
= 0.089	*(rounded to 2 significant figures)*
= 0.09	*(rounded to 1 significant figure)*

Note that

29.000	*is quoted to 5 significant figures*
= 29.0	*(to 3 significant figures)*
= 29	*(to 2 significant figures)*
= 30	*(to 1 significant figure)*

In the last case here, the 0 is not a significant figure but must be included (see below).

For large numbers like 283,000 it is impossible to say how many of the figures are significant (the first three must be) because the zeros have to be included to show the magnitude. This ambiguity is removed by using the **exponential notation** (see page 109).

* **Meniscus**, 115.

FIELDS AND FORCES

This table is a comparison of the three forces normally encountered in physics (excluding the **nuclear force**). In fact, most of the forces dealt with in physics, e.g. the **contact force** between two objects, are examples of the **electromagnetic force** which is a combination of the **magnetic** and **electric forces**. For more about these and all other forces, see pages 6-7.

Gravitational force

(see also pages 6 and 18)

Type of force

Note that a force can only exist between two masses, charges or currents, and that the size of the force is the same on both of them (see also **Newton's third law**, page 13). Note also that the forces only act between objects which are the same, e.g. there is a force between two masses, but not between a mass and a current.

Gravitational force: Force acts between two objects with mass. It is always attractive.

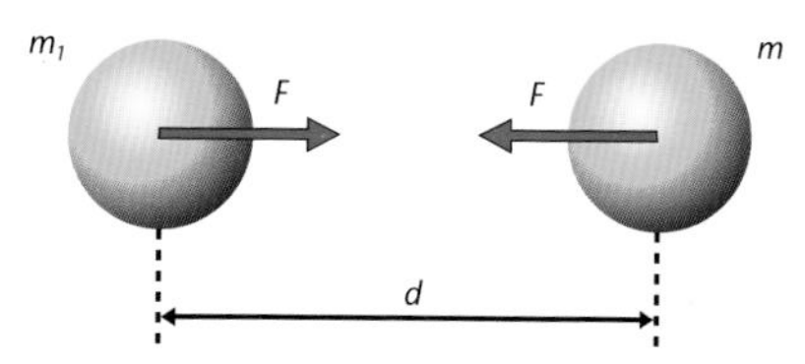

m_1
m
F
F
d

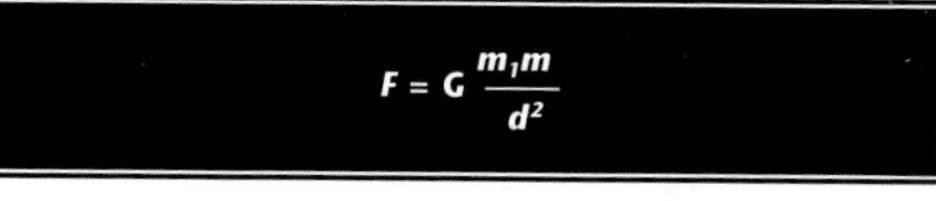

$$F = G\frac{m_1 m}{d^2}$$

$G = 6.7 \times 10^{-11} Nm^2\ kg^{-2}$

G is the **gravitational constant***. Its very small value means that the gravitational force is only noticeable when one of the objects is very large (e.g. a planet).

Description of force in terms of force field

The **force field** is the region around an object (mass, charge or current) in which its effects (gravitational, electric or magnetic) can be detected – see also page 6.

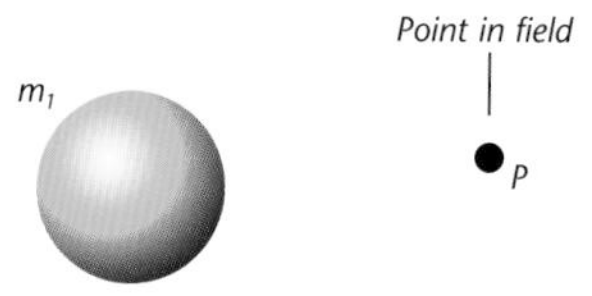

m_1
Point in field
P

Mass m_1 produces a **gravitational field** in the space around it (see **field intensity**, page 106).

A second mass experiences a gravitational force when placed at any point (e.g. P) in the gravitational field of m_1.

A mass thus produces a gravitational field and is acted upon by a gravitational field.

Field direction

This is found by observing the effect of the force field on an object (mass, charge or current) placed in it.

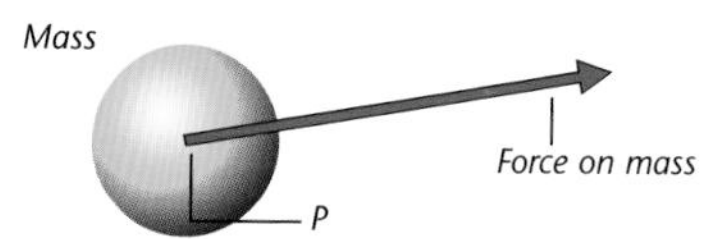

Mass
Force on mass
P

The direction of a gravitational field at a point P is the direction of the force on a mass placed at P.

* **Gravitational constant**, 18 (**Newton's law of gravitation**).

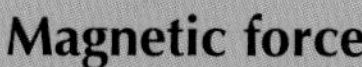

Electric force
(see also pages 6 and 58)

Force is between two charges. It is attractive if the charges are of the opposite sign, i.e. one negative and one positive, and repulsive if the charges are of the same sign.

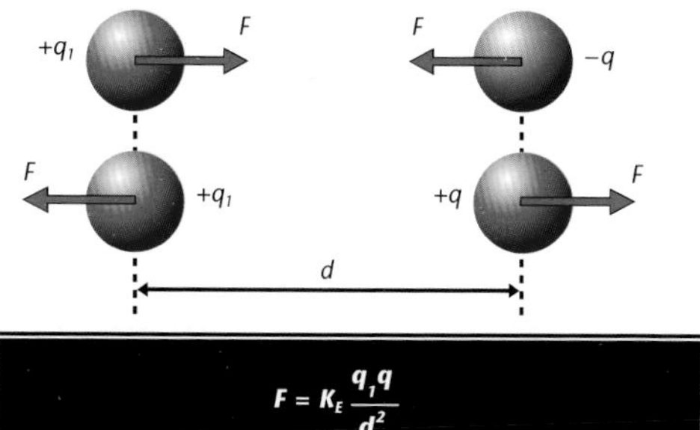
+q1
F
F
−q
F
+q1
+q
F
d

$$F = K_E \frac{q_1 q}{d^2}$$

In air $K_E = 9 \times 10^9 \text{Nm}^2\ \text{C}^{-2}$

This very large value means it is difficult to separate opposite charges.

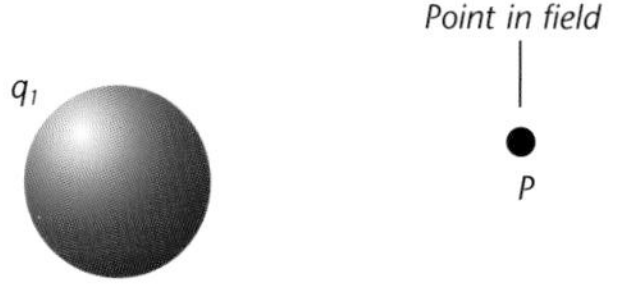
q1
Point in field
P

Charge q_1 produces an **electric field*** in the space around it (see **field intensity**, page 106).

A second charge experiences an electric force when placed at any point (e.g. P) in the electric field of q_1.

A charge thus produces an electric field and is acted upon by an electric field.

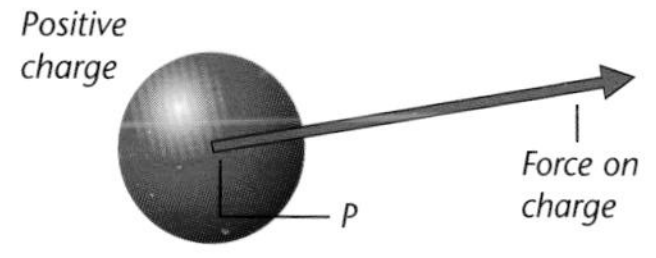
Positive
charge
P
Force on
charge

The direction of an electric field at a point P is the direction of the force on a positive charge placed at P.

Magnetic force
(see also pages 6 and 70)

Force is between two objects in which current is flowing. If the currents flow in the same direction, the force is attractive. If the currents flow in opposite directions, the force is repulsive.

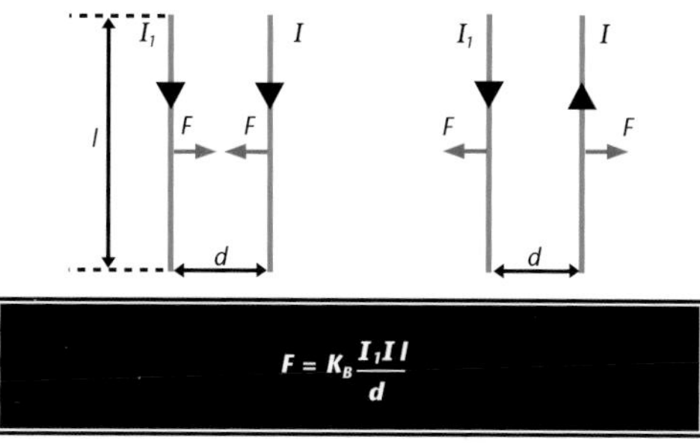
I1
I
I1
I
l
F
F
F
F
d
d

$$F = K_B \frac{I_1 I l}{d}$$

In air $K_B = 2.7 \times 10^{-7} \text{N A}^{-2}$

This small value indicates that the magnetic force is very small in comparison to the electric force.

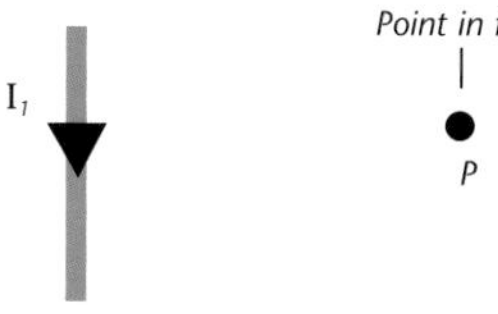
I1
Point in field
P

Current I_1 produces a **magnetic field*** in the space around it (see **field intensity**, page 106).

A second current experiences a magnetic force when placed at any point P in the magnetic field of I_1.

A current thus produces a magnetic field and is acted upon by a magnetic field.

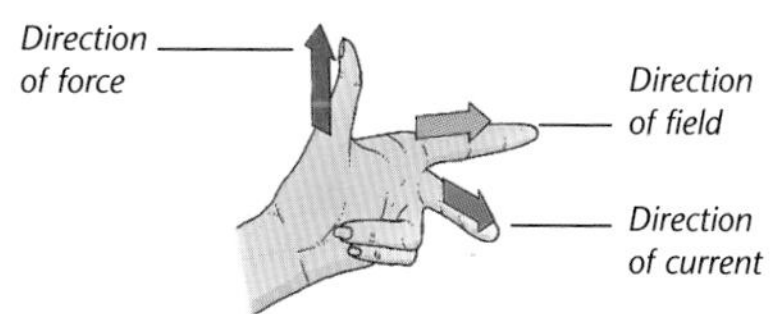
Direction
of force
Direction
of field
Direction
of current

The direction of a magnetic field at a point P is given by **Fleming's left hand rule***.

* **Electric field**, 58; **Fleming's left hand rule**, 76; **Magnetic field**, 72.

Fields and forces (continued)

Field intensity
This is found by measuring the effect of the force field on an object (mass, charge or current) placed in it.

Gravitational force

To measure the field intensity g of a gravitational field due to a mass m_1 at a point P, a test mass m is placed at P and the gravitational force F on it is measured. Then:

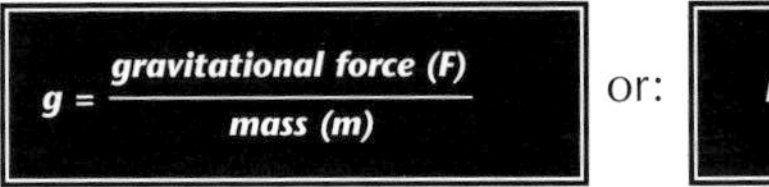

$$g = \frac{\text{gravitational force } (F)}{\text{mass } (m)} \quad \text{or:} \quad F = mg$$

By comparison with the equation above for the gravitational force, the field intensity g at a distance d from a mass m_1 is:

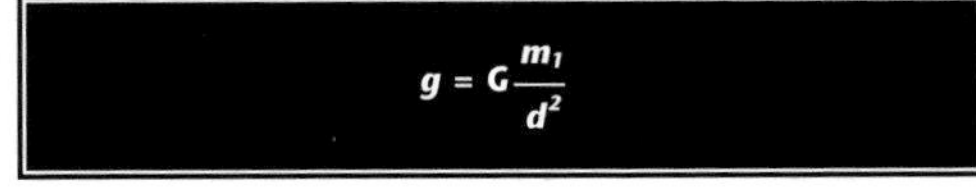

$$g = G\frac{m_1}{d^2}$$

Representation by field lines
Field lines (or **flux lines** or **lines of force** or **flux**) are used in all cases to represent the strength and direction of fields and to visualize them (see panel at bottom of page). Field lines never cross since the field would then have different directions at one point.

Gravitational field lines always end at a mass.

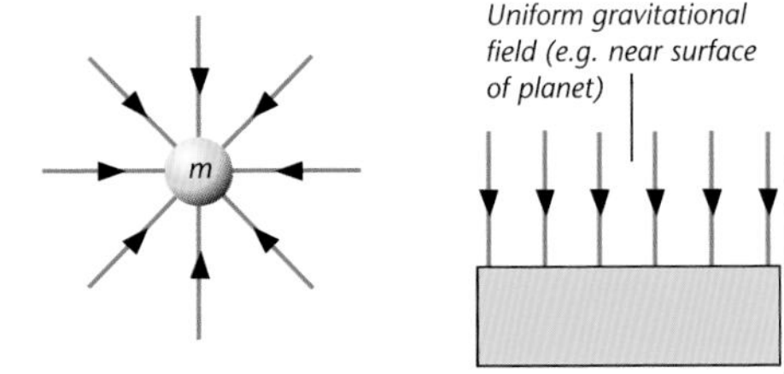

m
Uniform gravitational field (e.g. near surface of planet)

Potential energy (see also page 8)
This depends on **field intensity** and the object (its mass in a **gravitational field** or its charge in an **electric field***). The **potential*** at a point in a field is the energy per unit (of mass or charge) and depends upon the field only. Usually the only concern is the difference in potential, or **potential difference***, between two points. Potential can be defined by choosing a reference. The potential at a point is then the potential difference between the point and the reference point.

The gravitational potential difference between two points in a gravitational field is the work done against the forces of the field in moving a unit mass between the points.

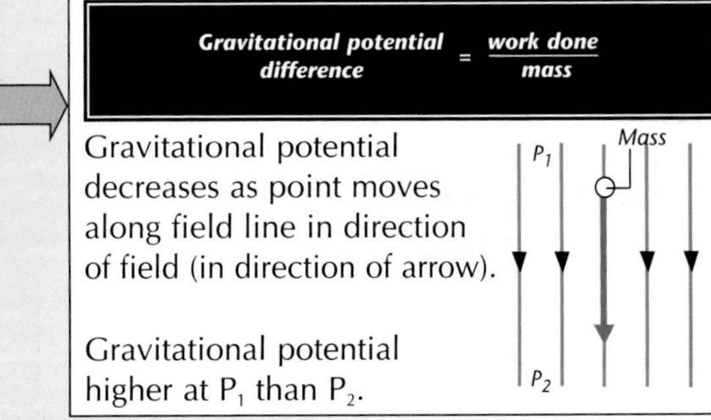

Mass
P_1
P_2

$$\text{Gravitational potential difference} = \frac{\text{work done}}{\text{mass}}$$

Gravitational potential decreases as point moves along field line in direction of field (in direction of arrow).

Gravitational potential higher at P_1 than P_2.

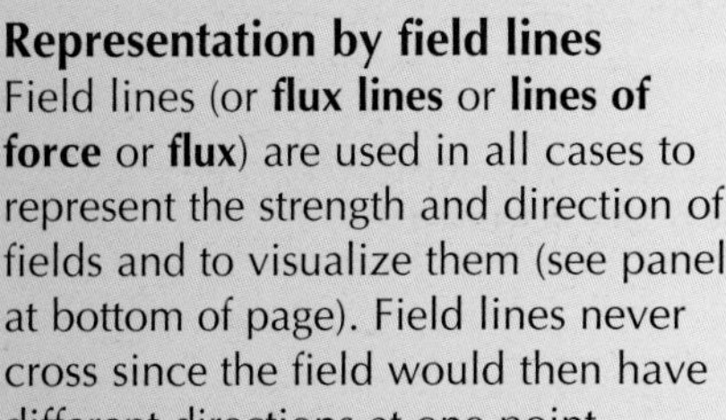

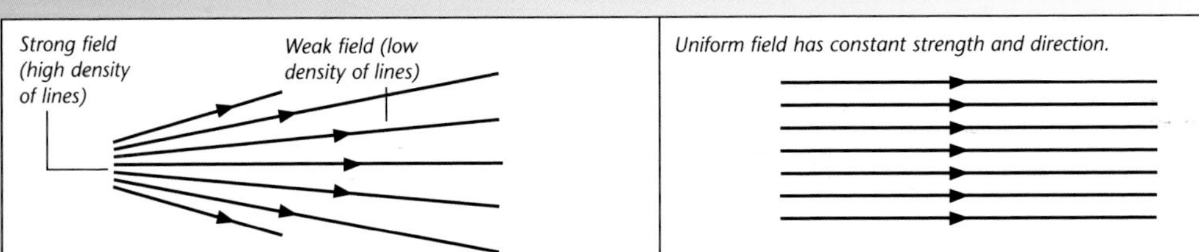

Strong field (high density of lines)
Weak field (low density of lines)

Uniform field has constant strength and direction.

* **Electric field, Potential, Potential difference**, 58.

Electric force

To measure the field intensity E of an electric field at a point P due to a charge q_1, a test positive charge q is placed at P and the electric force F on it is measured. Then:

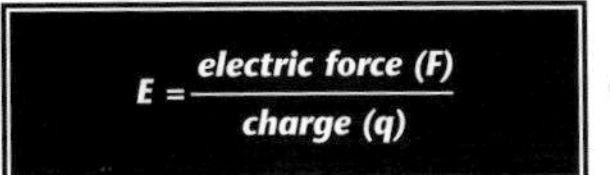

$$E = \frac{\text{electric force (F)}}{\text{charge (q)}}$$

or:

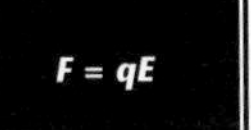

$$F = qE$$

By comparison with the equation above for the electric force, the field intensity E at a distance d from a charge q_1 is:

$$E = K_E \frac{q_1}{d^2}$$

Electric field lines always begin at a positive charge and end at an equal negative charge.

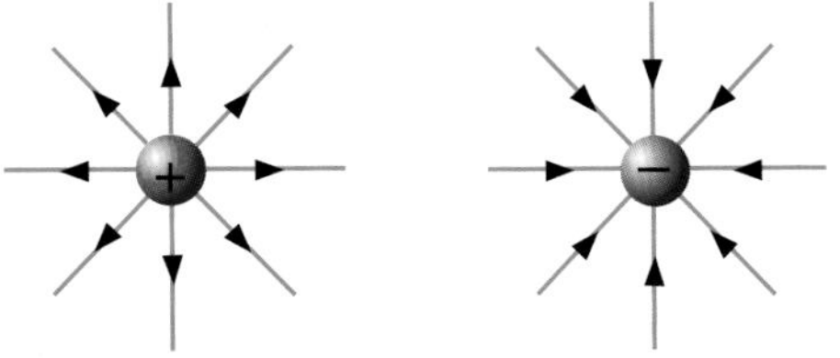
+
−

The electric potential difference between two points in an electric field is the work done against the forces of the field in moving a unit positive charge between them.

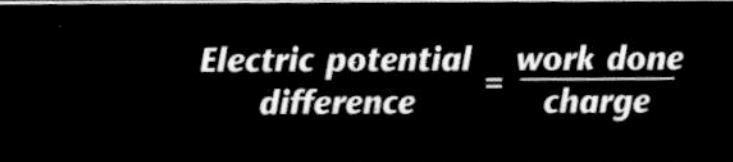

$$\text{Electric potential difference} = \frac{\text{work done}}{\text{charge}}$$

Electric potential decreases in direction of field (in direction of arrow).

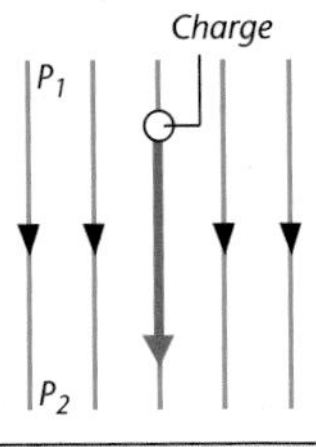
Charge
P_1
P_2

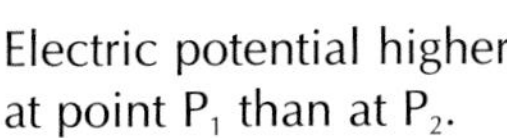

Electric potential higher at point P_1 than at P_2.

Magnetic force

To measure the field intensity B of a magnetic field due to I_1 at a point P, a conductor of length l carrying a current I is placed at P and the magnetic force F is measured. Then:

$$B = \frac{\text{magnetic force (F)}}{\text{current (I)} \times \text{length (l)}}$$

or:

$$F = BIl$$

By comparison with the equation above for the magnetic force, the field intensity B at a distance d from a current I_1 is:

$$B = K_B \frac{I_1}{d}$$

Magnetic field lines* have no beginning or end, but are always closed loops. This is because single north or south poles cannot exist. This is a fundamental difference compared to gravitational and electric fields.

Circular magnetic field lines around current-carrying wire.

Magnetic potential is much more difficult to define than for gravitational or electric fields because the field lines are circular. Note that if a point moves around a circular line in the diagram above, it returns to the same point, which must have the same potential, although it has moved along a field line. This means that magnetic potential is complicated to calculate.

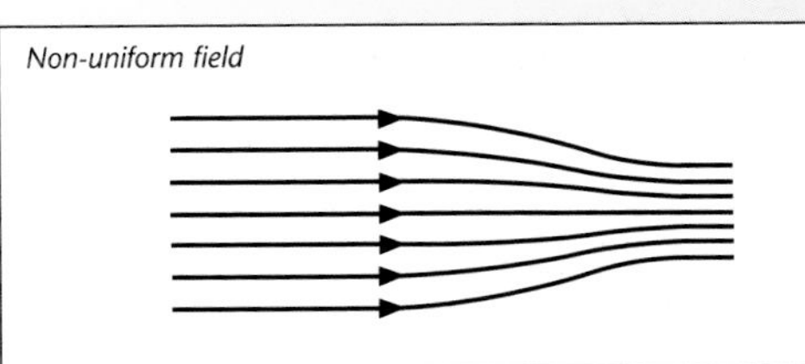
Non-uniform field

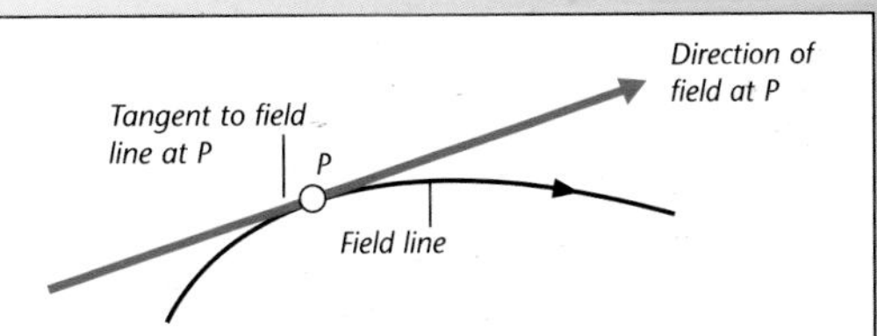
Direction of field at P
Tangent to field line at P
P
Field line

* **Magnetic field lines**, 72.

VECTORS AND SCALARS

All quantities in physics are either **scalar** or **vector quantities**, depending on whether the quantity has direction as well as magnitude.

Scalar quantity
Any quantity which has magnitude only, e.g. mass, time, energy, density.

Vector quantity
Any quantity which has both magnitude and direction, e.g. force, displacement, velocity and acceleration. When giving a value to a vector quantity, the direction must be given in some way as well as the magnitude. Usually, the quantity is represented graphically by an arrowed line. The length of the line indicates the magnitude of the quantity (on some chosen scale) and the direction of the arrow indicates the direction of the quantity.

Parallelogram rule
A rule used when adding together two **vector quantities**. The two vectors are drawn from one point to form two sides of a parallelogram which is then completed. The diagonal from the original common point gives the sum of the two vectors (the **resultant**).

The parallelogram rule is used to help navigation at sea. The direction and speed of the tide must be taken into account as the second vector quantity to be added to the direction and speed of the boat.

*Arrows represent forces (**vector quantities**). Length indicates magnitude of force.*

Scale is 1cm = 10 newtons

30N

3cm

2.1cm

21N

Forces act in opposite directions.

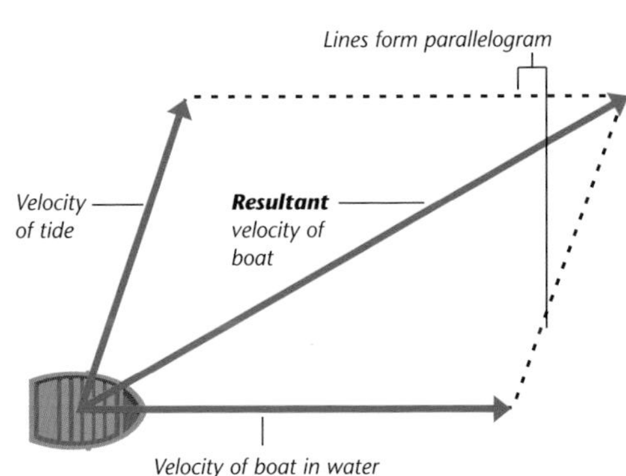

Lines form parallelogram
Velocity of tide
Resultant velocity of boat
Velocity of boat in water

Resolution
The process of splitting one **vector quantity** into two other vectors called its **components**. Normally, the two components are perpendicular to each other. Each component then represents the total effect of the vector in that direction.

Lift (**vector quantity**) from rotor of helicopter can be **resolved** into two **components**. The first acts upwards, in order to keep it airborne, and the second acts forwards, to move it along.

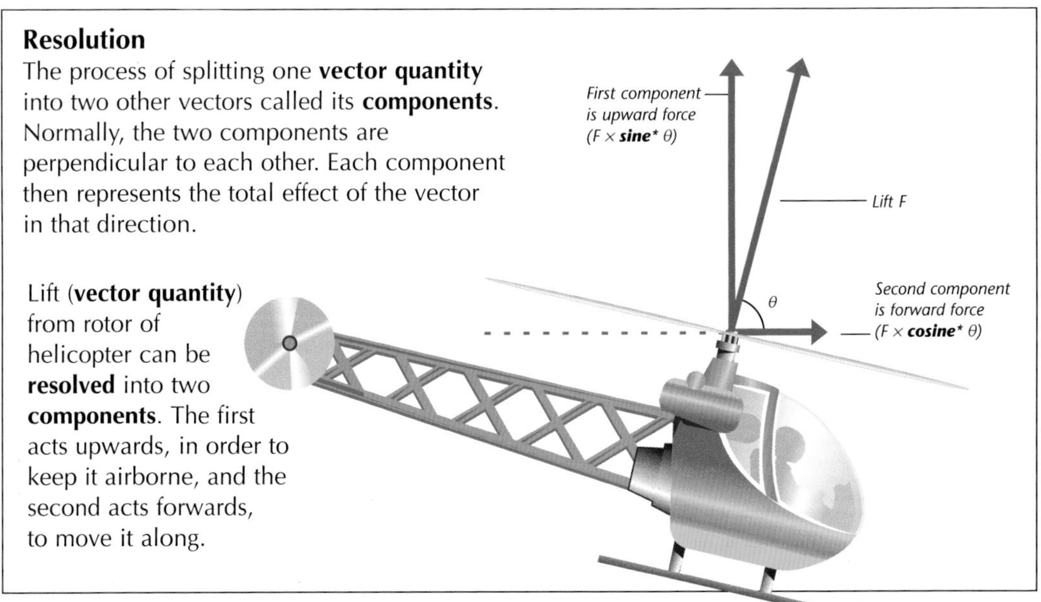

First component is upward force ($F \times$ **sine*** θ)
Lift F
θ
Second component is forward force ($F \times$ **cosine*** θ)

* **Cosine**, **Sine**, 115.

NUMBERS

Very large or very small numbers (e.g. 10 000 000 or 0.000 001) take a long time to write out and are difficult to read. The **exponential notation** is therefore used. In this notation, the position of the decimal point is shown by writing the power ten is raised to.

1 000 000	$= 10^6$	*or "ten to the six"*
100 000	$= 10^5$	*or "ten to the five"*
10 000	$= 10^4$	*or "ten to the four"*
1 000	$= 10^3$	*or "ten to the three"*
100	$= 10^2$	*or "ten to the two"*
10	$= 10^1$	*or "ten to the one"*
1	$= 10^0$	*any number "to the nought" equals one*
0.1	$= 10^{-1}$	*or "ten to the minus one"*
0.01	$= 10^{-2}$	*or "ten to the minus two"*
0.001	$= 10^{-3}$	*or "ten to the minus three"*
0.0001	$= 10^{-4}$	*or "ten to the minus four"*
0.000 01	$= 10^{-5}$	*or "ten to the minus five"*
0.000 001	$= 10^{-6}$	*or "ten to the minus six"*

Note that a negative exponent means "one over" so that $10^{-3} = {}^1/_{10^3} = {}^1/_{1\,000}$*. This also applies to units, e.g. kg* m^{-3} *means kg/*m^3 *or kg per* m^3*.*

Exponents are added when multiplying numbers, e.g. $10^5 \times 10^{-3}$ $(= 100\,000 \times {}^1/_{1\,000})$ $= 10^{5-3} = 10^2 = 100$*.*

Scientific notation

A form of expressing numbers in which the number always has one digit before the decimal point and is followed by a power of ten in **exponential notation** to show its magnitude (see also **significant figures**, page 103).

Examples of numbers written in scientific notation†

56 342	5.6342×10^4
4 000	4×10^3 *(assuming 0s are not significant)*
569	5.69×10^2
23.3	2.33×10^1
0.98	9.8×10^{-1}
0.00211	2.11×10^{-3}

Order of magnitude

A value which is accurate to within a factor of ten or so. It is important to have an idea of the order of magnitude of some physical quantities so that a figure which has been calculated can be judged. For example, the mass of a person is about 60kg. Therefore a calculated result of 50kg or 70kg is quite reasonable, but a result of 6kg or 600kg is obviously not correct.

Typical orders of magnitude

Item	Mass/kg
Earth	6×10^{24}
Car	5×10^3
Human	5×10^1
Bag of sugar	*1*
Orange	2×10^{-1}
Golf ball	5×10^{-2}
Table tennis ball	2×10^{-3}
Proton	2×10^{-27}
Electron	10^{-30}

Item	Length/m
Radius of Milky Way galaxy	10^{19}
Radius of Solar System	10^{11}
Radius of Earth	5×10^6
Height of Mount Everest	10^4
Height of human	*2*
Thickness of paper	10^{-4}
Wavelength of light	5×10^{-7}
Radius of atom	10^{-10}
Radius of nucleus	10^{-14}

Item	Time/s
Age of Earth	2×10^{17}
Time since emergence of man	10^{13}
Human life time	2×10^9
Time span of year	3×10^7
Time span of day	9×10^4
Time between heart beats	*1*
Camera shutter speed	10^{-2}
Half-life of polonium-214	1.5×10^{-4}
Time for light to travel 1m	3×10^{-9}

Item	Energy/J
Energy given out by Sun per second	10^{26}
Energy released by San Francisco earthquake (1906)	3×10^{17}
Energy released by fission of 1g of uranium	10^{11}
Energy of lightning discharge	10^9
Energy of 1kW fire per hour	4×10^6
Kinetic energy of golf ball	*20*

† *In scientific work, the convention is to print numbers up to 9999 closed up and without a comma. In numbers above this, small spaces are used to make the numbers easier to read at a glance. In non-technical writing, the convention is to add commas to numbers with four or more figures. The latter style is predominantly used in this book.*

CIRCUIT SYMBOLS

This table shows the main symbols used to represent the various components used in electric circuits (see also pages 60-65).

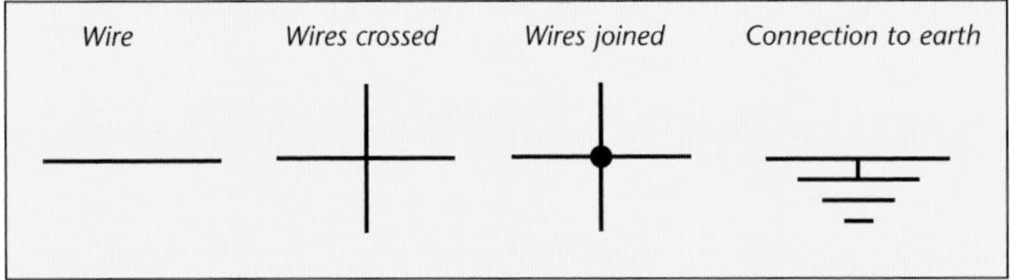
Wire
Wires crossed
Wires joined
Connection to earth

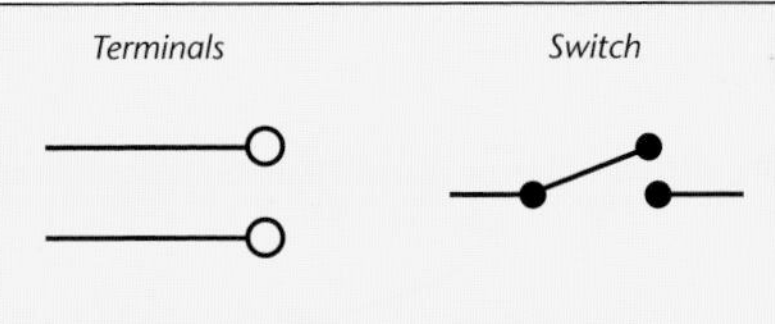
Terminals
Switch

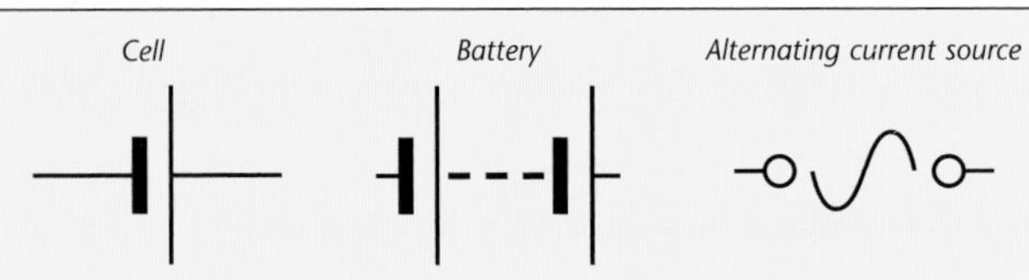
Cell
Battery
Alternating current source

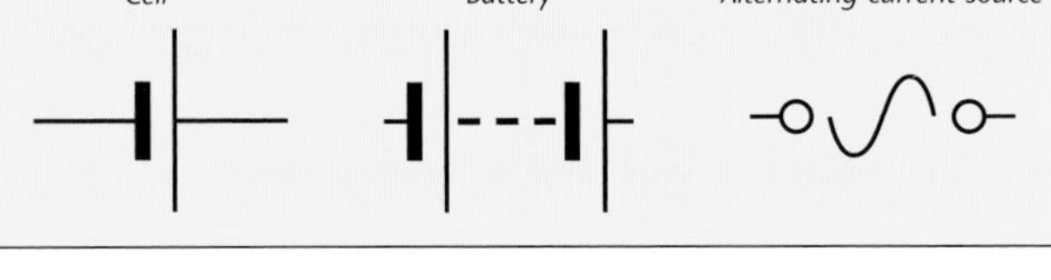

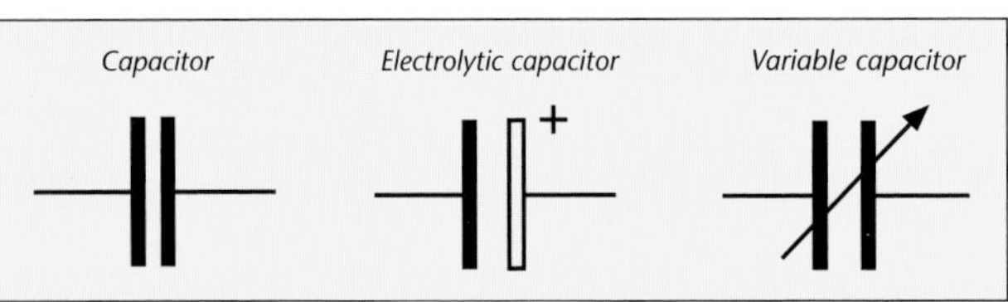
Capacitor
Electrolytic capacitor
+
Variable capacitor

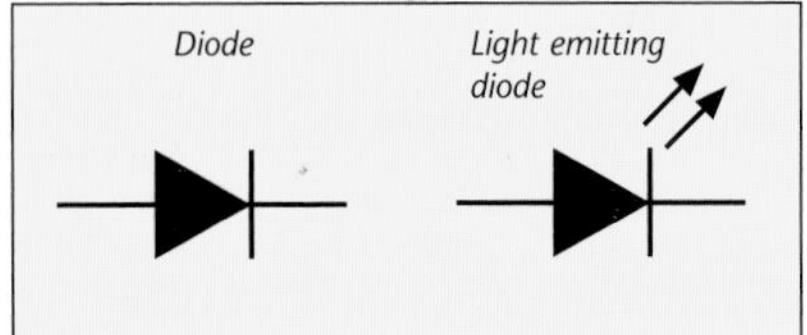
Diode
Light emitting diode

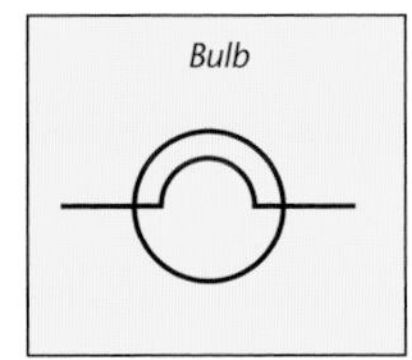
Bulb

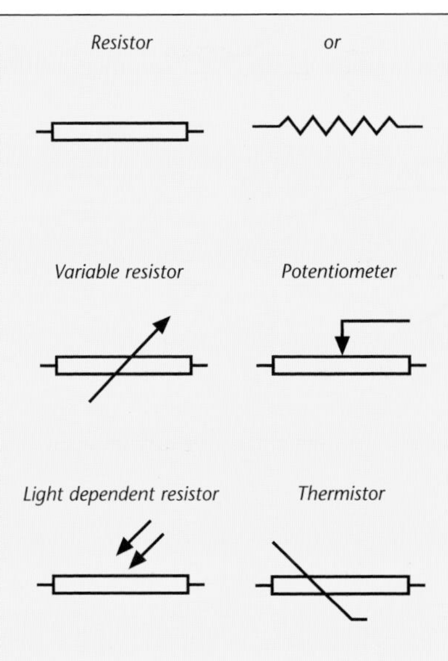
Resistor
or
Variable resistor
Potentiometer
Light dependent resistor
Thermistor

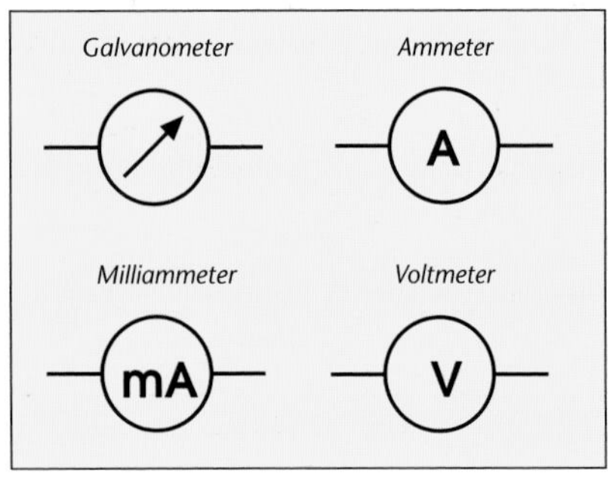
Galvanometer
Ammeter
A
Milliammeter
mA
Voltmeter
V

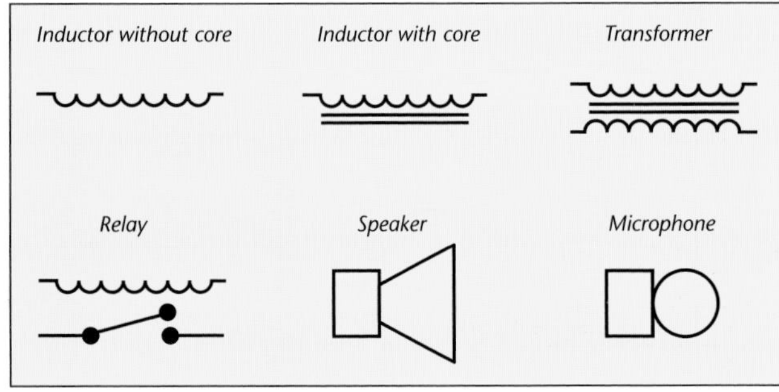
Inductor without core
Inductor with core
Transformer
Relay
Speaker
Microphone

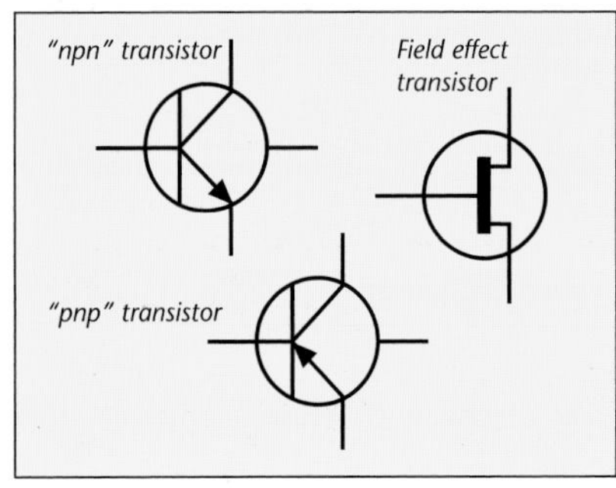
"npn" transistor
Field effect transistor
"pnp" transistor

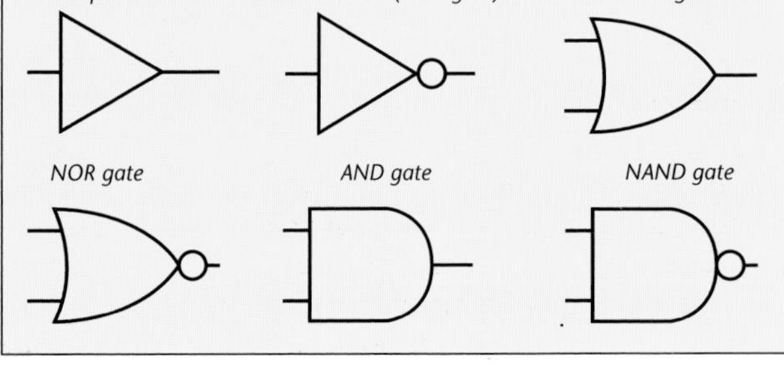
Amplifier
Inverter (NOT gate)
OR gate
NOR gate
AND gate
NAND gate

TRANSISTORS AND GATES

Transistors* can be used to amplify electrical signals, such as those from a microphone, and are also used as electronic switches. This has led to their use in complex circuits such as computers. They have replaced the much larger and slower valves and **relays***.

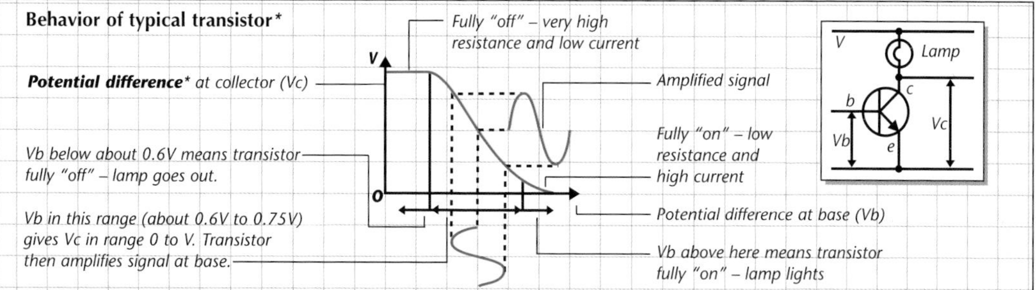

Behavior of typical transistor*
Potential difference* at collector (Vc)
Vb below about 0.6V means transistor fully "off" – lamp goes out.
Vb in this range (about 0.6V to 0.75V) gives Vc in range 0 to V. Transistor then amplifies signal at base.
V
0
Fully "off" – very high resistance and low current
Amplified signal
Fully "on" – low resistance and high current
Potential difference at base (Vb)
Vb above here means transistor fully "on" – lamp lights
V
Lamp
b
c
e
Vb
Vc

Logic gates

The on and off states of a transistor are used to indicate the numbers 1 and 0, respectively. The circuits are therefore known as **digital** (other circuits are called **analog**). Combinations of transistors with other components are used to make circuits which carry out logical operations.

Truth tables for basic logical operations

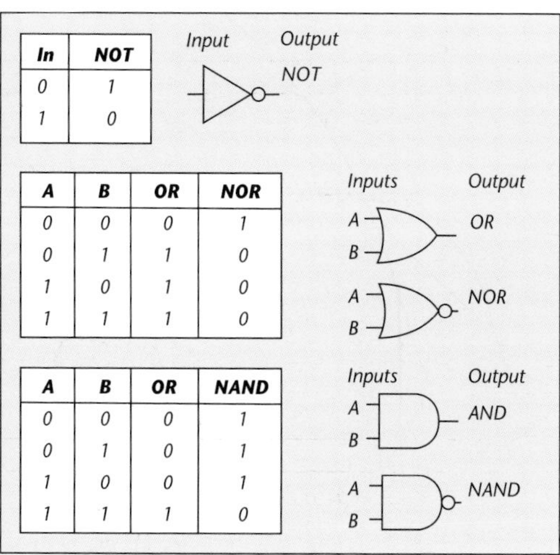

In	NOT
0	1
1	0

A	B	OR	NOR
0	0	0	1
0	1	1	0
1	0	1	0
1	1	1	0

A	B	OR	NAND
0	0	0	1
0	1	0	1
1	0	0	1
1	1	1	0

Input
Output
NOT
Inputs
Output
A
B
OR
A
B
NOR
Inputs
Output
A
B
AND
A
B
NAND

Combinations of these gates and other transistor circuits are used to make complex circuits which can perform mathematical operations, e.g. addition. These are called **integrated circuits**, and may contain many thousands of such components and connections, yet be built into a single slice of silicon.

Computers

Integrated circuits mean that many thousands of logic gates can be put onto a single tiny component called a microchip. The CPU of a computer (see below) can be put on one chip.

A personal computer with a CPU, monitor, keyboard and mouse

Typical computer system

*Disk and CD drives are examples of **input** and **output** devices. The disks can store many times more data than the **memory**, and also retain it when the computer is turned off (the information in the **read only memory** is lost).*

*Devices such as keyboard, mouse and screen are also **input** and **output** devices, from which data is put into the computer and to which it is sent. They are ways for the computer to link with the outside world.*

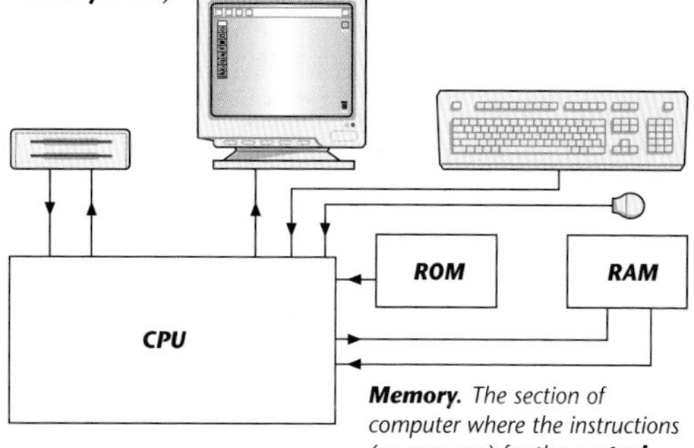

ROM
RAM
CPU

***Central processing unit (CPU).** The center of the computer. It takes data from **memory** and **input** devices, performs operations on it (it can do this millions of times per second) and sends the results to memory or **output** devices.*

***Memory.** The section of computer where the instructions (or program) for the **central processing unit** and the data are held. There are two types, **random access memory (RAM)**, where data can be stored (written) and retrieved (read), and **read only memory (ROM)**, from which "prerecorded" data can only be read.*

* **Potential difference**, 58; **Relay**, 75; **Transistor**, 65.

PROPERTIES OF SUBSTANCES

Substance	Density† / 10^3kg m^{-3}	Young's modulus / 10^{10}N m^{-2}	Specific heat capacity† / J kg^{-1} K^{-1}	Specific latent heat of fusion / 10^4J kg^{-1}	Linear co-efficient of expansion / $10^{-6}K^{-1}$	Thermal conductivity / W m^{-1} K^{-1}	Resistivity† / 10^{-8} ρ m
Aluminum	*2.70*	*7.0*	*908*	*40.0*	*25*	*242*	*2.67*
Antimony	*6.62*	*7.8*	*210*	*16.5*	*11*	*19*	*44*
Arsenic	*5.73*	–	*335*	–	*6.0*	–	*33.3*
Bismuth	*9.78*	*3.2*	*112*	*5.5*	*14*	*9*	*117*
Brass	*8.6 (approx)*	*9.0*	*389*	–	*19*	*109*	*8 (approx)*
Cadmium	*8.65*	*5.0*	*230*	*5.5*	*30*	*96*	–
Cobalt	*8.70*	–	*435*	*24.0*	*12*	*93*	*6.4*
Constantan	*8.90*	–	*420*	–	*16*	*23*	*49*
Copper	*8.89*	*11.0*	*385*	*20.0*	*16*	*383*	*1.72*
Gallium	*5.93*	–	*377*	–	*19*	*34*	*17.4*
Germanium	*5.40*	–	*324*	–	*5.7*	*59*	4.6×10^7
Gold	*19.3*	*8.0*	*128*	*6.7*	*14*	*300*	*2.20*
Iridium	*22.4*	–	*135*	–	*6.5*	*59*	*5.2*
Iron (cast)	*7.60*	*11.0*	*460*	*21.0*	*12*	*71*	*10.3*
Iron (wrought)	*7.85*	*21.0*	*460*	*21.0*	*12*	*71*	*10.3*
Lead	*11.3*	*1.6*	*127*	*2.5*	*29*	*36*	*20.6*
Magnesium	*1.74*	*4.1*	*1,030*	*30.0*	*26*	*154*	*4.24*
Mercury	*13.6*	–	*139*	*1.2*	*12*	*9*	*95.9*
Molybdenum	*10.1*	–	*301*	–	*5.0*	*142*	*5.7*
Nickel	*8.80*	*21.0*	*456*	*29.0*	*13*	*59*	*6.94*
Palladium	*12.2*	–	*247*	*15.0*	*12*	*74*	*10.7*
Platinum	*21.5*	*17.0*	*135*	*11.5*	*9.0*	*71*	*10.5*
Selenium	*4.79*	–	*324*	*35.0*	*26*	*0.24*	10^{12} *(approx)*
Silicon (amorphous)	*2.35*	*11.3*	*706*	–	*2.5*	*175*	10^{10} *(approx)*
Silver	*10.5*	*7.7*	*234*	*10.5*	*19*	*414*	*1.63*
Steel (mild)	*7.80*	*22.0*	*450*	–	*12*	*46*	*15 (approx)*
Tantalum	*16.6*	*19.0*	*151*	–	*6.5*	*56*	*13.4*
Tellurium	*6.2*	–	*201*	–	*17*	*50*	1.6×10^5
Tin	*7.3*	*5.3*	*225*	*5.8*	*23*	*63*	*11.4*
Tungsten	*19.3*	*39.0*	*142*	–	*4.3*	*185*	*5.5*
Water	*1.00*	–	*4,200*	*33.4*	*33.4*	*0.2*	–
Zinc	*7.10*	*8.0*	*387*	*10.5*	*11*	*111*	*5.92*

† *Density, specific heat capacity and resistivity all change with temperature. Values quoted here are for room temperature, i.e. 18-22°C.*

Useful constants

Quantity	Symbol	Value
Speed of light in vacuum	c	2.998×10^{8}m s^{-1}
Charge on electron	e	1.602×10^{-19}C
Mass of electron	m_e	9.109×10^{-31}kg
Mass of proton	m_p	1.673×10^{-27}kg
Mass of neutron	m_n	1.675×10^{-27}kg
Avogadro's number	N_A	6.023×10^{23}mol^{-1}
Faraday's constant	F	9.65×10^{4}C mol^{-1}
Gravitational constant	G	6.670×10^{-11}N m^{2} kg^{-2}
Gas constant	R	8.314J mol^{-1} K^{-1}

Values of common quantities

Quantity	Value
Acceleration due to gravity g (gravitational field strength)	9.81m s^{-2}
Density of water	1.00×10^{3}kg m^{-3}
Density of mercury	13.6×10^{3}kg m^{-3}
Ice point (standard temperature)	273K
Steam point	373K
Standard atmospheric pressure	1.01×10^{5}Pa
Length of Earth day	8.64×10^{4}s

The electromagnetic spectrum*

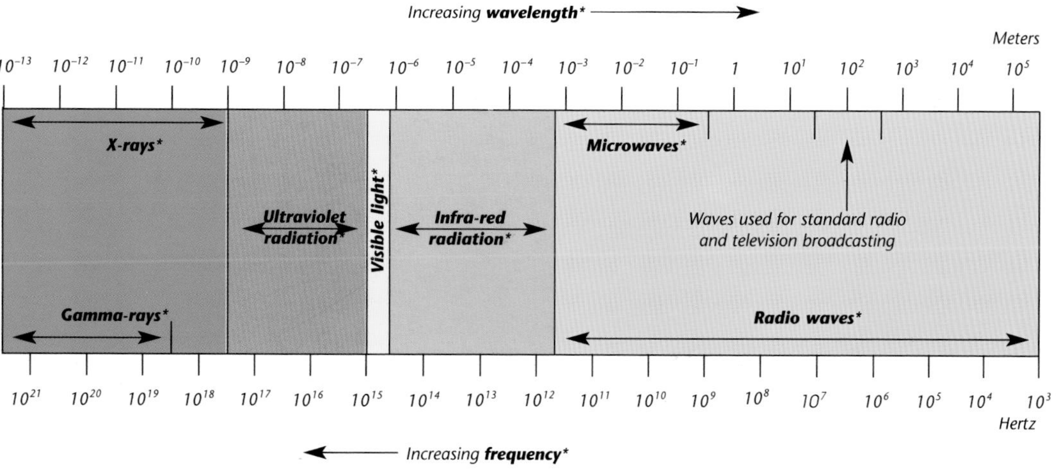

Increasing **wavelength***
Meters
10^{-13} 10^{-12} 10^{-11} 10^{-10} 10^{-9} 10^{-8} 10^{-7} 10^{-6} 10^{-5} 10^{-4} 10^{-3} 10^{-2} 10^{-1} 1 10^{1} 10^{2} 10^{3} 10^{4} 10^{5}
X-rays*
Microwaves*
Ultraviolet radiation*
Visible light*
Infra-red radiation*
Waves used for standard radio and television broadcasting
Gamma-rays*
Radio waves*
10^{21} 10^{20} 10^{19} 10^{18} 10^{17} 10^{16} 10^{15} 10^{14} 10^{13} 10^{12} 10^{11} 10^{10} 10^{9} 10^{8} 10^{7} 10^{6} 10^{5} 10^{4} 10^{3}
Hertz
Increasing **frequency***

* **Electromagnetic spectrum**, 44; **Frequency**, 35; **Gamma rays**, 44; **Infra-red radiation**, 45; **Microwaves**, **Radio waves**, 45; **Ultraviolet radiation**, 44; **Visible light**, 45; **Wavelength**, 34; **X-rays**, 44.

ELEMENTS

Element	Symbol	Atomic number*	Approximate relative atomic mass*
Actinium	***Ac***	*89*	*227*
Aluminum	***Al***	*13*	*27*
Americium	***Am***	*95*	*243*
Antimony	***Sb***	*51*	*122*
Argon	***Ar***	*18*	*40*
Arsenic	***As***	*33*	*75*
Astatine	***At***	*85*	*210*
Barium	***Ba***	*56*	*137*
Beryllium	***Be***	*4*	*9*
Bismuth	***Bi***	*83*	*209*
Boron	***B***	*5*	*11*
Bromine	***Br***	*35*	*80*
Cadmium	***Cd***	*48*	*112*
Calcium	***Ca***	*20*	*40*
Carbon	***C***	*6*	*12*
Cerium	***Ce***	*58*	*140*
Cesium	***Cs***	*55*	*133*
Chlorine	***Cl***	*17*	*35.5*
Chromium	***Cr***	*24*	*52*
Cobalt	***Co***	*27*	*59*
Copper	***Cu***	*29*	*64*
Dysprosium	***Dy***	*66*	*162*
Erbium	***Er***	*68*	*167*
Europium	***Eu***	*63*	*152*
Fluorine	***F***	*9*	*19*
Francium	***Fr***	*87*	*223*
Gadolinium	***Gd***	*64*	*157*
Gallium	***Ga***	*31*	*70*
Germanium	***Ge***	*32*	*73*
Gold	***Au***	*79*	*197*
Hafnium	***Hf***	*72*	*178.5*
Helium	***He***	*2*	*4*
Holmium	***Ho***	*67*	*165*
Hydrogen	***H***	*1*	*1*
Indium	***In***	*49*	*115*
Iodine	***I***	*53*	*127*
Iridium	***Ir***	*77*	*192*
Iron	***Fe***	*26*	*56*
Krypton	***Kr***	*36*	*84*
Lanthanum	***La***	*57*	*139*
Lead	***Pb***	*82*	*207*
Lithium	***Li***	*3*	*7*
Lutetium	***Lu***	*71*	*175*
Magnesium	***Mg***	*12*	*24*
Manganese	***Mn***	*25*	*55*
Mercury	***Hg***	*80*	*201*
Molybdenum	***Mo***	*42*	*96*
Neodymium	***Nd***	*60*	*144*
Neon	***Ne***	*10*	*20*
Neptunium	***Np***	*93*	*237*

Element	Symbol	Atomic number*	Approximate relative atomic mass*
Nickel	***Ni***	*28*	*59*
Niobium	***Nb***	*41*	*93*
Nitrogen	***N***	*7*	*14*
Osmium	***Os***	*76*	*190*
Oxygen	***O***	*8*	*16*
Palladium	***Pd***	*46*	*106*
Phosphorus	***P***	*15*	*31*
Platinum	***Pt***	*78*	*195*
Plutonium	***Pu***	*94*	*242*
Polonium	***Po***	*84*	*210*
Potassium	***K***	*19*	*39*
Praseodymium	***Pr***	*59*	*141*
Promethium	***Pm***	*61*	*147*
Protactinium	***Pa***	*91*	*231*
Radium	***Ra***	*88*	*226*
Radon	***Rn***	*86*	*222*
Rhenium	***Re***	*75*	*186*
Rhodium	***Rh***	*45*	*103*
Rubidium	***Rb***	*37*	*85*
Ruthenium	***Ru***	*44*	*101*
Samarium	***Sm***	*62*	*150*
Scandium	***Sc***	*21*	*45*
Selenium	***Se***	*34*	*79*
Silicon	***Si***	*14*	*28*
Silver	***Ag***	*47*	*108*
Sodium	***Na***	*11*	*23*
Strontium	***Sr***	*38*	*88*
Sulfur	***S***	*16*	*32*
Tantalum	***Ta***	*73*	*181*
Technetium	***Tc***	*43*	*99*
Tellurium	***Te***	*52*	*128*
Terbium	***Tb***	*65*	*159*
Thallium	***Tl***	*81*	*204*
Thorium	***Th***	*90*	*232*
Thulium	***Tm***	*69*	*169*
Tin	***Sn***	*50*	*119*
Titanium	***Ti***	*22*	*48*
Tungsten	***W***	*74*	*184*
Uranium	***U***	*92*	*238*
Vanadium	***V***	*23*	*51*
Xenon	***Xe***	*54*	*131*
Ytterbium	***Yb***	*70*	*173*
Yttrium	***Y***	*39*	*89*
Zinc	***Zn***	*30*	*65*
Zirconium	***Zr***	*40*	*91*

* **Atomic number**, 82; **Relative atomic mass**, 83.

GLOSSARY

Alloy
A mixture of two or more metals, or a metal and a non-metal. It has its own properties (which are metallic), independent of those of its constituents. For example, brass is an alloy of copper and zinc, and steel is an alloy of iron and carbon (different mixes give the steel different properties).

Amalgam
*An **alloy** of mercury with other metals. It is usually soft and may even be liquid.*

Calibration
The "setting up" of a measuring instrument so that it gives the correct reading. The instrument is normally adjusted during manufacture so that it reads the correct value when it is measuring a known standard quantity, e.g. a balance would be adjusted to read exactly 1kg when a standard 1kg mass was on it.

Calorimetry
*The measurement of heat change during a chemical reaction or event involving heat transfer. For example, measuring the temperature rise of a known mass of a substance when it is heated electrically is used to find **specific heat capacity***, and the temperature rise of a mass of water can be used to calculate the energy produced by a fuel when it is burned.*

Coefficient
*A constant for a substance, used to calculate quantities related to the substance by multiplying it by other quantities. For example, the force pushing two materials together multiplied by the **coefficient of friction*** for the surfaces gives the **frictional force***.*

Constant
*A numerical quantity that does not vary. For example, in the equation $E = mc^2$ (see also page 84), the quantity c (the speed of light in a vacuum) is the constant. E and m are **variables** because they can change.*

Coolant
*A fluid used for cooling in industry or in the home (e.g. in refrigerators). The fluid usually extracts heat from one source and transfers it to another. In a **nuclear power station***, the coolant transfers heat from the nuclear reaction to the steam generator, where the heat is used to produce steam. This turns **turbines** and generates electricity.*

Cosine (of an angle)
The ratio of the length of the side adjacent to the angle to the length of the hypotenuse (the longest side) in a right-angled triangle. It depends on the angle.

Ductile
*Describes a substance which can be stretched. It is normally used of metals which can be drawn out into thin wire, e.g. copper. Different substances show varying degrees of **ductility**. See also **yield point**, page 23.*

Graduations
*Marks used for measurement, e.g. those on a ruler, **micrometer screw gauge*** or **vernier scale***.*

Inversely proportional
*When applied to two quantities, this means that they have a relationship such that, for example, if one is doubled, the other is halved. See also **proportional**.*

Malleable
*Describes a substance which can be molded into different shapes. It is normally used of substances which can be hammered out into thin sheets, in particular many metals and **alloys** of metals. Different substances show varying degrees of **malleability**.*

Mean
A synonym for average, i.e. the sum of a collection of values divided by the number of values in the collection.

Medium (pl. **media**)
Any substance through which a physical effect is transmitted, e.g. glass is a medium when light travels through it.

Meniscus
*The concave or convex surface of a liquid, e.g. water or mercury. It is caused by the relative attraction of the molecules to each other and to those of the container (see also **adhesion** and **cohesion**, page 23 and **parallax error**, page 102).*

Photocell or **photoelectric cell**
A device used for the detection and measurement of light.

Proportional or **directly proportional**
When applied to two quantities, this means that they have a relationship such that, for example, if one is doubled, so is the other.

Rate
*The amount by which one quantity changes with respect to another, e.g. **acceleration*** is the rate of change of **velocity*** with time. Note that the second quantity is not necessarily time in all cases. If a graph of Y against X is plotted, the rate of change of Y with respect to X at a point is the gradient at that point.*

Reciprocal
The value obtained from a number when one is divided by it, i.e. the reciprocal number of x is $^1/_x$. For example, the reciprocal of 10 is 0.1.

Sine (of an angle)
The ratio of the length of the side opposite to the angle to the length of the hypotenuse (the longest side) in a right-angled triangle. It depends on the angle.

Spectrum (pl. **spectra**)
*A particular distribution of wavelengths and frequencies, e.g. the wavelengths in the **visible light spectrum*** range from 4×10^{-7}m to 7.5×10^{-7}m.*

System
A set of connected parts which have an effect on each other and form a whole unit.

Tangent (of an angle)
The ratio of the length of the side opposite to the angle to the length of the side adjacent to it in a right-angled triangle. It depends on the angle.

Turbine
*A device with rotating blades, turned by a force, e.g. jets of steam. The energy of the moving blades can be converted into electricity in a **generator***.*

Vacuum
*A space that is completely empty of matter. A **partial vacuum** can be created in a container by removing some of the air or gas inside. This makes the pressure inside the container less than the atmospheric pressure outside it.*

Variable
*A numerical quantity which can take any value. For example, in the equation $E = mc^2$ (see also page 84), E and m are variables since they can take any value (although the value of E depends on the value of m). The quantity c (the speed of light in a **vacuum**) is a **constant**.*

Volume
*A measurement of the space occupied by a body. See page 101 for calculations of volume. The **SI unit*** of volume is the cubic metre (m^3).*

* **Acceleration**, 11; **Coefficient of friction**, **Frictional force**, 7; **Generator**, 78; **Micrometer screw gauge**, 101; **Nuclear power station**, 94; **Velocity**, 10; **Vernier scale**, 100; **Visible light spectrum**, 54; **SI units**, 96; **Specific heat capacity**, 31.

INDEX

The page numbers listed in the index are of three different types. Those printed in bold type (e.g. **92**) indicate in each case where the main definition(s) of a word (or words) can be found. Those in lighter type (e.g. 92) refer to supplementary entries. Page numbers printed in italics (e.g. *92*) indicate pages where a word (or words) can be found as a small print label to a picture. If a page number is followed by a word in brackets, it means that the indexed word can be found inside the text of the definition indicated. If it is followed by (**I**), the indexed word can be found in the introductory text on the page given. Bracketed singulars, plurals, symbols and formulas are given where relevant after indexed words. Synonyms are indicated by the word "see", or by an oblique stroke (/) if the synonyms fall together alphabetically.

D

E

F

G

H

I

M

N

O

P

Q

R

S

T

U

V

W

X

Y

Z

ACKNOWLEDGEMENTS

Cover designers: Stephen Wright and Zöe Wray
Additional design by Chris Scollen, Stephen Wright and Roger Berry
American editor: Carrie A. Seay

Additional illustrations by:

Simone Abel, Andrew Beckett, Joyce Bee, Stephen Bennett, Roland Berry, Gary Bines, Kuo Kang Chen, Blue Chip Illustration, Isabel Bowring, Derek Brazell, John Brettoner, Peter Bull, Hilary Burn, Andy Burton, Sydney Cornford, Dan Courtney, Peter Dennis, Richard Draper, Brian Edwards, Malcolm English, Caroline Ewen, John Francis, Mark Franklin, Nigel Frey, Peter Froste, Peter Geissler, Nick Gibbard, William Giles, Mick Gillah, David Goldston, Peter Goodwin, Jeremy Gower, Terri Gower, Phil Green, Terry Hadler, Christine Howes, Ian Jackson, Elaine Keenan, Aziz Khan, Steven Kirk, Richard Lewington (The Garden Studio), Jason Lewis, Steve Lings (Linden Artists), Rachel Lockwood, Kevin Lyles, Chris Lyon, Kevin Maddison, Janos Marffy, Andy Martin, Rob McCaig, Joseph McEwan, David McGrail, Malcolm McGregor, Dee McLean (Linden Artists), Annabel Milne, Robert Morton (Linden Artists), Louise Nevett, Martin Newton, Louise Nixon, Steve Page, Justine Peek, Russell Punter, Kim Raymond, Barry Raynor, Michael Roffe, Michelle Ross, Mike Saunders (Tudor Art), John Scorey, John Shackell, Chris Shields (Wilcock Riley), Guy Smith, Peter Stebbing, Paul Sullivan, Stuart Trotter, Robert Walster, Ross Watton, Phil Weare, Wigwam Publishing Services, Sean Wilkinson, Ann Winterbotham, Gerald Wood, David Wright (Jillian Burgess).

Photograph credits:

Cover (clockwise from top left): Telegraph Colour Library; David Taylor / Science Photo Library; Omikron / Science Photo Library; Henry Dakin / Science Photo Library; David Parker / Science Photo Library.
The ultrasound scan on page 40 is reproduced with the kind permission of Charlotte Tomlins.
Page 45 (bottom left): Alfred Pasieka / Science Photo Library.
Page 45 (bottom right), page 93 (bottom right), page 206 (top right): Digital Vision.

This edition first published in 2006 by Usborne Publishing Ltd, Usborne House, 83-85 Saffron Hill, London EC1N 8RT, England. www.usborne.com

AE First published in America in 2007

Printed in Dubai.